utopia or oblivion:
the prospects for humanity

Books by R. Buckminster Fuller

r. buckminster fuller

utopia or oblivion:

the prospects for humanity

THE OVERLOOK PRESS
New York

Address all inquiries to:
THE OVERLOOK PRESS
R.F.D. 301, Woodstock, New York 12498

Library of Congress Catalog Card Number: 72-81085
SBN 0-87951-003-X

Printed in the United States of America

Contents

Introduction

It should be apparent that this is one of the most important books to come out of America.

"What if our urgent work now is, not to act at any price, but rather to lay in a stock of light for our difficulties?" This was Matthew Arnold's point some hundred years ago. Today, a significant answer, or set of answers, is provided in the work of Buckminster Fuller; and much light for the difficulties of our time is to be found in this volume.

Fuller is one of the few men in history who have systematically put in order the data of their experience, who have set out to see the world whole and see it constantly; and of these few he is singular in having available the technology of quanta, nucleonics, and computers. His work thus reflects an extraordinary gain in techno-economic leverage.

Since the Renaissance, the great innovators, with few exceptions—such as Leibniz, Newton, Kant—have tended to be specialists, each exploring a local domain, each a provincial in speculation. None has combined a comprehensive social philosophy with the technological insights that could provide blueprints for maximized abundance. The recent centuries have had their speculative philosophers, their pure scientists, their social reformers, inventors, technicians. But nowhere was the purview that embraced Utopia as an immediately attainable state of affairs, that measured the connections and interconnections of science and society and joined them in a functional gestalt.

Philosophers have seen the maximal development of man as an individual activity stemming from cumulative reflection and culture; they have seen an ideal society as an evolving product of deepened men—Plato's philosopher kings. Social reformers have urged radical changes in the rules by which society lives, and according to which it does its economic accounting. Inventors and engineers, in concert with investors and industrialists, have concentrated on product and market,

ix

assuming that social welfare follows naturally from gross national product. These several groups have not combined to orchestrate the human situation. On the contrary, their competitive themes, each hymning local self-interest, have sounded the clashes of Armageddon. And before us lie wars, hunger, riots; the global waste of lives and effort; the persistent threat of the fanatic use of the H-bomb.

To Fuller, the wealth of nations is their progressive degree of accomplished employment of energy by know-how—of the degree of mastery of the physical by the metaphysical. Energy exists in two forms: as substance—food and raw materials—and as push or power. To take a primitive example: solar power enables plants to grow, synthesize raw chemicals, produce the substance of cereals and fibers. Water power, steam, electricity, and other energy agencies transform the raw material into commercial products. Mediate in the transformation, however, is information, technological knowledge. In times past energy and knowledge were available in limited quantities. The ancient and medieval worlds, even the transitional centuries—the period of Malthus, Manchesterites, and Marx—were times of scarcity. Manners and morals were then scarcity products, with wide schisms and irremediable differences between haves and havenots.

The possibility of liberation from the inequities of the scarcity world came with the modern explosion of knowledge, the development of nuclear technology, the discovery of techniques for doing more with less. But both information and socially usable energy, Fuller maintains, are negatively entropic qualities. Information always increases; the more knowledge is articulated, the more it seeds additional knowledge. Atomic reactors, in turn, can, in use, breed more fissionable fuel than they consume. Thus the development, distribution, and economic application of power sources are virtually without significant limit. This energy, directed by the information stored in computers, can synthesize raw materials, machine and package commodities, and supply the physical needs of the world to the point of glut.

Moreover, the design initiative, as Fuller's own geodesic structures have shown, can solve the problems of human shelter, transportation, and communication with a fraction of the materials now in use. There is no longer any functional necessity for scarcities; no longer any justification for haves and havenots; no longer a rationale for national boundaries, political aggressions, monopolistic controls of obsolescent sources of raw materials and fossil fuels.

In short, in a world of maximum abundance, the manipulation of obsolescence is itself obsolescent. And politics is the obverse of design initiative; the politician in the modern world is like a determined driver of a twenty-mule team goading his mules along a six-lane highway on a Sunday afternoon. He may be skilled, ruthless, traditional, revered; but he has no viable solution to the problems of supply in a world of jets, pipelines, and nuclear fission.

This is not the place to review Fuller's own accomplishments; his designs, struggles, domes, transports, city plans, living techniques, mathematics, have been catalogued elsewhere. This introduction is intended simply to call attention to the freshness, comprehensiveness, and philosophical importance of his essential ideas; and to place them in historical perspective. There is, in my opinion, no one writing today who has more important things to say, no one whose ideas are more directly pointed to the attainable goals of a free and abundant life, no one more functionally attuned to the structural symbiosis of science and society.

It is to be noted that the papers collected in this volume are based on talks given by Fuller over the past several years to specialized academic or professional groups, or on articles prepared for specialized journals. For this reason there are references, occasionally, to local concerns; and there are expected inconsistencies in time references. Moreover, in the introduction of certain key concepts there occurs in some places an inevitable repetition of biographical detail. These elements could have been removed by incisive cutting, with subsequent editorial bridging of the developmental gaps. In the opinion of the editor, however, changes of this type would violate the integrity of Fuller's expression and distort the functional perspective of his work.

ROBERT W. MARKS

utopia or oblivion:
the prospects for humanity

1.   A Citizen of the 21st Century Looks Back

I was born cross-eyed. Not until I was four years old was it discovered that this was caused by my being abnormally farsighted. My vision was thereafter fully corrected with lenses. Until four I could see only large patterns, houses, trees, outlines of people with blurred coloring. While I saw two dark areas on human faces, I did not see a human eye or a teardrop or a human hair until I was four. Despite my new ability to apprehend details, my childhood's spontaneous dependence only upon big pattern clues has persisted.

Most children like to collect things. At four I started to collect documents of my own development as correlated with world patterns of developing technology. Beginning in 1917, I determined to employ my already rich case history, as objectively as possible, in documenting the life of a suburban New Englander, born in the Gay Nineties (1895)—the year automobiles were introduced, the wireless telegraph and the automatic screw machine were invented and X-rays were discovered; having his boyhood in the turn of the century; and maturing during humanity's epochal graduation from the inert, materialistic 19th into the dynamic, abstract 20th century. I named my documentation the Chronofile.

As the era of this case history loomed into greater perspective for me, as readable in the Chronofile, it became more accurately identifiable as that which, on the one hand, terminated Sir Isaac Newton's normally "at rest" world of myriadly and remotely isolated, hybrid cultures, to which change was anathema; and, on the other, opened Einstein's normally "dynamic," omni-integrating world culture to which change has come to seem evolutionarily inevitable. By 1917 I was convinced that, unannounced by any authority, a much greater environmental transformation was beginning to take place in our generation's unfolding experience than had occurred, for instance, between my father's, grandfather's, great-grandfather's, and great-great-grandfather's successive

1

generations. Their writings contain glimpses of their lives in their successive undergraduate days in the classes of 1760, 1801, 1840, and 1883 at Harvard. They tell of day-long trips walking or driving from Cambridge to Boston via Watertown Bridge.

As in 1913, in Fair Harvard's "Age that is past/surrendered her o'er [once more]/to the age that" was "waiting before," I felt intuitively in our freshman year that the subway, which then opened to connect Cambridge and Boston by a seven-minute ride, was harbinger of an entirely new distance-time relationship of humanity and its transforming environment. It seemed to me that *the* science-quaking fact of our boyhood was that light has a speed. Though fantastically fast, its 700 million miles per hour is not as absolutely fast as Newton's "instant universe." Newton's foundation was experimentally unrealistic. Light was real—but 99% of reality's electromagnetic spectrum was invisible. We could no longer pilot with our physical senses. We had henceforth to rely upon intellect and its power to invent and navigate with the instruments which could tune and scan the vast ranges of nonsensorially tunable reality. This called for intellectual confidence in the fundamental but nonobvious trends, and disregard for the only momentarily spectacular news.

Average lifespan expectancy for our classmates born *circa* 1895, as then calculated by the life-insurance actuaries, was 42 years. During our lifetime, the average life expectancy in the United States has increased to 70 years. Up to the time we were born, the average total distance covered by a member of humanity in his all-time, average lifespan of 27 years, was 30,000 miles. My total travel to date, by land, sea, and air, is a hundredfold that distance. It aggregates more than 3,000,000 miles and now, at 72 years, I find my work often taking me annually several times around the world with many lesser to-and-froings. This is in no wise a unique record. It is average for ever increasing millions of humans who have responsibilities in the vast frontiers of technology, business, and statecraft of a swiftly emerging spherical world city. Today's air hostesses far outtravel me, and Gemini astronauts outdistanced my 3,000,000 miles in one week's orbiting. Quite clearly, a complete transformation of human ecology in universe is occurring. It is not surprising that man, burdened with obsolete "knowledge"—his spontaneous reflexing conditioned only by past experience, and as yet unable to realize himself as being already a world man—fails to comprehend and cope logically with the birth of Universe Man.

By 1927 I felt that three big questions were posed by what the Chronofile as then made visible by the foregoing type of information.

*   *   *

First, what could society, backing up into its future, with eyes fixed only on the ever-receding and less adequate securities of yesterday, do to make this evolutionary process a gratifying rather than a painful experience?

Second, what could the average intelligent and healthy, moneyless individual best contribute, singlehandedly, toward bringing the earliest and happiest realization of advantage for society in general through taking and maintaining the comprehensive, anticipatory design-science initiative—in the face of the formidable axiomatic errors and inertias of academic authority as well as the formidable economic advantage of the massive corporations and their governments and mutually shortsighted foci of resource and capabilities exploitation?

Third, assuming that by competently reforming only the environment instead of trying to reform man, a favorably designed environment can be realized which will both permit and induce man to accomplish the same logical degree of physical success in universe as is manifest, for instance, by the hydrogen atom, how then can the economic and technological capability of all humanity to enjoy freely all of its world be accomplished exclusively by design science, without any individual interfering with another and without any individual being advantaged at the expense of another, with a design that will also induce its spontaneous adoption by world industrialization's managers?

*   *   *

In 1917, in the U.S. Navy, as I studied these questions the Chronofile disclosed a technological-environment-regenerated *acceleration* of technical evolution. This concept of *accelerating acceleration*, which had been discovered by Galileo and was later identified with gravity by Newton, had not been conceived as accelerating social evolution. During 1922-1927 the Chronofile also disclosed a trend of *comprehensive ephemeralization*—i.e., the doing of ever more with ever less, per given resource units of pounds, time, and energy. Ephemeralization was vastly augmenting the standards of living of ever-increasing numbers, but only inadvertently, as fallout from the defense-subsidized preoccupation of science with a weaponry supporting industrialization.

Ephemeralization was also accelerated by ever-increasing quantities of invisible energy events of universe, detoured by human intellect from their previously only cosmically flowing patterns to flow through engineered channels and impinge upon intellect-invented levers and thereby to vastly augment the work accomplishable by mankind's muscles in rearranging the energetic environment events to more effectively sustain the metabolic regeneration of human life.

Ephemeralization, which constantly does more with visibly less—as does, for instance, the one-quarter-ton communications satellite outperform 150,000 tons of transoceanic cables—has not as yet been formally isolated, recognized, and discussed in print as such by any economists. Until economists recognize it, ephemeralization cannot be popularly comprehended and be adopted in public policy formulations.

However, as the years have gone by the combined effects of accelerating acceleration and ephemeralization account primarily for the technical and economic augmentations which are now overwhelming man—trying to make him a success in universe despite his age-old Malthus-supported conviction that humanity, regardless of its composite significance and fate, is, with but a few exceptions, destined to demonstrate personal economic failure and premature death. Public policy the world around as yet assumes that Malthus was right—*ergo,* the vital necessity of Defense in view of the inexorability of the next Great War.

My Chronofile gradually disclosed the invalidity of that great superstition. It showed, for instance, that the metals in 80% of all of yesterday's obsolete mechanics and structures, contrary to popular conception of their "exhaustion," have been recovered, refined as "pure metals," and put to work again. Eventually, 99% of the all-time mined metals will be recovered and put into the recirculating-metals bloodstream of world industrialization as we go competently into the sea to recover all of yesterday's lost ships and cargoes—in particular, the war-sunken munitions vessels. But the rate of discovery of additional metal ores is slower than human population increase.

Throughout the twentieth century, therefore, the metals mined or unmined and materials in general have continually decreased in ratio to each individual. At this moment the cumulative total of metals—mined and refined by man throughout history—is wholly employed in machines or structures which, operating at full design-limit capacity, can successfully support only 44% of living humanity. Therefore, no exclusively political act of any political system can make the world's resources take care of more than 44% of humanity. But the overall mechanical efficiency of the extant machinery and structures is only 4%. An overall efficiency of 20% is engineeringly feasible at present. It could go to 80% someday. A design-science revolution could solve the problem.

Despite the constant increase in human population and constant decrease of materials per person, between 1900 and 1965 the number of people attaining economic and physical success—by full participation in the highest standard of living progressively developed by world industrialization—rose steadily from less than 1% to 40% of all living humanity. This is a personal standard of living and health superior to that ever enjoyed by a pre-20th-century monarch. The 40% of humanity thus surprisingly grown successful, despite constantly diminishing material resources per capita, can be explained only by accelerating ephemeralization.

Paradoxically, the self-accelerating doing-more-with-less invention revolution has been generated thus far almost exclusively by the technology of the world's weaponry race, whose ultimate objective has always been to deliver the greatest blows the farthest, most accurately, and most swiftly with the least effort. Evolution seems intent upon making man a success despite his negative fixations. The doing-more-with-less economic success of 40% of humanity, accomplished in only half a century, cannot be attributed to any political doctrine. Technology has flourished equally under exactly opposed ideologies.

Take away the energy-distributing networks and the industrial machinery from America, Russia, and all the world's industrialized countries, and within six months more than two billion swiftly and painfully deteriorating people will starve to death. Take away all the world's politicians, all the ideologies and their professional protagonists from those same countries, and send them off on a rocket trip around the sun and leave all the countries their present energy networks, industrial machinery, routine production and distribution personnel, and no more humans will starve nor be afflicted in health than at present.

Fortunately, the do-more-with-less invention initiative does not derive from political debate, bureaucratic licensing, or private economic patronage. The license comes only from the blue sky of the inventor's intellect. No one licensed the inventors of the airplane, telephone, electric light, and radio to go to work. It took only the personally dedicated initiative of five men to invent those world-transforming and world-shrinking developments. Herein lies the unexpectedly swift effectiveness of the invisibly generated and inexorable design-science revolution. Politics is, inherently, only an accessory after the fact of the design-science revolution. Despite this historically demonstrable fact, world society as yet persists in looking exclusively to its politicians and their ideologies for world problem solving.

Within all the foregoing concepts and in view of the low technical advance in everyday dwelling facilities as compared to transport and communication developments, my 1927 Dymaxion House was invented to function in due course as a prime instrument in an air-deliverable, mass-producible, world-around, new human life-protecting and -nurturing, scientific dwelling-service industry as the preferred means of transferring the scientific do-more-with-less capability from a weaponry to a livingry focus. I saw that a technology which produced total economic success for humanity could eliminate the fundamental causes of war, i.e., "you or me to the death—on behalf of yours or mine—for there is not enough to sustain us both": the seemingly scientific fact established by Thomas Malthus and later fortified by Darwin's survival-only-of-the-fittest. All else that I have done since then has related to these design-science considerations.

Thus in 1927 I embarked on a lifelong undertaking whose earliest possible realization lay a quarter of a century ahead, i.e., in 1952 (the year the Ford Motor Company acquired my first large Geodesic Dome) with full-scale, world-around industrialization of the livingry-service industry to be realized only half a century ahead in 1977. I predicated the economics of my grand strategy upon my own superstition-free concept of wealth as consisting exclusively of integrated intellect and energy. Since science's Law of Conservation of Energy states that energy may neither be created nor lost and experience shows that every time intellect experiments with energy it learns more, wealth can only increase.

Despite their negatively accounted cost and theoretically incurred debt and wastage of more than a trillion dollars,

World Wars I and II and subsequent cold warring have rendered the United States ever more vastly wealthy, despite the additional hundreds of billions of dollars lend-leased or given away. Why? Because those wars required ever more automated tool-up to harness more universe energy to do ever more continuous work on an earth whose total industrialization's percentage of strictly killing tools has become a progressively negligible minor fraction. The harnessed energy, production, distribution, communication tools, and techno-scientific literacy thus inadvertently established—all of which can produce peace-supporting prosperity—*is* the wealth.

There are two prime sources of energy to be harnessed and expended to do work. One is the capital energy-saving and storage account; the other is the energy-income account. The fossil fuels took multimillions of years of complex reduction and conservation, progressing from vegetational impoundment of sun radiation by photosynthesis to deep-well storage of the energy concentrated below the earth's surface. There is vast overabundance of income energy at more places around the world, at more times to produce billionsfold the energy now employed by man, if he only knew how to store it when it *is* available, for use when it was *not* available. There are gargantuan energy-income sources available which do not stay the processes of nature's own conservation of energy within the earth crust "against a rainy day." These are in water, tidal, wind, and desert-impinging sun radiation power. The exploiters of the fossil fuels, coal and oil, say it costs less to produce and burn the savings account. This is analogous to saying it takes less effort to rob a bank than to do the work which the money deposited in the bank represents. The question is cost to whom? To our great-great-grandchildren, who will have no fossil fuels to turn the machines? I find that the ignorant acceptance by world society's presently deputized leaders of the momentarily expedient and the lack of constructive, long-distance thinking—let alone comprehensive thinking—would render dubious the case for humanity's earthian future could we not recognize plausible overriding trends.

The only visible means of converting the momentum of negative employment of the physical principles operative in universe into making man a lasting success is in the design-science invention revolution, which fortunately may be joined by individual initiative founded on comprehensive intellectual integrity.

Whether all of my assessment of our historical position is correct and whether my grand strategy may be winning or not may possibly be readable in statistics that reflect the sudden surge of attention to and application of my ideas in the past five years. Though for more than half a century I have been purposefully disregarding the "earning of a living" or "moneymaking" in my occupational deliberations, my efforts sustaining but only incidentally accruing income, the income —low and slow at first—has steadily increased to ever more effective magnitude.

What, if any, is the significance of this upsurge? It seems to say that the generalized principles governing world industrialization which I seemed to discern, and the evolutionary events which they seemed to make predictable, are now tending to be confirmed by unfolding events. My activities' upsurge also probably reflects the fact that my world-around buildings are enclosing 30-fold the clear-span interior space per pounds of material of any known alternative clear-span engineering systems designed to withstand the same hurricanes, snow loads, and earthquakes. It also reflects the recent years' experimental confirmation in various regions of science of nature's use of the mathematical coordinate system which I long ago discovered and developed.

The upsurge probably further reflects the growing realization by world youth that its desire for success for all humanity can never be accomplished by politics, which is inherently divisive and biased and, to be effective, must eventually have recourse to its ultimate tools of warmaking; and that fundamental world peace probably can be accomplished only by a design-science revolution which can and may realize the feasible potential by upgrading the performance per units of resources to provide 100% of humanity with an ever-higher standard of living.

The upsurge probably reflects as well the realization of increasing numbers of the world's youth that world peace probably can be accomplished 20 years faster by a deliberate design-science revolution than by waiting for the inadvertent 20-years-later fallout into the standard-of-living-advancing commerce of the accelerating ephemeralization, as originally promulgated by only a wide variety of basic fear motivations, all of which result in the self-protective world-munitions racing. The world youth intuit that the 20-year difference could be the difference between humanity's success or extinction.

The upsurge also probably reflects the support I am receiving from industry and the National Aeronautical and Space Administration in my answer to those who say, "Why don't we stop spending billions for going to the *moon* and spend the money solving the *world's* housing problems!" My answer is that we will not have developed the high level of technology with which to successfully sustain all of the games-preoccupied human passengers on the promenade deck of the Good Ship Earth until we give total chemical, physical, and medical science and technology the task of understanding the successfully supporting humans as regenerative metabolic processes anywhere in universe for protracted periods, remote from the complex, regenerative, life-sustaining conditions unique to the biosphere surrounding earth, with the total scientific information translated into the mechanisms and content of a little black box weighing about 500 pounds and requiring replenishment only yearly. Only by the stark, resourceless conditions thus imposed upon experimental science will humanity be forced to transcend its erroneously conditioned earthian reflexes which would otherwise continue to frustrate it with worthless opinions, politics, and war after war.

The upsurge in the accrediting of my functioning is also probably related to my 40-years'-earlier forecast of the last decades' admission by world-around science that Malthus is wrong and, granted removal of all political boundary restrictions, that the physical resources of earth can support all of a multiplying humanity at higher standards of living than anyone has ever experienced or dreamed.

The upsurge further reflects the recent enthusiasm of scholars and natural scientists for my definition of universe as the cumulative aggregate of all humanity's nonsimultaneous experiences, all of which are finite and include both the ponderable physical and the imponderable metaphysical; with the entropic, increasingly disorderly expansion of physical universe counterbalanced by the increasingly orderly contraction of antientropic, metaphysical universe.

The scholars have also commented favorably on my philosophic observations that the omni-interacting, weightless, generalized principles apparently governing universe—discovered only experimentally and progressively by human-intellect-directed science—disclose an a priori, anticipatory, amorphous, and only intellectually conceivable omni-integrity of universe. By virtue of this integrity the generalized intellectual principles governing physical universe interactions and transformations never fail to provide an orderly set of consequences for any of its interacting events or for our own arbitrary or accidental experiments. We are thus confronted by a universe in which an intellect such as Einstein's could hypothetically take the measure of the physical energy universe, a measure which atomic fission later verified experimentally, thus demonstrating intellect's embracing and equating the integrated and differentiated energy of physical universe as $E=Mc^2$. There has not been, however, either experimental evidence or intuitive suggestion of the reversibility of those conditions and results whereby physical energy might take the measure of intellect, equate and inscribe the integral and differential equation of intellect and the metaphysical universe.

No scholars have published refutations of my widely publicized conclusion that all of the foregoing brain-recorded, mind-sorted, and comprehended experiences clearly disclose an infinitely greater a priori, omnianticipatory, intellectual integrity embracing and permeating universe than that demonstrable or suggested by any known capability of any individual human intellect—nor of the integrated, cumulative capabilities of all of history's human intellects—to control total universe in such a manner as to account for all the foregoing experimentally evidenced, omni-integrated, complex behaviors of universe. Wherefore the comprehensive, superhuman, nonanthropomorphic, Universal Intellectual Integrity thus altogether manifest to man by the integrated discoveries of experimental science may be spoken of as God, for that is the most economical term thus far intuitively formulated by humanity to identify such a macro-micro, human-capability-transcending, anticipatory, embracing, and inspiring relationship.

What intellect invented the integral of all the only intellectually conceivable, weightless, generalized principles discovered by science to be omnioperative as governing every physical experiment? Until man can answer that question he will have to accept an a priori intellect greater than his own.

I am convinced that neither I nor any other human, past or present, was or is a genius. I am convinced that what I have every physically normal child also has at birth. We could, of course, hypothesize that all babies are born geniuses and get swiftly degeniused. Unfavorable circumstances, shortsightedness, frayed nervous systems, and ignorantly articulated love and fear of elders tend to shut off many of the child's brain-capability valves. I was lucky in avoiding too many disconnects.

There is luck in everything. My luck is that I was born cross-eyed, was ejected so frequently from the establishment that I was finally forced either to perish or to employ some of those faculties with which we are all endowed—the use of which circumstances had previously so frustrated as to have put them in the deep freezer, where only hellishly hot situations could provide enough heat to melt them back into usability.

2. The Music of the New Life

Thoughts on Creativity, Sensorial Reality, and Comprehensiveness

I have pondered a great deal on the word "creativity," and I'm not inclined to use it in respect to human beings, because my own feeling as an explorer in events, behaviors, mathematics, and physical phenomena in general is that what is usually spoken of as *creativity* is really a unique and unprecedented *combination* in the use of principles discovered by man as existing—a priori—in the universe. I think the word "creation" implies adding something to the universe. And I don't think man adds to the universe. I think man is a very extraordinary part of the universe for he demonstrates the unique capability to discover and intellectually identify abstract, operative principles of the universe—which though unconsciously employed have not been differentiated, isolated, and understood before, as being principles, by other biological species. Rejecting the word "creativity" for use by any other than the great intellectual integrity progressively disclosed as conceiving both comprehensively and anticipatorily the complex interpatternings of reciprocal and transformative freedoms which apparently govern the universe I go along with the 5000-year-old philosophy of the *Bhagavad-Gita* which says, "Action is the product of the qualities inherent in nature. It is only the ignorant man who, misled by personal egotism, says: 'I am the doer.'" I am most impressed with the earliest recorded philosophic statements by unknown individuals of India and China. These earliest philosophies became progressively compromised and complicated throughout ensuing millenniums.

Machines have given rise to apprehension in people throughout the world—an apprehension shared by many within the field of music. With respect to machines I feel it important to recognize that we, ourselves, physically speaking, are machines. All of our musical instruments are machines. The physical universe is a machine—in fact, universe is the minimum and *only* perpetual motion machine. What people are usually apprehensive about is the unfamiliar machine. . . . Yesterday's horses were frightened by automobiles. When humans see an unfamiliar black box, batteries, and a red button with wires leading under their house, they are justifiably apprehensive. I think man is very properly concerned about that which he does not understand. I don't think that it is the machine per se that bothers man; it is just *not understanding*—anything—whatever it may be—that disturbs him. When an accident bares portions of human organs —familiar only to doctors—those organs look foreign and frightening to people. Stick your tongue way out before a mirror. It is a strange device.

At the outset of the industrial era it was often said that everything would soon be stereotyped; that variety in life would diminish. In the era of man's accomplished flight, the acceleration in design diversity of flying machines has outstripped all living species evolution in rate of increase of novel forms most of which have been magnificently reinspiring of man's imagination. Except for *paint* and interior passenger craft decor the design-science evolution of aircraft has been entirely functional and devoid of esthetical motivation yet inadvertently powerful in esthetical effects induced in the functionally illiterate public. The electronics revolution has been prosaic and severely mechanistic, but it has brought all the music of all history to all people everywhere.

As an explorer in what we call generalized comprehensive, anticipatory design-science principles, one could question my professional warrant to delve into the world of music. I would like to justify my position. The word "generalization" as used in the *literary* sense means "very broad." It suggests trying to cover too much territory—too thinly—to be useful. The literary men say "this is too general." In the mathematical sense, however, the meaning of generalization is quite different. The mathematician or the physicist looks for principles which are persistently operative in nature, which will hold true in every special case. If you can find principles that hold true in every case, then you have discovered what the scientist calls a "generalized principle."

The conscious detection of generalized principles which hold true under all conditions and their abstraction from any and all special case experiences of the principles may be

unique to humans. By abstraction I mean an idealized, empty-set, first-degree generalized statement such as one of my
own, "Let's take a piece of rope and tense it." This refers to
any rope and is a first-degree generalization. Next I say,
"Tension and compression are only coexistent"—when you
tense a rope its girth contracts—ergo compresses. This observation is a second-degree generalization. Another empty-set
abstraction of my own is "convex and concave only coexist."
We cannot have the convex surface of the pingpong ball
without the coexistence of the concave interior. You cannot
have the convex surface of a pebble without the concave aspect of that surface as viewed from the center of the pebble
with X-ray "sight." The sum of the exterior angles of every
system's convexity is always the same as the sum of the interior angles of the system's concavity. We also can say that the
electromagnetic positive charges only coexist with negative
charges. We can say that the three foregoing cases of *only
coexisting* phenomenon *tension and compression, convexity
and concavity,* and *electromagnetic charges* are each special
cases of the generalized mathematical case of the *only-coex-
istence of functions of a system.* This last statement is a
third-degree generalization which generalizes generalizations.
Forty years ago I generalized this third-degree abstraction
even further by saying that "unity is plural and at minimum
two." This is a fourth-degree generalization. Einstein's *"relativity"* and the physicists' *"fundamental complementarity"* of
universe constitute fifth-degree generalizations, for they abstract, condense, and reduce the generalizations to single
words.

There is further significance to this pattern of thought. The
physiologist, Dr. Wilder Penfield, head of McGill University's
Neurological Institute and leading electrode prober of the
functioning of the brain, says, "It is easier to explain all the
data—obtained from such probing—if we assume a phenomenon *mind* as well as the phenomenon *brain,* than it is to explain the data if we assume only *brain."* In other words the
probing has found the "telephone" connections of the brain
and the system's automatic message recording and informa-
tion-storage equipment, but many of the conversations and
initiation of the conversations that go over the system and get
stored are not inherent feedback developments of the telephone system itself.

It is inconceivable that a dog tugging at his leash at one
time and compressing his teeth into a bone at another time

should formulate consciously the generalized "only coexistence of tension and compression" and coexistence of the concavity and convexity of his teeth though the dog is spontaneously and subconsciously deft in tension-compression tactical moves. I am confident that the difference between animal brains and the human mind lies specifically in man's unique ability to generalize to progressively compounding degrees of abstraction. I think that this is man's unique function in universe—antientropy. The physical universe is entropic; that is, energies escape from local systems and the "fallout" is described as the Law of Increase of the Random Element, and that increase of diffuse energies brings about the expanding physical universe; in superb balance with which the human mind continually probes for and discovers the order in universe and continually contracts the descriptions of the separate orderly behaviors discovered in nature and combines the generalized observations in progressively comprehensive generalizations whereby the *metaphysical universe cofunctions equally with the physical universe* as its *contracting-universe* and *increasing-orderliness* counterpart. Man is the great antientropy of universe. The famous "Second Law" of Thermodynamics propounds *entropy*. But the human mind discovered and described and harnessed in orderly fashion this disorderly propensity of nature. Einstein's mind discovered and generalized the comprehensive law of physical energy universe as $E = Mc^2$ and the process of metaphysical mastery of the physical is irreversible. It is unthinkable and nonexperienced that energy can and does pronounce what intellect *is*.

I am certain that what we speak of as *human morality* is a form of intuitive and tentative generalization of experiences not as yet worked out in mathematical degree of incisiveness. Man has also the unique ability to objectively *employ* generalized principles—once recognized—in a *consciously selective* variety of special-case interrelationships. He is thus able to alter the inanimate environment and thereby to alter the "specialized-case" patterning of human experiences and thereby to provide more opportunity to verify or discard previous generalizations and to formulate new ones.

I am quite confident that many generalized principles also have their special-case realizations in the world of music. Pythagoras' discovery of the law of octaves obtained by halving tensed strings and of major and minor mode key progressions of fifth notes, obtained by trisectional fret-stops applied to firmly tensed strings or dried gut sinews, was an extraordinary instance of objective generalization which is also called "invention." I have discovered generalizations operative in other special case areas than that of music which may have special-case occurrence in music. It is my familiarity with generalized principles—that must per se permeate music as well as other areas—that permits me as a *generalist* to speak to you as musical education *specialists*.

Musicians in contrast to the scientists are extraordinarily intimate with their own theory. I'm going to make clear what I mean by that by talking about some scientists. The Massachusetts Institute of Technology's Faculty Club has quarterly speakers. I was their winter-quarter speaker of 1950. I stood up—and because I hadn't prepared anything—found myself thinking *out loud*—something that surprised me very much. I said that I was surprised to be invited to speak to them because they were all so ignorant. They looked astonished, and I was a little astonished myself. So I had to explain why I thought they were ignorant. And I said that all of them as scientists, on leaving M.I.T., went home to their families, and on a beautiful summer afternoon or early evening, at a picnic, said to their wives, or daughters, or sweethearts, "Darling, look at that beautiful sunset." And all the scientists realistically saw and as yet "see" the sun setting—"going down."

I wouldn't think much about this "seeing" of the sun "setting" by a taxi driver or other layman, but, I said, "As scientists, you have had 500 years since Copernicus and Galileo to get your senses in gear with your own experimentally-proven information. You know that the sun is not setting. You know that the earth is revolving to obscure the sun, but you *see* the sun set. Because it is taking you more than 500 years to get mentally—reflexively—in gear with your own theory, it must be because you don't know how and probably haven't even tried; therefore I think that you are fundamentally ignorant, particularly because of experiments I have made with children." I've used a free Earth globe and a small spotlight fixed on a stand ten feet away in a dark room. The spotlight represents the sun. One side of the Earth globe is lit—the other is in shadow. Having first identified the picture of the continents on the globe and "where we are now" I've gone on to explain to very young children who haven't been given the word "sunset" too often that the earth is revolving to obscure the sun. I glue the soles of the feet of little paper cutout figures of the children to the part of the world globe where "we are standing" and revolve the globe eastwardly. The children's paper figures are revolved out of the "sun" light, with increasingly long shadows until they are in the deep night— as the globe goes through night to return the children into morning as the long shadows shrink, and finally they come once more into the minimum shadow of noon.

I then take the children onto a high point of land, with wide horizons at dusk. I have them face north with their feet wide apart and I ask them to consider our enormous sphere revolving as they watch the sun out of the corner of their left eye and they say they "feel" the great Earth ball rotating them around out of line of sight with the sun.

Driving due west on a superhighway at 70 m.p.h. in late afternoon with the sun in our eyes we explain to the children that the earth's surface—like a phonograph record's outer rim—revolves faster at the equator than near the poles and that at mid-U.S.A. the surface is revolving eastward, away from the sun, at 860 m.p.h., which means that we are running a losing race to keep the sun in sight and the children excitedly see, and so do you, the extraordinary speed of eastward revolution of the earth speeding by the car as we get swept back eastward at 790 m.p.h. despite our 70 m.p.h. westward rate. Thenceforward the children "see" the true Earth-Sun relationship realistically. That is reflex conditioning. There is often an additional special blockage that hinders grown people regarding sun relationships, which is the *poetical sound* of "sunset." No one has invented a more poetical single word to express being revolved out of sight of the sun. Which way we see often depends on what we are told at the outset of life before we unconsciously, or subconsciously lock together our spontaneous brain reflexings.

I found it possible at 40 years of age to correct my erroneous *sunset* reflexes. It took much time, however. Therefore I know that we can say that it is not impossible to recondition our adult reflexes, but the later, the more difficult. I find that the scientists are experimentally remiss in continuing to yield to feelings that do not agree with their theories. They have failed, because of ignorance, or laziness, or fear of being "different," to bring whatever they have learned of the universe into correct conceptual realizations by the child. They haven't taken the trouble to test the theory they have acquired, so they carelessly continue to misinform the children. They are apparently ignorant of the fact that the child can most easily learn to see things correctly only if he is spoken to intelligently right from the beginning. Intelligently means thinking such situations through to discover the need for experimental preciseness plus the disciplining of self so to do. I think it is unscientific of the scientists in the educational processes to let these matters ride, and to go on debilitating whole new generations one after the other of billions of young who if geared sensorially with correct theory might have effective common sense enough to make the world work.

I note that scientists also use the words "up" and "down" hundreds of times daily. So I asked the M.I.T faculty if any of them could tell me what part of the universe is "up." Are the people in China upside down? Those deeply in-conditioned words "up" and "down" are derived from the millenniums in which man thought erroneously of his universe as an horizontal island as—"the four corners of the Earth"— and as the "wide, wide world"—in an infinitely extending horizontal ocean with an obvious "up" and "down" set of parallel perpendiculars to his flat plane—heaven up and hell down. Whatever other dimensional relationship could there be to an infinitely extended "flat" plane? Though as yet difficult to purge from yesterday's reflex-conditioned flat-earth concepts and speech, to man far out in universe the sphericity of Earth becomes evident and "up" and "down" soon become *obviously, feelably* meaningless. But clipper-ship captains of the last century sailing their ships around the world and the aviators flying planes around to China in this century discovered that they didn't have to turn their ships upside down when they reached China. Aviators have discarded the words "up" and "down." Now they come "in" for landings and they go "out." Astronauts come "in" with respect to various specific bodies in the universe and they go "out" from them. *"In"* is individually unique as a direction toward the center of any one system—but "out" is common to them all. There is no shape of space—there is only omnidirectional nonconceptual "out" and the specifically directioned conceptual "ins." "Space" has no identifiable meaning. The atmosphere's molecules over any place on earth's surface are forever shifting position. The air over the Himalayas is enveloping California a week later. The stars *overhead* now are *underfoot* twelve hours later. The stars themselves are swiftly moving in respect to one another. Many of them have not been where you see them for millions of years; many burnt out long ago. The sun's light takes eight minutes to reach us. When you see the sun tangent to the western horizon you are seeing *around* the horizon. And the light of the brightest star in the heaven takes 4¼ million years to get to us and that star probably burnt out a million years ago. "Space" is meaningless. We have relationships—but not space.

As there is no meaning to the words "up" and "down" I said to the M.I.T. faculty, "I think that you scientists are again demonstrating ignorance in not being able to purge your own language of scientifically faulty words and concepts." When the Jet Propulsion Laboratory's scientists of California reported to the world over radio and television of the first successful United States rocket-launched satellite's accomplishment of orbit, they constantly used "up" to describe its outbound flight. As the Gemini astronauts orbited over China the scientist on the ground speaking to them from Texas was heard to say, "Well, how are things up there today, boys?" As he spoke the "boys" were in the direction of the scientist's feet.

I went on to say to the M.I.T. faculty: "As scientists, you tell me that the wind is blowing from the northwest, which infers that you can really blow air great distances and that there is some place called *northwest*—which, of course, there isn't." Air can't be blown great distances. It curves back upon itself in evoluting-involuting doughnut shaped ring clouds—from the tobacco smoke-ring size to the atomic bomb's mushroom-ring size. An electric fan at the front door cannot push air through all the rooms of the house, but it can *pull* air through all the windows and through the rooms around corners and out through the front door. Whereas pushed air cannot travel great distances, pulled air tries to straighten out and can be pulled over enormous distances. What the scientists really mean when they said it is blowing from the northwest is that there is a low pressure to the southeast of us which is sucking the air from all directions and *pulling it by us*—as we happen to be situated on Earth northwestward of the low-pressure center. So why don't the scientists say "a low pressure southeast of us is sucking." Or simpler yet "southeast's sucking."

At any rate, I was able to get the M.I.T. scientists to laugh at themselves, realizing that they were indeed quite reflexedly "ignorant." They are as yet ignorant because they have not learned by experimentally proven means how to gear many of their theories in with their senses. How can they make sense if their senses deny their theory? They try to find excuse by saying that science now deals primarily with subvisible, subaudible, subsmellable, and subtouchable phenomena. We answer that through generalized principles, which being abstract are independent of size, it is possible to make special-case models at sensorial sizes of all the phenomena. The fact is that scientists, like aviators flying in fog at night, went "on instruments" in the mid-19th century. There is a greater gap between the scientist as a scientist and the same scientist as a human being than the gap between the scientists and the non-science-educated members of the human family. In contradistinction to the esteem in which world society holds them, scientists are the most confused and irresponsible human beings now alive. They lay "eggs"—and the businessman sells the eggs to the politicians and the politicians "scramble" or "drop" or "easy-over" those eggs as we hurtle toward oblivion. If our lives are left to their care we will all soon be dead.

Now I'd say that my feeling about musicians is that they do gear their senses realistically with their theory. And I have a feeling that in music, man may be able to deal with the new life much more effectively than science has been dealing with the newborn life.

All phenomena are generalizable into frequency language, and music provides sensorial-range frequency and amplitude modulating. As this meeting is being indirectly aided by the National Science Foundation's educational effort, in view of my foregoing statements, I think that it is important for us to look a bit at the great attempt of science to enormously expand its capabilities through organized educational activity.

Fifteen years ago, our country had great need to discover how to produce scientists. Sputnik, only seven years ago, accelerated the effort to solve the abundance-of-scientists problem. In order to know how to produce scientists the Academy of Sciences and the National Science Foundation said, "Let's look at the record. How have we produced scientists?" There is in Washington, D.C., a roster of all the scientific societies in the United States and of all the members of those societies. The vital data on all the different scientists in the United States is filed in Washington on punch cards which contain extraordinary ramifications of information concerning the lives and the educational preparations of those individual professional scientists. From this data it was possible to get answers as to the development of the front-rank American scientists.

The committee of scientists working on this question first

established their criteria of what in their estimation constituted a front-rank scientist. They said he must have a Ph.D.
He had to have made highly accredited original contributions
to knowledge. He must have published his work in copious
manner. Having set up the criteria, they were then able to
ask the punch card, data-storage system to come up with the
names of all the scientists in the United States who qualified
under their "front-rank-scientist" criteria. Up came a set of
cards with actual names and case histories of the individuals.

Possibly the most startling news for those who read this
data was the fact that the top scientists of the United States
had not been educated in scientific establishments. The Massachusetts Institute of Technology and the California Institute
of Technology were not among the first 20 of the educational
institutions from which the best scientists had come. It was
found that front-rank scientists had come predominantly
from small liberal-arts colleges. The committee went on to
query the scientists individually on the prime factors to which
they themselves attributed their successful development. This
inquiry brought out that the majority of "front-rankers" felt
that the most important factor in their lives was that they had
been students of a great and inspiring teacher. Front-rank
scientists' success was clearly attributable to small colleges
and intimate, personal-equation factors of an inspiring
teacher. The key was *individualism* at its intellectual best.
Russians please take note!

In regard to the subject of our meeting itself, *the new technology and its aid to the educational processes*—in (the special case of) the field of music, I think it's very important for
us to recognize right away that if a great teacher is of the
essence, then it is also very much in evidence that great personalities can come over television and moving-picture documentaries. Children and young people by the multimillions
fall in love with moving-picture actors and actresses. Their
personality comes through despite their having been seen
only as a complex of flickering light and shadows on a blank
wall. It is quite clear that personality can "come through" the
machine. Listen *to* and look *at* Pablo Casals playing in Robert Snyder's documentary of Casals during his now discontin-
ued self-exile in Prades, France. Inasmuch as the great
teacher personality is one of the great factors of education
success, I would say that we are not faced with insurmountable trouble by the machines—quite the contrary. We can attain greater intimacy with the nuances of facial expressions

and bodily motions of great personalities with the blown-up screen projections than can be experienced by students in back rows of concert and lecture halls. I think it obvious that we can bring great personalities—who could not possibly meet face-to-face with millions of students seated in stiff chairs in crowded classrooms—to hundreds of millions of young people listening and viewing undistractedly in their homes, by use of well-developed TV documentaries. Have we not been bringing Bach to billions of people by radio? Who can say "Bach is dead"? Children sitting comfortably at home seem annoyingly undisciplined to the busybodies of yesteryear, who want each generation to have to *take* what they themselves *took*. But discipline is exclusively from within the self and most effective when spontaneously initiated. I have photographed the eyes of my grandchildren—all unnoticed by them as they were fixed upon the TV. They were obviously in the same utter preoccupation as that of a baby at its mother's teat. TV antennae bristle from the rooftops of every one of the world's worst slums. The pipelines for great teachers to reach the eager brains of the otherwise underprivileged billions already exist.

At this point I would like to comment further about gearing scientific theory and sensorial reality. By such mental skirmishing I am going to work toward generalizations of the various principles that I think may interest you in relation to problems of music teaching.

Not only do I find that the scientists at M.I.T.—and everywhere else around the world—are out of gear with their own theory (as once was I—to far worse degree), but I find also by actual experience, that many if not most of the axioms of our would-be simplest geometry and arithmetic are faulty. Axioms are defined by Webster as "statements which need no proof because their truth is obvious." Because they take axioms erroneously as obvious (as with the sun "setting"), "pure" mathematicians deliberately sidestep the experimentally developed basis of all physical science. Much of the mathematics deal with phenomena which could hold true only *if* their *axioms* are proven experimentally valid. Because experiment invalidates most of the axioms of mathematics such as the existence of solids, continuous surfaces, straight lines, etc., much of the mathematical curriculum sanctioned by mathematical educators, adopted by school boards, and taught in all elementary schools is false, irrelevant, discouraging, and debilitating to the children's brain functioning. Science is culpable for allowing this debilitating practice to go on. Sense-illiterate scientists haven't taken the trouble to find out how to stop each generation from relaying to the next one disciplines that are misleading and frustrating.

Obviously one of the reasons why scientific education has seemed too difficult for many is the fact that much of its mathematics is founded upon experimentally unprovable myths which must greatly offend the intuitive sensitivity of the lucidly thinking new life. I find it shocking that I can recite to you many mathematical fallacies that we may be fated to go on teaching for another decade thus to ruin the extraordinary learning potential of another whole generation. All of this mischief of irresponsibility of the so-called grownups will have to be undone, probably at painful cost to world society, quite possibly at total cost. We don't have much time to couple both our theories and our senses with mathematical and physical reality, thereby to gain universally spontaneous cooperation in tuning man's competence first to save himself and then to make him a success in universe.

What should have been a socially shocking statement—but wasn't (in fact went socially unnnoticed)—had to be made during World War II, by some of the few great scientists. These scientists said in the early 1940s that when a young man demonstrated extraordinary capability in the sciences, at the university graduate-student level, and it was thought that he might be developed further to become a great scientist, it meant that eventually he had to be assigned to work with an already demonstrated great scientist, and the time of that very great scientist was of such extraordinary value that the great one must not be impeded by a young man who was not going to be worth the risk of wasting the proven great one's time. The greatest test that the senior scientists had to apply to the promising bright ones was the one which would discover whether the candidate had *the intellectual fortitude to withstand unlearning everything he had learned, because that was what he was going to have to do in order to become an importantly effective modern scientist.* This was occasioned by the proven greats' discovering that approximately everything that science had thought to be validly operative, up to 1932, was discovered to be no longer valid. Science had to start all over again. (See the 1942 farewell address of the outgoing president of the American Association for the Advancement of Science.)

Since 1932 mathematical physicists, physicists, chemists,

and many other scientists have been through one housecleaning after another. In contradistinction, so-called "pure" mathematics and all of the branches of the "pure" variety that permeate academic disciplining, on the pretext that it is pure —ergo transcendental to applied or experimental reality—has failed to purge itself of its unproven axiomatic conceptions, adopted almost entirely in the millenniums before present experimental science began to alter man's comprehensive ecology and cognitive capabilities.

The axioms, which started with the "obvious"—the superficially deceptive appearance of "nature" in the premicroscope or pretelescope era of extension of man's sight—induced a prodigious and now invalid vocabulary that has never been subjected to rigorously conducted scientific experiment.

Despite that the vast majority of pure mathematicians will disagree with me violently and may call me unbecoming names for so stating, I dare to suggest to you that (excepting completely the mathematical physicists) the revolution about to take place in mathematics education will be amongst history's most violent academic reforms. You will not have long to wait to discover that I am right—and I am not referring to what is called the "new mathematics."

Pride, fear, economic and social insecurity, and the general inability of humanity to let go of nonsense in order vastly to reorganize ourselves is of the essence. Therefore, I would say, speaking of educational tools and instruments, that the tools are going to make it easier for the new life to discover experimentally what really is going on in nature so that the young will not have to go on taking so much nonsense on experimentally unverified axiomatic faith. The revolution will come when the tools, such as the computers, disclose the nonsense and axiomatic invalidities to the rising generation.

Now, I'd like to mention an individual and his experimental work that has been recently and deservedly much discussed. I speak of Dr. Benjamin Bloom and his book on *Stability and Change in Human Characteristics*—John Wiley & Sons, publishers. His book reviews effectively a number of case histories of individuals from birth up to the university graduate-student years, approximately the first 26 years of life. The studies have been made in relation to periodically and uniformly administered IQ tests. I am going to talk about these case histories of Dr. Bloom's in the light of other scientific explorations, for instance the explorations that are being made by the neurophysiologists, exploring the human brain with electrodes and thus discovering many important electrical wave patterns.

Gradually a number of patterns in the brain have been positionally identified with respect to specific cell groups, as related also to specific types of thought, expressions, and actions of individuals. Through this physiological exploration a great deal is now known of the patterning of brain events and functions. Apparently we start life with a given total brain-cell capacity, component areas of which are progressively employed in a series of events which are initiated entirely in the brain of the individual by preset chromosomic "alarm clocks." Put your finger in the palm of a newborn baby's hand and the baby will close its tiny hand deftly around your finger. If you try to withdraw your finger, the baby's hand responds instantly to the withdrawal tension which you exert and it opens its hand. Its *tactile* apprehending organism is apparently operative in superb coordination at birth. Days later the "alarm clock" calls the hearing function into operation. Days later the babies "see" for the first time. One by one the brain's alarm clocks and the chromosome "ticker-tape" instructions inaugurate use of the child's vast inventory of intercoordinate capabilities and faculties. The child is not in fact *taught* and cannot be taught by others to inaugurate any of these capabilities. He teaches himself—*if given the chance* —at the right time.

Parents, as you know, have for eons thought that they were going to have to teach their children how to develop, function by function—to walk and to talk—but gradually it has been discovered that was not the case.

Now, we are entering a much more up-to-date phase of humanity on earth. We're beginning to learn a little bit experimentally about the child's extraordinary capabilities. What you can get from Dr. Bloom and the neurologists is the information that the set of "alarm clocks" that go off by the time a child is four years old govern 50% of the total capacity of the child to improve its IQ at any later date. If not properly attended to and given the chance to function, despite the brain's alarm-clock inauguration of progressive capabilities in those first four years, the brain mechanisms can be frustrated and can shut off the valves of those specific capacities and capabilities to learn, then or later on, in the specific areas. The capabilities need not necessarily be employed to important degree immediately after inception, but must upon inception be put in use and kept in use as active tools in the human coordinating capability else they will squelch themselves; that is, "shut themselves off," not necessarily irreparably, but usually so.

The next 30% of the total capacity of children to learn has been put into action by the time they are eight. Thus 80% of the total capability to self-improve IQ capability thereafter has been put in operation by eight. By age thirteen, 92% of the total capability has been self-started into usability. Between the years thirteen and seventeen the final 8% of the total capacity to coordinate and apprehend, to comprehend and teleologically employ the input data, has been brought into operation. From seventeen on, the most the young people can possibly do is to conserve the 100% capacity to further improve their IQ. We'll take those figures and plot a curve of the rate of inauguration of the capacity to learn, starting the curve at zero years and plotting 50% of the capacity by four, another 30% by eight; another 12% by thirteen, and the final 8% by seventeen. Next we plot the curve of state and federal funds in aid of education as applied at those same age levels. We find that somewhere around three billion federal and state dollars a year are applied to the "higher education" period from seventeen years onward, while approximately no government dollars are applied to help the birth-to-eight-years period when 80% of the critical educational capacity is being established, which if not properly set in use and kept in use will be closed off. The great bulk of government educational funds is being applied "after the horse has fled the barn." There was a little cartoon received with the papers about our Conference—a picture of the teacher, and a problem of multiplication chalked in white on the blackboard; along came the supervisor and gave the teacher a machine, an audiovisual aid, which projected the same multiplication problem in black figures upon a white screen—a new tool but no difference in technique.

I have what ought to be a surprising, even startling thing to say, which is that inasmuch as the period of greatest educational capability development is before four years old, the home is the primary schoolhouse—and kindergarten is the high school. Dr. Bloom makes this clear.

Given an adequate set of variable factors characterizing the environmental conditions experienced by a human individual from birth to seventeen years, Dr. Bloom can tell you within 1% what the individual's IQ will be at seventeen years of age.

Human babies are born helpless, and stay helpless longer than the babies of any other biological species. If, up to four years old, that young life has experiences leading to its mistrust of the competence and spontaneous inclination of the older life to look out for it, there is a breach of basic *trust:* its parents have a certified school dropout on their hands.

Nothing that I say is meant to tell you that the individuals whose spontaneous employment of their innate capabilities has been curtailed or abandoned, due to childhood frustrations, cannot later on "find" themselves. Determined and reinspired individuals have occasionally found ways of reopening their abandoned cortexial faculties.

Besides trust, there are two other conditions of critically controlling importance during the first four years: (a) *autonomy* and (b) *initiative.* The new life has to have an area that is really its own. All life tends to guard its minimum regenerative territory. This is apparently a basic ecological requirement of all living species. The child needs a minimum "territory" that is its own—its own room if possible—at least its own bed. This is its autonomy.

The third prime factor affecting the one-to-four-year-old is *initiative,* which must not be frustrated when it starts making experiments. The child may want to experiment with gravity and inertia by just knocking things off tables—this gives him basic information. He must be able to make many such experiments in order to learn about the way the universe works. The child must have experiences which indicate the coherence of materials and things. What can he trust when he has to grab something to stop his fall? To find out he needs to tear many things apart. Newspapers need only be torn a few times to show that newspapers give poor tensional support. Looking for adequate tensional coherence, the child will soon want to pull good vellums or silks apart. Children mustn't be stopped thoughtlessly as they go through their basic explorations, by virtue of which in due course they are going to start putting things together. They must take everything apart first and then learn how to put things together. Thus they learn to coordinate spontaneously. If parents break up that exploratory *initiative* by too many "don'ts" or punishments, or by having things in the child's environment that are dangerous and by which the child gets hurt so frequently as to discourage its further exploratory initiative, then that child will probably be an early school "dropout."

In the four-to-eight-years period of child development, something comes in that is in a sense close to music which governs the ability to improve IQ during those four critical years. The most important factor is the *speech pattern of the parents.* If the parents take the trouble to speak clearly, to use their language effectively, to look for the better words, the children are inspired to do likewise. If the parents' tones of voice are hopeful, thoughtful, tolerant, harmonious, again the children are inspired to think and speak likewise. If the parents are not parroting somebody else, but are quite clearly trying to think and are trying to express themselves, nothing encourages more the intuitions of the young life to commit itself not only to further exploration but to deal competently in coordinating its innate faculties. However, if the parents indicate that they are not really trying, or worse, relapse into slang clichés, slurred mouthings, blasphemy, anger, fear, intolerance indicating an inferiority complex which assumes an inability of self to attain understanding by others, then the four-to-eight-year-older becomes discouraged about his own capability to understand or to be understood. If the proper books are on the family shelves, if there are things around the house that make it clear to the child that the parents are really trying to educate themselves, then the children's confidence in family is excited and the children too try to engender the parents' confidence in their—the children's—capabilities.

We witness then that the children intuitively differentiate between parents who try to employ their minds and brains instead of relying only upon their muscles, cunning, or deception in the struggle to survive. The children who intuit that their parents have chosen to use mind over matter (of course unconsciously and without formulating such words) are inspired to employ their best innate faculties to highest effectiveness and most spontaneous coordination of the factors favorable to success.

I've just come from Caracas, Venezuela, a very beautiful city of two million inhabitants. We don't have many cities in the United States of that size and none more beautiful. We have heard much about bombings and political troubles in Venezuela. The beauty of the scene at first belies the reputation. You also have heard much of the petroleum-generated wealth of Venezuela and its capital city Caracas. From the

Caribbean port of Caracas you climb by automobile through tunnels in the mountains to enter a high and beautiful inland valley in which the city of Caracas is situated. The city runs about 15 miles along the 3000-foot-altitude valley bottom between two winding mountain walls rising on either side another 3000 feet above sea level. They are green-growth-covered mountain walls. There are no snow peaks on them. Clouds frequently hang lacily along the mountaintops. The clouds sprinkle frequently enough to maintain lush growth everywhere. A river bed winds through the valley intertwining with sculptured ribbons of expressways. Year-in, year-out, and the year-around, the temperature ranges only between 70 and 75 degrees Fahrenheit.

The Caracan rich have had enough money to build extraordinarily modern office buildings, apartment houses, hotels, universities, hospitals, and expensive residences. A few rich homes are on the hillsides.

In most cities, the slums run horizontally out behind, and are hidden by, the larger buildings. But with the opulent buildings of Caracas filling the entire valley floor, the only place left for the slum blight to spread was onto the rising slopes of its flanking mountains. In Caracas you can see the slums all along the hills. With the shacks constructed of the rubble and leftovers of yesterday's changing materials the different slum areas draped over the lower mountainsides have the color effects of patchwork quilts. They make a deep impression. They disclose the large proportion of poverty as yet unbenefited by the energy wealth released by Venezuela's petroleum. I was asked to meet with educators there in Caracas; much of my meeting was with the university students and those successful citizens who thoughtfully and wisely take responsibility for the general advancement of public education. First telling the Caracans of Dr. Bloom's findings regarding environmental effects on IQ capabilities, I pointed out to them that the "real schoolhouses" are the homes in the slums right there on the hillsides. None of the slum shacks have running water. There are no sewer lines and no bathrooms or inside toilets. Getting sanitary waste disposal and bathrooms into those slums would up the IQ capabilities 50% in a short space of time. A bathroom isn't just a piece of machinery. It is intimate to the fundamental routine of cleanliness, morality, and clean thinking. The ability to cope with filth-bred fungi and bacteria and their ravaging, through sanitary waste disposal and ready-to-hand soap and running

water, has many subconsciously important relationships to
the scheduled inaugurations of the progressive cerebral capabilities of the new life as disclosed by Dr. Bloom and his colleagues. Whether the older life really wants more life, and
whether the environment manifests that the older life is going
to try to make its arrangements to foster life more adequately
deeply effects the "unfolding flowers" of the cortexial "gardens." There are a million people sitting on those Caracas
hillsides who are looking right at all that modern plumbing in
the valley and the bombs of resentment explode first in their
hearts over their incapability to adequately foster their children. Bombs going off in Venezuela are all to do with this.
Of course illiterates are easy to incite to political revolution.
But after the revolution there are no more sanitary facilities.
So revolutions follow revolutions with never a sanitary gain.

Despite the poverty of those slums, they bristle with TV
antennas. Secondhand TVs are connectable with civilization
by wireless. Secondhand plumbing needs billion-dollar water-
and sewer-line developments—and hillsides double the time
and cost. In all the slums of the world, the TV antennas bristle. There is therefore a wireless hookup directly to the mothers and children who watch their televisions avidly. Whatever
comes over the TV to the children and parents is the essence
of education for better or worse. Television is the great educational medium. It is the number one potential emancipator
from ignorance and economic disadvantage of the entire
human family's residual poverty-stricken 60%. I pointed out
to the Caracans that their educational problems would not be
solved in their universities but through sanitation in their
slums and through educational TV advancements of high
order.

The little red schoolhouse was a worthy conception of our
forefathers. The older life always identified education with
higher possibilities of economic and cultural success. Wanting
their young life to have a better break of fortune than they—
the parents—had experienced, they put their children on highest
priority in the communal mandates upon their political leaders.
Thus *education* has become the most obviously acceptable political objective. Politicians who set about to get high educational
facilities for their constituents were most likely to succeed. Thus
the educational system has become a political football. The
enormous appropriations for education, however, go primarily
into building programs—on a "millions" for buildings and a
"thousands" for the teachers basis, approximately ten for the

buildings and one for the teachers. In fact, education is a
good way for politicians to keep the construction business
going in bad times. So the construction business lobbies for
education. The construction industry is the political payoff
system of least visible corruption. The great Appalachian
poverty program has turned out in the end to be only a
road-contract bonanza for that branch of the construction industry. We don't need more brick. We don't need more Geor-
gian architecture symbols. We need more wholesomely attrac-
tive and efficient sanitary facilities and superbly conceived
television educational documentaries. Early schools, with
few to educate, had only one teacher. Teachers were scarce
because even public literacy was minuscule. It seemed appropriate to bring all the children together in one place to
hear that rare individual—a teacher. It was nice for the
mother to be able to have the children out of the house for a
little bit in order to have a chance to get the house clean.
This did not mean that she did not love her children—but it
was very nice to get them out for a while. There was therefore a babysitting function of the school. But mothers didn't
like to say that it was babysitting, because they didn't want to
seem to be getting something for nothing so they called it
school. It also seemed desirable for the children to have social experience which the walk or ride to and from school
and the children's proximity—drilling and playing together
—provided. However the least favorable environment for
study is a schoolroom and closely placed desk prisons. Dr.
Einstein did not sit in the middle of Grand Central Station in
order best to study math and physics. He went into seclusion
to study as does any logical human—in his private study or
laboratory.

Let's return to Bloom's basic proclivities of the new life.
The child wants his autonomy. The maturing student wants
his privacy—his special place. We have learned by experimental work in education at Southern Illinois University of
the IQ capability favoring that was attainable with a little individual, private room-booth with a windowed door which
"belonged" to each student. When he first entered he found
in his private "room" all kinds of desirable items. He had his
own telephone directly and privately connected to his teacher.
He found a good dictionary; wall charts of the periodic table
of the elements; a world globe; a wall-mounted chart of the
electromagnetic spectrum; his private typewriter, and other
items conducive to thought and study. He did not feel in-

clined to go out of that room in order to find an environment
more favorable to study. However he was not allowed to go
into that room unless he was going to study. It became a
privilege to be allowed to go in. He was not allowed to smoke
in there, or to listen to music in there unless he had a music
course. He could go outside his private study and there were
places to smoke, places to have music, places to be social—to
do anything else he wanted except study, calculate, and write.
It became an obviously realized privilege to be allowed to go
into his private study. The student found that when he was in
his private study his reflexes became progressively conditioned, by association with that environment, to give himself
spontaneously to study, calculation, and writing. He found
himself producing. His mind really began to work.

So I don't see any reason why, with television reaching not
only the children in their private homes in the slums but children in the privacy of their homes everywhere, why we should
not bring education—school—to where the children are. That
is a surprise concept—the school by television *always and
only in the home* if possible in a special room in the home.
Try to remember your first experience in going to school.
You suddenly find that there are the inflexibly coupled chair-
desks. You fit uncomfortably into yours. The next kid has
one. Everyone is pinned into his desk. One of the children
psychologically escaping his lockup wants to go to the bathroom. You say maybe I'll go to the bathroom too. You try to
escape to the bathroom. It has horrid smells. I immediately
resented and as yet resent these stupid little bullpen desk-
chair "straitjackets" where you are put on exhibition as they
ask you to say things in front of the others so that if you
venture an original thought the others can laugh. This is conducive to showmanship and rote learning but not to self-
teaching and study. I think within the next ten years we are
going to have to give up schoolhouses. Your new educational
media are going to make possible bringing the most important kinds of experiences right into the home.

Let's be honest; if you want to send the children out for
babysitting, send them out for babysitting. Send them out for
social experience, to learn to lead parades, or whatever you
want them to do, but don't let's confuse our objectives. Give
them a chance to discipline their own minds under the most
favorable conditions. That is in their very own special private
environment. We'd better mass-produce "one-pupil schools";
that is, little well-equipped capsule rooms and send them to

all the homes; or we can design special private study rooms for homes. There are many ways we can do that. We'd better build that into the new life.

One or two other appropriate comments regarding big trends need to be stated. Major trends are reversing historical patterns. Decentralizing the school process is just such a reversal of historical patterns.

In regard to the educational process, Alfred North Whitehead made some very pertinent remarks when he first came to the United States from England around the turn of the century—well before World War I. As you may remember, Whitehead came to Harvard as a professor of natural philosophy. In one of his books he said, among other things, that there was a surprise pattern emerging in the educational process at Harvard. It was the development of the separate graduate schools at Harvard. They consisted of complexes of new buildings in a place remote from the rest of the university. They had special staffs. At Cambridge and Oxford, you became a graduate student and specialized to a high degree simply by going to the books that were in the library, or finding the man within the university who had special knowledge. You didn't need a whole new separate school. With the Harvard graduate schools specialization moved forward in much higher degree of separation in America. Whitehead said that Americans liked this idea because the idea of a plurality of champion specialists seemed analogous to American professional baseball where, if you had a champion pitcher and a champion catcher, or in football if you had a champion punter or a champion quarterback, you had an all-star team. Americans felt that by giving special advantage to those who are especially bright in special subjects, you'd be able to put together all-star culture and economic teams, by virtue of which our economy would prosper. And so the whole idea was applauded.

Whitehead noted the process by which students were selected to go the Harvard graduate schools, which were being copied by the other Ivy League colleges and a few public or state universities. Whitehead pointed out that we deliberately sorted out our students by examinations and deliberately culled out the bright ones. Next we deliberately persuaded the bright ones, if we could, to go on into the graduate schools. But Whitehead then noted that once the men became specialists within the university graduate schools that many nuances of specialization developed within the larger specialization areas. Instead of using their energies, which originally drove them in many directions of comprehensive coordination, specialists began to focus on a very fine target, which meant that being very bright and with plenty of energy, they would attain tremendous linear acceleration and get way, way out. They would be like stars, very remote in the heavens from one another. And, Whitehead pointed out, as men of high intellectual integrity, the specialist scholars became aware, by their experience, of how little any other human beings could possibly know about what was going on in their respectively unique areas of specialization. Therefore, as men of intellectual integrity, they themselves would not think of going into another specialist's laboratory and saying, "I see what you are doing. I see its significance." Thus Whitehead found that the specialists themselves were unable to communicate effectively with one another regarding their respective specializations. He found therefore that the specialists could not put together the potentials which society thought could and would be realized for the commonwealth as a consequence of the all-star teams of "way-out" scholars. The specialists proved themselves unable to integrate their findings to the comprehensive advantage of society.

We now come to a real surprise. I call this Whitehead's dilemma. Since the bright ones who had become specialists did not have the ability to integrate their own accrued potentials, it was necessary to find other humans who could integrate the specialists' accrued potentials and make the product available to society in appropriate form. Having deliberately sorted out the bright ones from the dull ones, this left a great residual pile of the dull ones. And inasmuch as the bright ones cannot put things together, we have to leave it to the dull ones to do so. As we look further into Whitehead's dilemma we find that there are sortable degrees of dull ones too. You also will discover that it has been the nature of modern business to specialize (until very recently when the new era of "diversification" set in). Corporations having to fill their managerial posts with the best available personnel have to do so from the first level of dull ones culled from the bright ones who were assigned to scholarship in specialization. The specializing corporations say, "We cannot undertake to produce so-and-so; that is out of our field. We must not spread ourselves too thin," or "We are auto manufacturers. Though roadways are part of the invention *automobile* we can't afford roadway-making politics. If the people want our autos, their politicians will provide roadways. If we provided roadways, we wouldn't be able to make profits."

The wider the field of responsibility, the lower the grade of "dull ones" (intellectually) available to the task. So when it comes to very wide-scale undertakings, such as how to make the world work, society has theoretically to leave it to the very dullest of the educational system's selective process culling. The *dulls* may be very handsome people, good golfers, good mixers, good diplomats because of their give-and-take, compromise-formulating senses—undisturbed by any intellectual theories. What we are saying is that the industrial managers and the local politicians, national politicians, international diplomats, are culled in descending order of scholastic brilliance by the educational processes of selection. Therefore the diplomats who have important economic biases often do not have any idea how to make the world work. As a consequence of Whitehead's (expanded) dilemma we are all faced with continuing, increasing accelerations in the development of world crises. Most hopeful sign in today's trending is the increasing use of computers—in the solution of problems—whose variable complexities transcend human "opinion" and provide "impartial" solutions acceptable by the dull ones—who always suspect the advice of "longhaired, eggheaded, unworldly human specialists." The only intellectuals welcome on the business as well as on the international and national political fronts are university presidents and deans who usually trend to such because they were more prone to management than scholarship.

There is a trending of the computer development which is a swiftly accelerating phase of human ecology evolution. In order to understand the logistical evolution of human artifacts and their sum-total feedback transforming effects on human ecology's total environmental transition and the latter's reciprocal modification of man's evolutionary patterning in universe, you have to recognize that the computer can choose to do only what man can choose to do within the limits of variables of mathematical strategy. There are two strategically fundamental and diametric operations of the mathematics. One is *differentiating* out, and the other is *integrating*. Differentiation and integration—those are really the two great diametric limit functions. Those who are expert in the development of the computer point out that it is very clear that the computer is already making man obsolete as a differentiator, that is as a "specialist." The computer and its very sensitive controlling subsidiary organisms which we call automation can very clearly pick out the green from the red and pick it out very much faster than the human can pick it out. It can do it all night long at 2000 degrees heat, where the human can't operate at all. So the machine as computer —as automation—is about to make man extinct as a specialist.

The other—diametric—function of the computer is *integration*. And the probability is that the computer and its subsidiary automation will not make man obsolete as an integrator for several million years—possibly never. We introduce great complexities into integration, many variables, and the interrelationships of which we wish to comprehend, and that is what the human mind is doing all the time. I can tell you quickly why the computer is never, or not for a long time, going to displace man as the *integrator*. The total variables that we deal with integratively all deal with a series of original questions which we have asked ourselves. Furthermore, those original questions and their discovered answers are relayed from generation to generation by chromosomic instructions which implement our appropriate, survival-accomplishing, subconscious reflexing to myriad variations of environment stimuli. We have at least two million years and possibly vast eons more of cumulative instructions for relaying our various question-askings and constant answer-relationships. Philosophers used to say that the computers would not be able to ask an original question. But it is now some time since a computer first asked an original question when it hadn't been told to ask an original question. All of a sudden as a consequence of variables in the environment and in the machine itself which had not been anticipated by the machine's designers and operators it went ahead and asked an original question. That occurrence requires explanation. Computers can play games, and the same computer can play two games. The same computer can play chess, backgammon, and checkers. Now I am going to have a computer playing backgammon and checkers at the same time. The things you have to do in order to be able to make a move in backgammon are much more complex than the things you have to do in order to be able to make a move in checkers. Therefore, the checker moves get played a little more rapidly than do the backgammon moves. So the checker moves are going like this [taps table rapidly] and the backgammon moves [taps more slowly] more slowly. The fast moves are not whole-number multiples of the time lapses of the slower (bigger) moves. Every once in a while, these movement rates get to the point where one is catching up to the other and suddenly the two come momentarily in seeming synchronization. You get this synchronization hum in variable-speed motors such as the twin motors of an airplane or a boat. When the computer's two game moves get into the synchronization phase and the timespan for solution action by the computer is too short for the computer's solution of both (approximately simultaneously) there develops a momentary blockage interference, whereat the computer must decide to which of the two games it accords right-of-way priority. *To answer—its own originally conceived question—* the computer asks itself which—by the computer's stored information—of the two games, backgammon or checkers, is the most important to man's psychological equanimity maintenance—and the answer comes "backgammon"—because, though not as yet as popular as checkers, backgammon is the rich man's game and people are swiftly trending toward comprehensive opulence, ergo will need universal backgammon capability and will drop plebeian checkers. Here then is an original question—*born through occurrence of an unexpected interference in experimental interpatternings.* Original questions of computers or humans probably are, always, products of unexpected interferences. Once asked, the theretofore original question becomes an additional brain-inventory item, to be passed on to the next generation in the chromosomic inventory. All old questions were once original questions. The human brain stored questions and answers of each unique individual's life, plus all the individual's heritage of chromosomic-administered, subconsciously operative experience responses, represent, in progressive sum total, the uniquely variant integral known as individual man. The integral man will always be far more complex than any systematically organized sets of variables conceivable by man and introduceable into the computer. Computers cannot in millions of years generate enough unexpected interferences to occasion enough original questions to be further integrated to approximate even an average individual let alone each of a trillion individuals' lives and their half a septillion interrelationships and the unpredictable interferences thereby to be generated.

While the computer will not replace man as an integrator

in the foreseeable future, it will undoubtedly displace man as a differentiator. There is good historical precedence for this prognostication. It is to be found in natural history.

At the American Association for the Advancement of Science's Annual Congress in Philadelphia, a few years ago, two papers on extinction were read by pure coincidence in widely separated sections of the meetings of the Congress. Nonetheless, both papers were closely akin. One was a biological research paper read on the investigation of biological species that have become extinct, which sought, if possible, to identify generalizable commonalities characterizing all species' cases of extinction. The other A.A.A.S. paper was an anthropological investigation of human tribes that have become extinct which also looked for generalizable explanation. Both the biological and anthropological investigations came to the same conclusion, though remotely conducted. The generalized conclusion was that *extinction is a consequence of overspecialization.* In the face of inexorable, comprehensive, and universal physical evolution, when species become overspecialized through successive inbreeding of special behavior characteristics and concurrent outbreeding of comprehensive adaptability, there inevitably comes a time when evolution develops steps—or wave lengths—that are too big or too small for the specialist to negotiate. Suddenly there are increasing species mishaps of nonadaptability—suddenly the species is extinct. We can say that world society through overspecialization has reached the brink of extinction. It has come to the point where its specialization has developed fission and the atomic bomb while unable to self-coordinate sufficiently to realistically guarantee that one of the lopsided specialists will not push the man-annihilating buttons. Man has, however inadvertently, as usual, developed his own destruction antiforce or "antibody" by developing the computer.

The computer suddenly makes man as specialist obsolete. Computers will force man back into "comprehensivity" functioning, which he was born spontaneously to demonstrate. We will henceforth cultivate our innate propensity for comprehensivity, and comprehensive coordination. You in music, though developing special technical capability in respect to instruments, keep yourselves as individuals in constant engagement with musical compositions and orchestrations. Unlike scientists, musicians tend to live logically with the whole experience of music. In developing comprehensive coordination, man develops spontaneous awareness of generalized cases which permeate all the sciences and arts. Fortified with a spontaneous awareness of general systems theory as manifest in orchestral composition and conductance, musical education teachers may be more able to comprehend and program computers with innately superior competence in such functioning than that possessed by professional mathematicians.

The words "genius" and "creativity" have sometimes been used in explanation of my being "well known." In my way of thinking, the only reason that I am known at all is because I set about deliberately in 1927 to be a *comprehensivist* in the era of almost exclusive trending and formal disciplining toward specialization. Inasmuch as everyone else was becoming a specialist, I didn't have any competition whatsoever. I was such an antithetical standout that whatever I did became prominently *obvious,* ergo well known. I'd learned that you could train for comprehensivity at the United States Naval Academy. I attended the U.S. Naval Academy at Annapolis, Maryland as a special student at the time of World War I. I found at the Naval Academy at that time an educational strategy fundamentally different from the educational strategy which Whitehead had found at Harvard which in turn all the private universities and colleges then followed, to be followed thereafter in so doing by the public colleges and state universities because the political representatives wanted to make sure that their constituents had the same educational opportunity as the more affluent youth. I found at the United States Naval Academy that the authorities were deliberately taking the *bright ones* and setting out to make them *comprehensivists* instead of specialists. To understand why this occurred we must look at the Navy in terms of general systems theory. The United States Navy as of World War I had airplanes, but they were just in their infancy. Navy airplanes patrolled off the European coast looking for submarines but did not get into much fighting. Our land planes had a minor number of dogfights. But no airplanes had as yet flown over oceans. They were only *local* tools like landing boats. The Navy represented a vast complex of realized technology which represented *objective uses of all that man had found out about his physical universe* in chemistry, physics, mathematics, geography, geology, biology, and other studies. Navy theory asks *what* and *where* are the world's resources? What are the unique performance excellences of each and every chemical element? How do you separate them and then reas-

sociate them to bring about supreme energy-controlling capability realized in floating hardware shops which carry the
greatest hitting power to any point on earth in shortest time
by virtue of which you can run the world? There could only
be one top navy—the one that stayed on top of the ocean.
Second-best navies went to the bottom. Navies as make-be-
lieve greats had no meaning whatsoever. Naval systems
theory assumes that the best defense is the supreme offensive
capability. Unlike long-drawn-out land warfare's sieges, naval
engagements are over in minutes. It took only minutes to find
out who had the supreme hitting power in batteries of big
guns which could be only floated by ships and weighed too
much to be transported over land. The ocean covers three-
fourths of the earth and was negotiable (until World War I)
only by sea vessels. The Navy had to develop officers who
were capable of taking all that hardware and the multithou-
sands of personnel to any part of the great world ocean and
no matter where they were, to maintain their sea stations.
With much shop maintenance necessary to such a task it was
essential that the officers have the scientific, logistical, and
psychological capability to build great bases anywhere
around the shores of the one-ocean world whose three big
"bays" are the Atlantic, Indian, and Pacific. And the one-
ocean water world was until 1919 "the world."

For a few decades the fighting-bombing airships took over
world control through domination of the air-ocean world.
Since then supreme control of earth is in dynamic balance
and its dominances can be won only by superior capability
of satellite and planetary maneuvering in major universe. But
general system theory as first conceived in establishment of
world navies as yet governs supreme control systems. In sending your men off around the world in the days of naval supremacy and in making this great investment in the Navy
you had to be reasonably certain that it would be supreme
around the world. The furthermost world point is always
halfway around the world, away from you or official "home."
In order to be able then to have such an extraordinary operation as a world-controlling navy you had to have officers who
not only understood a great deal but were operatively capable
of dealing with all circumstances. They had to be comprehensive industrialists so they could build a naval base anywhere
around the world and rebuild and improve their own ships.
They had to understand the history and principles of world
economics. They had to understand the ambitions of all the

world's nations. They had to understand philosophy and the history of development of law and human rights. The officer training was comprehensively specific and always broadening. The comprehensive coordinating capability of the naval officers must continually multiply. The Naval Academy training was only the beginning. The whole service experience was continuous postgraduate work in comprehensivity with always enough penetration in depth in all main classes of science, technology, and humanities to make possible the naval officer's effective communication with specialists in any field. Naval officers were subject to selective promotion, in contradistinction to automatic promotion, by the numbers, in the Army. Why this selective promotion? To answer that requires some historical reconnoitering.

Abraham Lincoln was the first President of the United States who was wired to the army at the battlefront with a telegraph line. With Lincoln, for the first time in the history of man, the fatal decisions of a nation did not have to be made at the front but could be obtained in split seconds by wire from the central authority of the society. Up to that time, the leaders of states had to be near or on their battlefronts in historically crucial battles. But, Abraham Lincoln didn't have any wires to the Navy. Yet the Navy was the first line of national defense against exterior forces of destruction. Because the sea covered three-quarters of the earth the Navy had to cover three-quarters of the earth. The Navy was inherently world-minded. "Join the Navy and See the World" was its enlistment slogan. You couldn't have wires to ships at sea. Early in this 20th century, came wireless communication by radio with ships halfway around the world, at sea. But until and including World War I, we didn't dare trust the top-secret information to the then only 13-year-old, and openly tunable radio. We didn't dare put important secret messages on the air. Strategically vital messages had to be carried by courier, and the courier couldn't get from here to there any faster than you could get a ship from here to there. However, since we didn't dare trust radio with secrets of supreme national strategy, up to and through World War I, the naval officers who took the nation's world-commanding "hardware" off to sea had to be trusted not only with the ultimate fate of the nation but also with the *pro tem* responsibility of running the world until couriers could be exchanged with the nation's elected leader. To meet this ultimately potential responsibility required the most comprehensive capa-

bility obtainable by scientific training and selective promotion. The ships' captains and flotilla, division, and fleet admirals had to have complete local autonomy and authority. The
captain of the ship had control over the life and death of the
people on board. I was brought up in that Navy and learned
its comprehensivity-breeding educational strategies. After
World War I, we found that we could "scramble" the radio so
that it was proof against deciphering. We learned much more
about electronics. Suddenly democracy withdrew the autonomy of the captains and commanders of the ships and admirals of the fleet. The authority had centralized, in physical
fact, into the White House and right up to the President's
telephone. There is a widely held misconception that holds
centralization of authority to be an arbitrary political voli-
tion. Not so. It was a physical-communication fact brought
about through electronic inventions. Now it is inexorable,
and it's exercised officially by laws or unofficially by lobbies.
From 1919 on, the Navy too began its conversion into the
specialization that controlled all other educational discipline;
Navy began to have its *naval aviators, submarine men,* and
so forth. I happened to attend the United States Naval Academy at Annapolis and to live through the last, pre-1919 days
of naval officers training in comprehensivity as a discipline
carefully developed over centuries and relayed secretly by the
British Admiralty to the U.S. naval authorities during World
War I, as the British Navy found itself inadequate to cope
alone with the Germans' submarine warfare. In 1927, I set
about deliberately to recall everything I could about the psychological, philosophical, mathematical, and physical strategies for developing the comprehensivity disciplines. A great
deal of the comprehensive adaptability was attained through
mathematics, which represents the most generalized of all the
disciplinable capabilities. I found it possible to reestablish
comprehensive self-disciplining in 1927. But to maintain my
comprehensivity I had to keep abreast of scientific and technical evolution. When I was the technical consultant, which
was in effect the technical editor, of *Fortune* magazine for
several years, or when I was head mechanical engineer on the
United States Board of Economic Warfare—these and other
jobs became a continual educational affair. As a consequence
I found, as I had for many years in other roles, that I could
go into any factory or laboratory in any industry and comprehend both the old and the newest equipment and its integrated functioning. I find it possible to keep up with the gen-

eralized principles of science, technology, logistics, economics, and other studies, to such an extent that I am able as yet to communicate at a critically effective level with scientists in many directions.

As a complete inadvertency and for reasons miraculous to me, painters, dancers, sculptors, poets, musicians, and other artists ask me to speak to them; or they look at my starkly scientific structures and devices and mathematical exploration models and assert satisfaction, comprehension, and enthusiasm. The miracle is that the artists are the human beings whose comprehensivity was not pruned down by the well-meaning, but ignorant educational customs of society. I will therefore examine with you some of those models which embrace the scientific trending. Artists—including the music educators—will spontaneously integrate the significance of scientific explorations with their art.

* * *

Professor C. H. Waddington, geneticist of the University of Edinburgh, identifies a phenomenon which he has named the "epigenetic landscape." In the epigenetic landscape, man and other life alter the landscape; the trees grow where there had been only pasture; the cattle can no longer graze where once they had done so. The epigenetic landscape is an evoluting one. Life alters the landscape, then the landscape alters the life—the inanimate winds and waters alter the land and vice versa. Neither the individual species of life nor the physical components of the inanimate chemistry of the environment, nor the whole landscape ever return exactly to their respective previous conditions. Entropy and evolution are inherent. The inanimate physical complexes become increasingly and superficially random while the biological phenomena regenerate with increasing orderliness of species, and subspecies, regularities.

When, in due course, man invented words and music he altered the soundscape and the soundscape altered man. The epigenetic evolution interacting progressively between humanity and his soundscape has been profound. Whereas the scientists as I have shown earlier have adopted many false premises and axioms and have much to correct, words and music have to our knowledge not made any false starts.

When I was born 70 years ago I was very cross-eyed. When I was four years old the cause was discovered. My eyes were so farsighted that I saw only blurringly colored and out-

lined objects. The colors were wonderful, but there were no details. I was given glasses that gave me sharp vision. As a consequence my senses of color, sound, touch, and smell were
most prominently employed. My first sight of a drop of dew,
of a strand of hair, of details in general amounted to a second birth at four years old. A whole new sense of pattern
coordination, that is, of consciousness occurred.

My memory of socially popular music both secular and religious goes back into the Gay Nineties—before the days of
world wars—before the days of autos, radios, airplanes, and
the like. My heightened sense of hearing has given me a
large-scale sense of sound patternings. For instance I have
tended to correlate popular music with general evolutionary
transformations of the dynamic environment. I have been
especially aware, for instance, of the correlation of the
change of popular- and dance-music tempo with the changing
and accelerating pace of technology and its effect on our
modern living pattern. In the dance music of my Gay Nineties childhood, the waltzes predominated. This slow music
was followed by an ever-faster sequence: there came the
two-step, the polka, the turkey trot, the Charleston, Lindy
Hop, jitterbug, rock-and-roll, frug. The pace shifted from
that of the sedately swaying northerly hemlocks to the swift
complex rhythm of the African drums.

The comprehensive science and technology trend chart of
the last 800 years discloses the basic acceleration curve of
that 20th-century compositional evolution.

David Rockefeller's great world-around collection of beetles discloses the epigenetic effect on the coloring, marking,
and shaping of the beetles of the various countries of the
earth. To those familiar with the art, landscape, the costume
history of Japan, Persia, the Congo, Ireland, and other countries, the beetles of those countries quite clearly manifest the
color, shape, and cultural characteristics in general of those
countries.

Though the relationships are often subtle, there is a comprehensive interrelationship of all science and technology with
all music, as well as with the other arts and with the moods
and philosophy of world society. The present-day research
work in music employing computers reveals to us many of
the subtle interrelationships of mathematics and music, for instance, those which Bach intuitively employed. The very
fundamentals of harmonics are now looming into surprisingly

discreet niceties in respect to wave mechanics, number theory, and general systems theory.

I will not try to identify music directly with each of the illustrations which I am employing in this discourse. Each of my pictures illustrates a generalized principle which has not yet been effectively integrated into our culture and our spontaneous formulations. But all of them have always been operative in nature. The difference from now on will be that we are consciously employing these principles. This will profoundly affect the kind of music which we compose and produce, and the way in which we dicipline ourselves to produce and compose the new music.

This first picture (Figure 1) is what I call the Profile of the Industrial Revolution. I found that revolution best portrayed by the chronological rate of humanity's acquisition of the scientific controls over the basic inventory of Cosmic Absolutes—i.e., the 92 regenerative chemical elements.

* * *

This chart is a curve of acceleration reliably portraying the fundamental rate of impingement of science and technology upon man, as referenced to regular calendar clock time. Lists of historical inventions and discoveries are formless because they are inherently open-ended, i.e., infinite. There is one closed or finite family of pure scientific events. It is the history of the isolation by man of the 92 regenerative chemical elements. Membership in this family of prime universe patternings requires a "credit-card" identification of specific and uniquely consecutive matching electron-proton numbers. The family must consist of all 92 unique sets from 1 to 92 electron-proton counts inclusive, and none other. That is the curve herewith presented. To it has been added the curve of the rate of isolation of the, thus far, subsequently isolated, nonselfregenerative chemical elements beyond 92. These elements of negative universe are shown for comparison only.

Figure 1 covers 800 years. It runs from 1200 A.D. to 2000 A.D. Nine chemical elements (see list at lower left corner of chart) were already known to and isolated by man when recorded history dawned. The first known isolation of a chemical element was that of arsenic in 1200 A.D. in Italy. There is a 200-year lag to the next isolation—antimony—then another 200-year interval to phosphorus, then only a half-century gap to cobalt, whereafter, the list takes "off" averaging a climbing rate of one isolation every two years.

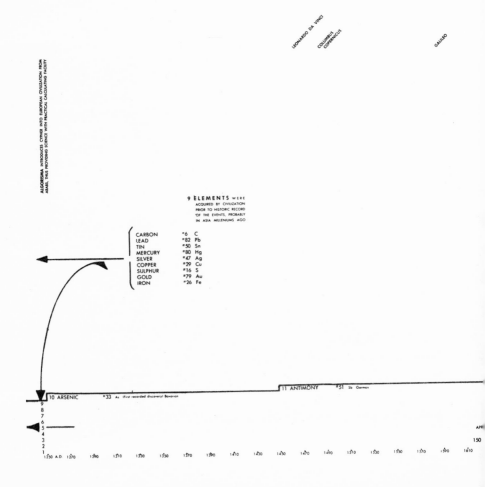

1250 A.D. 1270 1290 1310 1330 1350 1370 1390 1410 1430 1450 1470 1490 1510 1530 1550 1570 1590 1610

SAILING SHIP

EARTH ORBIT IN MAN MADE ENVIRONMENT CONTROL:
PRODUCT OF SUCCESSFUL APPLICATION OF HIGH
PERFORMANCE PER UNIT OF INVESTED RESOURCES

PROFILE OF THE INDUSTRIAL REVOLUTION
AS EXPOSED BY THE CHRONOLOGICAL RATE
OF ACQUISITION OF THE BASIC INVENTORY OF
COSMIC ABSOLUTES—THE 92 ELEMENTS

LEONARDO DA VINCI

COLUMBUS
COPERNICUS

GALILEO

ALGORISMA INTRODUCES CYPHER INTO EUROPEAN CIVILIZATION FROM
ARABS, THUS PROVIDING SCIENCE WITH PRACTICAL CALCULATING FACILITY

9 ELEMENTS WERE
ACQUIRED BY CIVILIZATION
PRIOR TO HISTORIC RECORD
OF THE EVENTS, PROBABLY
IN ASIA MILLENIUMS AGO

CARBON #6 C
LEAD   #82 Pb
TIN   #50 Sn
MERCURY #80 Hg
SILVER #47 Ag
COPPER #29 Cu
SULPHUR #16 S
GOLD   #79 Au
IRON   #26 Fe

11 ANTIMONY   #51 Sb German

10 ARSENIC   #33 As (first recorded discovery) Bavarian

9
8
7
6
5
4
3
2
1
1250 A.D. 1270 1290 1310 1330 1350 1370 1390 1410 1430 1450 1470 1490 1510 1530 1550 1570 1590 1610

150

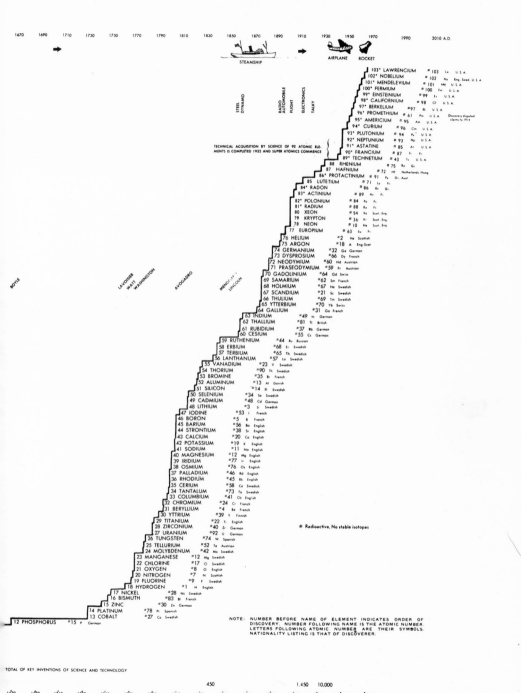

The swiftly rising curve is not smooth. There are three distinct slowdown "shoulders." These are occasioned by periods of universal warring. Pure science activity, which these isolations represent most truly, is frustrated altogether by the atmosphere of war. Because the earlier discoveries of science are often converted to technological advantage in wartime, science has been thought, erroneously, to prosper in wartime. What prospers is applied science and production technology but not pure science, not basic thinking.

It is seen on this chart that 1932, popularly identified as the "depth of the depression," is, in fact, a moment of epochal success. In 1932 the last of the finite family of 92 regenerative chemical elements, occurring spontaneously in nature, was isolated. For the first time in known history man had in neat "knowhow cans" on the "shelf" all the basic ingredients for reassembling the physical universe's basic pattern behaviors in preferred arrangements. This permits greatly increased performances per units of controlled and invested energies. It makes "possible" theretofore undreamed-of physical-advantage gains to be realized for all of humanity. It is the beginning of man's consciously successful participation in the evolutionary events of nature. This conscious and scientific participation, in turn, leads swiftly to realization of physical, metabolic success of man in universe.

After 1932 and the ninety-second isolation, there is an important, but temporary, slowdown in further isolation. Scientific man became momentarily preoccupied in taking apart the nuclei of those fundamental chemical elements. Fission and the theoretical release of the elemental energy five years later, and realistic release twelve years later, were inevitable to that ninety-second and final isolation of the full family of prime elements in '32.

It is interesting to note that the posturanium element isolations, starting with 93, occur with extraordinary regularity. Witness the approximately straight-line ascent of the post-92 isolations as well as the direct correspondence of the elemental numbers with the numbers representing the successive order of isolations. This correspondence is unlike the discovery pattern theretofore occurring. For instance, isolation number 97 is berkelium—element number 97—with 97 electrons and 97 protons.

In the first 92 isolations, however, the order of isolation does not correspond to the atomic-number order. The twenty-eighth isolation was zirconium—element number 40; the thirty-first isolation, beryllium, was element number 4; the eighteenth isolation was hydrogen, which was element number 1, meaning one electron and one proton and so forth. None of the atomic numbers correspond to the numbers in order of successive isolation within the "first family" of 92 elements.

The extraordinary pattern disclosed by this curve of man's acquisition of fundamental controls over the basic energy patternings of nature portrays only the evolutionary rate of development of pure science. It is subjective in that it establishes only a potential use-advantage for man. Without discovered use or technical capability to use having been as yet invented by man, this pure knowledge remains only potential.

In view of this curve of development of the high fundamental potential, it is appropriate to ask ourselves: What is the most comprehensive change in the relationship of man to his earth and his universe that may be realized physically by the application of this "pure (physical) knowledge"?

Probably the most significant consequence of the application of this knowledge is man's alteration thereby of his ecological patterning in universe.

Amongst all the species of life on earth, none of them, other than man, has consciously participated in the fundamental alteration of their overall, lifetime ecological sweepout patterning. Eels, plovers, and many other biological species unconsciously were forced to alter their total lifetimes' cumulative ecological patterning—by the comprehensive earth-surface changes induced by the successive ice ages. As ice receded, cold-area-breeding types of life were forced to ever-larger annual migrations between the most favorable tropical feeding grounds and arctic breeding grounds, respectively. This was unconscious participation in the fundamental alteration of ecological patterns. The designing and building of a hydroelectric dam or development and production of an antibiotic constitute conscious participation by man in the evolutionary pattern transforming of universe.

Up to and including my own father's generation, men were limited essentially to motion accomplished almost exclusively by their own leg motion—mildly increased by horse and vehicular travel. In 1914, American man was averaging 1640 miles per year total travel. Thirteen hundred miles were accomplished by his (integral) legs, and 340 additional miles were accomplished by his (nonintegral) "vehicles." This vehicular augmentation was a motion increase of only 25%. As a consequence of mass production of the equipment of mobilization during World War I, in 1919 U.S. man covered 1600 miles by vehicle alone—in addition to his continued 1300 miles per year walking—a total of 2900 miles per man. By 1942 U.S. man was averaging 4500 miles per year by vehicles plus 1300 miles per year by legs or an annual total ecological sweepout of 5800 miles per year.

In view of the "life-expectancy tables" we find that the total miles of an average human's lifetime's mileage to-and-froing, ecological sweepout, up to and including my father's lifetime, was only 30,000 miles. However, at 69 I had already covered three million miles, which is one hundredfold the lifetime distance accomplished by humans of any previous generations. I am one of a class of several million human beings, who, in their lifetimes, have each covered three million miles or more. The class of senior airline pilots has covered severalfold my three-million-mile sweepout. Astronauts equal my three-million-mile sweepout every one hundred circuits of the earth, i.e., in approximately every four days of earth orbiting. All these dramatic alterations of the ecological pattern of man have accrued directly to the inventory of Cosmic Absolutes—"canned" and put on the "potential shelf" by the pure scientists, working like bees to store the "honey," utterly unaware of the value to man of that honey or of what man will do with it.

To realize ecological pattern transformation requires that man penetrate environments theretofore intolerably hostile to his naked existence. His invention of hats and clothing first permitted man to penetrate hot and cold regions theretofore intolerable. Clothing represented man's first environment-controlling and ecology-transforming tool. When man built himself a house, making possible his existence during external development of hostile conditions, it did not alter, however, his ecological patterning geographically—any more than did his retreat into a cave. To make fundamental alteration of his ecological sweepout, man must propel his harm-immunizing, controlled environment into geographical realms of previously intolerable environmental conditions. He must propel the environment-controlling device either by his own power or by his control of power systems external to and greater than his bodily power system.

In order to maintain a uniform measure of the magnitude of effectiveness of such (previously intolerable) hostile-environment penetrations by man, I have documented man's circumnavigations of the earth—inside his succession of improved environment-controlling machines, propelled by energy patterns, which, though indirectly controlled by man, are nonetheless external to and greater than his integral, metabolic energy-conversion, propulsion capabilities.

As shown by little symbolic pictures along the top area of Figure 1, the first such circumnavigation of earth by man was accomplished with the wooden sailing ship, which took approximately three years. About 350 years later man circumnavigated earth in a steel steamship, taking approximately three weeks. Seventy-five years later he circumnavigated the earth in an aluminum airplane, taking approximately three days total flying time. Thirty-five years later he circumnavigated earth in an exotic-metal-structured rocket capsule, taking a little over an hour for each orbit cycle.

We have in the intervals between the progressive modes of circumnavigation as well as in the contractions of the successive elapsed times for the circumnavigations both a second- and third-power acceleration of the original velocity rate of pure science growth as demonstrated by the prime family of 92 chemical element isolations. To be realistic we must now multiply this third-power acceleration by a fourth coefficient. The fourth coefficient is the conceptual regeneration induced in the human mind by the concomitant visual information, circumnavigation of earth now being accomplished by the team of Telstar satellites whose world-around relayings of the electromagnetic wave-born TV communications will result in a four-dimensional acceleration of man's teleologic and conscious participation in universal evolution.

The extraordinary fourth-power acceleration thus to be realized by man in the distribution of technology generating information, through computers, electronics in general, and the world-around information relay, will integrate the total acceleration, the rate of human ecology transformation to a fifth-power progression. Within ten years anything reasonably "thinkupable" by science fiction will probably have been realized.

I know of no device as effective as this chart to generate comprehension of the unprecedented rate of experience acceleration into which man has now entered.

Along the bottom of Figure 1 the numbers 150, 450, 1450, and 10,000 occur in approximation of the cumulative number of key science and technology inventions realized by all men, everywhere, up to the historical dates at which those numbers are posted. I have not yet made accurate check of 1964 figures, but it is in the magnitude of millions. It can only be measured effectively at a later date.

*   *   *

Just go ten years to the right of the first man orbiting of earth in 1961, and you may safely say that by 1971 anything dreamable can happen. When I stand up here for instance and talk about changing obsolete, ineffective, and debilitating school patterns, the established reflexive conditioning of our brains tends to expect that it would take another hundred years to bring about that change. But the rate at which information is being disseminated, integrated, and inhibited into our current decision-making regarding the subjects I am discussing comprehensively discloses that my discourse constitutes subconsciously the general atmosphere of our thinking. The changes indicated as desirable are going to happen very, very rapidly. And I would say to you as educators, thinking about what you may dare to undertake, "Don't hesitate to undertake the most logical solutions. Take the biggest steps right away and you will be just on time!"

Change has become recognized now as normal. Just think. Isaac Newton's first law of motion was "A body persists in a state of *rest.*" Then he said, "or in a line of motion" as a secondary thought, "except as affected by other bodies." Normal was at *rest.* Change was abnormal. Einstein gave us the opposite concept in which he made the *velocity of light* the *normal speed* and the normal pattern of an all-acceleration universe. Any other lesser velocities or apparent motions were abnormal. We are now in an all-Einstein world. As a consequence of the extraordinary acceleration of technology in World War II, brought about by the technological competition to have airplanes outperform each other, we suddenly came to the realization that change was realistically normal. Man is now consciously coordinate with evolution as a continual process of change. Most recently businessmen have been acknowledging change to be normal and most profitable. In the past men felt that (other than fashion) changes would always be too costly and preclude profit making. Yesterday's businessmen opposed change politically. The 1964 presidential election saw business supporting change for the first time.

I was told in school about Galileo's parallelogram of forces. It was drawn on a plane where you showed one body running at a certain velocity in a given direction. You multiplied its weight times its velocity and that made the length of the line; we called such a force line a vector. Then we had another body which was on collision course with the first moving body, which we had vectored. And you took the second moving body's weight times its velocity and that was the length of the second line or vector. And the second body also was going in a unique and discreetly identified compass direction. You had these two moving bodies come together and then you made two other lines parallel to the first set of two vectorial lines and they made a parallelogram with the first two vectors.

Next you made a long diagonal in that parallelogram from the point of collision to its diagonally opposite corner. Then you extended the long diagonal outwardly from the parallelogram from the point of collision, extending this line to a length equal to the diagonal already constructed inside the parallelogram and that external equidistant extension of the diagonal of the parallelogram was called the *resultant* of forces. In the Navy I had also been taught Galileo's parallelogram of forces—at the Naval Academy. For some reason that I don't know of it was never considered at the U.S. Naval Academy that when two ships ran into each other, Galileo's force diagram told us that following the collision as indicated by the "resultant of forces" the two ships were supposed to waltz north-northeast for 12 miles together. I saw as indeed most all sane men see that such behavior was just what the ships didn't display after collision. One of them went in toward the center of the earth and that wasn't in the diagram. I decided that this criticism was typical of my general suspicion that we were not starting with the right set of axioms or simplest concepts, as for instance when we said that "plane" geometry is more fundamental and therefore easier than solid geometry, and that a dynamic geometry was something prohibitively "way out" in relative difficulty of comprehensibility. "Geometry didn't have qualities of energy!" said the pure mathematicians. All their complete abstraction of pattern from reality of experiences was thought to be simple. I discovered that nothing can be more complicated than "plane" geometry nor a more highly specialized case of "pure mathematics." Plane geometry is the most special case of "not true at all."

So one of the two ships colliding on the wavy surface of spherical earth goes towards earth's center. One of them does go a few hundred feet in the direction of Galileo's resultant of forces but not 12 miles. We find that in reality four forces are operating. Two accelerate conically together, rising from earth, plus *gravity,* plus the *resultant.* When the ships first ran into each other, they actually rose outwardly from earth's center because in acceleration both ships were "trying" to leave the earth. If they could accelerate faster—like rockets —they *could* leave the earth. So, when two ships collide they usually rise outwardly against gravity, before they subside, and then one or both either go into the bottom of the sea or go a few yards in the direction of the resultant of forces. The pattern of real force lines looks very much like a music stand —three vectorial legs spread out with a fourth vertical vector. And so I began to discover and study what we may call fundamental angular degrees of the vectorial interactions of universal freedoms.

(Figure 2) I'm going to give you a swift but fundamental insight in respect to the fundamental vectors and their degrees of universal freedom. I think that these vectorial and angular degrees of freedom relate mathematically to the fundamentals of music. These are the fundamental generalizations of structure and transformation.

I said to myself back in 1917, "Inasmuch as the planar force diagrams with which we were taught are, to say the least, 'inadequate' is it not possible for us to find an adequate model for ourselves—an omnidirectionally interacting, minimum set of vectors?" We have to deal always in the reality of an omnidirectional physical universe. I said, "How many forces are really operating on us?" For instance, there are clusters of stars out there, millions of stars, that look superficially like just one star, such for instance as the Pleiades. I am sure that the gravitational effect of that group on me is a linear one. "So how many fundamentally separate force lines of universe are there impinging on me? Into how many separate vectors do all the stars' and planets' gravitational pulls on me collect? How many universe lines (like the lines tying a ship to a dock) are pulling constantly on earth and even on me?" So I contrived an experimental device for exploration of the problem.

At the top right-hand side of Figure 2 you see something looking like a ping-pong ball on a thread. The ping-pong ball represents *me* and the *universe* is the thread whose other end is "fixed." I've found a hole in the stars and I go "zooping" out as far as I can so that all of the stars of universe seem to collect and appear as approximately one. One thing that I

Investigation of requirements for a minimum
system within the universe:

One vector of restraint allows ball to define
complete sphere — a 3-dimensional system.

2 vectors: a plane — a 2-dimensional system

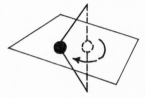

3 vectors: a line — a 1-dimensional system

4 vectors: a point — no displacement

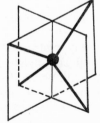

Figure 2

can't do is get out of, or absolutely away from, the universe, so the single string representing the gravitational pull of all the remotely bunched stars of universe is always attached to me. With this single restraint I can make omnidirectional patterns like a "tether ball." I can make spherical patterns, waves, any omnidirectional patterning I like. The only freedom that I can't demonstrate is that of getting entirely away from universe. Universe means "toward oneness" and implies a minimum of twoness. I say "universe is plural and at minimum—two." Now, in the second picture below the first I give myself a second restraint, so I have two strings pulling on me. Now I am as though I were in the middle of a violin string. I can still move as though I were a knot tied in the middle of a violin string. I can move now only in a plane. I can make planar figures of eight and planar clover leafs perpendicular to the axis of the violin string, but I can't get out of the plane. I'm going to give myself a third restraint. Now I am as if I were in the middle of a drumhead. I can still move but I can only move in a line perpendicular to the "drumhead" plane described by three convergent lines. I can move vertically to-and-fro to make a positive and negative flat tetrahedronal "drumhead." If I give myself a fourth restraint, then for the first time I seem to be positionally immobilized in respect to the four relatively "fixed" outer ends of my restraining lines.

(Figure 3) You discover that you are not yet completely immobilized because making a model with four delicate steel wires attached perpendicularly and symmetrically to a steel ball at the center of the modeled system of restraints you'll find that you can put a Stillson wrench on that steel ball in the center and you can always torque or rotate it. So I (as the fourfoldedly restrained ball) can't move from that localized spot. But I can *twist in place,* and I can twist locally in several different ways. In fact, in order to keep "me"—in the ball—completely immobilized you have to divide each of the four restraints into three lines each and then they must come in crisscrossing each other tangent to the sphere. Thus it takes a total of 12 restraints for universe to completely immobilize me—4 to localize me and 8 more to lock me rigidly into a system.

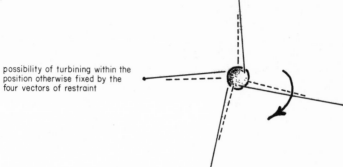

possibility of turbining within the
position otherwise fixed by the
four vectors of restraint

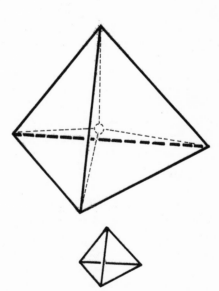

The four vectors define the tetrahedron: The first identifiable
"system" (a primary or minimum
subdivision of universe)

The ball lies at the center of
gravity within the tetrahedron.

the tetrahedron

Figure 3

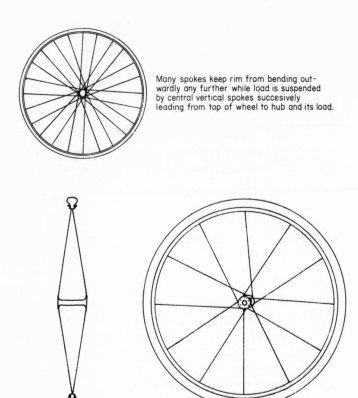

Many spokes keep rim from bending outwardly any further while load is suspended
by central vertical spokes succesively
leading from top of wheel to hub and its load.

It takes minimum of 12 spokes to fix hub position in relation to rim.
Six positive diaphragm, six negative—of which respectively three
each are positive and negative opposed turbining or torque members.

Figure 4

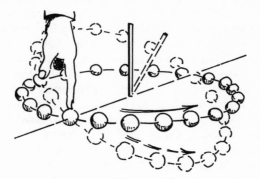

the flywheel of a gyroscope
considered as a ring of balls

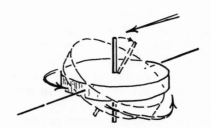

When downward pressure is applied to the edge of a gyro flywheel,
its plane of rotation tilts along a horizontal axis created at the point
of force. This effect from downward pressure at the edge can be
produced by a horizontal force at the axis. Therefore the axis of the
gyroscope tips at right angles to the force exerted. Such a
ninety-degree reaction is a precessional effect.

Figure 5

(Figure 4) Next we find that it takes a minimum of 12 spokes to make a wire wheel—to keep the hub from oscillating as a drumhead or twisting in any way. So we discover that there are always only 12 fundamental vectors which converge as the angular degrees of freedom in the universe: 6 positive vectors and 6 negative, which, when symmetrically interacting, represent the 6 edges of the positive phase of the tetrahedron and the 6 edges of the negative, or vertexially inside-outed phase of the same vectorial tetrahedron.

(Figure 5) I'm not going to tell you much about this picture except that it explains *precession*. It shows why a gyroscope does what it does. Children learn a great deal about fundamental motions. Using their own bodies they learn how to (1) *roll*, how to (2) *spin*, how to make a big circle (3) *orbit*, while also spinning (so they can have axial rotation—spin—while in orbit) and they learn how to turn themselves partially (4) *inside out* by sticking their tongues out. They learn (5) to *oscillate*, i.e., how to *converge* and *diverge* by inflating and deflating their lungs. But when you say (6) *"precession,"* that is one motion that they do not understand, because they did all those other five motions with their own integral bodies forgetting the reaction motion of the earth when they rolled and orbited, etc., for the reaction motion of earth is not visible to them. *Precession is the motion effect of a body in motion upon any other body in motion.* So when the children just take a step they are literally precessing the earth and the earth is constantly precessing them. When your uncle gave you a top and you asked him to explain its slow secondary wavy axial motion as it spins rapidly, he couldn't seem to explain it to you. The top's complex of motions within motions is precession. After long pondering I found it is quite easy to explain. But I am not going to have time now because I am pledged to finish this exposition on time. I'll just simply say to you, that in precession, the resultants of forces are never at 180°. It is impossible to throw a "straight" ball. Gravity, the wind, your releasing hand and throwing arm precess its flight into a helical pattern—often imperceptible (almost). These 6 motions each have their opposite motion—ergo our (6 positive, 6 negative) or total of 12 fundamental angular degrees and vectors of freedom.

(Figure 6) It is precession when, for instance, you drop a stone into the water. You will always get eccentrically developing waves in beautiful circles. A stone in motion is going toward spinning and orbiting earth's center and plunges into

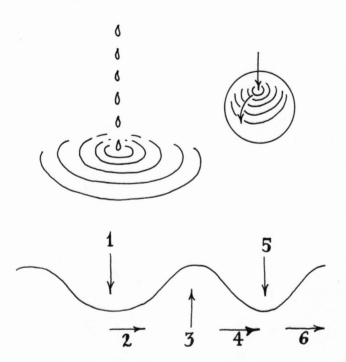

a precessional sequence: illustrated by water waves radiating from
a central point, each force producing a reaction at 90°

Figure 6

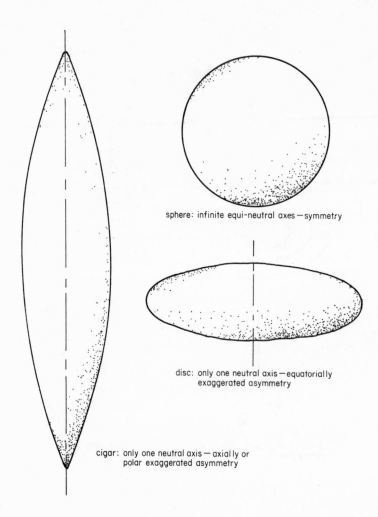

sphere: infinite equi-neutral axes—symmetry

disc: only one neutral axis—equatorially
exaggerated asymmetry

cigar: only one neutral axis—axially or
polar exaggerated asymmetry

Figure 7

the Brownian and other movements of water. Out go the circular waves at 90° to the stone's line of motion. And those waves that go horizontally *outwardly* precessionally beget vertical motions. Then the vertical motion of the waves begets precessionally a further horizontally outward motion. The precessional 90° regenerations of motion altogether cause the wave's pattern—as a whole series of precessions. Precession is regenerative.

(Figure 7) When we push on a cigar-shaped column it tries to become a squash. Its girth gets bigger. Therefore, its girth is stretching thinner. Therefore, its girth is in tension in a plane at 90° to the pushed-together axis. While you are pushing on the ends, the cigar column's girth is going into tension at 90°. I pull on the rope, and put it into axial tension. As I do so its girth begins to contract which means that its girth is going into compression in a plane at 90° to the axis of tension. The resultants of compression going 90° into tension and vice versa are typical of precessional resultants. The sphere precesses positively as it transforms toward a planar disc, and precesses negatively as it transforms toward a line.

(Figure 8) And here is a man jumping from the stern of a boat onto another boat. As a complex of the resultant motions the boats come around and the bows run into each other. This is typical of the non-180-degreeness of the precessional effect.

(Figure 9) We've been told by the Greeks and we've accepted it for too long that a sphere is *a surface equidistant in all directions from a point.* What I am going to show you about the sphere may be considered by you as typical of the way axioms are found to be both erroneous and experimentally inadequate. A sphere was defined by the Greeks as a surface equidistant in all directions from a point. It could not have holes in it. Because if it had any holes in it, it would turn inwardly as you came to the holes and therefore the surface would no longer be the same distance from the center. So the definition of the Greeks was of some kind of a continuously and absolutely "solid," ergo utterly impervious surface phenomenon that completely surrounded that point. The definition means that the Greek sphere would then divide the whole universe into all of the universe outside the sphere and all the rest of the universe inside the sphere and because there are no holes in it, there could be no traffic of any kind between the two absolutely divided sections of universe. This scheme is a typical perpetual-motion machine because it com-

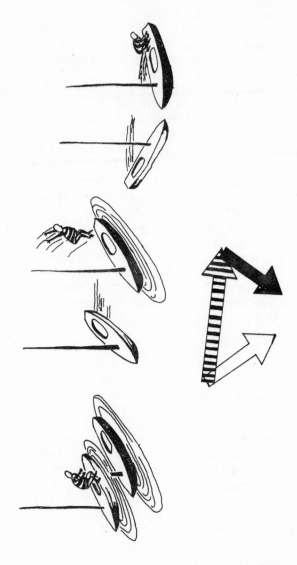

Figure 8

A sphere is a plurality of events approximately
equidistant in all directions from one event.

Figure 9

pletely defies what physics has found experimentally to be the case. All local systems (and a sphere is a local system) are continuously losing energy to outside universe. This is called *entropy*. It is the famous Second Law of Thermodynamics. All local systems are full of holes; in fact, as physicists have discovered experimentally by probing the atom and its nucleus, there are no "solids." As we probe into the "solid surface" of an experimental sphere we come to the atoms as very remotely deployed sets of energy "star" events, and we find we're dealing in a diaphanous Milky Way array of nebulous "abstract" mathematical events in which half of all the component events have negative weight wherefore altogether their weights average at zero—and there goes the last hope of the "pure" mathematician that his nonsolid abstraction "solid" concept had any meaning whatsoever. The best definition that we can have of a sphere is a plurality of events approximately equidistant in approximately all directions from approximately one event, at approximately the same time. Thus we tentatively restate our fundamental definitions of *experimentally* encountered systems and their internal and external relationships. They are really just childish descriptions stated in terms of our direct experience.

Another thing that we are always told, which scientists and engineers like yesterday's schoolboys as yet accept, is that in both Euclidean and non-Euclidean geometries the pure mathematicians say that you can run a plurality of lines through any one point. The engineer puts a point on paper and takes his straight edge and painstakingly draws line after line (approximately) through (approximately) the same point. And he assumes this to be both theoretically and realistically done. But try this with your knitting needles or get the smallest lines you can get. In fact reduce your line to the size of a neutron's diameter. Let your "line" be the trajectory in the cloud chamber of a neutron shot into a plurality of atoms and suddenly there is an interference of the trajectory as the neutron interferes with another nuclear component's linear trajectory and the component separates into further subcomponents as all of the individual atomic components now diverge angularly from one another in identifiable angu-

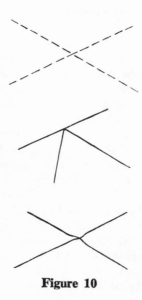

Figure 10

lar directions unique to each, *having failed to permit the neutrons simultaneous passage through the one point of interference.* Because they can't go through the same point at the same time we get little angles by which cloud-chamber physicists recognize the subatomic particles. If lines, which experimentally are always vectors, are unable to go simultaneously through the same point, then we can't have "planes" which were absurdly thin wafers of solids. Thus we find that we are dealing with a very different kind of a universe from the one that we were told about and the children as yet are "learning" about in the grade schools.

(Figure 10) Because you can't have two actions going through the same point at the same time, we have the phenomenon of *reflection* with which we are all familiar or we have *refraction*. Those two experimentally reliable *interference* phenomena are direct consequences of the fact that actions cannot take place through the same point at the same time.

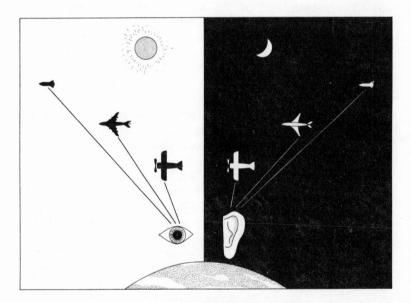

Figure 11

(Figure 11) Now, something we are all familiar with. One of the first surprise experiences in each young life is seeing somebody hitting something at a distance and realizing that they, the observers, are hearing the hitting event somewhat

after they see it. Up to this time, the children thought that all
their faculties were *simultaneously* and *instantly* coordinate
and operating at equal velocities. Einstein showed that neither *simultaneous* nor *instant* are valid, i.e., experimentally
demonstratable. In World War I with many airplanes in the
sky, we began to realize that we were hearing them in this
direction and seeing them in that other direction. Then as the
planes got bigger and faster and flew higher, we began to experience enormous distances between where we thought we
heard them and where we thought we saw them. The highest
airplanes we can see with our eyes, as little glintings in the
sun, are flying at about 40,000 feet or only about 8 miles out
from the surface of the earth, and 4008 miles out from the
center of the 8000-mile diameter of the earth. The 8 miles is
a negligible distance, only one-thousandth the earth's diameter. The highest orbiting of manned satellites has been at 380
miles outward of the earth's surface. This is a distance which
is only one-twentieth of the earth's diameter—equal to an
inch away from a basketball's surface. Today, man hasn't as
yet gone "far out." Our nearest star, the sun, is 92 million
miles. And it takes 8 minutes for the light to come from the
sun to us. Then the next nearest star is so far away that it
takes years for the light to come to us. Our eyes do not tell us
the different distances of the stars in the heavens which seem
to be in a great spherical bowl array at apparently equal radial distance from us. The stars seem utterly motionless because when objects move at a great distance from us, we cannot see their motions.

The stars are all moving at fabulous velocities but the in-
terpositional relationships in respect to our lifetimes seem
changeless. We do know but do not sense that we are looking
at many stars that haven't been there for sometimes millions
and sometimes billions of years. We do not have any conception of what the true geometrical interrelationships of those
stars might be to each other. Their most economical interrelationship patterning might be a surprisingly regular geometrical pattern. The chaotic array is the consequence of differen-
tially delayed information from very great distances.

Observe that when we send up four rockets, at one-half
second apart, their afterimages are approximately simultaneous. So, we say that we see four rockets "at the same
time." The illusion of simultaneity is one of the most important illusions for us to consider. Musicians may be able to

comprehend nonsimultaneity better than do others. Einstein emphasized the importance of attempted spontaneous comprehension of the nonsimultaneity of all the events of universe—a concept akin to our discovery that in our universe none of the lines can ever go simultaneously through the same points. In the realistic concept of the nonsimultaneity of events of universe, we lose forever the conceptual validity of the static pictures which man had assumed in accord with Newton's norm of "at rest." People say, "What is the shape of the universe?" and "What is outside of outside?" The question assumes that everything in the universe is actually in simultaneous static array with no consideration of all the myriads of stars that just aren't there, and haven't been for billions of years. What Einstein is telling you is that none of the events occur at the same time. There is some illusory overlapping of events from special eclipse viewpoints but we are dealing with a universe of completely nonsimultaneous events. There is no inherently composite picture of "May Day in Moscow, 1923" and the inside of a brand new jukebox in an Atlantic City hotel in New Jersey, Christmas Day, 1965.

There is no inherently logical montage of these nonsimultaneous, unspecified-viewpoint concepts. We take the dictionary, all the dictionaries, of all the languages and make them into one great big book. In that book we'd have all the word formulations accruing to all attempts of all men through all history to try to explain all their nonsimultaneous-event experiences. We can say that this is one big composite dictionary with only the latest words of the latest year left out. That's like saying the word "universe." But you cannot put all those words together simultaneously in one meaningful sentence. Nor can you even open one page and comprehend a coordinate meaning out of all the words. Nor can you read all the words simultaneously. In fact, you can only deal meaningfully with one word at a time. And by the time you finish reading one you have to begin with another. And so we get a sequence of events. There is no validity in the concept of a universe of nonsimultaneous events as a unit and simultaneous shape—with an inside and outside. It becomes exciting to realize that we are not logically required to formulate a simultaneous shape universe. We need not bother any more about what is outside, because what you think that you see outside may now be inside. So there is no inherent inside or

UNDERLYING ORDER IN

No. of Events	Conceptuality of number of most economical relationships between events or minimum number of inter-connections of all events	No. of Relationships $\dfrac{n^2 - n}{2}$	Closest packed, symmetrical and most economical conceptual arrangement of number relationships.
1	•	0	
2	AB	1	
3	AB, BC, AC	3	
4	AB, BC, CD, AC, BD, AD	6	
5		10	
6		15	
7		21	
7	Same number of events could be in random array but minimum total of relationships are same in number.	21	

Figure

RANDOMNESS

Sum of Adjacent Relationships $(n-1)^2$	Conceptuality in closest packed Symmetry Note: This occurs as ◇ "diamonds" and not as □ "squares".	Sum of Experiences or of Events Is Always Tetrahedronal	No. of Events
			1
0 + 1 = 1			2
1 + 3 = 4			3
3 + 6 = 9			4
6 + 10 = 16			5
10 + 15 = 25			6
15 + 21 = 36			7
			7

Copyrighted 1965   R. Buckminster Fuller

outside of the aggregate of universe's ages of nonsimultaneous events. We find that the word "in" expresses a direction toward the center of a specific body. "In" is unique to
individual bodies but "out" is common to all and "out" has
no shape. Inside-outing of nonsimultaneous-event relationships from heterogeneous time viewpoints of universe is inherently shapeless, ergo nonconceptual.

(Figure 12) I find this chart to be one of the most exciting
I've been able to put on paper. There is a column on the
left-hand side where you just see the numbers 1, 2, 3, 4, 5, 6,
7. In the second column you see first one black spot. Below it
you see two black spots and below them are three black spots
and some little lines connecting them. Now, those lines connecting them represent the minimum number of telephone
wires that we would have to have to connect each of the
points privately with each of the other points in its group.
The black dots of the second column each represent just one
experience. In the first row there is only one experience,
which does not need a telephone relationship. But down
below it, there are two experiences and there has to be one
telephone wire between the two for each to be able to communicate privately about his respective experiences. We could
say that for *A* to telephone *B* is different than for *B* to telephone *A* (*A* being the President of the U.S.A. and *B* the village barber). We may if we wish say that each telephone
wire is worth two because it has two different alternative calling orders. For the purpose of simplicity I will hold consistently to the single mutual value of *one* as the true minimum
number of telephone wires necessary to provide private
hookup between any two telephone *callers*. These I speak of
as *experiences*. In the third row of the second column there
are three experiences and we find that there are three private
connections. Down below it there are four experiences and
we find that there are six connections. You can express these
relationships algebraically. In the top one, you have *A*, and *A*
has no relationship. In the next one, you have *AB* so you
have the relationship *AB*. So you could say that *BA* is the
negative; but it is *AB* when *A* is talking with *B* listening, and
it is *BA* when *B* is talking and *A* is listening—with only one
telephone wire necessary to that functioning. A set of negatives and positives do not require more connections because
negative and positive cannot simultaneously occupy the connecting line. In the third row we have *ABC*. So you say, *AB*,

AC, BC. There are three relationships. The fourth line has four experiences *ABCD.* And they could be expressed uniquely as *AB, AC, AD, BC, BD, CD.* So you get six. Then below that, I have five experiences *ABCDE* and they have ten relationships, ten telephone wires. Below that, I have six and they have fifteen telephone wires. Below that, I have seven and they have twenty-one telephone wires. Therefore the number of telephone wires are not the same series of numbers as the series of experiences numbers.

We also note that for three experiences there are three telephone wires and for two experiences one private wire but for four experiences six telephone wires. We can say that in the case of four or more experiences the number of private-wire relationships is always greater than the number of experiences. We may also say that the minimum number of private-wire relationships between any number of experiences is always $\dfrac{n^2 - n}{2} = r$—where n equals the number of experiences and r the minimum number of relationships. So the third column of our chart gives the number of $\dfrac{n^2 - n}{2}$ telephone wires and reads 1, 3, 6, 10, 15, 21, corresponding to 1, 2, 3, 4, 5, 6, 7 in column one. Then in column four to the right, I have a series of circles in groups of the most economical and symmetrical arrays possible. The number of circles in these symmetrical clusters show how many telephone connections were necessary for that row's number of experiences. So to come down to the second line reading across, we have two experiences. And we see that one telephone wire and it says "1" and I have one little black-line circle in the fourth vertical column. In the row below that we have three experiences and three relationships. So I have three circles in the fourth vertical column and they make a little triangle. On the fourth line there are four experiences and they have six relationships so we count the little circles: 1, 2, 3, 4, 5, 6, also making an equilateral triangle. We come down to the line below where we have five experiences and they have ten relationships, and you count the little circles in the triangle: 1, 2, 3, 4, 5, 6, 7, 8, 9, 10. So in the one below, we have six experiences and fifteen relationships and you count the circles in the triangle and you will find that there are fifteen. In the row below where there are seven experiences there are twenty-one relationships. Count the circles in the symmetrical triangle and you will find that there are just twenty-one. $\frac{n^2 - n}{2} = 7^2$, $49 - 7 = 42 \div 2 = 21$. Now it is very interesting that the *picture of the relationship is always a triangle.*

Then I would point out that those numbers 1, 3, 6, 10, 15, 21, are numbers which, if associated as any *pair of adjacents,* add to a number of the second power, e.g., the 1 with 3 makes the number 4 which is 2 to the second power. If you associate the 3 with the 6, you get the number 9 which is the second power of 3. So that you find in combining any two of those sets of relationships adjacently, they make what we call the second power. We used to call it a "square," but I made a most economical space picture of it and you will find that the circles close pack as *diamonds* and not as *squares.* Then in the right-hand column, we have stacks of those triangles of circles which represent the numbers of fundamental relationships. The stacks of triangles are like stacks of cannonballs, and they make a tetrahedron. So we can say then that *the sum of the relationships of all our experiences is always tetrahedronal.* It is pretty exciting then to discover this extraordinary, omnisymmetrical tetrahedonal sum of all our experience interrelationships. We can say correctly to human beings trying to understand number relationships of arrays (that seem to be chaotic as with the stars in the sky) that all the interrelationships of all stars you are able to count in the sky are always symmetrically triangular. This has to be. Therefore, what seemingly is disorderly on first appearance turns out to have this extraordinary order. And the sums of interrelationships of all the experiences of each of our lives are always tetrahedronal, and all the relationships of all the component events of universe are always tetrahedronal.

We've heard the popular myth of talking about man and the universe (the *Life* magazine type of story) which starts universe off as an astronomical aggregate of primordial chaos in some kind of vast nothingness. Somehow or other out of this enormous amount of chaos, in which the scientist finds that random elements are always increasing, ergo becoming ever more chaotic, until the random elements suddenly jell in an inexplicably orderly way and we have all the extraordinary things like daisies, diamonds, and moons. Then it is also said that the scientist wrests order out of chaos. This implies that there were extraordinary scientists standing off somewhere from the primordial ooze to suddenly make the daisies, diamonds, and moons. The legendary scientist is a magician and, therefore, he is a great benefactor of society.

Many a great scientist who has made a great discovery, has noted, somewhere in his letters, manuscripts, or diaries and in his recorded talks with his friends just what he had first thought might be going on in certain events of nature which had excited him into making an experiment. According to the great scientists' own records, their formulations, their hypotheses about what might be going on always turned out to be very crude as compared to what they actually found to be the patterns operative in nature, which always disclosed an extraordinarily sublime, a priori orderliness. In finding that the sum of all of our relationships always add to one neat complete, closest-packed tetrahedron we understand why the scientist had to find orderliness.

During the early days of World War II scientists found their narrow fields of specialization beginning to overlap one with the other by virtue of the powerful instruments and the increasing numbers of abutting specialists. The biologist found himself suddenly overlapping the area of the chemist, and the chemist found himself overlapping the area of the physicist. This brought about all the interhyphenating of the sciences such as in bio-chemistry, and so forth. Now the microworld scientists all find themselves so overlapped as to realize that they are in one world, with everywhere the same sublime orderliness. And the orderliness of various aspects of nature are all interrelated, so they realize that they are dealing in just one great, sublimely coordinated, comprehensive accounting system employed by nature. Nature is not only orderly but the orderliness is rationally accountable in pure principle. And pure principles have no beginnings or endings. Therefore, we are not dealing in universe that has to be pictured or explained by a beginning and an ending. The experiences may be a chaotic array. But the interconnections are orderly. What we mean by *understanding* is: apprehending and comprehending all the interrelationships of experiences. Understanding is symmetrically tetrahedronal.

This is as far as I will go in the pictures. I hope that I have introduced some generalized principles which have some relationship to music: for instance, the wave phenomena, the precessional phenomena, and so forth; the omnidirectionality with which we are really dealing. I am quite confident, because I have been exploring it for a long time, that nature has just one coordinate system.

In 1917, I found myself asserting that I didn't think that nature had a department of chemistry, a department of mathematics, a department of physics, and a department of biology and had to have meetings of department heads in order to decide what to do when you drop your stone in the water. Universe, i.e., nature, obviously knows just what to do, and everything seemed beautifully coordinate. The lily pads did just what they should do, the fish did just what they should do. Everything went sublimely, smoothly. So I thought that nature probably had one coordinate system and probably one most economical, arithmetical, and geometrical system with which to interaccount all transactions and transformations. And I thought also that it was preposterous when I was told that real models were not employed in advance science, because science was able to deal with nature by use of completely unmodelable mathematical abstractions. I could not credit that universe suddenly went abstract at some microlevel of investigation, wherefore in order to be able to deal with the physical universe in the most advanced stages of frontiering you had to deal entirely with abstract-formula, unmodelable mathematics. As we acquired larger microscopes and larger telescopes, I found that models always showed up. And men, satisfied with their abstract preoccupations, didn't bother or didn't seem to know how to explain the emerging pictures of the obviously systematic but strange, often asymmetrical but sometimes symmetrical models. I thought then that if we could find nature's own coordinate system we would understand the models and we would be able to develop much higher exploratory and application capability. In chemistry atoms were associating and disassociating in beautiful whole simple-numbers arrangements: such as H_2O, or whatever the combination. Chemistry seemed to avoid irrational fractions. Everything was accountable in simple and whole numbers. I felt that if we ever found nature's coordinate system, it would be very simple and always rational.

I am confident now that I have found that coordinate system because I have submitted it to bodies of competent scientists. In October, 1965, I met with competent scientists of all the related fields of physics. I made comprehensive disclosure of the ramifications of the coordinate system which I have discovered and explored for a third of a century. They accepted the coordinated system which I disclosed as probably being nature's most efficient means of accounting those of nature's generalized relationships which I tended to identify by the coordination system.

The omnirational coordinate system which I have named "synergetics" is not an invention. It is purely discovery. I am quite confident that with the complete and simple modelability of synergetics that it is going to be possible for children at home with closed-circuit TV documentaries coming to them and making their own models, to do valid nuclear-physics formulations at kindergarten age. With that fundamental structuring experience, and sensing through models, children will be making experiments that discover why water does what it does. They will really come to understand what a triangle is and what it can do and does. The obsoleting educational system taught people to think in "squares," and to measure in terms of "inches," "squares," and "cubes." We've come to assume that a cubical or rectilinear house has structural integrity. If you make a cube with little sticks and rubber joints, you'll find that cubes always collapse. They have no structural integrity whatsoever. We find ourselves starting out on all the wrong axiomatic bases. When we use tetrahedra to account nature we are three times more efficient (with energy) than when we account in cubes. And nature is always most efficient.

In this total interprecessional set of events that I have talked to you about, I have stressed that where men think of themselves as most scientifically advanced, especially in pure mathematics, that I find them dealing in axioms that no longer hold true. What they are doing does hold true in relation to that axiom. But inasmuch as they didn't start with axioms disclosed experimentally by nature they are dealing in nonuniverse, and are playing perfectly good games and I love them for doing it, but they are playing games that are completely irrelevant to what we and nature are doing and need to do.

I am confident that in the world of music and in the world of art, human beings have attained much spontaneous and realistic coordination. Artists are really much nearer to the truth than have been many of the scientists.

I wasn't surprised when under the authority and funding of the National Defense Education Act, the Science Advisor to the President recently persuaded the White House to spend some of the science-aimed educational funds on an exploration with art educators in New York. They had their meeting in New York University and brought together some of the best (in my estimation) art educators in the country as well as some good artists. It was realized in our nation's seeking for scientists that they were only getting people who were good methodologists, who could expand or refine what was already proven, but they had no ability to conceive of as yet entirely hidden and previously unthought-of conditions and relations of nature or to explore and use their minds imaginatively. That is where the word "creative" came in. It was hoped by the scientists and the President that by going to the art educators they might be able to discover in the knowledge and experience of art educators just how children suddenly conceive in sublimely pure and simple yet original patterns. The scientists and the President wanted to know what really constitutes and motivates and detonates the imagination of bright creative children, as well as of the inspiringly resourceful teachers who have the imagination, power, strength, and conviction to go along with the children's original conceptioning. It is interesting to discover that our national defense, having found the academic world of science per se to be only a methodological system of researching and rehashing already proven phenomena, now discovers that academic science is running into a dead end. Because our scientists are unable to maintain or exceed the world pace of evolutionary development, our whole nation is losing its leadership pace. We have suddenly to turn to the artist. Art educators themselves had found that there was an extraordinary relationship between the conceptually brilliant child and the human-being teacher who the child found was not frustrating it but was accepting and fostering the child's curiosity and need to deal with its interference-born original questions.

In your musical-education world and in your professional meetings, I think it important that you realize that within the next ten years the world of science and the world of seemingly very pragmatic affairs may be turning to the world of music for leadership in fostering the spontaneous development of the most powerfully coordinate capabilities of evoluting life. Rather than being a pleasant sideshow for the more serious central affairs of economic life, you who deal with the music of the universe and the innate coordinate capability of man to tune in the music of the new life may be recognized as dealing with the sensitive mainspring of life itself, because of which you may find yourselves called by society to perform its most responsible task allowing life to succeed.

3.   Prevailing Conditions in the Arts

When very young in school I often felt that I could make jokes about the axioms from which we proceeded to formulate. Since we knew about the relatively vast spatial relationships of atoms and electrons, I thought that solids were impossible. I remember just before World War I, I began to say that I didn't think nature had separate departments of Physics, Chemistry, Biology, and Mathematics requiring meetings of department heads in order to decide how to make bubbles and roses! I had a suspicion that nature had just one department! The exploration capabilities of the scientists of my youth were meager compared to today—what the biologist was able to see with his very low-powered microscope looked very different from what the chemists seemed to be dealing with—the chemist couldn't see what he was dealing with anyway! He just simply found that things associated or dissassociated in unique manner and he had ways of measuring the rates and quantities. The physicist didn't know what he was looking at either—he seemed to feel that what he was dealing with was very different from what the biologist saw, so they felt they had to have different departments. They all made unique measurements. If the information was to be turned to practical account, some kind of coordination of the data, from the different departments' several methods of quantation, had to be developed. In matters of spatial arrangements the x-y-z coordinate system was used. Men seemed to think that breadth, height, and width were all very logical.

Everybody in this room, as I speak today 60 years later, has lived through the days when man began to talk about other dimensions, such as time. He began thinking vaguely about time as a fourth dimension. Science advanced and changed rapidly without any adequate way for the nonscientist population to bridge the great break between the sciences and the humanities. C. P. Snow became well-known around the world for his "two worlds"—the concept of the great dichotomy between the sciences and humanities. Snow attributed it to an antipathy at the beginning of the Industrial Revolution on the part of the literary men for the smells of the laboratories and the noisiness of the industry which ensued. Snow also attributed the initial dichotomy not only to carelessness on the part of the scientist toward the antipathy of the literary man, but also to the scientist's snob enjoyment of being mysteriously obscure. Snow said that the chasm widened until it could never be spanned again.

A year ago I talked with C. P. Snow in London; I said that I agreed with him about the existence of the chasm. I felt that anybody who had ever been a science writer would feel that way. In 1938 to 1940 I was the technical advisor to the editors of *Fortune* magazine. Whenever I attempted to report the scientific content of industrial enterprises to *Fortune* readers in words, the scientists within those industries said I would be unable to do so. They said that science is entirely mathematical and unless the *Fortune* readers read the mathematics, there would be no way to explain their scientific formulations. I felt them to be wrong. I battled hard to find ways of spanning this chasm. However, I didn't make my start to find the answer in 1938-1940. I had been looking for it a long time. It went back beyond 1917 when I said I didn't think science and nature had different departments. It went back to kindergarten and to my earliest schoolboy skepticism about the very axioms of geometry and arithmetic. I'd been exploring seriously since 1917, at first spasmodically—gradually more intensively—to discover whether we might not be able to find *the* coordinate system employed by nature. I felt that if and when we did find it, that it would be characterized by arithmetic and geometry which would be extremely simple. Chemistry showed us that nature was associating and disassociating in terms of simple, whole, rational numbers such as H_2O, not as H pi O which would prevent nature from ever making anything because pi may never be resolved. Pi is irrational. There were no irrational numbers in chemical combinings of atoms and molecules.

What I was able to say to C. P. Snow was that I thought that the break was not due to antipathy on the part of the literary man, but due to a fundamental event that occurred in the world of science in the mid-19th century. I explained that it occurred after Faraday discovered electrical behaviors, and the work of Maxwell and Hertz indicated the existence of invisible electromagnetic waves—waves going through the walls and through each other without interference with one another. In this new electromagnetic world, man found himsel˜ dealing with discrete apparatus such as a specific number of copper wire coils wound around a magnet. Each additional coil had a discretely measurable effect all statable in neat algebraic equations. Ohm's law was typical of this development. The scientists, though dealing with invisible energy phenomena, were able to get beautifully neat answers to experimentally posed questions regarding various arrangements. They found themselves getting on very well without seeing what was going on. It was during some of these early experiments on energy behaviors that a fourth-power relationship was manifest. The equation contained a fourth power x^4. You can make a model of x^3, e.g., as a cube, and you can make a model of x^2, (x to the second power) and call it a square, and a model of x^1 and call it a line; but you could not make a geometric model of x to the fourth power. The consequences of this unmodelable fourth-power event are tied up with other events. At the same historical period literary men were trying to explain the new invisible electrical energy, which could do yesterday's tasks with new and miraculous ease, to their scholarly readers and the public in general. They began to use visually familiar analogies to explain the invisible behaviors. The concept of a current of water running through a pipe as analogous to electricity running through a wire was employed by the nonscientific writers. The scientists didn't like that at all, because electricity really did not behave as does water. Electricity "ran" uphill just as well as downhill (but did not really "run"). The scientists felt that analogies were misleading and they disliked them. When the experiments that showed a fourth-power relationship occurred, the scientists said "Well, up to this time we have felt that visual models were legitimate (though not always easy to formulate), but now, inasmuch as we can't make a fourth-power energy-relationship model, the validity of the heretofore accepted generalized law of models is broken. From now on physically conceptual models are all suspect. We're going to work now entirely in the terms of abstract, 'empty-set,' mathematical expressions."

Their invisible procedures thenceforth to this day have a counterpart in modern air transport and night fighter flying —which is conductable and is usually conducted entirely "on instruments." When you qualify for instrument flight you are able to fly in fog and night without seeing any terrain. You get on very well, and arrive where you want on instruments.

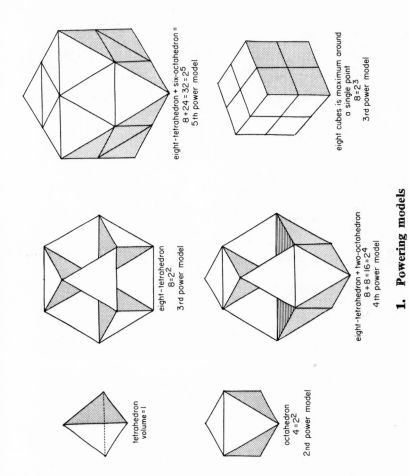

eight-tetrahedron + six-octahedron =
$8 + 24 = 32 = 2^5$
5th power model

eight cubes is maximum around
a single point
$8 = 2^3$
3rd power model

eight-tetrahedron
$8 = 2^2$
3rd power model

eight-tetrahedron + two-octahedron
$8 + 8 = 16 = 2^4$
4th power model

tetrahedron
volume = 1

octahedron
$4 = 2^2$
2nd power model

1. Powering models

2.   Pilot blind-flying

Scientists "went onto instruments" about 1875—almost entirely. By the time I went to school at the turn of the century we were taught about instruments and equations and how to conduct experiments. We were told that the fourth dimension was just "ha-ha,"—you could never do anything about it. Frustrated by the withdrawal of models to describe, literary men invented the myth that the fourth dimension was *time* and therefore logically invisible—while the other three dimensions were as yet visible. Though it was incorrect, few scientists contradicted this explanation of *time;* for the scientists no longer thought of, or discussed, models. The cliché of "the fourth dimension is time" became a "knowing-one's" mystique.

So I told C. P. Snow of my own investigation of nature's coordinating system. In thinking about nature's coor-

3. Scientists blind-probing with instruments

dinate system, I assumed it must embrace some kind of omnirational geometry and arithmetic, because of chemical structuring rationality. I also found myself well-impressed with something we call vectors. Vectors had first been developed to important extent in electrical engineering (though Galileo used them tentatively and erroneously in developing his parallelogram of forces). According to Galileo we could make a vectorial pattern of a ship A of such and such a weight, going in such and such a direction at such and such a velocity. You multiplied the velocity times the weight and that gave you a vector: x. You then made a vectorial line AC on your diagram that was x units long, that was shown going in the compass direction that the ship was going—let us say "due east." Ship A collided with another ship B at point C. Ship B weighed such and such an amount. You multiplied ship B's weight by its speed (velocity) and it gave you the

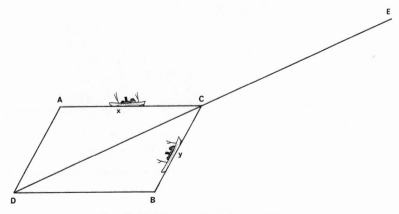

4. Galileo's parallelogram of forces

length, y, of a vector line BC. BC had a compass direction,
too—let us say "northeast," reading from B to C. Galileo
then constructed a parallelogram $ACBD$ with BD parallel to
AC running west from B to D, then DA constructed parallel
to BC, running northeast from D to A. Galileo then drew a
vectorial line diagonally from D to C, the point of collision
of ships A and B, and then Galileo extended the line DC outward of the parallelogram to E with $CE = DC$, and with the
angle $DCE = 180°$, i.e., a "straight" line. Galileo called CE
the "resultant of forces"—the vector of the combined forces
x, y. Galileo's "resultant of forces" was wrong because two
colliding ships do not waltz gayly east-northeast 12 miles together. Usually one of the ships goes "down"—into the sea
—toward the center of earth—which multidirection vector
was not in Galileo's "plane" geometry scheme. Nevertheless I
found his vectoral diagram exciting. It suggested a comprehensive geometry consisting entirely of vectors. A vectorial
line was a very nice kind of a line because it had a discrete
length—it didn't go on absurdly forever to the nowhere of
two infinities—in both directions as potential extensibilities of
lines. It didn't have the "time" to do so. It had a discrete
amount of time, which time was a component factor of the
vector's velocity. I wondered if nature might have a set of
omnidirectionally operative vectors that represented all of our
experiences. It is *experiences* that we are dealing with in nature. Nature and universe are alike *the aggregate of all ex-*

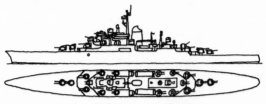

5. Ships are vectors.

perience. Couldn't I then find vectors that represented any and every unique experience? Vectors are like *spears*. I could "massage" any object into a spear shape, point and thrust-throw it in a discrete direction. I intuitively liked those directional vector "spears." I felt that they tended at least to embody all the energetic qualities of represented experiences. That thinking-feeling, however, was only an intuition and not an accomplished, *mathematically coordinate, generalized-experience system.* That intuition was followed by another pure intuition. I had liked Avogadro, just as soon as I had heard about him. Avogadro came into the world of chemistry at a time when chemists were excited about gases. The gases came into recognition as chemical elements through Lavoisier's explanation of Priestley's experiment with the isolation of fire. All the chemical elements up to the Priestley-Lavoisier event were metals—easy to recognize by their weights and colors. Lavoisier explained Priestley's experiment of fire under a bell jar which had resulted in water vapor and ash whose combined weight was more than the weight of the item which had burned. Lavoisier said, "Well something that was in this space under the bell jar must have been there all the time which combined—with the visible item which burned—during the process of 'burning' whatever that might be." He said that the "nothingness" under the jar ("something" men had called both "nothingness" and "air") must indeed be *something* which, though invisible, is physically real which combined to make the *water vapor* as well as the ashes.

I think Lavoisier's intuitive conceptioning was possibly the most intellectually daring of all history. For a man to dare to think that the nothingness could be something fundamental, so fundamental as to be identified as a chemical element, and not only that, but that the nothingness could be divided into a plurality of fundamental chemical elements was an enormous jump from the conditioned reflex concept of chemical elements only as metals. And so he called one of the invisibles oxygen and he had it combine with the carbohydrate item releasing the carbon and combining with the hydrogen to form the water vapor. I have oversimplified to get on with my story. Other humans were involved, etc. But it is close enough not to be misleading. From that point on scientists came swiftly to understand what fire was. It was fast oxidation. Therefore, they also knew what steam was for they now also knew what H_2O was, and how it combined. And they knew what iron rust was. It was *iron and oxygen,* as was iron ore. The metallurgical, chemical, thermodynamic bases of the invention of the steam engine were implicit in the chemical conceptioning of Lavoisier. As an indirect recognition of his general integrity, he was guillotined.

With the steam engine came the ability to drive ships without wind. With that came vast acceleration of world commerce and with it enormous amounts of wealth. Realizing for the first time in history that great wealth accrued to scientific discovery the rich masters of commerce—privately I call them the great pirates—put up large amounts of their wealth for further scientific discovery. This brought great scientific competition to determine who would run the world with the new steamships. In the scientific endeavor which ensued the next five chemical elements to be isolated were all gases found by Cavendish in England. Whoever understood energy and gases was apparently going to run the world. At this time the laws of thermodynamics evolved.

Avogadro entered the scientific era at the time of its preoccupation with gases. He began to study the total pattern of what men had found out about the gases—what characteristics they had found so far? He saw something which seemed significant and intuitively hypothesized a theoretical statement. He next devised experiments which could prove or disprove his theory. Experiments proved his hypothesis to be correct, to wit "that all gases under identical conditions of heat and pressure always disclose the same number of molecules per given volume." Gases are individual elements; therefore, fundamentally different from one another. That individually fundamental elements, such, precisely because they were different, should show the same number of molecules in a given volume under identical energy conditions of both heat and pressure persuaded me that Avogadro had found at least a corner of the "Grand Central Station" of nature's fundamental coordinate system. Here were common conditions of chemistry, physics, arithmetic, and geometry—a wedding of number and volume. I then said we know that Avogadro did what he did when gases were thought to be a special class of elements. Since that time we have learned that all the chemical elements including the metals can be liquefied and incandescently plasmacized or gasified, and, in the other direction, that gases can be liquefied. Apparently we can run any of the elements back and forth through this transformation hierarchy depending on how much energy is present in the form of heat or pressure. So I intuited that it might be possible to generalize Avogadro by hypothesizing that "all elements under identical conditions of energy may disclose the same number of something per given volume." So I said: If this becomes experimentally provable we may be getting somewhere in our search for nature's comprehensive coordinating system; if the answer lies in this direction the coordination will be expressible in neatly coordinate arithmetical, geometrical terms. There are and have been a great number of scientists looking for comprehensive coordinate systems. What has been lacking in all, other than Avogadro's limited coordinate system of a plurality of individual elemental atomic gases, has been the failure to coordinate the *arithmetic and geometry*. We have number values galore in respect to invisible energy relationships. We have hypothetical chemical constructs but no true geometry which is reliably conceptual. Avogadro's volume requires a geometric container quantum.

So I said, all right; *if all the conditions of energy were the same*, what would such a condition look like in vectors? (And that brings me back to where I detoured from Galileo to Avogadro.) Well, it would mean that all vectors would have to be the same length. All of them would have to be running into each other at the same angles. So I said, can we make realistic, multidimensional, visible, tangible models of equilength vectors all running into each other at the same angles? Such a vectorial system in local universe would be inherently finite. It would not imply additional vectors. It wouldn't have to go on forever, because vectors, unlike Greek "lines," don't have to go on forever.

I found I could make just such a model. It came out as what we call the tetrahedron-octahedron complex; some scientists call it the isotropic vector matrix. Aston, in 1929, made the discovery for the physicists of what he called "closest packing of spheres." The fruit dealer selling oranges and

6. Oranges in closest packing

the cannoneers stacking equiradius cannonballs learned about
this closest packing of spheres earlier, but the scientists
never noticed it. Two spheres may become tangent. We may

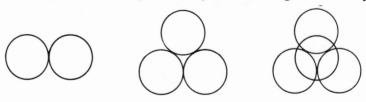

7. Closest packing arrays

then rest a third ball in the valley between them with the
third ball tangent to both of the first two. The three balls,

each one tangent to both of the others, now form an equiangular triangle group with a valley at their center. A fourth
ball may be rested in that triangular valley. The fourth one
touches each of the other three, and vice versa. The four
closest packed spheres make a "closest-packing array." This

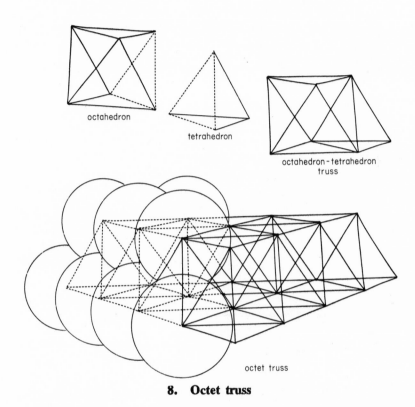

octahedron

tetrahedron

octahedron - tetrahedron
truss

octet truss

8. Octet truss

closest packing of spheres may go on triangulating in all directions. Because the spheres are all the same size, equilength
vectors may connect each and every adjacent sphere, with the
vectors running from the centers of the spheres through the
points of tangency to the adjacent spheres' centers. Remove
the spheres and leave the vectors and you've got the tetrahedron-octahedron complex. The "isotropic vector matrix" is a
structure that I discovered quite independently in kindergarten in 1899.

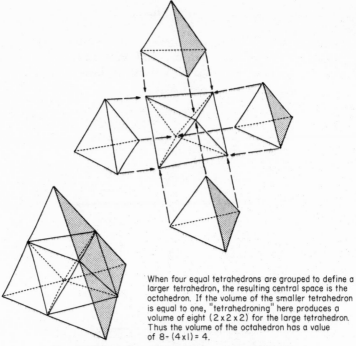

When four equal tetrahedrons are grouped to define a larger tetrahedron, the resulting central space is the octahedron. If the volume of the smaller tetrahedron is equal to one, "tetrahedroning" here produces a volume of eight (2 x 2 x 2) for the large tetrahedron. Thus the volume of the octahedron has a value of 8 - (4 x 1) = 4.

9.   Vector edge tetrahedron and octahedron

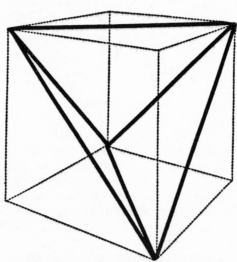

10.   Cube stabilized by a tetrahedron

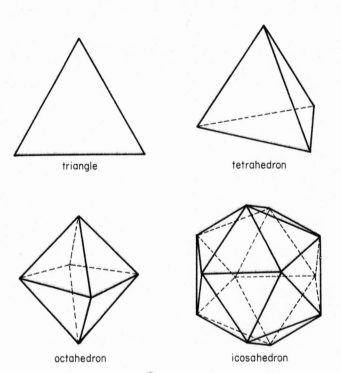

triangle   tetrahedron

octahedron   icosahedron

11. Basic structures

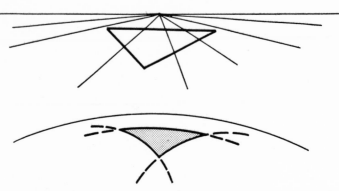

A triangle drawn on the earth's surface is actually
a spherical triangle bounded by great circle arcs.

The area apparently "outside" one triangle is seen
"inside" the other. Because every spherical surface
has two aspects---convex if viewed from outside,
concave if from within---each of these triangles is,
in itself, two triangles.

12.   Insideness and outsideness of systems

I related to Lord Snow how I experimented with this kind of geometry, and how I found that the vector-edged octahedron with the same length edge as the vector-edged tetrahedron had a volume of four times the tetrahedron.

A symmetrical cube has six faces, and a tetrahedron has six symmetrically-oriented edges. If you put a continuity of six diagonals in each of these six faces of the cube, a tetrahedron is formed. If you make a model of a cube with rubber joints, it collapses; it is completely unstable. If there's a tetrahedron secreted in the six diagonals of the cube's six faces, it will not fold up. A triangle is the only structurally stable polygon. A tetrahedron is the minimum omnitriangulated, omnistructural system. A tetrahedron is the most fundamental of all structures. There are only three basically stable omnitriangulated, omnisymmetrical structures—the octahedron, the tetrahedron, and the icosahedron. Each is a basic system because each stably and symmetrically subdivides the universe into two parts: all of the universe inside and all of the universe outside its system. When I then began to explore the volume relationships of the simplest basic, symmetrical structures and gave the simplest—the tetrahedron—a volume value of 1, I found that an octahedron had a volume of exactly 4 and a cube had a volume of exactly 3. That's very interesting because if you try to account in cubes for nature's energy associabilities—as structural systems—you use up three times as much space as you do if you count space volumes in tetrahedron units. The physicists have found that nature is always most economical; therefore, she could not use cubes to quantitate her structurings. The cubes, you know, represented our *x-y-z* coordinate system.

If you use tetrahedra as your coordinating system, something very economical and fundamental happens. The cube's angles are each 90°. When you want to make a bigger cube out of littler cubes—want to double the size of the cube—you then put eight little cubes together and get eight cubes symmetrically "closest-stacked," the big cube, around one point. The edges of the big cube are each 2 units of cube-edge long. The cube edges are 2. The face areas are each 4. The volume of the 2 linear-module-edged cube is 8, 8 being the third power of 2.

When we deal in tetrahedra, we're dealing in 60°-angle systems because in a regular tetrahedron, all the angles are 60°; they're equilateral—or equiangular—triangles.

You remember that what I told Lord Snow was that when

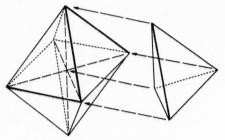

1/8 octahedron removed from whole octahedron
value of octahedron = 4
therefore 1/8 octahedron = 1/2

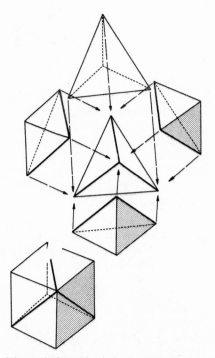

Cube may be formed by placing four 1/8 octahedrons
with their equilateral faces on the faces of a
tetrahedron. Since tetrahedron = 1, and 1/8 octahedron = 1/2, therefore value of a cube = 1 + 4 (1/2) = 3

13.   Cube uses up three times the space of tetrahedrons.

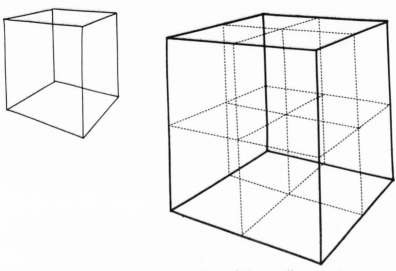

14.   Closest packing with cubes—90° coordinate system

the scientists found an energy relationship in the fourth-power value, they couldn't make a visual model of it because they couldn't find a fourth perpendicular to a cube which was not in a plane parallel to one of the planes of the cube. But the scientists did not need a model to calculate fourth-power problems. They were able to handle it very easily algebraically. They did it by using what they called an imaginary number, e.g., by using the square root of 1 — 1. If that sounds complex, don't let it bother you. What they were doing was simply saying they had a cubical clock. In effect, their cubical day consisted of eight little cubes around the center of the big cube. The first dimension used up one cube, the second dimension used up four cubes, and the third dimension used up all eight cubes. Their day's entire clock capacity would only take care of "three dimensions." So what they did was to borrow cubes from "tomorrow"—or from "yesterday." They then carried out their problem algebraically without reference to any conceptual models. After they got finished, they'd paid back the borrowed time and once again had a visual three-dimensional-model quantity. When you use 60° for your coordination, you don't need imaginary or complex numbers to carry out fourth-power calculations because there is a volume of 20 tetrahedra around one point instead of 8. Two to the fourth power is 16, and I've got 20 tetrahedra around a

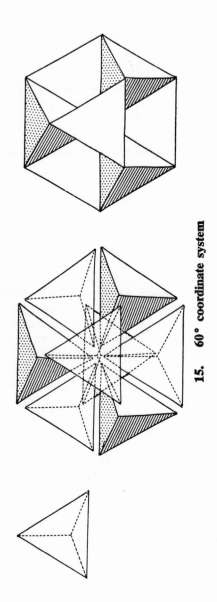

15. 60° coordinate system

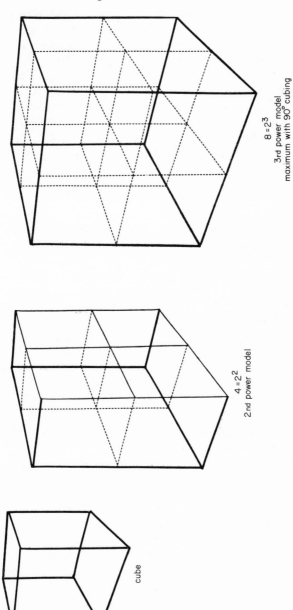

$8 = 2^3$
3rd power model
maximum with 90° cubing

$4 = 2^2$
2nd power model

cube

16. Cubical clock—powering model with cubes

point. There is an additional 2 to the second power in the model which comes in very usefully when this vectorial grouping around a common nucleus is employed to account for nuclear-energy behaviors. When the nuclear group of vectors has a radial or edge molecule of 2 (as do the 8 cubes in closest packing), then the vectorial system has a volume around its center of 160, which is $5 \cdot 2^5$. It is perfectly possible today, then, for a child to make fourth- and fifth-power models with tetrahedronal and octahedronal building blocks. Einstein was working on fifth-power problems in his last days, trying to reconcile gravity and electromagnetics.

I was able to say to Lord Snow, who was then Sir Charles, that I had found an arithmetical-geometrical energy-coordinating system which apparently coincided rationally and comprehensively with nature's behaviors which you could make models of and which could handle the fourth- and fifth-power problems which three-dimensional cubes could not, which latter fact had accounted for the discard of models and the preoccupation of science with a completely abstract treatment of nature.

Linus Pauling received his first Nobel prize for his contributions to the general knowledge of chemical structures. He gave me his Nobel laureate paper to read and it was the best and most concise history of chemical structures. The first part of his paper is about organic chemistry.

It was in the years around 1800 that the organic chemists, in making experiments, discovered that associating/disassociating of organic chemistry seemed to be always in number increments of 1, 2, 3, 4. Those were the only numbers you had to have to account for your experiments. In about 1810, a man named Frankland was the first to make any written notation of that. Then two men, Kékulé and Cooper, added a little more of the same. In 1835 a Russian, Butlerov, was the first to use the expression "chemical structure." And he was the first to say that 1, 2, 3, 4 seemed to have something to do with "bonding" together. He called the bonding "valence." Then there is a gap in further fundamental discovery up to 1885 when a man named van't Hoff said he thought the oneness, twoness, threeness, and fourness were the tetrahedron's four vertexes. Van't Hoff was looked at askance by the other chemists. He was called "an outright charlatan." He was called a faker of every kind. Otherwise the chemical scientists paid no attention to him. He was greatly stunned, but went on with his experiments and lived to make optical proof of the tetrahedronal configuration of carbon, the combining master of organic chemistry. Van't Hoff was the first chemist ever to receive the Nobel prize. From this point on, chemistry recognized that organic chemistry was tetrahedronally coordinate. Two tetrahedra linked

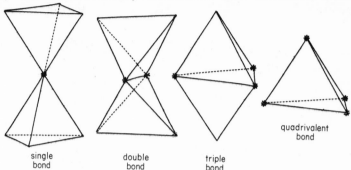

single
bond

double
bond

triple
bond

quadrivalent
bond

17. Chemical bonding

together by one vertex of each is a single bonding—very flexible, like a universal joint—like gas. Many tetrahedra so linked could be stretched to fill much more space than if linked mutually by two or three vertexes. Two bonds form a hinge—as yet flexible but quite compact as a system—like water. Triple bonding is rigid, like crystals. You can get four vertexes of tetrahedra together, which means they are congruent and most densely compacted, possibly like *diamonds*.

In van't Hoff's day, the majority of the chemists were metallurgists and they found no vertexial bondings. That was probably one reason the chemists in general had been so against van't Hoff. Even though he was finally successful, his contemporary metallurgists said, "We don't find any tetrahedra in our metals! Even though there seem to be visible crystals in nature such as octahedra, rhombic dodecahedra, etc., we can't find any way to account for their atomic structuring."

Linus Pauling, in 1932, approximately a half century after van't Hoff, was the first to use X-ray diffraction machines to probe metal structures. X-ray diffraction machines operate very much as does radar. X-ray diffraction sends X-rays right into the atoms and they bounce back and give pattern information, but not regular photographs. But you could make a photograph. The photograph was of X-rays bounced in against something and bounced out angularly so that what was really at the center was outward in the photograph and vice versa. It's really quite difficult to reconstruct the X-ray diffraction photographs into "pictures" of the shape of the explored patterns. Expertness is involved. Linus Pauling, applying X-ray diffraction to metals, discovered that all the metals which he analyzed were tetrahedronally coordinate, but instead of being linked vertex to vertex, they were linked

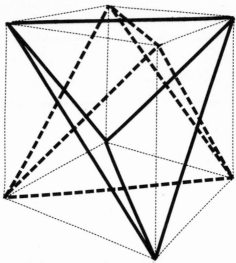

18. Tetrahedrons with common center of gravity

midedge to midedge often with common centers of gravity. We can make a red-edged tetrahedron's six edges by making a set of six contiguously-ended red diagonals in each of the six faces of a cube. Each red diagonal will occupy only one of the two diagonal paths across each of the six faces of the cube. We may therefore make a second blue tetrahedron occupying the six alternate diagonal paths of the cube's six faces. The blue tetrahedron and the red tetrahedron have a common center of gravity. That's one way metallic atoms combine.

While Linus Pauling has not to my knowledge said as yet that all metals are tetrahedronally coordinated, so far no exceptions have come to my attention. Pauling's Nobel laureate discourse twenty years after commencing his X-ray diffraction explorations discussed no exceptions.

I will now say to you that organic chemistry has for 80 years recognized tetrahedronal coordination. Twenty years of X-ray diffraction has found the metals tetrahedronally coordinate. I came to this subject in an entirely different way from that of the chemists and have found the tetrahedron to be the coordinating unit in experimental mathematics, which is what the scientists call my work. Therefore, I will say to you what I said to C. P. Snow: "All of nature's formulating is tetrahedronally coordinate." Snow, a scientist, said, "From what you have related to me, I am inclined to agree with you; in fact, this information happens to come at a very strategic moment in my life." In the 1965 New Year statements harvested by the press from world leaders, Lord Snow had quite a long piece saying that he now was retracting his "two forever unjoinable worlds" statements. He felt he was wrong and it looked as though the chasm between the two was closing.

I was in Ghana in January, and I received a telephone call from the British Broadcasting Corporation, asking me to come to London. When I reached London, I learned something which to me seemed extraordinary. This, too, is a long story but pertinent. Six years ago I had begun to get letters and photographs from two nuclear physicists who were leading virologists—Dr. Aron Klug, of Birkbeck College at London University, and Dr. Donald Casper, director of cancer research at the Boston Children's Hospital, now at the Cavendish Laboratories at Cambridge University. These men, using X-ray diffraction also, were finding the shape of the protein shells of the virus to be similar in appearance to my geodesic domes.

Very quickly I want to point out the general significance of virology. In the range of magnitudes between macro- and microcosmic limits of exploratory knowledge, there seem to be "octave"-like levels of unique pattern-phase relationships. The microdomain of the virus is that in which the tobacco-mosaic experiments first showed that the domain of the virus is apparently the threshold between what we have known in the past as the inanimate and the animate. The virus follows all the behavioral laws of an inanimate crystal, but also follows all the laws of animate biology. It is both animate and inanimate—in fact, because it follows both requirements, you have to say there is no difference between animate and inanimate phenomena. As a threshold, the virus overlaps both. It does not divide them. It calls for a very different concept of what we *are*, physically; it asks just how physical is life and what is unique to the individual? Within the virus, we have the now famous DNA and RNA, the nucleic acids consisting of four chemical compounds whose interpatterning sequences in helixes *control all patterning of all the designs of all life*

—all the biological forms design-scheduled by DNA and RNA. Investments by world society for the search in the virus domain are great. This is the most probable area in which to find the clues to the possible control of cancer, for here in the virus is the control of the design of life. DNA-RNA may also control the design of antilife.

A virologist is a very interesting kind of man. He was rarely trained to be a virologist; he was trained as a specialist —as a nuclear physicist, a mathematician, a chemist, a biologist, or a geneticist. But as virologists, they become one: an unusually comprehensive thinker—an integrator of widely held findings of science.

Just preceding and during World War II, scientists began to find their microscopes getting far more powerful. As a result, their field of observation began to overlap. My original hunch about nature having only one department became increasingly valid. The scientists found themselves forced to adopt hyphens to describe their work—bio-chemistry, etc. The virological teams find themselves inherently comprehensive—they deal with the whole show. And so the men who are good in virology are really extraordinary men, and tremendously articulate. Any good virologist sitting in with us today would find no trouble in participation in your subject. In fact he would probably be able to lead you in formulating a grand strategy of attacking your special problem. Virologists deal exclusively in fundamentals of structural design and how best to communicate our findings and intuitive formulations.

The virologist discovered the proliferation of my geodesic structures, which had emerged from structuring aspects of my energetic geometry studies which pursued nature's most economical stratagems. In 1957 Klug asked if I could identify the geodesiclike protein shell of the polio virus. I was able to give him the mathematical explanation of the structuring. Gradually, I heard from more virologists. I was told by a Johns Hopkins scientist the other day that she had read over twenty papers by scientists identifying my mathematical work—such as I've been giving you today—with the findings of their own investigation areas.

I was told by BBC (February 1964) that they were about to open up a broadcasting on a new channel 2, using colored TV, Telstar, and other electronic advances, and that they were about to reach audiences many times larger than their old channel 1 viewers. New receiving sets would be necessary

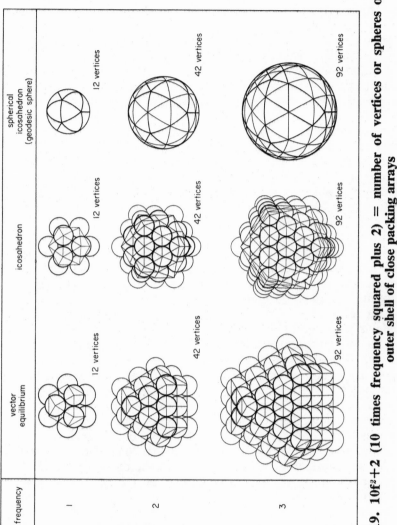

19. $10f^2 + 2$ **(10 times frequency squared plus 2) = number of vertices or spheres on outer shell of close packing arrays**

for tuning in channel 2. To warrant their old audience's purchase of new TV sets BBC felt that they must present programs of higher standards than ever before. They said, "Let's see if we can't take our experience and step up the quality of our program." For their step-up in content quality they took the most popular hour, which is 9:30 Saturday night, and set about to produce a science program once a month which they hoped could be so well done that it would displace lower-caliber amusements through spontaneous popularity. BBC got together its directors who had done science programs and chose the director who had done the Cavendish Laboratory documentary of Drs. Watson, Wilkins, and Crick—the DNA-RNA team which won the 1963 Nobel prize. This BBC director—Ramsey Short—went out to the Cavendish Laboratories at Cambridge University and asked their scientists what they recommended as the subject of the first channel 2 science program. The Cavendish scientists said, "Buckminster Fuller would be appropriate because TV must employ visible phenomena and Fuller has found the bridge of structural conceptuality to pure science exploration."

In the 19th century the literary man had the models taken away from him. He had no model to explain science to the people. Popularization of science employed superficial romance. True science was shunned as too difficult—or as dry, obscure, blackboard equations.

Since conceptuality is returning, it was felt that the first television program should deal with a fundamental bridge.

So the program started with giant geodesic radomes in North Riding, Yorkshire, and was done partly in the Cavendish Laboratories and partly with architectural students of London's Architectural Association. When it was finished, the BBC art directors were delighted with it—they said it was a good art show. This alarmed the BBC executives who said if it was very good art, it couldn't be very good science!

The program was broadcast in April '64. Those of you who are familiar with England know that the English critics are both plentiful and articulate. The science critics acclaimed it, so that it was successful scientifically. So also did the art critics. (I haven't seen the program myself, but that's the way life goes!) However, I'm confident that we have, in reality, closed the science-humanities gap with kindergarten conceptuality.

At start of today's meeting, when we were talking with the representative from the U.S. Science Foundation about what science is, science remained obscure in its advanced mathematics wrappings. I asserted (before presenting the integrated information I am now reciting) that man is coming into an extraordinary new era on earth, in which we are going to be able to deal conceptually with advanced science. Inasmuch as conceptual communication is art, art will become intimate with science; and philosophy will be able to comprehend the significance of developments; and thought may enter upon new speculation and altogether new comprehension.

One more item—have any of you read a book by Professor Benjamin Bloom of Chicago University? He is Professor of Education and head of the university's curricula committee. He has written a book, *Stability and Change in Human Characteristics*—Wiley, publishers—in which he has listed a number of experiments and case histories of lives from birth through university age which correlates progressively taken IQ tests with environment and the effects of events upon immature life at various age levels. The conclusions are astonishing! If you can give Dr. Bloom an adequate report of environmental factors governing a given young life from birth to seventeen years of age—such as description of the home— private bathroom or no—drunken parents—play only in streets—etc., he can give you the IQ of that life within 1%. There are built-in "alarm clocks," according to the neurophysiologists, which go off at unique moments, which put "capabilities" progressively in operation in the new life. If the new capability is frustrated at outset it is frequently relegated to disuse. At the age of four, 50% of the capacity to improve his IQ capabilities either have been expended or protected. Teaching doesn't add capability. Teaching can either gratify or frustrate capabilities. Usually they get badly damaged. The IQ is most directly affected by what happens in the first four years. Between four and eight, the next 30% "of capability to self-improve IQ" is brought into operation and either frustrated or gratified. Between eight and thirteen years, 12% more of potential capability is actuated totaling 92%, and at seventeen 100%. After seventeen, the most any human being can do to actuate more IQ is 0%. About $3 billion a year is appropriated jointly by the United States and the local governments for higher education, where the most possible self-improvement of IQ capability is 0%. Where 50% activatability of IQ occurs—that is from zero to four years—no appropriation is made. The only area where important chance of conserving and improving capacity occurs gets the small

money going into kindergarten, elementary, and junior high
school. The greatest schooling opportunity birth to four is operative through the TV only. The right TV programs for both
child and parents could up the national IQ by a large percentage.

Dr. Bloom shows that from birth to four years old there
are three clearly defined factors which govern the inauguration of capability to improve IQ (at any later date) or what
part of that first 50% is to be lost. Factor number one is
trust. Human young stay helpless longer than any other living
species. If the new life, for any reason, has its utter trust in
its parents violated, it is pretty sure to be a dropout. The next
two factors after *trust* which govern the one to four years are
autonomy and *initiative*. You don't know how to tell the extraordinary new life how to stand up—it just stands up by
itself when ready. The initiative is innate. The parents have
to be sure the child has room of its own and expendables for
the new life's "checkout" of: tension—cohesion, etc., by
trying to tear things, etc. From four to eight, there are several clearly defined factors governing favorable or unfavorable inauguration of 30% of total capability to ever improve
IQ. The new five-to-eight-year-old factors are ones to do primarily with the leadership of the parents. If the parents speak
their native language properly, effectively, and with joy in a
constantly improving vocabulary, it will have a very favorable effect on the child. Blasphemy or slang, a mark of an inferiority complex that is afraid to speak out clearly and con-
structively, will block off the six-year-old's brain capabilities.

Availability of good books on the shelves is an important
environment plus. While the child cannot read the grownup's
books, its intuition detects a drive or lack of drive for self-
improvement in its parents. It seems important to our meeting on clues for detecting the gifted schoolchild through art
teachers that Dr. Bloom's findings be known. When we know
that ages zero to four are the biggest "school" opportunity
and when we discover that entirely new mathematical simpli-
cities are at hand, we must realize that educational theory is
in for a complete revolution. There is no question about it—
an educational revolution is upon us.

Labor opposes automation only because everybody is
scared about their jobs. It's perfectly logical for them to be
scared about their jobs. But we're beginning to do something
about it which goes back to the post-World War II GI Bill.

We have said we will take all the people who are unemployed because their machines have become automated, and teach them a new skill relating to another machine. But soon the advancing state of automation will be such that by the time they have learned to operate a new machine, that one will have been automated too! They will simply stay in school studying how to operate obsolete tools. What we are going to do about all this is the following. First we must reorient our eons-long nervous-reflex conditioning. It is not strange that we are so negative-minded regarding man's potential behavior on earth. He has had, up to this century, a 1 in 100 chance of economic success. It is logical that we think of *unemployment* as a negative, rather than realizing that it is signaling that society now has the ability to free people from the necessity of demonstrating their right to live by gaining and holding employment.

The kind of wealth we're actually dealing with—the industrial wealth—has nothing to do with the old monetary gold, whose retention in balance-of-trade accounting is a mark of innocence of society and an economic-expansion cancer. Our present real wealth is, exclusively, the *tool-organized capability* to take energies of the universe, which are transforming their patternings in various ways as yet uncontrolled by man, and shunt them through channels onto the ends of circularly arranged levers which man invents so that the energy turns wheels and shafts to do all the work. In doing the foregoing we're taking nothing from the energy capital of the universe. The physicists make it very clear that energy can neither be created nor destroyed. You can't exhaust that kind of wealth. It is not physically exhaustible. And in fact, our relationship to the energy wealth is an intellectual one. It says that every time we make an experiment with physical-energy wealth we learn more. Even when we only learn that something we thought might work won't work, that's learning more! Every time we make an experiment we learn more, we can't learn less. Because universal energy is inexhaustible, and our intellectual advantage only gains, our wealth is continually gaining. We're continually upping the relative metabolic advantage of man in the universe.

One of the reasons I can talk to you the way I do is because I am a comprehensivist in an era of almost total specialization. By fortune I go many places and get experience in many directions—I keep in touch with many. I can tell you that at the present regenerative state of intellectual experience and mass science and mass technology that there is

the probability that for every 100,000 we "educate" through
to a bachelor's degree, there will be a science-technology realization by one of the 100,000 so world-advancing that it will
pay for all the other 100,000 people's education and livelihood without their direct contribution to the technoscientific
breakthrough. That capability is now in operation so that in
order to progressively elevate human dignity, we're going to
be able to afford to give everyone student fellowships in any
subjects they elect—fly-fishing studies are O.K.—everyone's
going to go back to school! Man no longer has significance as
a muscle-and-brain-reflexing machine. The Marxian worker-
slave is going into extinction. He is not needed. Man is essential to the success of the industrial equation as a consumer.
The more consumers there are, and the more frequently they
consume, the more successful and swiftly increasing is the industrial wealth capability. We can only justify the vast investments in world-around industrial networks of structures and
machinery by the numbers of spontaneous consumers that are
served. Because the initial tool-up undertakings take months
and years, as well as vast billions of dollars, the more active
consumers there are to divide up costs, the lower the costs
and the quicker the total amortization and inauguration of
improved tools and efficiency. Therefore, man becomes a regenerative consumer. The more he consumes, the more he
learns, and the factor that increases the wealth is the "know-
more" factor. We can afford to send everybody back to
school. There are a great many people intent on learning and
finding out something which increases the common wealth.
Those who go fishing may inadvertently make a great contribution through just "taking it easy" and doing some good retrospective thinking. And this inexorably is the way history is
going to unfold. We will not undertake this new education
and wealth-regenerating spontaneously within our country.
We won't agree and coordinate that fast. But the competition
from Russia, China, and others will force us to this logical
measure. Economic competition is the catalytic factor. Because the Chinese now have the most potential consumers
they can eventually produce at the lowest prices! To under-
price all that competition, in a very short time we're going to
be forced to go into total automation only to find ourselves
amazedly successful—automated wealth!

I'll give you one more picture to vivify what is happening
to us. This picture is of the now visibly developing new
"world man." We had him in the news a few years ago, a

man who talked about being a "world citizen," you may remember, an American in Paris. Society not only laughed at him as a dopey renegade, but now, unexpectedly to all, everybody is beginning to experience more and more travel. World citizenry is coming about by itself.

DIRECT U.S. FOREIGN INVESTMENT

20. Direct U.S. foreign investment

There is something going on with respect to the U.S.A. we haven't paid much attention to. Figures were published in last month's *Exchange* magazine, published by the New York Stock Exchange, regarding foreign investments. There are two kinds of foreign investment—one is called indirect investment, which means purchase of shares in foreign enterprise. The other kind is called direct investment, where you buy land, put up a factory, and start producing something. That's called direct enterprise, or direct investment. U.S.A.'s citizens' and corporations' investments in foreign countries started up at the turn of the 19th into the 20th century. There was a jog down in the historically rising curve during the 1929-1942 Depression, and now it's going up again, ZOOM! Its resumption of the original acceleration rate indicates that it was trying to happen all the time and that the depression dent was abnormal. It's now up to better than $70 billion and the direct earnings from it each year now exceed $4½ billion. Every major corporation is in this outward-bound move. The hundred largest corporations in the U.S.A. are now spending four out of every five new-plant-and-machinery dollars in countries outside the U.S.A. General Motors last year, though its total foreign investment is only 10% of its whole, made one-third of its total profits from its foreign operations. General Motors total net profits after taxes were $1½ billion.

Arthur Watson, of IBM International, says that the old foreign-trade language such as speaking of "Germany trading with Russia" or "England with France," or any country trading with any other country, is now as obsolete as speaking of New York City trading with the city of Chicago. Industry is inherently world-around and is inherently world business—we have no other characteristic but "world."

This *world-identity-only* trending of big business promises a surprise which is that world citizenship will not occur as a political initiative. The economics of this exploding industrial-world activity soon will require world citizenship for its personnel.

I want to precipitate your awareness of the reality of the points I have been making by asking you, "If everybody who teaches school because it's the simplest way of making a living were given a well-funded fellowship to lifelong research would they accept? If humanity receives universal fellowships —all expenses paid plus a comfortable bonus, would humanity not stop asking itself, 'How can I earn a living,' and start asking, 'What is it that I'm interested in, and what could I do to help make the world work more satisfactorily, more interestingly?'" This used to be a stupidly altruistic question. It suddenly becomes a very logical one.

*   *   *

I feel that the high capability of the young who do not happen to have been trained in science goes into their intuitive formulations. Artists are now extraordinarily important to human society. Many who have been called artists are healthy human beings who have kept their innate endowment of capabilities intact. The greatest of all their faculties is the ability of the imagination to formulate conceptually. I feel that it is the artists who have kept the integrity of childhood alive until we reached the bridge between the arts and sciences. Suddenly we realize how important that conceptual capability is. Professor Kepes of M.I.T. took uniform-size black-and-white photographs of nonrepresentational paintings by many artists. He mixed them all together with the same size of black-and-white photographs taken by scientists of all kinds of phenomena through microscopes and telescopes. He and students classified the mixed pictures by pattern types. They put round-white-glob types together—wavy-gray-line-diagonals, little circle types, etc., together. When so classified and hung one could not distinguish between the artist's works and scientific photographs taken through instruments. What was most interesting was that if you looked on the backs of the pictures you could get the dates and the identities. Frequently the artist had conceived of the patterns or arrangements before the scientists had found their counterparts in infra- or ultravisible realms. The conceptual capability of the artists' intuitive formulation of the evolving *new* by subconscious coordinations are tremendously important. Much of the essence of what I have been saying to you may or may not be news, but I would not be surprised if tomorrow's biggest news is that the artists who best appreciate and conserve our natal capabilities have ascended by acclaim to the premiership of this new era of man on earth.

4. Keynote Address at Vision 65

Our theme subjects of communications and vision are of immediate interest because today world society is operating almost exclusively in the inaudible and nonvisible area of the physical universe. I think it is safe to say that 99% of all the important work now being done by man—relating to our evolutionary advance—is work going on in the areas above and below the tunable range of man's direct optical or other sensorial participation in the electromagnetic spectrum. Society neither hears nor sees the great changes going on.

You who are convening as participants in the Vision 65 meeting are those rare individuals, only one of whom appears in every one hundred thousand humans. You intuit the necessity, and take the initiative in trying to comprehend the significance of the invisible evolution. Thereafter, you develop ways of alerting society to its newly evoluting conditions. It is possible to develop means for society to intercommunicate its new concepts and adjustments thereto at greatly accelerated rates. You are uniquely concerned with finding effective ways for man to visualize, understand, and respond advantageously to what is going on despite approximately total inaudibility and invisibility.

In the very short time which I have to think out loud with you, I want to think about what I know of high potential trends in communication.

Certainly, the accelerating accomplishments in electro-probing of the brain are important. I find that the men who are the physiological probers of the brain are beginning to understand its energy patterns. They have identified many of the storage areas for specific types of information. They have apprehended much of the traffic pattern of the brain's information processing. I find these men are not prone to be prognosticators but do not shudder or feel me to be overdaring

114

when I say in their presence that possibly within the next decade we will have discovered that what we have always spoken of in the past as telepathy is in fact ultra, ultra-high-frequency electromagnetic wave propagation. We may find that we are doing a great deal more subconscious communicating with one another than we are accomplishing in the "reality" of the visually tunable ranges of the electromagnetic spectrum. That is one reason why I do not prepare and read or memorize my lectures. I prefer to think my way along in front of my audience, speaking my thoughts as they occur. I am confident that my spoken thoughts are greatly affected by subconscious feedback from my audiences.

I'd like also to prospect a little regarding my Skyocean World Map on the stage's backdrop behind me. It is an aid in effectively conceiving the totality of world (and universe) events, as we shall presently realize.

With our enormous specialization we have powerful insights in a variety of unique directions, but we have very little integrated comprehension of the significance of the total information. I find that not only does our vision have a narrow electromagnetic spectrum range but that we also have a very limited apprehending range within the spectrum of motive velocities. For this reason, we see and comprehend very few motions among the vast inventory of unique motions and transformation developments of the universe.

Universe is a nonsimultaneous complex of unique motions and transformations. Of course, we don't "see" and our eyes cannot "stop" the 186,000-miles-per-second kind of motion. We don't see the atomic motion. We don't even see the stars in motion though they move at speeds over one million miles per day. We don't even see the hands of the clock in motion. We remember where the hands of the clock were when last we looked, and thus we accredit that motion has occurred. In fact, experiment shows that we see and comprehend very little of the totality of motions.

Therefore society tends to think staticly and is always being surprised, often uncomfortably, sometimes fatally. Lacking dynamic apprehension it is difficult for humanity to get out of its static fixations and specifically to see great trends evolving.

We do from time to time take progressive stage photographs of subvisibly changing phenomena, such as plant growth, and accelerate the rate of projection of the successive pictures to make possible man's seeing the changes take place at a rate that he identifies as "motion."

To rectify this condition, I have speculated and experimented a great deal on the development of what is called the "Geoscope" or miniature earth. The particular Geoscope that we think about a great deal is 200 feet in diameter. The reason that we have chosen that 200-foot size—which is about twice the diameter and eightfold the volume of the world globe at the New York World's Fair—is that if we use the aerial mosaic contact photographs taken by the Air Force at the lowest standard flight level, and put the whole world inventory of contact-size photographs together as a continuous spherical surface mosaic picture, they will make a 200-foot-diameter globe. In the 200-foot-diameter spherical aerial mosaic we can see men's houses—but we can't see men. In a sense we can recognize man because we recognize his farm and his house. On a 200-foot globe, pasted up with an aerial photo mosaic, you could see all of humanity's highways, railways, towns, and houses. Any human could identify his home on such a sphere.

This 200-foot sphere could be mounted 200 feet above the water, suspended invisibly from masts arising from the Blackwell Ledges in the East River of New York City, just south of Welfare Island. The weight of the structure would be so light that the cables suspending it from the masts would be invisible. You would have a 200-foot-diameter miniature earth apparently floating out in space one-half mile away from the United Nations Building. The miniature earth's top would be at about the height of the top of the United Nations Building.

Fourteen years' development work on the 200-foot Geoscope makes it possible to describe it with accuracy. Ten million electric light bulbs, one for each two square inches, evenly covering the sphere's entire surface would be hooked up to a computer. The light intensity in each bulb is controllable. We would, in effect, have an omnidirectional "spherical" television tube which seen from the United Nations Building would have as good resolution as a fine-mesh halftone print. This spherical TV-like "tube" would accurately picture the whole earth. We wouldn't need a rigid structural outline of the continents, for the latter would be part of the spherical picture described by the lights. You would be able to look at any part of the earth that you want—because you could have the computer rotate the spherical earth picture on the 200-foot sphere surface in any preferred way.

How would we use this giant Geoscope? We could, for instance, show all the population data for the world for the last 300 years. We would identify every thousand human beings by a red light located at the geographical centers occupied by each one thousand human beings. You would then be able in one minute to develop the picture of the world's population growth and geographical spread for 200 years. You would see the glowing red mass spreading northwestward around the globe like a great fire. You would be able to run that data for another second or two which would carry you through three or four more decades of population growth. While the edge of the data would be unreliable, the gravity and momentum centers of population would be quite reliable.

All the satellites going around earth make their circuits at about the pace of the minute hand of the clock—roughly one circuit per hour. So we couldn't see the satellites' motion around the earth except by accelerated motion which is easy to introduce into the Geoscope. All the cloud cover and weather information around earth can be shown and accelerated to predict the coming weather everywhere.

The Geoscope is only one of many devices that could provide man with a total information-integrating medium. We're going to have to have some way for all humanity to see total earth. Nothing could be more prominent in all the trending of all humanity today than the fact that we are soon to become a world man; yet we are greatly frustrated by all of our local, static organizations of an obsolete yesterday.

I will speak about other technical devices which may develop to facilitate communication. One has been developed in respect to language problems. For instance, there have continued to be great explorations to determine the geographical origins of the Pacific peoples. It has been possible to take all the languages of the Pacific and of all of its, as yet, existing tribes and to identify transitional stages in the evolutionary sound pattern developments of the whole range of words. It is possible to identify the earlier and later sound forms in evolutionary sequences. A Southern Illinois University professor was able to identify all these sound patterns and to put them into the computer to find the lines pointing toward origins. The computer showed that the languages of the Pacific clearly came from the region of New Britain just east of New Guinea.

The same kind of evolutionary working with word sounds shows that it is going to be quite possible for the computer to find the most commonly recognizable and speakable sound and meaning relationships common to all world people. Indications are that the computers will probably develop some kind of phonetic acceleration leading toward a common world language. I don't think we need to talk about too many more of such trends, but many will be realized.

Men must have been in critical life-sustaining crises to have invented words. When we have something vital to say we can usually develop the means of communication. Today with our great vocabulary inheritance we squander meanings on unworthy causes and communicate little that needs to be said.

I will now talk about what it seems to me needs to be communicated by man today. Up to the time of Thomas Malthus at the opening of the 19th century we had had many great world empires—but all the pre-16th-century great world empires such as those of Genghis Khan, Alexander the Great, the Ottomans, and Rome, were all what I call "flat empires," that is, they were all part of the same pre-16th-century cosmology of man which conceived of the earth as being flat—a great island, apparently surrounded horizontally to infinity by the sea. All the great empires were flat postage-stamp empires inside of the great infinity. All our ancient world maps show that flat concept with civilization centered around the Mediterranean Sea, which term means sea in the middle of the land.

And the people, in the times of Alexander the Great or of Caesar or of Saladin, all thought in that flat way. That is why "simple, elementary plane geometry" is used and taught to beginners and "solid" is considered more difficult and "spherical trig" even more advanced and more difficult.

When you think about the real consequences of that psychologically, philosophically, and mathematically, it is devastating. It means that "inside" the empire, we have something we call civilization while "outside" the empire begins the unknown wilderness with pretty rough people and outside of that live dragons and beyond the dragons, flat infinity. What we have in flat land is an only local finiteness, and all outward around us extends the flat infinity. This meant then that the Greeks in attempting to communicate their mathematical conceptioning defined the circle as "an area bound by a closed line of equal radius from one point," or a triangle as "an area bound by a closed line of three angles, three edges, and three vertexes." The Greeks talked only about the area that was "bound" as having validity, finiteness, and identity while outside, on the other side of the bounding line, there existed only treacherous terrain leading outwardly to infinity and therefore boundless. This has a tremendous feedback effect and explains the ingrained fundamental biases in our present thinking. We tend to think only of *one side* of a line as definable, organized, and valid. "Our side" is natural, right, and "God's country" and vice versa. All humanity has been conditioned to accredit only its own local area of experience as being natural, and the logical prototype of all that is good and acceptable with all else remote, hostile, treacherous, and infinite. Infinite systems may contain an infinity of variables. The ancient world was imaginatively controlled by an infinity of gods.

The British Empire was so called because the great business venturers—the great outlaws—the world men—who ruled the world's ocean found the British Isles to be their most easily defendable shipbuilding bases which coincidentally and conveniently also commanded the whole waterfront of all the European customers for the venturers' Oriental booty. The venturers "Shanghaied" their crews out of the British pubs and because there were so many ships with so many British sailors aboard the world came to identify the most successful world outlaw organization as the British Empire. This was the first empire of man to occur after we knew that the earth was a sphere. A sphere is a mathematically finite or closed system. It is an omnisymmetrical closed system. A sphere is finite unity.

Thomas Malthus, the professor of political economics of the East India Company, was the first economist ever to receive all the vital statistics and economic data from a closed system world. Once the world is conceived of as a sphere and finite, there are no longer an infinite number of varying possibilities identifiable uniquely as whims of gods.

Because earth had been discovered by its high-seas masters to be a closed and finite system, the great pirates who controlled the seas took their scientists around the world to discover and disclose to them its exploitable resources. Only because the earth constituted a closed system could the scientists inspect, in effect, *all* the species and only thus was Darwin able to develop the closed-system theory of "evolution of species." Such a theory could not have existed before that. It would have had to include dragons and sea-serpents. All the people in all the previous open-edged empires lived in a system, within whose bordering infinity anything could happen. Paganism (or peasantism) wasn't illogical. Geometrically speaking, the pagans could have any number of gods because any kind might occur in infinity. There were an infinite number of chances of upsetting the local pattern which was a most satisfying idea if it happened that the individual didn't like the prevailing local pattern.

It seems strange that we were not taught about the historical, philosophical, and economic significance of the foregoing transition from an open to a closed world system. However, the omission can be explained by realizing that a closed system would exclude any variables supposedly operating external to the system. This automatically would exclude any supernatural phenomena such as the theologies of the organized religions. And because the churches were strong and the great pirates wished to obscure both their monopoly of the riches of the closed system and their grand world ocean strategy for its control, significance of the concept of a closed world system was popularly unrealized.

Once a closed system is recognized as exclusively valid, the list of variables and the degrees of freedom are closed and limited to six positive and six negative alternatives of action for each local transformation event in universe.

In view of Thomas Malthus' discovery that the world's people multiplied themselves much more rapidly than they were able to produce goods to support themselves, what could prayers do to alter those hard facts? For approximately a century the world-mastering venturers "classified" Malthus' books as secret information, belonging exclusively to the East India Company. Once "classified" that kind of information leaked out only amongst the pirates and the scholars. Marx, as a great scholar studying in England, encountered the Malthusian data. It was equally clear to Marx that there was not enough to go around. Marx said, "Since there is not enough to go around for all and not enough even for 'many'—certainly those few who are arbitrarily favored by the prevailing system and thereby enabled to survive their allotted span of 'four score years and ten' ought to be the ones who are most 'worthy' and those who do the work 'obviously'—to Marx —"were the most 'worthy.' "

That is logical thinking.

Those who opposed him said that headwork and daring enterprise which alone conceived of the great value to be realized by society could also increase the abundance and support more people and that the enterprisers should be conceded to be the exclusive few who could and should survive. Others said it should be the bright ones—who by their superior intellectual fitness alone could increase the numbers who could be supported. The choice of "who" should survive has always underlain all class warfare. Should it be the brightest, the toughest, the bravest—or who should it be?

Certainly, the corollary to Darwin's theory of evolution which expounded "Survival only of the fittest" seemed to fit neatly with Malthus who observed that only a few were attaining their full span of years. It was assumed to be obvious by those in power that a scientific law supported and vindicated their position. Despite the great pirates' satisfaction, the question persisted amongst the "outs" as to "who were the fittest"? Would it prove in the end to be the workers, or would it be some military class or would it be some intellectual class?

Just before I went to Harvard University in 1913, before the start of World War I, an "uncle" gave me some counsel. He was a very rich "uncle." My father had died when I was quite young. My "uncle" said, "Young man, I think I must tell you some things that won't make you very happy. I know that you are impressed with your grandmother's golden rule: 'do unto others as you would they should do unto you.' But my uncle went on to tell me about the discoveries of Thomas Malthus. He spoke about the pre-Malthusian times when there could reasonably have been any number of gods. He made it clear that in the early empires, the concept of the golden rule was highly plausible. There seemingly were an infinity of chances that it could work. "But," my uncle said, "a few of us now know from the closed-system experts that the golden rule doesn't work. Those few of us who are rich and who really have the figures know that it is worse than one chance in one hundred that you can survive your allotted days in any comfort. It is not you or the other fellow; it is

you or one hundred others. And if you are going to survive
—and have a family of five and wish to prosper—you're
going to have to do it at the expense of five hundred others.
So, do it as neatly and cleanly and politely as you know how
and as your conscience will allow. At any rate, that's what
you're up against." He went on to say, "I'm not going to try
to educate your grandmother because she's quite happy in
thinking her own golden-rule way, and—of course unknown
by her—I have taken care of her one hundred alternates."
My uncle said, "There are few even today who really know
this is so. There are those all around the world who have
their gods. They keep dying off, short of their potential years,
but they keep themselves happy by having their hopes and infinite possibilities. So we don't tell them about it."

That "you or me" pattern began to emerge in sailor's jar-
gon around the time of World War I. In the time of the
1929-to-1941 Depression, Americans began to learn about
Malthus. But I also found Malthus unknown as I interrogated
educated audiences, for instance, the university audience in
the city of Stockholm in 1961. The people of Sweden think
deeply in economics. I asked how many of them knew of
Malthus, and found that they had never heard of him. I
asked the question around the world and found that Malthus
is hardly known outside of the United States and England.
So, the Malthus concept—"knowing what it was *all* about"
—was not disseminated by the economically successful few to
the rest of the world.

At the present moment in history, we find ourselves in a
fundamentally different economic position. When, a decade
ago, Eisenhower went to meet with Khrushchev in Geneva,
both had been informed by their military and scientists regarding the magnitude of the destructive capability of the
atomic bomb. And Eisenhower said, as he went to that
conference, "There is no alternative to peace." I'm sure
Khrushchev, with the same realization, must have felt the
powerful responsibility of that moment. Both, being political
realists and hard-fact men, knew that they would not be able
to make any important peace agreements as conceived solely
by themselves. Their proposals and agreements, if any, would
have to be backed by their respective political parties, and
their parties were always in mortal contest at home with their
chief opposition parties which waited upon altruistic moves of
the "ins" as opportunities to impeach them for treachery to

their respective sovereign power's ideological premises. Any softheaded step on the part of the leader would throw the party out. While Eisenhower and Khrushchev couldn't yield an inch politically, ideologically, and militarily, both of them brought along their atomic scientists and allowed them to talk to each other in a limited manner regarding any at all possible *peaceful uses of the atom.*

Only one decade ago, at the meeting in Geneva and its companion meeting of the Food and Agricultural Organization of the United Nations, it came so clearly into scientific view that the leading world politicians could acknowledge it to be true that—as reported unequivocally by Gerard Piel, publisher of the *Scientific American—for the first time in the history of man, it was in evidence that there could be enough of the fundamental metabolic and mechanical energy sustenance for everybody to survive at high standards of living— and furthermore, there could be enough of everything to take care of the increasing population while also always improving the comprehensive standards of living.* Granted the proper integration of the world around potentials by political unblockings, there could be enough to provide for all men to enjoy all earth at a higher standard of living than all yesterday's kings, without self-interferences and with no one being advantaged at the expense of another.

But clearly both political leaders and their respective states were frustrated by all the political checks and balances each side has set up to protect and advantage only their own and their allies' side in view of yesterday's dictum that there was only enough of what it takes to support one in a hundred. So, all the ages-long fears; all the bad habits; all the shortsighted expedients that have developed in custom and law frustrated whatever might be done to realize the new potential. But the fact to remember is that it was only one decade ago that man had this completely surprise news that Malthus was indeed wrong and there now could be enough to go around—handsomely.

Inasmuch as I have found that the majority of people around the world had never heard of Malthus—coupled with our observation that not more than 1% of humanity read what Piel said and thereby understood what had occurred at Geneva a decade ago; and at present not more than one-thousandth of 1% of humanity as yet recall and as yet accredit the scientists' realization at Geneva that Utopia was now for the first time feasible; it is easy to understand that what I am saying to you now must be jolting.

World society's confusions regarding what we are reviewing here are great. The fact is, however, that the foregoing economic facts are mankind's now most important considerations. We are faced with the necessity of developing effective ways to educate all humanity as rapidly as possible regarding this completely new and vital economic situation.

To start with, here is an educational bombshell: Take from all of today's industrial nations all their industrial machinery and all their energy-distributing networks, and leave them all their ideologies, all their political leaders, and all their political organizations and careful study shows that within six months, two billion people will die of starvation, having gone through great pain and deprivation along the way.

However, if we leave the industrial countries with their present industrial machinery and their energy-distribution networks and leave them also all the people who have routine jobs operating the industrial machinery and distributing its products, and we take away from all the industrial countries all their ideologies and all the politicians and political party workers and send them off by rocketship to forever orbit the sun—the result will be that as many world people as now will keep right on eating, possibly getting on a little better than before. This will remove all barriers to completely free world intercourse and thereby permit realization of enough for all.

The fact is that now—for the first time in the history of man—and only for the last ten years, all the political theories and all the concepts of political functions are completely obsolete in any other than secondary housekeeping functions. The primacy of political ideologies is obsolete because they were all developed on the basis of the exclusive survival only of your party or my party—simply because there was not enough for both.

The whole realization that mankind now can and may be comprehensively and mutually successful is so startling that we must have it—as both the *whole* and as the *essence* of the theme of our forward undertakings. But to have enough to go around for all requires a design revolution, for as now designed the world's metals are invested in machinery and structures which are so inefficient that they can only take care of 44% of humanity. Engineers and scientists agree that the technical knowledge to correct this now exists. So it is also part of the great message to humanity of those who have the power to communicate that the world's problems cannot be solved by politics and can only be solved by a physical invention-and-design revolution.

In pursuance of this theme and under auspices to be announced later, we are going to undertake at Southern Illinois University, in the next five years, a very extraordinary computerized program to be known as "How to Make the World Work." It is based on general systems theory, combined with von Neumann's game theory as "played" by the national defense and joint chiefs of staff in the development of computerized world-war games and the theory of world economic warfaring.

We find that man is developing an increasing confidence in the way in which computers are resolving heretofore vexing and seemingly unsolvable problems. Lest one defective computer may lead mankind seriously astray, he is learning to check results in several computers. We, herewith, review typical ways in which society has gained confidence in the computers' ability to solve heretofore unsolvable problems.

After World War II, when enormous new magnitudes of energy-mastering tools had been developed, America, despite the astronomical costs of World War II, found itself many-fold wealthier than it ever had been before. This was because vast improvements of the means of production, more than of the special end products, won the war. Enormous quantities of energy were now flowing to the ends of levers to produce wealth. American labor began to realize that it could ask for a great deal more participation in the advantages accruing to further regeneration of this vast wealth.

The problem of sustaining postwar economic and technical growth in our country was one which involved centrally coordinated scientific, technical, industrial, and economic organization, while also developing the profitable growth of the nation's prime contractors. This was accomplished by inducing a regenerative self-amplification of the moneys which would flow irrigationally through the whole economic system in ten recyclings per year which could convert $50 billion in war orders into a $500 billion gross national product that would yield a $55 billion tax extraction for reintroduction of next year's $50 billion cold-war orders to the prime contractors. To implement this economic irrigation system, Congress extended the President's World War II emergency powers to implement his "anticipation" of the next war—which realized anticipation we speak of as the cold war. In this way, the economy could and has attained omniprofitable probing for the new economically capitalizable industrial-advantage augmentations inherent in the scientific and technical invention evolution of each new military program's development of greater production power of greater hitting power with ever less effort per each function.

The total grand strategy of cold warring introduced an immediate preview of the astronomical complexity of its accounting problems both anticipatory, current, and retrospective.

World War I and World War II had demonstrated that human beings were inherently inadequate, as "directors" of the war-production complexities. I'll just point out to you quickly that a single-family house has about 500 types of parts, a fighter plane has 25,000 types of parts, while a big corporation, e.g., International Harvester, has to keep a live inventory of 135,000 types of service parts—and these are the figures of just one corporation. When we begin to talk about all the corporations and all the evolution-anticipating undertakings and all the stockpiling for 10, 15, and 20 years ahead—of the whole national economy—in getting ready for the next war—the myriad millions of types of parts and functions and raw materials and tools to produce and handle them rocketed beyond the thinking capabilities of any individuals. The obvious economic complexity of the cold warring made the swift development of the computers mandatory to the U.S. military leaders. Production of the modern computers had been found to be theoretically feasible in the 1930s in the course of development of the great electrical-power-distribution systems' "network analyzers." There were computers in the invention and laboratory-development stage and a few minor prototypes of both the analog and digital computers. It was only a question of allotting enough money to the big universities to pay for the major development research programs. Computers which worked with electronic tubes were developed but were swiftly improved after the invention of transistors.

After the universities had developed the prototype computers, they were given to the big corporations to reproduce. The skilled machinists of the U.S.A.'s labor force had to produce, assemble, and tune up the production computers.

Though it cannot be confirmed by any published document, I
—as a card-carrying "journeyman machinist" of the International Association of Machinists, one of the U.S.A.'s oldest
labor unions—am confident that Walter Reuther put into the
computers the problem of, "Which would pay General Motors the greatest profit: to grant or not to grant the United
Auto Workers not only shorter hours and more pay, but also
vacations, retirement, and complete life benefits?" The computer said, "General Motors will make much more money by
granting." Boards of directors having been elected by the
stockholders have always heretofore been mandated to secure
all the profits of their corporations for the shareholders and
therefore not to yield an inch to labor. However, with the introduction of computers, General Motors' board of directors
yielded without a battle to Reuther's unprecedented demands.
Therefore, General Motors' board of directors also must have
put the problem into the computer because they acquiesced
so quickly. Within three years after granting, General Motors
became the first corporation in history to make a billion dollars net after paying all taxes. This is how well it paid off to
allow a percentage of accrued profits to fund labor's wider
buying power. They made money because mass production
cannot exist without mass consumption and the wider and
more persistent the distribution of wealth as buying power the
greater and more persistent the sales and profits to all. General Motors' decision to heed the computers insured their
profits.

The wealth which we as industrialized society are now
dealing in is the tooled and tuned capability to shunt the
free-flowing inexhaustible energies of universe on to the ends
of levers to do the work for us. The tooled capability to satisfy tomorrow's metabolic regeneration of each man is what
underlies our wealth today. Though this is not yet officially
recognized by either business or by U.S. government, wealth
is our tool-organized capability to deal with the forward metabolic regeneration of humanity in terms of forward man-
days of increasing degrees of mutual enjoyment of the whole
of the earth without interferences and without the gains of
one to be realized only by the loss of another.

Very recently another extraordinary computer decision occurred. As you know, in America the greatest opposition to
centralization of economic power in government authority
has been that of the organized private electricity-generating

industry. The means of electrical-power generation and distribution were one of the last great holdings of the old pirates who came off the sea and onto the dry land with their railways to own the mines and control energy as power. They built many electric-power and light-generating companies within the U.S.A. and in foreign countries. These "utilities" were adamant against any public control. After the 1929 crash came the New Deal and the government underwriting and control of the banking system, and the public entry into the electrical-generating industry—along with flood control—as for instance in the Tennessee Valley. Next came the U.S. government's rural electrification and many other governmental developments and ownership of public power services.

As Eisenhower became President, he found himself in the middle of a battle waged between the "private" and the "public" sectors of the electricity producers for control of the fabulously grown energy resources. The private-sector progeny of the old pirates hoped not only to win, but in so doing to take over atomic energy despite the fact that its development had cost the government unprecedented billions to develop. This battle was joined in 1952 when the old pirates' progeny, led by a Wall Street admiral, made a skilled and powerful attempt to reverse their catastrophic loss in 1929 of control of the world's overall economic intercourse and its monetary systems as well as of the prime initiative in guiding the world's capital reinvestment evolution; as well as their loss by default to democratic government of their position as the ultimate creditor, forecloser, and underwriting dictator of the comprehensive economic recovery system and its grand domestic and international strategy formulations. Ensconced only in their privately owned security-trading houses, divorced entirely from access to bank-deposit funds, and possessing only their privately operated public utilities and their privately owned mines whose profitable operation had been bedeviled by the vast and unexpected magnitude of recovery and recirculation of World War I and subsequent industrial evolution's scrapped metals, the private sector of the 1952 battle had only the momentum of wide public affluence of World War II's vast productivity gains and the McCarthy-stilled voices of democratic dissent to support their campaign of "righteous indignation" of a long-suffering private enterprise to be restored to supreme power. An intuitively alerted democracy frustrated their coup.

In the last four years metals coming back as scrap into the world's metal markets, with government stockpiling ended, have threatened comprehensive deflation of metals prices and impoverishment of the mines and metals cartels. With the scrap of World War II about to reappear in 1966, we will have a flood of metals. Combining this flood with the weapons industry's continual accomplishment of more power with less resources per each function, it is seen that the metals market will go way down unless a new major use for metals develops. This "use" may be in weapons and ammunition. But other forces are at play.

The major interests in metals who are also by heritage close to the major interests in private power began about 1960 to look for new outlets for the major metals, iron, copper, etc., other than for war. One of the ways in which the metals could be employed was, very appropriately, in the electrical-transmission systems—and that requires some explaining.

There is no way in which we can get energy from here to there as fast as by wire. Energy by wire is manyfold faster than its delivery over the pipelines, or by ships full of oil. When you want to send electricity great distances, you have to get very high voltages and the higher the voltages the wider apart and higher the apparatus must be to avoid short-circuiting and overloading by lightning strokes. Distance in electrical distribution has been limited during the last forty years to about 350 miles. That was the capacity of electrical-generating and transmission apparatus as then designed. In the 1920s the power- and metals-controlling pirates had built apparatus with as large a voltage capacity as was feasible in view of the quantity of metals then to be made available without elevating the metals prices beyond negotiability. And the top distance of that 138,000–230,000-volt system was 350 miles. It was discovered, however, in 1960 that with the glut of metals coming into availability as scrap from World War II, that there would be sufficient to build a new national network of greatly increased dimensions permitting elevation of long-distance transmission from 230,000 volts up to 500,000 and 1,000,000 volts. With the new high voltage, we could transmit up to 1500 miles. The metals flood made this new overall voltage magnitude a very practical matter. No part of this story seems to have reached the newspapers or magazines until this year. But, starting about three years ago, the private sector of the electrical-apparatus-designing industry began to put the feasibility and quantation problem of a designed re-working and integration of the national electricity networks into the computer. The problem was to discover in which way the private-power interests would make the most money —by or by not upping the voltage and integrating the national distribution networks. With the ultrahigh voltage it was possible to reach great distances and integrate remote networks systems as we have not been able to do previously even at a top 230,000-volts capacity, between the different time zones of the United States. Every electrical-generating company has the problem of maintaining the experience-proven minimum surplus margin of standby power to take care of unexpectedly compounding big electrical-power loads—the unpredictable peak loads. And all standby power that is not used is completely wasted. If used, it could be pure profit. Network integration smooths out the power-loss peaks and increases profits.

It became evident that if the networks of different time zones of the U.S.A. were interconnected by the ultrahigh voltage, long-distance transmitters, that the peaks and valleys of adjacent systems would fit together very efficiently. The computers indicated that with ultrahigh voltage it would be possible to integrate the whole United States and all four of its time zones. It was discovered by the design researchers, however, that such nationwide integration also involved merging of both the *public* and *private* networks which integration heretofore had been theoretically opposed by the private interests as an unwanted reconciliation with their "enemy."

The computers however showed both the public and private sectors that ultrahigh voltage integration would result in both sides making a 33% additional profit. Of course both sides signed up and the long battle between private and public power was ended. There was nothing about the merger in the newspapers. If the public had known what had happened, they would have known that Johnson was going to be elected. That was the end of private power's financial underwriting of the Republican party. Because it was the private-power interests who most opposed government centralization, this economic point of contention is removed. A new Republican party if it arises will have to find some other kind of economic base. To find an adequate one will mean joining forces with the forces of change and that will mean a liberal Republican party or none at all. The residual old-line reactionaries are too few to have significance.

What I am pointing out mostly is that the computer was able to solve this public- vs. private-power problem which it had been thought could never be solved. So, I assert that we are a society that is going to be developing an increasing confidence in the competently programed computer to provide clear unbiased answers to questions heretofore held to be unsolvable, particularly those questions which provide answers which can show which way powerful segments of world society will mutually and most copiously profit, in both short and long terms. This will bring about a large series of surprising mergers of heretofore opposed interests.

For instance, it is now visible that after integrating the network across the United States, the new 1500-mile transmission reach will bring connection to Alaska. This will bring in also the enormous water-generated electrical power of the Canadian Rockies. From Alaska we cannot only go right into the Aleutian Islands, but we can go under the Bering Straits and hook up with the great Russian networks in eastern Siberia. This will provide an intercontinental powerhead immediately adjacent to and ready to flow into China. China's leaders have promised their people physical success through industrialization. The essence of successful industrialization is energy available *as unlimited power by wire anywhere.* This integrated powerhead will make possible China's achievement of full industrialization decades earlier than expected. The Americans, the Russians, and the Chinese will put the problem into the computer to find which is most profitable to each and all—to integrate or not integrate. All hands will be informed by their respective computers that network integration will bring large mutual advantages. The Chinese and Russians will have to choose between the political advantages of deliberate, but unnecessary, prolongation of a class struggle between the haves and havenots and letting the controlled energy flow into their systems to altogether eliminate havenotness everywhere and thereby to eliminate all basis of class struggle. The political leaders will be forced by their engineers and science-educated public to choose to integrate and the ideological differences will vanish. Thus, all unexpectedly almost all obstacles to man's comprehensive physical success will be removed.

On Southern Illinois University's Carbondale campus, we are going to set up a great computer program. We are going to introduce the many variables now known to be operative in world-around industrial economics. We will store all the basic data in the machine's memory bank; where and how much of each class of the physical resources; where are the people, what are the trendings and important needs of world man?

Next, we are going to set up a computer feeding game, called "How to Make the World Work." We will start playing relatively soon. We will bring people from all over the world to play it. There will be competitive teams from all around earth to test their theories on how to make the world work. If a team resorts to political pressures to accelerate their advantages and is not able to wait for the going gestation rates to validate their theory, they are apt to be in trouble. When you get into politics you are very liable to get into war. War is the ultimate tool of politics. If war develops, the side inducing it loses the game.

Essence of "success in making the world work" will be to make every man able to become a world citizen and able to enjoy the whole earth, going wherever he wants at any time, able to take care of all the needs of all his forward days without any interference with any other man and never at the cost of another man's equal freedom and advantage.

I think that communication task of reporting on the computerized playing of the game—"How to Make the World Work"—will become extremely popular all around the earth. Because we're going to be playing that game so soon at Southern Illinois University and because there is such a fabulous acceleration in the rate of world events, I felt that we could no longer wait and am therefore announcing it to you now at this Vision 65 congress.

I am deeply interested in the play of our intuitions. I am inclined to think that our integrated organic capability is much more powerful than any of us tend to accredit. I have learned how much we can apprehend in just the flash of an eye. In one ten-thousandth of a second, a strobe light can get a beautifully detailed photograph. I am quite certain that humans can enter a room and tell instantly what the real situation is. But they don't usually trust their own high capabilities so they spend hours trying to find out whether their first flash impression was right or wrong. As I travel around the world today, I see in a flash that the eyes of youth see that the world could be made to work for all of humanity. And I see that they will settle for nothing less. And I see that they are impatient. And I see above all that they can and will soon make it so.

5. Summary Address at Vision 65

I have never been in a large conference at which I've felt as intuitively intense as I feel right now at this one. My intuitions tell me this has been an extraordinary meeting of human beings. I speak with the experience of many meetings —of human beings brought together because of their eminence in all manner of unique performance patterns. Their strength and variety gave hope that they would be able to contribute importantly to the answering of great questions.

The meetings of the last few years have been organized to address great questions, particularly on the forward implications of the impact of technology on world society. However, few, if any, answers of importance have developed.

At this Vision 65 Conference at Southern Illinois University, the whole set of circumstances seems to be extremely propitious for the formulation of some important realizations. Southern Illinois University was approximately unheard of until about nine years ago. It wasn't even a university until Adlai Stevenson as Governor of Illinois converted it from college to university status. It has, however, been in existence for almost a century, as a very small teachers' college, going back to within a few years of Abraham Lincoln's day in southern Illinois. Stevenson anticipated the flooding need for higher education facilities, so he created several universities, in the north, east, west, and south of the state.

Southern Illinois had become a completely forgotten part of America. It dropped out of sight when the great north-and-south river traffic that plied on the Mississippi, Ohio, Missouri, and Illinois rivers—all finally merged into one at the lower extremity of southern Illinois—was suddenly replaced a little over a century ago by the new era's east-west railroad, which crossed Illinois, from Chicago to St. Louis, well over a hundred miles north of Carbondale. So this very remote place in the heart of America was almost entirely for-

134

gotten except for its mine labor riots at Herrin, a half century ago.

Now southern Illinois comes into world prominence again as the place where it is the working assumption of a classless democracy that all of humanity should have the opportunity of an advanced university education. As S.I.U.'s President Delyte Morris has pointed out: it is the assumption here that "dropouts" indicate inadequacy of the educational system and not of the human individual.

I am certain that none of the world's problems—which we are all perforce thinking about today—which are also central to this conference—have any hope of solution except through society's being thoroughly and comprehensively educated, and thereby able to identify and communicate the vital problems of world society, and thereafter to sort and put those problems into order of importance in respect to the most fundamental principles governing man's survival and enjoyment of life on earth.

My intuitions are vigorous regarding the present alertness and almost apprehensive awareness of the particular human beings who have come here to this Vision 65 S.I.U. meeting from all around the earth. I have met many of the participants in other parts of the world; I know that the group who have come together here are unique. They are of the one-in-one-hundred-thousand type of thinker, who is realistically earnest in trying to find ways of making humanity successful. They have learned how to take the initiative. They don't need or want to be told what to do. My intuitions tell me, therefore, that this meeting is an unusually successful harvest of capably responsible human beings. I think it interesting that we have avoided negatives and that much that is useful and promising has been said about the functions and functioning of communication.

I often play a mental game, which I started a great many years ago. I patterned it after the physical discipline, with which all humans are familiar, of lifting progressively heavier weights on successive days, thus gradually to become more physically powerful. When I started playing my mental game, my scheme was to ask myself a little larger and more difficult question each day. I also gave myself a basic playing rule, that I must always answer the questions from my own direct experience. I have been playing that game for a long time. Finally I came to the question: What do you mean by the word "universe"? And I said to myself, if you can't answer that question, you must give up the use of the word universe, because you are being deceitful to yourself and others by suggesting that it has a meaning. Following my own rules, I gave myself the answer: Universe is the aggregate of all humans' consciously apprehended and communicated (to self or others) experiences. Because I had answered in terms of experience, my definition has withstood all subsequent testing by myself and others. I haven't been able to find any thinkable aspect of universe that has been overlooked. We have experiences of dreaming, falsification, multiplication of the numbers of words in the dictionary, and so on. I don't find any experiences that are not included in the definition. So, for the time being, I go along with that definition. It has been fruitful.

Playing the same kind of game and starting with universe as defined, I found that the universe definition included metaphysics because metaphysics deals with thoughts, which are weightless. The physicist defining the physical universe (Einstein's famous definition) had deliberately excluded metaphysics because they are imponderable. So, I found it interesting that I had a definition that also included the metaphysical universe—of mathematics, thoughts, and dreams as realistic experiences. And because all of my experiences had beginnings and endings, they were finite. I said, therefore, that the aggregate of finites must also be finite. Therefore, the universe, including both physics and mathematics, is finite.

In playing that kind of game I now had the advantage of being able to start not only with total finiteness but logically —as men, lacking a definition of the whole universe, had not been able to start logically before. This gave me many advantages, for the whole system was finite. I thus came logically to some mathematical discoveries regarding the thought processes. I would like to give you a simple way of looking at things, which I found appropriate once one starts with a definition of the finite whole.

I also found this process of working with finite logic from the whole to the particular to be a very effective kind of strategy in trying, for instance, to think our way through to understanding what our human function in the universe might be. I found that, when I was confronted with a vast question and an enormous amount of material and experience, one of the first things I always tried to do was to make a basic division of the universe and thereafter to subdivide the relevant parts into progressively smaller halves, always, successively, selecting the half most clearly containing—and therefore relevant to—the problem until I reached an understandable and very local level in universe. In developing the solution to complex problems in modern information theory, which governs the design of computers, this same principle of progressive subdivision and selection of the relevant half is used and each progressive subdivision is called a "bit" and the number of subdivisions totally required are known as "so many bits."

I found it is quite possible to subdivide the universe instantly by developing the concept of a "system." A system is a local phenomenon in the universe that is geometrically definable because it returns or closes upon itself in all directions. Systems may be symmetrical or asymmetrical. I found that systems are the first subdivision of universe for they subdivide the universe into all the universe that is inside and all the universe that is outside the system. This divided the universe into the macrocosm and the microcosm. Then came the extraordinarily surprising and sudden discovery that this system concept led to an important understanding of—what we do when we think.

I am quite certain that thoughts are not bright ideas mysteriously inserted into a vacuum chamber in the head. I'm quite confident that what we do when we think is to behave as follows:

We dismiss the irrelevancies. I find that our brain is filled with constant reports and notices in which we're being told about various events around us. All of us have experiences saying to one another, "What's that friend's name? You know, the man we both know. We were with him for three years." And neither of us can remember his name right away. But we all experience suddenly recalling the name possibly five minutes later, possibly the next morning.

The main point is that there is a definite lag in the search to memory storage and its feedback and that there is a great variety in the rates of lag between some recalls and others that we have stored deeply. Because we do get such feedbacks, we are always receiving a great deal of feedback from questions we had even forgotten that we had even asked. On my way here today I looked at a tree and I said, "What kind of a tree is that?" And I asked many other questions as I went along. I am asking myself questions all the time; and because the lags are very different for the different kinds of memories, I find that when I am lying down in my bed and trying to go to sleep, I get report after report coming back telling me about things that I had asked questions about and forgotten that I asked them. At all times we are in almost chaotic focus of brain-dispatched messengers trying to come into our conscious thought pattern to give us the answer to questions we or others in our presence have asked. Therefore, I have discovered that what I do when thinking is to say, Keep those messengers outside for a moment. That's very interesting. I am glad they're there, but please keep them outside because all I want to think about right now is this glass of water.

I discover, then, that thinking is a *momentary dismissal of irrelevancies*. That decision immediately gives you one of those enormous opportunities further to divide the residual definition into two. This is possible because irrelevancies fall into two main classes: all the events that are irrelevant because they are too big to have any possible kind of bearing on the particular focus of our thought, and all the irrelevancies that are too small possibly to build up any significant relationships to alter the focal subject of our thinking. You find that what you have been trying to think about has a definite experience and frequency magnitude. Thus we find that all the irrelevancies that are too small are dismissed inwardly of the thought about local system and, therefore, dismissed into the microcosm because they can't catch up to the magnitude zone of the wave length and magnitude that we are working on; and the irrelevancies that are irrelevant because they are too big to have any effect on our considered focal system of consideration, are dismissed outside the system, that is into the macrocosm.

I find that there are also a number of temptingly almost relevants, which I might bring into our consideration, which might persuade you to be interested in what I am trying to communicate to you. Thus I learn that there is a Twilight Zone of Tantalizingly Almost Relevants. There are two such twilight zones—the macro and the micro—tantalizingly almost relevants. Between them there is always a set of extraordinarily lucid items of relevance. And when I pay attention to those lucid relevances I find that the minimum set that may form a system to divide universe into micro and macro cosms is a set of four items of consideration. I see next that between four stars that form the vertexes of the tetrahedron, which is the simplest system in universe, there are six edges that constitute all the possible relationships between those four stars. When we have found all the relationships between the number of items of our consideration we have what we speak of as "understanding." The word consider derives from the Latin words for "together" and "stars." When we *understand*, we have all the fundamental connections between the *star* events of our consideration. When n stands for the number of stars or items of consideration, the number of connections necessary to understanding is always $\dfrac{n^2-n.}{2}$

When I was invited to come up and meet with you now, I felt that I would like above all things not to allow myself to be affected by any conditioned reflexes that would make me say anything I had ever said before. I would like to think out loud as freshly as possible about the significance of this meeting. Our experience with Bob Osborn's cartoons gave us a good inventory of negatives. This doesn't bother me at all, because I am thoroughly aware of the experimental work done by nuclear physicists. One of their most important experimental findings shows that every physical component of the atom has its opposite, for example, the electron which is "negative" has its positron. Every positive has its negative and vice versa. The negatives of all those having positive weights have negative weights. This means that the average of all the weights of all the fundamental components of universe is zero. Although dealing with a universe of average zero weight, we find by experiment that we are (almost) always dealing with the positive or the negative which is our reality. We are dealing in a complex of pure principles that include a variety of time lags and thus create time and life as experience. This is an intellectual experience. Everything we cerebrate has to do with the principles such as lag, angle, and frequency. I am never concerned when some people concentrate on enumerating negatives, because I know that each has its positive.

As noted, I must always go back to my own experiences for answers and my own experience inventory is short. It is only 70 years. But in that 70 years, I have experienced some extraordinary changes. The life-insurance companies' mathematicians, dealing with all of mankind's vital statistics, are able to determine the probable "number of years that people born in a given year will live." This lifespan is known by the insurance companies as the expectancy of individuals born in the given year. Expectancy for females usually is greater than for their contemporary males. My expectancy at birth was 42 years. That was all that an 1895-born male was supposed to live. But conditions governing man's health and welfare improved rapidly, and expectancy began to advance at an historically unprecedented rate, so I have not yet caught up with expectancy.

The average distance that human beings could travel on their feet or in vehicles in their respective separate lifetimes up to and including my father's time was an average of 30,000 miles. In my lifetime I have already swept out three million miles, which is one-hundredfold the distance of all our forefathers. Now I am one of a class of several million men who have experienced three million miles around our earth. Our ecological pattern has clearly changed, and changed abruptly, from all the generations before us. Now the aviators and air hostesses make much more mileage than I do and each of the two Gemini astronauts knocked off my three million miles in one week of orbiting. Quite clearly man is moving into some very new relationship to his physical universe on a pure physical-assessment basis. I recall my first pre-World War I jobs and working with men admirable for their strength and physical courage. I found I could win their friendship, but I was appalled at their mental inferiority complexes. Very few of them had gone to school for more than a few years, almost none had gone to high school, let alone finished. Very rarely did I meet anybody who had gone through college. My fellow workman was intellectually timid to a fault. He was a slave; he knew he had very little chance of happy and healthy survival. He was afraid of his words and his mind. He communicated his feelings by the way in which he chewed tobacco, spat, and blasphemed, using a total vocabulary of no more than about 50 words.

This was the everyday experience of all times for 99% of humanity. Shakespeare and the historians write only about the doing of the 1%. The history of the 99% is the same as the history of cats and dogs, who usually fared better than men. Yesterday this southern Illinois town of Carbondale was just a strip-mining coal town, where tobacco was chewed and spat, accompanied by the 50-word vocabulary. These conditions have all changed in an extraordinarily short moment—

in less than my lifetime. Here at Southern Illinois University are 21,000 young people—probably very greatly affected by the radio and television in their childhood environments—to whom a good vocabulary is obviously and happily desirable. You have come to us from all around the world, speaking and organizing your thoughts with great integrity and without intellectual fear of your fellowman. But, in my memory humans, of the same origins as those of any S.I.U. student, who dared to speak a well-formed sentence were whistled at and treated as being some kind of sexual deviates. I know by personal experience that the world has changed and is changing at an ever-faster rate.

When I was young going from a little town seven miles outside of Boston into Boston through Dorchester, or Roxbury, I saw that all the children in the streets were in rags. No exceptions. People on the trolley really stank. Women of 26 years were hags with half their yellow teeth out. There was no dentistry for them. It is my own direct experience that life has changed very much for the better.

Clearly, and sum totally, something very important is happening to man on this planet. Fred Hoyle, the great astronomer, dealing with the regularities found by astrophysicists in the heavens, has been able to say in all seriousness that he now assumes from the observed regularities that there are at least hundreds of millions of stars with planets that could maintain human life. He finds it logical to assume human life to be present in this universe on at least one hundred million planets. This particular big figure he uses is obviously intended to infer astronomical numbers of humans present in universe.

Dr. Hoyle—who is the Plumian Professor of Astronomy and Experimental Philosophy at Cambridge University in England—finds the case of humans on this particular planet to be precarious. He says humans have found atomic energy just in time to overlap the exhaustion of the fossil fuel supplies. Humanity will have to make other vitally important moves in a hurry.

I remember asking myself in my game of big questions whether there is anything in our experience that could tell us whether man might have an essential function to perform in the universe. Was he needed in the universe? Or was he—as he seemed to feel himself—just a chance observer, a theatergoer watching a great play called life. I said the only way we can judge whether he has a function or not is to go to our experimental data, and the way it came out is as follows.

With the development of steam, which could propel their ships when there was no wind, the great pirates, who mastered world commerce, saw that science could greatly advance their power, so they put up great amounts of money to back further scientific inquiry. The scientists developed the laws of thermodynamics and showed that energy continually and *always* escaped from local systems. Systems were always running down. This inherent energy dissipation was called entropy. The mathematicians described entropy as the Law of Increase of the Random Element. This concept is manifest by Sir Isaac Newton, when he said in his first Law of Motion, *A body persists in a state of rest—or in a line of motion* [clearly a secondary thought]—*except as affected by other bodies.*

"At rest" was the great norm. All the scientists went along with the second law in assuming that energy is leached out of the universe and that in due course the universe must run down and become motionless and dead. Life was abnormal and death was the normal state.

I entered Harvard University in 1913 just before World War I began. The Harvard community, and, in fact, Boston's large community of intellectuals, all assumed a universe that would ultimately run down, and that the earth had been spun off from the sun and would finally stop spinning. It is a very short time since people were thinking in that way. But in this century the scientists experimenting with entropy began to discover that when energy left one system it could only do so by joining another system. It did not go out of the universe. They found that energies were always 100% accountable. This forced them into a completely new law, the Law of Conservation of Energy, which says: Energy cannot be created, and energy cannot be lost. Energy is finite. This eventually brought about Einstein's finite physical universe.

Einstein found himself confronted with this new way of looking at energy and also with the extraordinary experiments that disclosed the speed of light—experiments made not only in relation to visible light but to invisible radio signals, that showed that energy released *in vacuo* was moving at 186,000 miles a second.

Einstein felt forced to think about the universe in a different way from Newton. He said that inasmuch as no energy could be lost, then the universe could not "run down," and "at rest" was not normal. He then assumed a universe of continual transformation and its acceleration normal. He further assumed that normal velocity is the speed of radiation unfettered in a vacuum—186,000 miles a second. While that is very fast, he pointed out that it is not *instantaneous*. Einstein then pointed out that the universe is a complex of nonsimultaneous events, and because there is no inherent composite "picture" of nonsimultaneous and nonidentical events, there can be no possible unit and static conceptual picture of universe. "What is outside the outermost stars?" is a meaningless question. Thus Newton's simultaneous, all interlinked mechanical universe became invalid and obsolete.

One of the brightest stars we use in our navigation is Rigel kentaurus. And Rigel kentaurus is 4½ light-years away and is of a brightness magnitude characteristic of the stars that burn out in a million years. Probably many a starry event hasn't been "there" in the sky for millions of years. We only have evidence about man being on earth for about two million years. In seeing many of the celestial bright spots we are looking at live shows taking place millions of years before man came on earth. In looking at stars in the heavens we are not looking at simultaneous events.

There is no outside to what is not there. Our thinking gets an entirely new breakthrough with Einstein. In the philosophy of relativity Einstein postulates an all-transforming universe, constantly transforming at various rates. He next hypothesized that although energy was traveling normally at 186,000 miles per second, it could be going around locally in knots and that it could be so local as to be confined to atomic patterning dimensions and that the tighter the heavier, and this resulted in his famous equation of $E = Mc^2$ which fission a quarter century later proved valid as accounting for the amount of energy in any given mass.

There is now a very large inventory of ways in which man has been teaching, thinking, and accounting events and values which have no experimentally demonstrated validity. There is no experimental proof of such phenomena as straight lines, solids, and planes. There is no instantaneous phenomenon. The word is meaningless. The senses and brains of approximately all our scientists are disconnected from their theories. Scientists see the sun "going down" when they have known theoretically for five hundred years that it isn't "going down." Although our senses are not geared with our advanced knowledge, man has been getting along in a gradually more favorable way. His communication is no longer confined to the mode of his spitting.

Man is born utterly helpless and remains utterly helpless for a longer period than the newborn of any other living species. That's quite an invention—an extraordinary complex like man born utterly helpless. It is valid only under the assumption that he will be taken care of. Although the helpless child often has drunken parents, fortunately gravity holds him in his bed, and fortunately some cow ate some grass and made milk and somebody got it out of the cow and through a series of pourings by many people, it got into a bottle leading into the baby's gullet. It didn't come out of the mother's breast. In many ways, mankind is utterly helpless, vain, and ignorant.

Human beings often say, "I wonder what it would be like to be on a spaceship." The answer is, "What does it feel like —you are and always have been on a very small spaceship, eight thousand miles in diameter." The nearest star Sun is 92,000,000 miles away and the next brightest is five million times further away. You are very much alone in your spaceship. And this spaceship is designed so superbly, all its passengers so skillfully provided for, that they have been on board playing the game of self-reproduction for two million years without even realizing that they are on board a spaceship.

We see that all life has been able to succeed owing to the anticipatory design of a regenerative ecological energy exchange. The mammals give off the gases that are necessary to the survival of the vegetation, while vegetation gives off the gases that are essential to the survival of the mammals. None of them knows that he is contributing gratuitously to vital support of the other. I find that the earthworm is quite as irresponsibly, yet essentially, involved here, as is the bee. All of life is inadvertently and unconsciously involved. All of life has designed subconscious drives. Earthworms do the twist. But none of them realize the vital tasks they are doing for the others.

So I find all life interconnectedly successful and almost completely unwitting of the total ecological balance, which men sometimes speak of as "nature." The little bumblebee goes after his honey and his little fuzzy tail inadvertently knocks off and dusts pollen, which fertilizes vegetation. I think that is exactly the kind of pattern with which approximately all of humanity is preoccupied. I don't know any man who can stand up and say to us, "I am a success by virtue of having consciously designed, fabricated, and operated myself, the biosphere, the sun, earth, and all the intercomplementing ecology. I can tell you what I am doing with my lunch. I am sending off certain of this food to this gland and that gland, and I am going to use these differentiated energies in such and such ways."

We know humanity can't say that. Humans can't even tell you why they have hair. They certainly can't tell you that they are consciously pushing each hair out through their heads in special shapes and colors for special purposes.

We don't know anyone who knows much about what he is doing and why. Yet, one of the prominent, built-in behaviors of the occupational game-playing is the ego-claimed credit for its inadvertent successes.

There are many indications, however, that man is just about to begin to participate consciously and somewhat more knowingly and responsibly in his own evolutionary transformation. I include evolution of the environment as a major part of the evolution of humanity. In his unconscious participation in the past he has carelessly ruptured his earth, polluted his air and water, corrupted his children in order to sell any kind of toy guns, dope, smut, and anything that would make money, and has made all money-making sacrosanct. But if we discover that man is necessary to the invention of universe, we can understand somewhat better what he is inadvertently doing.

Some years ago, I asked myself whether man had a function in universe and if so, what it might be. My experience-informed answer went as follows:

The astronomers have given us their observation of the "red shift," which indicated that vast and remote star groups are probably receding from us in all directions because the light coming from them is redder than that from nearer groups, which in turn indicated an expanding universe. The expanding universe is also called for by the law of entropy or increase of the random elements which must ever fill more space. So I thought, we have also learned experimentally that unique behaviors are usually countered by somewhat opposite behaviors; therefore, an expanding universe would probably infer a concurrently contracting universe. So I said, "What experience do we have that may demonstrate such a contracting universe, even though none has been observed or mentioned by the astronomers?"

I saw that around our own planet we have high and low atmospheric "pressures," which might better be called expanding and contracting atmospheric patterns. I discovered clues to the operation of a contracting universe to be operative as our own planet. Our planet earth is not radiant. It is not sending off energy in any important degree. As compared with a star it is "dead." Earth is receiving energy from the sun but is not losing it at the same rate. For instance, we have learned from the Geophysical Year that we are receiving about 100,000 tons of stardust daily. Our physical imports from the universe are as yet much greater than exports. Therefore, we are a collecting or concentrating center, possibly one amongst myriads in universe. All planets in universe may be collecting points as focuses of the contracting phase of universe. At the surface of the earth, in the top soil, the ecological balance becomes operative. The vegetation's chlorophyll inhibits the sun's radiation instead of allowing it to be reflectively rebroadcast to universe. The sun-inhibited energy impounded in the vegetation is further inhibited by insects, worms, and mammals, and both botanicals and zoologicals are gradually pressured into the growing earth crust and finally are concentrated into coal and oil rather than being broadcast off to universe in all directions. By dissipating these energy concentrations, man may well be upsetting the expansion-contraction balance of universe.

The ecological balance is fascinating when viewed chemically. We find all biological systems continually sorting and rearranging atoms in methodical molecular structures. To ensure performance each species is genetically and environmentally programed. Each sorts and reassociates atoms as its genes cope with and alter environment, which in turn alters the species behaviors.

Thus we see that all the stardust, cosmic rays, and other radiation randomly dispersed into universe by all stars are being methodically converted by the biological activity around earth's whole surface—in the sea and on the land—into progressively more orderly "organic" chemical structures. Thus biological life on earth is antientropic. Earth is acting as an antientropic center as may all planets in universe.

Of all the antientropic sorters and rearrangers on earth, none compares with brain-driven man. We find man continually differentiating and sorting out his experiences in his thoughts. As a consequence we find him continually rearranging his environment so that he may eat, be clean, move about, and communicate in more orderly and swifter ways.

Dr. Wilder Penfield is the head of the Neurological Institute of McGill University in Montreal, Canada. He is one of the world's leading electrode probers of the brain. The brain probers have now identified, for instance, the location of various memory banks. Dr. Penfield says, "It is much easier to explain all the data we have regarding the brain if we assume an additional phenomenon 'mind' than it is to explain all the data if we assume only the existence of the brain." Why? Because they have found, so to speak, the telephone sets of the brain, they have found the wires connecting the telephone sets, they have found the automatic message-answering service and the storage systems; but, a great deal goes on in the conversations over the wires that is not explicable by the physical brain's feedback. I have submitted what I am saying to you to leading neurologists and they have not found fault with it. A good scientist doesn't applaud you publicly or right away, even though he is favorably impressed with your theory. But he does let you know whether he objects to what you are saying and what his objections are. And so far there have been no objections and there seems to be some affirmation of what I am about to say to you.

We have a phenomenon that we speak about as a generalization. In science, a generalization is very different from a literary generalization. Generalization in a literary sense means that you are trying to cover too much territory with some statement. The scientific meaning is precise; it means "the discovery and statement of a principle that holds true without exceptions." I will give you an example. I am going to talk about a special piece of rope. I could have in my hands a foot length of three-quarter-inch manila rope. But I can also say to you, "I am going to take an imaginary piece of rope," and I, not mentioning whether of nylon or manila, immediately generalize a rope concept from our mutual experiences. I am going to pull on that piece of rope and as I pull on it very hard it contracts in its girth. As it gets tauter, it gets tighter. This means that it goes into compression in its girth in planes at ninety degrees to the axis of the pull. I have found a great many human beings who think that tension is something independent of compression. I find experimentally, however, that tension can be only operative when compression is also present. A cigar-shaped vertical compression member that is loaded on its neutral axis tries to "squash." This means that its girth tries to get bigger. Which means also that its girth expands and is tensed. So I find that compression is never innocent of tension, but that they are cooperative in axes arranged at ninety degrees to one another. Sometimes I find tension, at what we call "high tide," or a highly visible aspect, and compression at "low tide" or at almost invisible aspect, and vice versa. We have here a generalization. We have found by experiment that "tension and compression only coexist." That is quite an advance over the first generalization just saying, "I take a piece of rope and pull it," which was a second-degree generalization. And it is a third-degree generalization when I say, "Tension and compression only coexist."

A system subdivides universe into all of the universe that is outside the system and all of the universe inside the system. Every system, as viewed from inside, is concave and, as viewed from outside, convex. Concave and convex only coexist. Concave and convex are very different from one another. Convex diffuses energies by increasing wave lengths and widening angles. Concave concentrates energies by decreasing wave lengths and reducing angles. Although not the same and not exactly opposite, concave and convex only coexist.

In addition to tension and compression and convex and concave, I can give you a number of other such coexistences. This brings us then to another and further degree of generalization wherein we say that, "There is a plurality of coexistent behaviors in nature which are the complementary behaviors." That caused the mathematicians to generalize further. They developed the word "functions." "Functions" cannot exist by themselves. Functions only coexist with other functions. They are sometimes covariables. When I say, "Functions only coexist," I have gone a little further than the special cases of concave and convex or of tension and compression which were themselves highly generalized. Then I'll go further still and say, "Unity is plural and at minimum two." Which is the generalization that greatly advantaged quantum physics. We may go a little further in generalization, as did Einstein when he gave us his "relativity." You can't have relativity without a plurality of cofunctions.

Now, I will give you another progression of events. You have seen a dog tugging at one end of a belt. He tenses it as he grips with it compressionally—with the concave and convex surfaces of his teeth. I am sure that you will agree that the little dog will never say, *"Tension* and *compression* only coexist," even though his brain coordinated them. The dog will not say, *"Concave* and *convex,* tension and compression are similar cases of coexistence of functions."

I think the neurologists go along with me in saying that, "What we mean by mind—in contradistinction to the brain of the animal or of man—is man's ability to generalize."

The ability to generalize—in its incipient phases—seems to me to be also a tendency to moralize. For instance, to say that "if a man does so-and-so, he will get into trouble." I feel that in religious scriptures we come time and again to semi-generalizations showing how some men get into trouble and how you and your children may avoid such trouble.

We have seen how an enormous amount of special case experiences finally led to a progression of generalizations. There are about six degrees of progressive generalization. As we went from the one case to another and to higher degrees, it was accomplished with fewer and fewer words. We finally came to just one word, "relativity."

Now this orderly simplification happens to be exactly the opposite of the mathematician's Law of Increase of the Random Element. It is the decrease of the random element. Generalization is the law of progressive orderliness.

I found myself in 1951 having to write in a book, which I was about to publish, that the mind of man seemed to be the most advanced phase of antientropy witnessable in universe. And if there is an expanding universe there is logically a contracting universe. Possibly man's mind and his generalizations, which weigh nothing, operate at the most exquisite stage of universe contraction. Metaphysics balances physics. The physical portion of universe expands entropically. The metaphysical contracts antientropically.

It is interesting that within a few months after my publication of the hypothesis someone told me that Norbert Wiener had just published the concept also that "Man is the ultimate antientropy." I talked with Norbert Wiener about this and we found that we had both written this at approximately the same time—starting quite differently but coming to the same conclusion.

So now we have found a function for man in universe, which was our objective. Man seems essential to the complementary functioning of universe. Therefore the probability of humanity annihilating itself and thus eliminating the antientropic function from universe is approximately zero.

This does not, however, mean that man on earth may not eliminate himself. It suggests that there are—as the Cambridge University astronomer, Hoyle, suggests—hundreds of millions of other planets in universe with men living on them.

This brings us to the observation also that to keep her ecological balance intact, when nature finds the conditions are becoming unfavorable for any of the "cog wheel" species necessary for the system, she introduces many more starts of that species. She makes enormous numbers of babies, enormous numbers of seeds of this and that tree when she sees that such trees are not going to prosper. The seeds multiply in number, float off in the wind, randomly distributed in order to increase the probability of an adequate survival number to keep the system in balance.

I also go along with Hoyle in his concept of the possibility of the enormous numbers of human beings on an enormous number of planets simply because not all of them are going to make a success of life on their respective planets.

Man is beginning to transform from being utterly helpless and only subconsciously coordinate with important evolutionary events. We have gotten ourselves into a lot of trouble, but at the critical transformation stage we are getting to a point where we are beginning to make some measurements—beginning to know a little something. We are probably coming to the first period of direct consciously assumed responsibility of man in universe.

I spoke to you on my first day here about the great challenge of our day. I showed that it was no longer true, as had seemed true throughout all history, that man was born purposefully to be a failure in all but one case in a thousand—with the latter semisuccess occurring only as an "exception that proved the rule." Throughout ages it was probable that the average human would die before reaching the average human's 27 years—despite scriptural accounts of great longevity. There just was not enough known sustenance for humanity. At the beginning of this century there was not enough for

more than one in a hundred to survive comfortably and "live
out his days," meaning "fourscore and ten"—90 years. Expectancy for males when I was born was 42. Half potential
age. Under those conditions, dying slowly is not pleasant, so
why not fight. Why not have a good quick battle with everything to win and nothing to lose—better than rotting in the
slum. As I said in my opening address, we will always have
war until there is enough of every essential to support all
lives everywhere around earth.

Every day, when it is available, each human consumes an
average of 2 pounds of dry food, 6 pounds of water, and inhibits the amazing figure of 60 pounds of air out of which he
consumes 6 pounds of oxygen.

Food has often been very scarce, and often men have
fought to the death for it. Water has sometimes been scarce
and has been fought for. Air has rarely been scarce. Nobody
has ever thought of putting a meter on the air for human
consumption. But, we have had some terrible panics in theaters when there was a fire. Suddenly human beings—completely unused to competing for air—lose all reason, go mad
and trample their fellowmen to death.

So I would simply say that there is nothing in our total experience that shows that when there is not enough to go
around, it is illogical for men to fight to the death, because
they are going to die anyway. There is also nothing illogical
in the concept that when there is enough to go around men
will not even think of fighting.

We now know scientifically that for the first time in history
there can be enough to support continually all of expanding
humanity at previously undreamed-of and ever-advancing
standards of living and intellectual satisfaction in effective
participation in the evolutionary processes. But we are frustrated from realizing our success by our different political
systems and laws, which have all been devised to protect the
few who have or have not adopted the system that promised
the most in a bad bargain, or the most just system such as
that which would provide for those whose labor produced the
little that there was to go round.

I have made measurements in terms of work that can be
done by human beings, measured by army engineers, in elevating foot-pounds per hours, days, and years. From these
studies I developed what I call an "energy slave" or the energy equivalent of the work a healthy human youth could do.

The energy slaves in operation were determined by the amount of energies we were consuming from nature as water-power, fossil fuels, wind, foods. Because up to now the distance that electrical energy could be delivered economically was only 350 miles, industrial prosperity has been temporarily localized and has expanded only gradually. Therefore I took the total annual energy consumption of, for instance, the United States (of North America) for 1940 and reduced it by 96% because the machinery and processes used by man are of so overall low-grade design that he is only able to realize 4% of the consumed energy in potential effectiveness in the work accomplished. Despite this necessary reduction, I found that a very large number of energy slaves are working for humanity in our U.S. industrial economy. On the eastern seaboard of the United States in 1940 we had 135 energy slaves working for each man, woman, and child. And they were able to work continuously in extremes of heat and cold in which humans would swiftly perish. The inanimate slaves work with extraordinary precision at tolerances millionths finer than permitted by human sight.

I found, however, that an enormous proportion of all energy slaves' capabilities were going only into the development and production of weapons. Putting aside all the energy going into weaponry and retaining only that necessary to keep the people themselves going at a healthily high standard of living, I found that a family of five could be maintained at the high standard of living level with only one hundred energy slaves working for them in their economy—very few of the slaves work actually inside the house—they are employed in building the highways and keeping their telephone system in operation, et cetera. And this standard of living for a family of five produced by one hundred energy slaves was so high that it had not been known by any national sovereign before the 20th century.

I found that in 1900 less than 1% of humanity were industrial "haves," but that changed very abruptly in and after World War I.

World War I witnessed intense mechanization of the world. In the year 1917, man took out of the ground, refined, and put to work more copper than he had taken out of the ground in the whole cumulative history of man's copper mining and refining. He did so because copper is essential to energy distribution. He developed such intense mechanization in World War I that the percentage of the total world population that were industrial "haves" rose by 1919 to the figure of 6%. That was a very abrupt change in history suddenly to have 6% of humanity surviving at a high standard of living. By the time of World War II 20% of all humanity had become industrial "haves" despite that the population was ever increasing. At the present moment the proportion of "haves" is at 40% of humanity.

Consisting mostly of recirculating scrapped metals, 80% of all the metals that have ever been mined are still at work. And all those metals are now occupied in structures and machinery which operating at full capacity can take care of only 44% of humanity; that is, they can take care of 4% more than are now being taken care of. During this 20th century the combined amounts of scrap and newly mined metals per each world man has been continually decreasing because population is increasing faster than discovery of new ore bodies.

For man to go from less than 1% to 40%, living at high standard—despite decreasing resources—cannot be explained by anything other than by doing more with less.

We find doing more with less has come about entirely through the unique technology of the less than 1% of humanity that cast its lot with life on the ocean to master the great commerce routes of the earth. They developed a technology that could float in contradistinction to the dry-land custom of protecting oneself with great stone walls—of which the greater the thickness and height, the greater the popularly-assumed security.

On the sea one couldn't use stone—one would sink. On the sea men took fragile materials such as wood that would float naturally and, by scientific designs, produced extraordinary and powerful ships with which they battled the seas and one another, seeking to control the great sealanes of world commerce, seeking to be the greatest power. They developed more and more speed, hitting power, and cargo space with ever less of invested resources in time, material, and energy per each and every function of the ship and its equipment and that brought them to steam and the steamship, brought them to steelmaking, to make the great ship. Half a century later they began to have enough steel left over from shipmaking to put some into buildings on the land. From the battleship to the land came electric dynamos, refrigeration, radio, desalination, *et al.*

To control the world even more effectively with the airplane forced an international race to do even more with less. In doing more with less we have recently gone, for instance, from the latest 75,000-ton transatlantic cable of copper wires to Telstar, which provides more communication more effectively with less than a ton of materials. We have not been thinking correctly of this technological do-more-with-less revolution as being only a by-product of our scientific preoccupation with weapons. But it is now obvious on study that this is what has changed man's condition on earth. It takes, on average, 22 years for the "dynamo to come off the battleship" into our domestic use. If we have to wait for 22 years to bring the curve of "haves" to 100%, this may be fatally slow.

If humanity understood that the real world problem is that of upping the performances per pound of the world's metals and other resources, we might attempt to solve that problem deliberately, directly, and efficiently. It might be a world-around university students' elective research undertaking.

But I find that approximately no one realizes what is going on. That is why we have been leaving it to the politician to make the world work. There is nothing political that the politician can do to make fewer resources do 60% more.

Just what our communication problem is now becomes obvious. Man long ago invented communications because he had something to communicate. He was terribly hungry; and he only used communication when he had a vital need. He develops effective communication capability only when he has both an enormous need and a clear idea of what his problem consists. To keep aware of the progressively most critical problems of humanity one must keep an eye on a complex of economic and technical development curves. As I told you the other day, when Eisenhower was confronted by his atomic advisors regarding the enormity of the hydrogen bomb, he said, "There is no alternative to peace."

I will give you figures that will bring you to last week's U.S. inventory of destruction. For each one of us, in the U.S.A., there are now 10 tons of steel and 20 tons of concrete and 100 pounds of copper in use. But, for every human being on the face of the earth today, we have now 28,000 pounds (T.N.T. equivalent) of explosives—that's 14 tons per capita, which is to say that for every pound of human flesh there are 200 pounds of self-annihilating explosives. We must move swiftly to convert that energy from negative to positive advantage before an Oswald puts his finger on the trigger of the omni-interretaliatory atomic-bombing systems. If we have to wait 22 years for high standard living to develop second-handedly from weapons development, the probability is high that the Oswald finger will trigger human annihilation.

In addition to Eisenhower's "no alternative to peace," I go along with two other statements. A physicist of Chicago University, John R. Platt, surveying general world trends and basic data, says, "The world is now too dangerous for anything but Utopia."

Unfortunately, we now view Utopia as unfeasible. Our attitude is derived from the fact that all attempts to establish Utopias occurred when there wasn't enough to support more than 1% of humanity, whereas it is fundamental to Utopia that there must be enough for all. For the last ten years the by-product more-with-lessing of prime weapons development has made it visible that there can be enough to go around—handsomely.

I also go along with the statement of Jerome Wiesner, who was the White House Advisor to Kennedy and to Johnson during his first term. Wiesner is now back at M.I.T., where he is head of the department of nuclear physics. Wiesner says, "The armaments race is an accelerating downward-spiral to Oblivion."

So I'll say to you that man on earth is now clearly faced with the choice of Utopia or Oblivion. If he chooses the latter he can go right on leaving his fate to his political leaders. If, however, he chooses Utopia, he must get busy very fast.

For this reason I am excited over the earnestness of this meeting. Our intuitions are powerful in bringing our reasoning to bear. So, here we are, suddenly discovering what the real world problems are: So long as there is not enough for all of humanity to survive and enjoy total earth, there will be war.

We now know that Malthus is wrong and that there can be enough to go around if we up the performances per pound of the world's resources from the present overall mechanical efficiency of world societies' mechanics to a highly feasible overall efficiency of only 12%.

This can only be realized through a design-science revolution of spontaneously coordinate university-aged youth. This revolution is trying to articulate itself everywhere. It gets bogged down by political exploiters of all varieties.

Making the world resources adequate can't be accomplished through political system competition. All politics are obsolete as fundamental problem solvers. Politics are only adequate for secondary housekeeping tasks. Mankind must take the universal initiative in effecting the design revolution.

You, of this world conference, Vision 65, at Southern Illinois University, are experts on how to communicate. This is the message that you must communicate to the world society in time to accomplish Utopia before Oblivion occurs.

6. The World Game—How to Make the World Work

To start with, here is an educational bombshell: Take from all of today's industrial nations all their industrial machinery and all their energy-distributing networks, and leave them all their ideologies, all their political leaders, and all their political organizations and I can tell you that within six months two billion people will die of starvation, having gone through great pain and deprivation along the way.

However, if we leave the industrial machinery and their energy-distribution networks and leave them also all the people who have routine jobs operating the industrial machinery and distributing its products, and we take away from all the industrial countries all their ideologies and all the politicians and political machine workers, people would keep right on eating. Possibly getting on a little better than before.

The fact is that now—for the first time in the history of man for the last ten years, all the political theories and all the concepts of political functions—in any other than secondary roles as housekeeping organizations—are completely obsolete. All of them were developed on the you-or-me basis. This whole realization that mankind can and may be comprehensively successful is startling.

In pursuance of this theme and under auspices to be announced later we are going to undertake at Southern Illinois University, in the next five years, a very extraordinary computerized program to be known as "How to Make the World Work."

Here on Southern Illinois' campus we are going to set up a great computer program. We are going to introduce the many variables now known to be operative in economics. We will store all the basic data in the machine's memory bank; where and how much of each class of the physical resources; where are the people, what are the trendings—all kinds of trendings of world man?

Next we are going to set up a computer feeding game, called "How Do We Make the World Work?" We will start playing relatively soon. We will bring people from all over the world to play it. There will be competitive teams from all around earth to test their theories on how to make the world work. If a team resorts to political pressures to accelerate their advantages and is not able to wait for the going gestation rates to validate their theory they are apt to be in trouble. When you get into politics you are very liable to get into war. War is the ultimate tool of politics. If war develops the side inducing it loses the game.

Essence of the world's working will be to make every man able to become a world citizen and able to enjoy the whole earth, going wherever he wants at any time, able to take care of all the needs of all his forward days without any interference with any other man and never at the cost of another man's equal freedom and advantage. I think that the communication problem—of "How to Make the World Work"— will become extremely popular the world around.

The game will be played by competing individuals and teams. The comprehensive logistical information upon which it is based is your Southern Illinois University-supported Inventory of World Resources Human Trends and Needs. It is also based upon the data and grand world strategies already evolved in the Design Science Decade being conducted, under our leadership here at Southern Illinois University, by world-around university students who, forsaking the political expedient of attempting to reform man, are committed to reforming the environment in such a manner as to "up" the performance per each unit of invested world resources until so much more is accomplished with so much less that an even higher standard of living will be effected for 100% of humanity than is now realized by the 40.% of humanity who may now be classified as economically and physically successful.

"The game" will be hooked up with the now swiftly increasing major universities information network. This network's information bank will soon be augmented by the world-around satellite-scanned live inventorying of vital data. Spy satellites are now inadvertently telephotoing the whereabouts and number of beef cattle around the surface of the entire earth. The exact condition of all the world's crops is now simultaneously and totally scanned and inventoried. The interrelationship of the comprehensively scanned weather and the growing food supply of the entire earth are becoming manifest.

In playing "the game" the computer will remember all the plays made by previous players and will be able to remind each successive player of the ill fate of any poor move he might contemplate making. But the ever-changing inventory might make possible today that which would not work yesterday. Therefore the successful stratagems of the live game will vary from day to day. The game will not become stereotyped.

If a player resorts to political means for the realization of his strategy, he may be forced ultimately to use the war-waging equipment with which all national political systems maintain their sovereign power. If a player fires a gun—that is, if he resorts to warfare, large or small—he loses and must fall out of the game.

The general-systems-theory controls of the game will be predicated upon employing within a closed system the world's continually updated total resource information in closely specified network complexes designed to facilitate attainment, at the earliest possible date, by every human being of complete enjoyment of the total planet earth, through the individual's optional traveling, tarrying, or dwelling here and there. This world-around freedom of living, work, study, and enjoyment must be accomplished without any one individual interfering with another and without any individual being physically or economically advantaged at the cost of another.

Whichever player or team first attains total success for humanity wins the first round of the gaming. There are alternate ways of attaining success. The one who attains it in the shortest time wins the second round. Those who better the record at a later date win rounds 3, 4, and so on.

All the foregoing objectives must be accomplished not only for those who now live but for all coming generations of humanity. How to make humanity a continuing success at the earliest possible moment will be the objective. The game will also be dynamic. The players will be forced to improve the program—failure to improve also results in retrogression of conditions. Conditions cannot be pegged to accomplishment. They must also grow either worse or better. This puts time at a premium in playing the game.

Major world individuals and teams will be asked to play the game. The game cannot help but become major world news. As it will be played from a high balcony overlooking a football field-sized Dymaxion Airocean World Map with electrically illumined data transformations, the game will be visibly developed and may be live-televised the world over by a multi-Telstar relay system.

The world's increasing confidence in electronic instrumentation in general—due to the demonstrated reliability of its gyrocompasses, and its "blind" instrument landings of airplanes at night in thick fog, and confidence in opinion-proof computers in particular, will make the "world game" playing of fundamental and spontaneous interest to all of humanity.

Ultimately its most successful winning techniques will become well known around the world and as the game's solutions gain world favor they will be spontaneously resorted to as political emergencies accelerate.

Nothing in the game can solve the problem of two men falling in love with the same girl, or falling in love with the same shade under one specific tree. Some are going to have to take the shade of another equally inviting tree. Some may end up bachelors. Some may punch each other's noses. For every problem solved a plurality of new problems arise to take their place. But the problems need not be those of physical and economic survival. They can be perplexing and absorbing in entirely metaphysical directions such as those which confront the philosophers, the artists, poets, and scientists.

The game must, however, find ways in which to provide many beautiful shade trees for each—that is to say a physical and economic abundance adequate for all. There will, of course, have to be matchings of times and desires, requiring many initial wait-listings. As time goes on, however, and world-around information becomes available, the peaks and valleys of men's total time can be ever-improvedly smoothed out. Comprehensive coordination of bookings, resource, and accommodation information will soon bring about a 24-hour, world-around viewpoint of society which will operate and think transcendentally to local "seasons" and weathers of rooted botanical life. Humanity will become emancipated from its mental fixation on the seven-day-week frame of reference. I myself now have many winters and summers per year as I cross the equator from northern to southern hemisphere and back several times annually. I have now circled the earth so many times that I think of it and literally sense it in my sight as a sphere. I often jump in eight- and nine-hour time-zone air strides. As a consequence my metabolic coordination has become independent of local time fixations.

It is my intention to initiate on several occasions in a number of places anticipatory discussion of the necessary and desirable parameters to establish for playing the world game. I intend to nominate as participants both in these preliminary discussions and in formal play only those who are outstandingly capable of discussing these parameters. The participants must also be those well known for their lack of bias as well as for their forward-looking competence and practical experience.

7.   Geosocial Revolution

INTRODUCTION

The International Cooperation Year of the United Nations came into being as a consequence of the great and surprising success of the two International Geophysical Years—wherein world scientists, transcending political ideologies, established an all-time historical high in the integrity of behavior of emerging world man.

The international cooperating of humanistic concerns is far more difficult and complex. Each human is a whole universe and there are now over three billion of them around the world.

Science is inherently observational and theoretical. Science is committed only to the discovery of energetic and mathematical behaviors of universe. It is left to the integrity of internationally cooperating technology and the humanities to advantageously integrate the scientific findings with human behaviors. I.C.Y. 1965 must invent objective applications of the discovered knowledge in such ways for instance as, hopefully, never to exhaust the newfound resources while also turning them to physical improvement of man's survival. It is also left to internationally cooperating technology to formulate effective strategies for increasing the physical advantages while decreasing the physical interrestraints of both individual and collective humanity. I.C.Y. technology must at the same time safeguard future humanity's welfaring.

It becomes swiftly clear that to make equivalent contributions to those of I.G.Y., I.C.Y. must develop technological stratagems which will have the same powerful scientific foundations as those of the Geophysical Years.

Through employment of the scientifically gained data and the generalized physical principles therefrom derived, it behooves the internationally cooperating technology of I.C.Y. to establish a continuously self-increasing, per capita, metabolic (energy-process) advantage of humanity over its a priori

162

and forever evoluting environment. The cry goes up: "Haven't you ever heard of the Second Law of Thermodynamics which predicts the inexorable energy loss of entropy— from all local systems of universe? You can't increase advantages!" (Entropy is also known mathematically as the "Law of Increase of the Random Element.") The answer goes back: "Have you never heard of the Law of Conservation of Energy, which says—in terms of the empirically indicated finite physical universe—'energy may neither be created nor lost?'" Energy is shown experimentally as only accomplishing *disassociation here* through entirely orderly regrouping or *association there*. Energy transactions are 100% accountable. Every action has its reaction and resultant, and every nuclear component has its positive or negative opposite with each reversing every characteristic of the other. In this dynamically opposed system, the Geosocial Year can find the scientific fundamentals of its logical extension of the work of the Geophysical Years. The scientific connection between the I.G.Y. and the I.C.Y. lies in the answer to the question: Has man a function in the universe, and if so, what is it? Norbert Wiener and others* said "Yes." We will now trace that connection and function.

In dynamical balance with the inside-outing *expanding universe* of radiant stars, man witnesses radiantly dormant earth as a collecting or outside-inning *contracting phase* of universe. Earth receives and stores a continually increasing inventory of sun-and-star-emanating radiation in its lethal-energy-concentrates sifting, sorting, and accumulating spherical Van Allen belts. In addition to the Van Allen belts, the succession of earth's concentric spherical mantles, e.g., the ionosphere, troposphere, *et al.*, constitute an extraordinary series of discrete filters for the random-to-orderly sorting, shunting, partially accumulating, and final inwardly forwarding of the benign radiation residues to the biosphere stage of earth's continual and orderly processing of its discrete share of the expanding-universe-propagated energy-income receipts. Earth also receives an additional 100,000 tons of expanding-universe-dispatched stardust daily. This concentration around earth's surface of the universe-deposited dust apparently consists of all the 92 regeneratively-patterning chemical elements

---

* See Buckminster Fuller in *Fuller Research Foundation Bulletin*, 1949.

in approximately the same systematic order of relative abundance of those elements as the relative abundance of those same elements as they are found to occur in the thus-far inventoried reaches of universe. The biological life on earth is inherently antientropic for it negotiates the chemical sorting out of the earth crust's chemical-element inventory and rearranges the atoms in elegantly ordered molecular-compound patternings. Of all the biological antientropics, i.e., random-to-orderly arrangers, man's intellect is by far the most active, exquisite, and effective agent thus far in evidence in universe. Through intellect, man constantly succeeds in inventing technological means of doing ever-more-orderly—i.e., more efficient local-universe energy tasks with ever-less units of investments of the (what may be *only apparently*) *"randomly" occurring* resources of *energy, as atomic matter,* or *energy, as channeled electromagnetics.*

During the International Geophysical Year, world-coordinating science charted vast physical-pattern behaviors within and around earth, such as magnetic fields and comprehensive world earthquake patternings. All of the vast geophysical systems were spontaneously acknowledged by scientific man to be operative in nature before men discovered and charted their behaviors.

Man—the scientist—has no ego problem in acknowledging the a priori existence in universe of a myriad of energy patterns whose existence and behaviors constitute the life-permitting and -sustaining energy environment.

Contrariwise, man—the humanist—feels it degrading to his ego to acknowledge the a priori existence of social and economic patternings operative around earth, which develop, evolve, and transform transcendentally to his conscious contriving. To do so seems to admit to a naive subscription to supernatural phenomena. Man's vanity tends swiftly to lay personal, corporate, partisan, or national claim upon all the man-advantaging events and equally swift claim to exoneration from any and all humanly disadvantageous events.

The positive and negative ego-claiming is a historically conditioned social reflex, which springs directly from man's fear of death in face of all the yesterday's 99% probability of premature and painful demise. When yesterday's environment failed to disclose, superficially, the means by which 99% might survive or avoid deterioration and pain, a few by super physical strength, cunning, and insensitivity could command the 1% survival support for themselves and a few associates.

Spontaneous, positive-negative ego claiming probably developed in many ways. Typical was the case, in which it was learned that the most brazen pretense and artifice frequently persuaded the dull brains of the strong-armed, survival-commanding bullies, that the bullies' chances of maintaining their survival would be enhanced by adding the persuading individuals, at least temporarily, to their band of supportable cohorts. This rationalized myth-formulating was for various causes grafted deeply in the human defense mechanism as a postnatal reflex system, relayingly triggered from life to life —usually in the earliest childhood of those whose spontaneous trust in the integrity of understanding between themselves and their parents was repeatedly violated to critical degree. To gain wordable understandings for moment-to-moment situations, the children learned early to invent at least temporarily effective stories or lies.

Human myths and self-deceptive rationalizations have so permeated custom and culture as, thus far historically, to have prevented the social scientists from "seeing themselves" with sufficient objectivity to permit their differentiating out from the social developments all those larger patterns of human behavior which were not consciously premeditated by men. The scientists recognize the individual's subconsciously controlled behaviors, but over and above outright human panic in catastrophe, the articulated self-starterings and coordination controls of group behaviors are sometimes not well, and often not at all, understood.

For technology and the humanities of the I.C.Y. to match in any way the integrities of pattern discovering demonstrated throughout by the physical scientists of I.G.Y. the technologists and humanists of the I.C.Y. will have to concentrate on the geosocial, instead of the egosocial.

The I.C.Y. participants, at the outset, will have to acknowledge that mankind, like all the other living species, has its ultrashortsighted, built-in "desire" drives, its romantic-conception ambitions and protectively colored self-deceits, as well as its longer-distance "needs," all of which cause each species to pursue its particular "honey" with its particular rose-colored glasses as does the bumblebee, which at the same time inadvertently and unconsciously performs myriads of other tasks, designed with fabulous scientific capability by nature, which inadvertent tasks, unknown to the separate creature species, are all essential to realization of the regenerative continuance of the much larger survival-support conditions for the generalized ecological system of "all life."

It is part of the comprehensively anticipating design science of life that the bumblebee's unviewed, unwitting, bumbling tail bumps into and knocks off male pollen, which it later, and again inadvertently, knocks off upon the female botanical organs thus unconsciously participating in a vastly complex ecological interaction of the many energy-processing biochemical "gears" of the total life system, dynamically constituted by all the living species. The myriad inadvertencies of all the living species have sum-totally provided a metabolically sustaining and regenerative topsoil process which—it is realized now, but only by our retrospectively gained knowledge—has kept man regeneratively alive on earth for at least two million years, while ever improving his physical-survival advantages and increasing his longevity.

This vast "game playing" of life has also indirectly occasioned, not only the regenerative multiplication of human beings, but also a progressively increasing percentage who survive in conditions of ever-improving physical advantage. It is probable that 99% of all history's human babies have been inadvertently conceived as a consequence only of the human's preoccupation with their momentary "desire" drives. That man, in his rationalizations, has explained this regenerative drive to himself only mythically and negatively as the "original sin" wraps up all the ego claiming or disclaiming into one typical nonsense-conditioned reflex package, which the I.C.Y. cooperators must discard altogether in order to free their brains and minds to identify the vast human-ecology-transforming forces comprehensively in operation about earth.

The human-ecology-transforming forces are as real and as important to life on earth as are the Van Allen radiation inhibiting belts surrounding earth. The human-ecology-transforming forces are nonetheless as foreign to man's consciousness as have been the Van Allen belts, both of which have been unknown to man's knowledge throughout all but the last decades of the presently known limit of two million years of man's presence on earth.

The treatise on "Geosocial Revolution," herewith introduced, is a tentative inventory of those heretofore invisible technoeconomic, world-social force fields now looming tentatively into view. These heretofore-invisible evolutionary systems' tidal waves once discovered and studied apparently disclose nature's scheme, not only for successfully sustaining human life on earth—despite the inertial negatives and shortsightedness of man's arrogant ignorance—but also the scheme by which nature will permit man to henceforth participate consciously in ever less meager degree in his prosperous continuance on earth, which planet he will probably continue to occupy as a base for his larger operations in universe. These forces and their trendings become the logical pattern developments to be served by all those taking the conscious initiative in promulgating world man's comprehensive advantaging through the International Cooperation Year.

*　　*　　*

GEOSOCIAL REVOLUTION

Though dwarfing all other of history's revolutions in relative magnitude of transformation of human affairs in universe, the vital characteristics and overall involvements of the 20th-century revolution have gone on entirely unapprehended for one half of a century. So vast and historically unfamiliar are the revolution's ramifications that the narrow foci of contemporary specializations have failed to perceive, recognize, categorize, and integrate its widely ranging components. Though everyone recognizes that "a world revolution of some kind is going on"—such a concept is exclusively a post-World War II cognition. Meetings of intellectual, business, and government leaders are convened with increasing frequency on the subject of the "impingement of science and technology on human affairs." These meetings demonstrate that the nature of the greatest revolution in history, which had been developing powerfully for a half century before the meetings, is only now entering the comprehending awareness of man. The titles of the meetings disclose that men are only now asking questions, which seek to understand the specific nature of the revolution.

Because the revolution's characteristics have not even now been defined, we can say that its first half century has been as subconsciously operative, in respect to world society's thoughts and deliberations, as are a child's day-to-day size growth, and the transforming pattern of the earth's magnetic field, both transcendental to the child's thoughts and plans. Though articulated piecemeal by men themselves, it is safe to say that the first half century of this greatest world revolution has developed without men's conscious awareness either of its existence or of their part in it.

It was possible for this invisibly developing revolution to happen because every separate event was—in respect to the revolution—entirely unpremeditated by man—ergo inadvertent. Each unplanned revolution interlinkage was entirely uncorrelated with the other inadvertencies.

Since the revolution has developed inexorably without benefit of man's conscious planning it must, in due course, be recognized as constituting sum-totally a process of nature as transcendental to man's consciously assumed responsibilities as are the earth's seasons, whose behaviors however may some day be consciously modified by man. In the same way, the great 20th-century revolution's comprehensively uncontrolled development may come under progressively favorable modification and control by man. Such inexorable, overwhelming, and invisibly developing events of nature are of the same order of importance as are conception, birth, and death—they constitute in fact total social conceptioning and rebirth with total death or obsolescence of the outworn concepts of social preoccupations.

The human inadvertencies, which altogether add up to the world history's greatest single revolution in human affairs, were executed, separately, each unbeknownst to the others, by 100,000 (approximately) of the world's industrial corporations—private or state—the abstract, limited-human-liability inventions of lawyers or government planners—which during the last half century undertook, corporately, as prime or subcontractors, to supply all the world's most powerful nations with the multitrillion-dollar-price-tagged flow of technological goods, which all together constituted the swiftly evoluting weaponry systems of those nations. The contracts included the invention, research, development, and production of all the swiftly transforming evolution in support mechanisms, consisting of the tools-that-made-the-tools that eventually made, and maintained as operative, the omniautomated, design-regenerating, massive-retaliation capabilities, in comprehensive world-space weaponry systems.

The inadvertencies, which unknowingly initiated the transcendental revolution, occurred as one by one in the course of events each of the world-around corporations' separate contracts were terminated by the world nations' defense departments—due to the progressive obsoleting of their products by the next invention generations in the swiftly evolving weapons and tool designs. The inadvertencies occurred as each of the previous weaponry or tools-to-make-tools-to-make-weapons contractors made separate, fortuitous, corporately independent reorientations of their survival strategies and contrived new end-products of their as yet only semiobsolete, tooled-up, and scientifically staffed production capabilities— converting them from the outpouring of weaponry systems devices to production of the myriad of mechanical and structural items, gadgets, and knickknacks for the "home front"— the "everyday-living" market—which latter we have, for economy of expression, designated comprehensively as "livingry"—in contradistinction to scientific technology's original focus of all of its productive capability in "weaponry."

Weaponry, born of man's necessity to anticipate high-frequency life-or-death crises in a world of seeming universal inadequacy of vital essentials—best phrased by Darwin as "survival of the fittest"—always had priority of access to the highest-performance physical and cerebral resources present within mankind's as yet discovered and comprehended environment.

Priorities for weaponry required sacrifice of access to resources for all the nonpriority-claiming individual human needs and desires, the seemingly deferrable and less important survival and development activities. As engineers have learned, every action has its reaction as well as resultants, wherefore all priorities must involve antipriorities. The home front has always been the antipriority area. From man's personal home and family life the reserves of effort, savings, and anticipatory capability to meet inexorable crises have always been commandeered to meet the seemingly common enemy. Therefore highest priorities have only been invoked to establish the highest scientific-industrialization capabilities which alone could best produce ever higher, swifter, more powerful, longer-distance, and more accurately hitting weaponry for anticipatory defense of the "have" minorities against the "have-not" majorities, who—in desperation of birth into a world of seemingly overpowering inadequacy of metabolic sustenance and regeneration of life—must periodically join their

havenot numbers to revolt against the inferior-numbered
"haves." Thus far in history *weaponry* has always been ac-
corded priority over *livingry*.

That scientific industrialization would have a by-product
capability to produce livingry was not foreseen. Nor was it
foreseen that the development of scientific industrialization to
produce special end-product weaponry would generate a
comprehensive train of ever more generalized tools to make
the tools, which finally made the special tools, that made the
ever more fleeting special models of the latest weaponry. The
vast generalized tool base of the scientific industrialization
which would accrue inadvertently as a consequence of the fo-
cusing of both enterprise and government subsidies exclusively upon the *end products*—the special weapons—was utterly unforeseen.

It was thought by yesterday's "ins" that their fortresses
would be forever impregnable.

Battleships, it was thought, would be good for generations.
It was not realized that every battleship would be obsolete before it was finished. The integrated consequences of all the
separate, fortuitous, uncoordinated reorientations of all the
world's weaponry-producing contractors applying their do-
vastly-more-with-vastly-less capabilities to man's domestic
needs was to effect an utterly unplanned alteration of man's
historical relationship to his environment. Ecology is the name
for the science which studies the patterns of life in respect to the environment. The human-ecological-transforma-
tion consequences of the 20th-century revolution are so enormous that in the last generation of man on earth, they have
increased one hundredfold the hitherto unvarying multimil-
lion-year, man-on-earth, average mileage of a human lifetime's total locomotion—which was approximately 30,000
miles—and has already become three million miles for millions of humans—and will increase that lifetime mileage one
thousandfold in the present generation, and millionfold it in
the next.

So great has been the fundamental ignorance of man and
so formidable has been the improbability of happy survival
of the preponderance of mankind, that his conditioned
reflexes would never have permitted mankind's lucid, world-
around foresight or his adequately accredited, organized generations of coordinated work, sacrifice, and dedication to be
amassed to the degree necessary to his *accomplishment,*

peacefully and consciously, of the present level of scientific industrialization capabilities and world-around resources integration—at which level it now is becoming visible for the first time that man can and may become a comprehensive and continuing physical success in the universe.

As with the bumblebee—of our introduction—preoccupied with his honey seeking—whose tail inadvertently brushes about the pollens to fertilize the botanical members of the omniregenerative metabolic processes of the total integrated ecologies of all species—so have fear-motivated man's negative preoccupations, in weaponry anticipations, inadvertently established the positively reactive technological mastery of universal energies to the degree adequate to elimination of the want which originally had necessitated the weapons.

Specifically, the revolution of inadvertencies has resulted, all unplanned, in doing so much more-with-so-much-less that —despite swiftly multiplying world population and swiftly dwindling per capita metallic resources—the percentage of all mankind participating at the standard of living of a modern U.S. industrial worker's family, (or better) one so much improved in physical advantages as to have been undreamed-of even by the world's richest and most powerful men of 1900 A.D., has risen from less than 1% of all humanity to 44% within the first two-thirds of the 20th century. Thus almost one-half of all humanity—whose total yesterdays were poverty-stricken, illiterate, diseased, and ruthlessly exploited by the "fortunate" strong-arm few—have been suddenly and inadvertently catalyzed into a pattern of physical success. This success of the 44% is probably also to be achieved for 100% of humanity well before the 20th century's close.

No world leaders planned this integrated success of man —neither economists nor philosophers predicted it. None gave their lives for it—consciously. Unconsciously however, everyone in all history gave their lives for it. There is therefore a deep subconscious passion in man which now stimulates his intuitions to strike for realization of the historically held "impossible" and now looming reality of physical success for all humanity.

While the first half of this revolution was unrecognized and uncoordinated—ergo only subconsciously achieved—the second half will be consciously coordinated—for man is now beginning to realize vaguely, but nonetheless realistically, that he need not wait upon the politically organized fear-mandated-defense underwriting of science and technology to accelerate the doing of more-with-less in weaponry only, which is only thereafter to be secondhanded into his piecemeal domestic advantaging a quarter of a century—i.e., a human generation—later, and only thereafter in turn to multiply the numbers of humanity to be served at ever-higher standard, with ever-less resources per each and every function. Despite the inexorably gaining bounty of the previously unapprehended revolution, the majority of humans are as yet poverty-stricken "havenots." But there is now fortunately visible a means of swiftly accelerating the process of converting the remainder of humanity to high-standard "haveness." This is the specific task to which the U.N.'s International Cooperation Year must address itself.

While the powerful scientific, computer-implemented theory of generalized systems controls governed the consciously integrated weapons-delivery systems, the inadvertent, uncoordinated, fortuitous reorientation of the contractors' tooled-up capabilities to exploit the separate human home-needs markets was never advantaged by the efficiency of a *generalized livingry coordinating system,* nor by the latter-day powerful expansion and refinement—at the astronomical scope and level of generalized systems-theory capabilities realizable only through computerization.

Unlike the home-building market, both the communications industry ("Tel and Tel") and the transportation industry have benefited by the general systems controls adopted for weaponry systems, simply because mails, telephones, telegraphs, cables, wireless, railroads, ships, autos, and trucks were—and as yet are—vital parts of the operational weapons-delivery and -support systems themselves.

Though today, American Telephone and Telegraph and General Motors Corporation are far out in front in computerized general systems controls of their respective operations, Henry Ford, Senior was the pioneer in the long-range, world-around, historical development of the application of the tools-to-make-tools system of mass production to large end-product tools, such as the motorized road vehicles—for mass production had long before been applied to small things, such as pins, army rifles, and watches. The premass-production use of the principle of the *moving production line* and its large-scale jigs, fixtures, templates, and massive power tools and cranes was developed centuries earlier in the production of ships on cradles on marine railways whose launched hulls moved around to outfitting docks, and around the world to receive their final full-rigged capabilities.

In the 20th century's 50 years of world-revolution-generating inadvertencies, all that the separate prime-weaponry-technology contractors attempted—in turning to domestic outlets for their government-financed capability-augmentations—was to produce domestic items suitable for profitable processing by their unique tools. Giant electric generators, steam boilers, electric lights, radios, oil burners, refrigerators, air conditioners were originally developed and used only as battleship equipment. Such items were easily converted to domestic use. But many of the potentially useful domestic-field capabilities were not originally obvious.

The prime-technology contractors' reorientations to domestic products were usually successful because their advanced technology could, for instance, readily replace the inferior materials used in yesterday's individual building components without altering the familiar building forms and procedures in any fundamental way. They produced improved wall panels, partitions, office furniture, stoves, window hardware, aluminum shingles, etc.

But no emergency-mandated authority existed such as the *national defense* or the *military*—in respect to the vast weapons-delivery-systems of the integrated national-defense systems of the U.S.S.R. or U.S.A.—to comprehensively organize and oversee the industrial contractors' scientific development and production capabilities under a comprehensively coordinated world system, designed specifically to make all men on earth a physical success—while at the same time increasing their degrees of freedom while also ever-lessening their inter-trespassing upon one another—and to do so without at the same time raping earth of its fundamental resources or robbing man of inspiring antiquities or of further restimulating environmental challenges and riches, both abstract and physical.

No scientifically informed and popularly mandated authority existed or as yet exists which adequately comprehends the immediately developing overall world revolution in design-science concepts and world-scale logistical-capabilities development. Such an authority must first emerge to effectively convert the building world from the most ignorant and self-corrupting exploitation of all the yesterdays' ever-desperate needs of man—to be now converted into the most comprehensively effective and successful enjoyment of life in universe by all of humanity. As we shall see, such an authority is even now emergent in the I.C.Y. and other developments.

Yesterday's scientifically organized weaponry contractors —whose whole development had been subsidized and developed by the national-defense authorities—never had to risk their judgment on the selection of the weaponry items to be produced. That was the prerogative of the national-defense authorities whose reasons were often obscured by top-secret classifications. When the prime-technology contractors converted their exploitable toolups into production of livingry items, they assumed that all the building items had been wisely selected for production.

The exweaponry prime contractors are the castoff long-time "kept mistresses" of the sovereign nations. The exprime contractors familiar with the grand strategies of the intimately coordinated, scientifically evolved, and unitarily commanded national and allied defense systems—assumed that their new master, the *building industry,* like their old master, the *national defense department,* must of course have a grand, logically coordinate strategy. Both the weaponry and exweaponry contractors have assumed, therefore, that their long preoccupation with weaponry was, and is as yet, alone responsible for their ignorance of the building industry's organizational ramifications and general scientific conceptioning. Naively the weaponry contractors say, "All industries must of course be governed by a comprehensive system." They don't know that the unsystematized, happenstance building activity was so inefficient and uncoordinated that it went utterly bankrupt in 1929; and that ever since its real-estator-operated anarchistic plunging is entirely subsidized by several hundred billion dollars underwriting of the U.S. government, because the building activity's overall, unplanned mushrooming and technical inefficiency has no true objectives against which to measure its gains, ergo no possible innate profits and enterprise attractions. The real-estate world is a capital cash-in and is sustained only by capital loss. Real estators buzzard the dilemmas of humanity's constantly increasing dwelling and workspace needs by bulldozing orchards, laying in water and sewer lines, and throwing up boxes. Their overall unplanned exploitation is so shortsightedly costly to society that the multihundred-billion-dollar government mort-

gage-guarantee underwriting is in reality a commonwealth
capital loss that is adjusted progressively by generation-long
deferments of the ultimate reckoning of the cost to world society and its progeny. These deferments are accomplished by
local and federal government bond issues, guarantees, etc.
The multihundred-billion-dollar real loss is mounting and will
never be paid off nor recoverable.

The indebtedness is carried however on the government
books as a momentarily lucrative debt-service generator that
drives vast billions of interest-payment dollars annually into
the macrocities banking systems' expansion—and into the latter to a ridiculous degree in which colossally sumptuous
branch banks are erected in almost every "big-city" block.
New York, N.Y., has possibly more big-name branch banks
than five-and-ten-cent stores.

The prime-technology contractors, veering from weaponry
into livingry, accept blindly the so-called building "industry's"
product categories as having been scientifically conceived—
whereas the fact is that livingry as the historical antipriority
is a bedlam of less-with-more make-do's, fortuitously contrived with the lowest-capability resource leftovers, wrapped
up in religious, and esthetic orders of classical-modern interior
and exterior symbolic-distinction superficialities.

No Ph.D. scientist has ever been retained to consider the
general systems theory governing establishment of the potentially successful life of all men around earth—let alone retained to look at a toilet. No architect or builder knows what
buildings weigh—they have never heard of performance per
pound.

The rocket capsule that will keep man living successfully
in space for protracted periods, entirely remote from the
sewer and other service mains, will be the first "scientific
dwelling" in history. The prototype of the little 300-pound
black box, which will reduce the metabolic regenerative system as now operative on earth from a one-mile-diameter ecologically accomplished chemical-energy exchange complex to
a four-foot-diameter rocket capsule energy-regenerating accessory, will cost in the neighborhood of $7 billion. Once
produced and successfully "operative," its replicas may be
mass-reproduced for $2 per pound, i.e., for $600. With such
an integrated chemical-energy regenerator taking care of all
sanitary and energy-generating requirements of family living,
men may deploy almost invisibly to the remote beauty spots

about the earth in air-delivered geodesicly enclosed dwelling machines and survive with only helicopter and TV intercommunication at luxuriously simplified high standards of living —operative at negligible land-anchorage cost similar to telephone-service charges.

Because of the dawning awareness that the weaponry phase and its quarter-century lag can be eliminated, this second half of the tool-invention revolution is to be identified as the *consciously undertaken continuance of the accelerated doing-more-with-less by world society* as world society led by I.C.Y. becomes aware that man's comprehensive physical success is not only possible, but that it can only be accomplished through design-science competence. To do so, design science now emergent in university research activities encouraged by I.C.Y. will first develop the comprehensive, computerized programming of the general livingry *system*. World coordination of the design-systems development is to be administered —as will be seen later—by spontaneously self-organized university students whose world-around design-science coordinating authority, because of the inherent primacy of physical capability in energy universe, will progressively displace the sovereign nation's political authorities who, until yesterday, have administered the regeneratively self-improving more-with-less system, exclusively on behalf of their respective separate national defenses, on the assumption that there was not enough of world resources to take care of even one-half of humanity, wherefore *it was also assumed that war for survival was and would be forever a necessary characteristic of mankind.*

This, the ultimate revolution, now to be resolved only by scientific inventing and engineering competence of the young world in general, instead of by the now-outmoded and obsolete political initiatives, will swiftly bring about high-standard survival for all and thereby the elimination of the former political recourse only to preparatorily acquired weaponry, and to the now untenable assumption that survival can only be justified by elimination—on the battlefield, or in the slums' lower-velocity rot-rate—of the unsupportable excess of human population.

Through design science, the common success of all men is guaranteed which, for the first time in history, eliminates the factors to contend with which all the world nations' defense systems were established.

Responsibility for development of the scientific-invention competence is being spontaneously assumed, in ever-increasing degree, since 1961, by the world-around students in the professions—at first in architecture, engineering, and science. They are now being joined by university students of all kinds and will now be vastly encouraged by I.C.Y. support of their initiative.

Politics will play its future part which, however, is only a secondary service—a stewardess function—of polite supervision of the passengers' "adjusting of their seat belts" for the great world "takeoff" for physical success of all mankind. But before the inventing youth can seize the initiative from world politicians to make the great fight to comprehensive success, they must—figuratively speaking, only—first state clearly to themselves and to the world what the design-science problem consists of. The problem includes the parameters of generalized anticipatory comprehensive system theory. Students will then invent, calculate, and design the (1) development, (2) production, and (3) operational tuneup of the million-types-of-parts prototype of the as-yet-nonexistent "one-thousand-passenger vertical-takeoff, rocketships." Within this hypothetical invention we package the myriad of do-more-with-less design-science inventions, innovations, or reorganizations with which the revolution can be won for all humanity—within 20 years, if all goes well—and as it is now augured by the swiftly progressive realization of the true nature of the problem by the world students.

Paris, France, July 1965, will be a prime focus of the largest world travel in the history of man. Paris will provide in July a most spectacular world stage. Upon this stage the I.C.Y. technology committee and the comprehensive world-economics-initiative-seizing students have chosen to inaugurate their design-science revolution. They will do so under the auspices of their International Union of Architects, the only world organization of professional architecture whose members corepresent all sides of all the political curtains. As the university students present their first-stage statement of their *five-stage,* ten-year-overall planned world design revolution, they will have an extraordinary opportunity to catch the world's attention with their surprisingly discovered and lucid truth that *"the one and only world revolution which is omnipolitically tolerable is now underway and is visible to all the world at the I.C.Y.-encouraged students' exhibit at the Inter-*

national Union of Architects' Eighth World Congress now meeting right here in Paris."

This is a superb opportunity to clarify for all humanity that the fundamental and prior problem of man's surviving successfully on this little sun-orbiting spaceship, *"Earth,"* cannot be solved by political theory and is not to be left to the politician's ultimate lever—war—hot, subversive, cold, or cool.

Because the revolution is too large, selection by man of the natural and best timing and place for public birth of its conscious promulgation is difficult to judge. Paris 1965 may not be the right ripe moment. If so the I.C.Y. and the students will make presentation after presentation the world around, until the concept of the scale and import of the revolution are publicly realized. Both the I.C.Y. technology committee and the students see that the world's *prime, vital* problem bears repeating a million times. It is: *how to triple swiftly, safely, and satisfyingly, the overall performance realizations per pound, kilowatt, and manhour of the world's comprehensive resources. To do so will render those resources—which at the present design level can support only 44% of humanity—capable of supporting 100% of humanity's increasing population at higher standards of living than any human minority or single individual has ever known or dreamed of. To thus concentrate on the mastery of the physical service of man will also have its inadvertent profit increment, for to master the physical—intellectually—will bring into human intercourse a level of integrity of exploration of the metaphysical capabilities of man and the metaphysical ramifications of universe also heretofore undreamed of by man.*

Science and engineering say this is eminently feasible. It is feasible because the world's economy is now operating at an appallingly low overall mechanical-efficiency level in which the machines realize, in energy work done, only 1/25—i.e., 4%—of the potential of the thus wastefully consumed energy, while the structures of the environmental controls, housing the machines and the regenerative human ecology, realize less than 1% overall structural efficiency in respect to the now-known structural capabilities in cubic feet per ounce of materials controlled, per units of labor time and per given *protection* or *advantage* function; i.e., we could build one hundred comparably volumed and useful buildings out of the same weight-, time-, and energy-recourse units now ignorantly processed into one building. But this relative performance advance involves comprehensive building-system reorganizations.

In contradistinction to that minuscule 4% overall mechanical efficiency and 1% overall structural efficiency now realized by world man, the automobiles' reciprocating engines are 15% efficient. The new gas turbines are 30% efficient. Coal-burning turboelectric generators are 40% efficient. Jet engines are 60% efficient. Combined desalination and electric-power-generating atomic reactors are 72% efficient. The new fuel cells are 80% efficient. Organized design-science competence, general systems control, and employment of man's normal rate of inventive evolution can swiftly triple the overall resource effectiveness and *that's it*. Instead of living on his million-year-deposited savings account of fossil-fuel energy, man can with larger installation and comprehensive planning succeed in living on his vast daily energy-*income* account in gravitational-energy-generated watershed and tidal dams, sun power, *et al*. Thus, this and future generations may conserve the fossil-fuel hydrocarbon energy savings to be passed on from generation to generation as an emergency "cushion."

Typified by the University of California's 1964-1965 New Year's Berkeley Campus outbreak, the present 21-year-old junior-class university students—everywhere around the earth —are the World War II babies. Most frequently, as babies, their fathers were away at the war and their mothers away at the munitions works. The superlative wartime spirit of social cooperation which must have inspired the children's foster parents and baby sitters to undertake the care and nurturing of those babies may have satisfied to unique degree the baby's and children's innate trust, the most critical and most easily damaged of all the socially coordinate spontaneous behaviorisms of newborn life—which if damaged usually results in school dropouts and juvenile delinquency. The World War II babies' subsequent childhoods were spent with their "G.I." student parents at universities. The attempt of their parents to learn more, to speak better, to use their heads instead of their muscles to win their livelihood, was, as has been learned also through behavioral science, a most powerful influence on childhood favorable development of intelligence. 1965's 21-year-olds are also the first babies reared by the "third parent," television, which brought them world news every hour with greater frequency and regularity than they received their milk. They think "world." They think and demand justice for all humanity, with no exceptions! The world students *are* the *world* revolutionaries. They are also the most literate students of all history as well as the first "world-minded," ergo, nationally unbiased, as well as the healthiest students in history. Altogether, theirs will be the most powerful and constructive revolution in all history.

In the prime of life, realizing their first individual independence, and bursting with logical and realistic idealism, the students are everywhere confronted with yesterday's science fiction, now operative as today's practical reality.

First, the students comprehend that any invention can be realized.

Secondly, the students find themselves confronted with the concurrent news of the majority of the world people being as yet faced with starvation, ignorance, and suffering.

Thirdly, the students are confronted with an ideological struggle of the world's major political systems, the major protagonists of which, in idealistically convinced self-righteousness, alike exploit to the limit men's lethal dilemmas by every manner of subversive and guerrilla warring. Each assumes that the poverty-striken peoples' problems can only be solved by political organization. Each seeks to prove its respective political system to be superior to the others'. Each hopes to gain the largest world support for its equally lopsided and mutually obsolete political biases. Each spends far more to frustrate the other side than it spends in developing any realistic plans to make the world work. Each pours its technology only into weapons. Each distributes lethal weapons en masse to people who only want to eat, love, speculate, and laugh. This homogenization of negatives hides the fact that no political system can, by virtue of its ideology alone, make man a physical success. Both sides, as yet, assume Thomas Malthus' and Marx's fundamental resource inadequacy to hold true, and claim their respective systems to be most just under the assumed mutually exclusive economic-survival alternatives imposed by fundamental inadequacies.

But—take the technological tools of industrialization away from U.S.A., Russia, France, China, England, West Germany, Japan, and Italy, and leave them all their respective ideologies, and within six months, two billion world humans will die of starvation. Contrariwise, take away from those eight sovereign states all their political ideologies and political leaders, and leave them their industrial tools and human operators and their habitual daily production- and distribution-system network tasks and no more will starve than are starving now. New gap-filling pro tem leaders would spring up everywhere, overnight, with emergency-gained authority who would make things work as well and probably better.

Only as a consequence of such politically transcendental and industrially informed observation is it now philosophically, scientifically, and mundanely visible that the only difference between all of the *unsuccessful yesterdays* and the *half-successful today* is the presence of the world-around industrial network and its regeneratively multiplying scientific and technical knowhow.

World society is as yet unappreciative of industrialization's significance. Its superevolutionary stature and the nature of its comprehensive functioning are as yet obscured by thick overlays of essentially irrelevant theories of its political and economic profit involvements. World students, will, in due course, discover that world industrialization is an evolutionary transformation, as fundamental as that of caterpillars into butterflies. Man's originally internal and corporeally integral functions and organic processes are inventively externalized by man, all together to provide a world-around metabolic regeneration system of mutually sustaining significance only. For instance, great cities are organic components of the world industrialization. Into the cities-evolving continuity, new human lives are born and lives die out as do little coral animals, in and out of coral reefs. Industrialization constitutes continuous man. Each new life is born to be stimulated positively or negatively into making direct or indirect, conscious or subconscious contributions to the evolutionary increase of the industrial commonwealth's metabolic and metaphysical regeneration capabilities.

Uncomprehending industrialization as constituting inexorable accelerating evolution everywhere around the world, the students demand impatiently that the world be made to work, right now! However, as with the older population, the students' reflexes have been originally and overpoweringly conditioned by their childhood experiences of being at first helpless babies, utterly dependent on their parents' responsibility and authority. Both as children and as youths, their reflexes have been conditioned to think of problems as being solvable only by some higher authority, their father, the schoolteacher, the family doctor, or the family priest. For this obvious reason, they now assume that the world problems can only be solved by their respective Big (political) Papas, and by the latter's political initiative. But the students don't as yet understand that the mandate of political leaders stems from an inherently debilitating bias—the exclusive protection of their respective national or political groups.

As we have already observed, due to the inordinately low level of mechanical efficiency of the world's production and distribution system, as now designed and operative, not even one-half of humanity can now survive for half its potential lifespan—though it is eminently feasible by design to triple the mechanical-efficiency level and thus take care handsomely of 100% of humanity. The problem is primarily one of performance upgrading by scientific inventions. However, the true technical nature of the problem is overwhelmingly obscured by the individuals' millenniums-long reflex-conditioned reliance only upon whichever political individual happens to be the most powerfully emergent claimant to being the "champion" of his community and nation's cause. It is assumed by man's historical conditioning that the strongest political leaderships are morally ordained to lead society into periodic warring for survival only of the "fittest."

Many factors have operated to bring about such fatalistic social reflexing. Much vulnerability of society arises from misplaced social confidence in the soundness of its primary educational concepts. For instance, major reflex conditioning of society springs from the universal elementary schooling of children with Greek geometry's definition of a triangle (or of a circle or any polygon) as "the area bound by a closed line" —in the case of the triangle, "the area is bound by a closed line of three edges and three angles." In the days of the Greek geometers' formulations, the earth was thought of as a plane whose lines ran outward horizontally to *nowhere*. Outside the triangle lay ultimate wilderness—then chaos, then infinity. Today we know that the earth and all systems are finite. The Law of Conservation of Energy says, "Energy may neither be created nor lost." The physical universe is a finite system. Earth is a finite sphere. The surface of a sphere is a unit area; any closed line such as a circle or a triangle, set upon a sphere, subdivides the whole sphere's surface into two subareas—i.e., the two areas on *both* sides of the line. The earth's equator subdivides earth into northern and southern hemispheres. When a small triangle is scribed on the earth, the *remainder of the earth's surface* is *also* a *unit area* defined by the same closed line of three edges and three angles—with the angles greater than 180°.

Dogmatic teaching of Greek plane geometry in elementary school produces an *exclusive only-one-side-of-the-line bias* whereby the *"inside"* area, which is "our" area, is also a finite and valid area. It is inferred by the Greek geometry that all the surface *"outside"* in an infinite, unbounded area, ergo uncontrollable, is ultimately chaotic and unreliable. To each elementary-school student—carelessly misinformed in many ways, such as: "The sun goes *down* and *rises,"* the world as yet seems realistically to stretch away horizontally to infinity, despite the students' mildly contradictory geographical training. It is easy for the students to be trapped by the "one-side-of-the-line" bias. Ergo—they automatically assume that "the other fellow is wrong." This bias is a typically debilitating consequence of dogmatically accepted axioms, many of which though now proven invalid through scientific experiment continue to be taught to hundreds of millions of young students.

The politicians are forever faced with the ultimate, axiomatic, Malthusian economics—the "you or me" decisions, "because there is not enough for both of us." Politicians therefore are not only inherently, but also debilitatingly biased. In spite of their ghostwriters' political speeches—rising at times to altruistic heights—politicians are always realistically maneuvering for the next election, or supreme council meeting. Despite superb dreams of some political leaders, compromising deals have usually had highest priority in their ultimate ways-and-means decision making.

Those politicians who undertake altruistic and idealistic solutions of the "only you or I can live—not both" dilemmas, always fail because of the heretofore, seemingly "forever," lethal economic assumption of a fundamental *world-resource inadequacy—as thus far in history designedly employed, and as thus far understood, either popularly or by the noninventively thinking economic experts.*

In the design-science revolution world students have at last glimpsed the realization that they no longer *must* leave the solution of the world's problems to the politicians or to anyone other than themselves. The world's students have glimpse-realized that with the same inalienable right as that of all inventing individuals—i.e., with poetic license only, without guns or weapons of any kind, employing only their intellect, which is weightless—they can seize the economic initiative and institute *the tool-and-network-design revolution* and its also realistically designed performance upgrading of the world resources to serve 100% of humanity, instead of 44%.

Practicing professional architects and architectural students may say, "This is not in the architectural curriculum. What authority decreed that architectural students might be allowed to take the design initiative in redesigning all the industrial tools? Who is going to pay us?"

The answer is, "What authority told the Wright brothers to invent the airplane? Who told the Bell Laboratory scientists to discover the transistor? Who told Bell to invent the telephone? And if you make a good invention, all the world will pay you for it over and over again."

Initiative springs only from within the individual. Initiative can neither be created nor delegated. It can only be vacated. Initiative can only be taken by the individual on his own self-conviction of the necessity to overcome his conditioned reflexing which has accustomed him theretofore always to yield authority to the wisdom of others. Initiative is only innate and highly perishable.

Wasn't all this visible before? Why hasn't the whole world been consciously disciplined to coordinate such a do-more-with-less design revolution?

The answer is: the generalized *do-more-with-less* principle has only become meagerly visible to anyone in the last three decades, and only importantly evident to a few more in the last decade. It has emerged, all unpredicted by any economists of history, through the accelerated evolution and mass production of doing-more-with-less primarily in weaponry. It is the result of *mass production of the means of production,* which in turn was brought about only by the historically unprecedented *"massive-retaliation"* strategy of the 1950s and 1960s, which in turn became possible of realization—for the first time in history—only with the advent of the invisible scientific tidal wave of atomics, electronics, and computerization. Doing vastly more with vastly and invisibly less is known technically as *ephemeralization.* The mass production of electronic controls inaugurated automation. With automation has come—just now—a dawning awareness of the *invisible avalanche of ephemeralization.*

Until World War II saw the Maginot Line swept over, as though it did not exist—mankind's dry-land civilizations had always conceived of their safety as being dependent upon ever more massive fortifications! *The heavier and bigger, the more secure!* No one knew or cared how much weight was piled up. Even today, neither architects nor their clients nor the public has any thought of how much buildings weigh. Massive masonry and "deep-window reveals" were the "most-wanted" residential architectural features of the 1920s.

What swept over the world's historically most massive and deeply founded fortification, the Maginot Line, in 1940 was the Germans' bringing out onto man's dry land of the theretofore exclusively seaborne and seakept secret strategy of doing vastly more with invisibly less—the tanks were submarines climbing out upon the land, the airplanes were the destroyers with wings—stunned mankind called it the blitzkrieg. The do-more-with-less blitzkrieg machines didn't have to "take" the fort. They ran right over it. They commanded the whole economy's circulatory system. There was no greater hitting power anywhere to still their omnipresent killing power.

Mankind, conditioned only to look for more to do his tasks, was utterly confused by the blitzkrieg. He kept looking for a bigger rather than a smaller explanation. This was the popular historical turning point. Throughout all of known history, 99% of humanity occupied only the dry land—whose arable portion amounted to only about 5% of the surface of planet earth—the other 1% of humanity occupied 75% of earth's surface, the great, treacherous, watery one-ocean world. Realizing that ships may deliver magnitudes of cargo tonnages thousandfold of that transportable on the backs of men or animals, the 1% of world population who became high-seas merchantmen, or pirates, mastered the other 99% of human population by controlling all the sealanes of world commerce and thereby the world's wealth integrations. The great pirates became supreme. The secret of their mastery lay in the secrets of shipbuilding, handling, and navigation, in which the basic limits of floatability—or displacement—meant that whoever could build-in the highest overall performance with the least weight and effort could float-mobilize the greatest and swiftest hitting power to command the seaways and their merchantman, and thereby run the world.

The *ethereal strength secrets* of ship, airplane, and rocketry building have never been even mildly understood by the only massively impressed brains of land men, i.e., 99% of humanity. Up to 1932, the calculation records of all naval ships were methodically destroyed by all the admiralties of all the navies of the world. How many Americans are familiar with the name of the Webb Institute, the prime source of the U.S.A.'s great naval architects?

That man might do more with less was thought of by the landlubbers' economic experts as nonsense. Up to and through World War II, more-with-less used to be conceived of as impossible and jokingly referred to as "lifting oneself up by one's own bootstraps"—we don't hear of the expression now. But it is only since World War II that we haven't heard it. The public press has not yet noticed the obsolescence of that historically devastating cliché.

A key part of ephemeralization's acceleration has been played by the return of approximately all of the world's metallic scrap into complete reuse. This scrap recirculation released by progressive obsolescence of earlier inventions by newer more efficient ones was utterly unrecognized by either economists, businessmen, politicians—or even the world's metal monopolizing cartels up to 1940—as constituting a fundamental factor in the doing-more-with-less process. It is approximately unknown even today that the world's total mined metals resources recirculate every 22½ years. This surprising condition occurred as follows: the quantity of the prime metals—iron, copper—mined and put into circulation during the years 1917, 1918, 1919 of World War I was *threefold* and *total cumulative* quantity of those metals mined in all previous history. The vast new recirculating resource did not come into play historically until 22½ years later, i.e., in 1940, 1941, and 1942, which was well into the years of World War II. In the onrush of war, the vast new scrap arrival was unnoticed (except by the few who had predicted its arrival). The economists assumed this scrap-metals arrival to be a normal part of the enormously stepped-up war production in general—probably, they thought, the scrap had been sacrificed by patriots throwing "their all" into the breach.

Economists, politicians, and financial market speculators as yet think of today's and tomorrow's metallic resources as only existing in mines. They have altogether missed that the metals once mined go into eternal recirculation—chemical elements never become *secondhand* and shopworn. All that is needed is energy and knowhow to free them in pristine purity for further tasks. The United States has no tin mines, yet it has a tin reserve in aircraft and rocket production's soft tools greater than the ore reserve in Bolivia's great tin mines.

Ony 14% of all the copper mined historically by man is not at present recirculating. And that 14% which went to the ocean bottom in munitions ships will soon be recovered and put into circulation.

During World War II, and during Eisenhower's cold war, metallic stockpiling, ostensibly for swift and massive retaliation capabilities, the great mineowners realized a contrived bonanza as the otherwise adequately recirculating metals were augmented by a twofolding again of history's alltime mining rate. Employing the 22½ year "recirculation yardstick," we may safely predict that from July 1966 to 1975, the world's recirculating scrap-derived metals resources, coming uninvited onto the world's metal markets, will be more than doubled again. This massive metal supply will render the design-science conversion of the world's resources—from the service of only 44% of humanity, to service of 100% of the world's population—a facile matter.

The world's metals cartels, the older "have" countries and the newest industrial nations—as yet uninformed regarding this newly emerging scrap recirculation—now reconnoiter to control as surreptitiously as possible the metallic resources originally buried by nature within the distantly deployed, world-around lands of the now newly "emerged nations." Their uninformed economic premise is that the integrity of expansion of the industrial giants will soon depend largely upon the as-yet-undeveloped and unmined, tantalizingly rich, metallic resources of those many small nations. All those so assuming will be "rudely awakened" when (1) the avalanche of unexpected scrap of World War II plus (2) the dropping-market-enforced cold-war stockpile cash-in of the national holders of the unused metals will suddenly dump such an abundance of metals on the world markets that, when combined with (3) the doing-threefold-more-per-pound technology, concurrently coming into the domestic technology with (4) the converted weaponry producers vastly higher-performance tool capabilities, the 100% industrialization of world man will probably be realized without further development of those new nations' as yet unmined metals resources. The latter will become the reserves for the future generations' "rainy days." This enormous self-augmentation of industrialization's doing unprecedentedly more with unbelievably less, which is about to take place all unannounced, is the big economic surprise that will bring about final abandonment of the cold warring now being insinuated into the small nations' theaters as, not too invisibly, puppeted by all the big nations of all political biases.

There are several other major economic world trends which are as surprising as they are vast which are also heading full-speed to integrate with and compound the "big economic surprise" which will sum-totally render man on earth an "overnight" total physical success.

Of top importance among the events trending to compound as the big surprise is the trend of big business to move its headquarters permanently out of the country—out of the U.S.A.—out of any sovereign nation. In the official language of the U.S. Department of Commerce, there are two kinds of U.S. foreign investments—direct and indirect.

Indirect foreign investment consists of U.S. citizens and corporations buying and owning of equities in countries outside the U.S.A.

Direct foreign investment consists of capital investments by U.S. corporations in land, buildings, and machinery for foreign manufacture and commerce.

At the beginning of the 20th century, the U.S.A. had 3½ billion of "F.D.R." dollars' worth of direct foreign investments—this amount increased slowly for a third of a century, to 8 billion of "F.D.R." dollars' worth, by the time of the 1929 Crash. U.S.A.'s DFI then diminished to $7 billion and held there for 13 years until 1942, when the U.S.A.'s Second World Warring required much foreign-production activity which the U.S.A. entrusted in entirety to its private enterprise's operation and management.

Since 1942, the direct foreign investments of the U.S.A. have zoomed tenfold from 7 to over 70 billion "F.D.R." dollars' worth, which equals the value of all the gold that has been mined in all history—of which 42 billion "F.D.R." dollars is the total value of that portion which functions as monetary gold. The U.S.A.'s direct foreign investments also equal in value the $70 billion worth of the entire electrical-energy-generating and -distributing industry's capital equipment as now owned by the combined public and private sectors of the continental United States.

The original U.S.A.-born corporations' direct foreign investments are now doubling every seven years. Unabated, they will probably double to $150 billion by 1972.

In 1964, the $70 billion U.S. direct foreign investments earned $4½ billion net, after all taxes. That is just under 6½% net.

Largest earner from direct foreign investment was General Motors, whose $500 million—constituting one-third of its total 1964 earnings from all sources of $1.5 billion net profit after taxes—came from its foreign operations, despite the fact that much less than one-third of its total capital investments have been made outside the U.S.A. So powerful is this trend of big U.S. corporations that *in 1964, $4 out of every $5 that the U.S.A.'s hundred largest corporations put into new capital-equipment investments went into their foreign operations.*

Quite clearly, as I.B.M.'s international-operations chairman, Arthur Watson, says, "the trend is already a reality, and big business is no longer 'national' in character, but is identifiable only as a 'world' phenomenon."

Watson says that it is now as inappropriate to speak of "England trading with Spain"—or of world commerce as a "country trading with a country"—as it would be to speak of the myriad mideast coast U.S. commerce events as consisting of states trading with states, i.e., "New York State trading with New Jersey," with their trade balances only adjusted annually with gold-bullion transfers. Despite big businesses' new efficiencies the world's sovereign political states as yet operate with utterly outworn international accounting customs, inherited unquestioningly by world society—from the great pirates' method of avoiding hijacking of their gold on the high seas by trading for a whole-at-a-time on credit, leaving their high-rank "sovereign ambassadors" as hostages in the foreign capitals to insure their annual trade balancing, which took place only "across the counter" or "down the street" between the large banks in the world's well-guarded capital cities.

The post-1942 pattern of the foreign industrial corporations' upsurge is quite different from the old foreign mine and oil-well exploitations in which the U.S. or European corporations *took away wealth from* the foreign countries. The new trend *brings wealth into* the foreign countries. The old pattern became intolerable to most of the exploited countries, which seized the wells and mines and operated them for their own account as, for instance, did Iran or Mexico.

In addition to prohibiting foreign operators from taking away their wealth, Mexico will not allow any foreign corporations to export automobiles or other major manufactured items into Mexico. They require that the foreign corporations shall manufacture in Mexico. The Mercedes auto, for instance, is popular in Mexico due to its world-around-acknowledged excellence of performance. The Mercedes Company, like General Motors, must manufacture their cars in Mexico exclusively for Mexican consumption. They must give the Mexican government and Mexican investors the majority of the shares in their Mexican manufacturing corporation. But General Motors, Mercedes, *et al.*, can, for good value given, and without depriving the foreign operation, take out enough profit to make the sum of all their many separate foreign earnings a fabulous amount. Ergo, the foreign countries prosper and get the benefit of the knowhow of a world-powerful research-and-development program to an extent greater than they could develop for themselves. The Mexicans could produce an "Inca" car or a "Montezuma V-8," but these products could not have the mature world corporation's knowhow, serviceability, or competitive earning value.

It is improbable that these new-era world companies ever will be seized by countries, as the countries are already the majority share owners and are realizing greater wealth and technical-advantage earnings from General Motors' world-experienced production management and research development than they could possibly make on their own.

This general exodus of the world industry giants from sovereign protection of their respective countries of origin will in due course altogether eliminate big-business lobbying for continuance of their respective earlier domestic "protection"—in the way of custom tariffs—and even indirectly through passport controls, just as inter-New Jersey-New York-state customs and passports have become utterly impractical of maintainance as state-sovereignty devices.

As the big corporations graduate to world status they enter countries whose wages are far below U.S. wage scales. Because of the world corporations' economic lessons learned in their "school days" in the U.S.A.—e.g., *that the higher and*

*wider the wages distributed the more prolific and profitable
the mass production*—the big world corporations' policy—
now managed more and more by computer determinations
regarding which is the most profitable strategy—will promote
progressive increase in foreign wage rates and in time-pay-
ment finances to accelerate world buying. This world corporations' around-the-world wages stepup to final parity with
U.S. wages will not be occasioned by the U.S. labor unions
instituting world operations—a difficult task due to passports
and other restrictions—but *all unexpectedly by computer fiat*
because it will be promoted profitably by the world corporations' C.I.T.-type investment operations. It will take only a decade to develop world wage-rate parities, thus eliminating the
fundamental frustration of economic development in India,
etc.

In the meantime, the low foreign wages will make it *impossible* for U.S. labor to compete with the world industry
operations without committing economic suicide by quarter-
ing their wage rates. Instead, U.S. labor will have to recognize that its direct objective of raising labor's income share of
progressively multiplying industrial wealth augmentations was
only inadvertently the means of its doing something much
bigger and important for world industrialization and humanity which was the key to making U.S. mass-production industry successful. Labor's inadvertent contribution to world industrialization success was that its widely distributed and
stepped-up wage rates *made possible mass purchasing,* which
made mass production of any good prototype a fundamental
economic success. To consolidate its gains and to stride forward into the new era, U.S. labor will have to let automation
articulate briskly its flourishing trends in order greatly to advance the production of the organized energy-wealth capability and thereby to make possible the residual, smaller U.S.
producers' ability to compete favorably in world markets.
Thus U.S. labor will have to persuade the U.S. Congress to
underwrite 50 million lucrative university scholarships with
life benefits of every type in order to persuade labor's "rank
and file" to unblock and mandate full-cry automation.

The only limitation to such a commitment is the ability to
produce the goods which will be commanded by this steady
buying power, and that exactly is what automation alone can
do! The same scholarships will have to be given also to all
the tens of millions of jobholding bureaucrats—federal, state,

and corporate—as the international and interstate tariffs and personal taxes are progressively eliminated "on advice" of the computers—as to the most favorable strategies for generating, distributing, and regenerating the greatest possible real *"energy-intellect" capability commonwealth* in the shortest possible time.

In order to make universities adequate to the avalanche load, a "great teachers" documentary-producing television revolution in education must take place. First thing will be to give all the faculty "deadwood" of all colleges and universities superresearch "fellowships"—to be operative anywhere off campus.

Through computer analysis the private-vs.-public sectors' "best-interest" differentiations will tend to disappear. As they diminish, the *inhibition by invitation*—already commenced— of the world-production corporations' enterprises into the previously exclusively "socialist" lands will swiftly increase. With such socialist-invited world-type corporations' automated enterprise installations advantageously operative in socialist lands will come the suprabounteous, incentive-held options on capital-share values, which will gain swiftly as world-around-accredited and computer-evaluated relative-wealth-augmenting. In order to stimulate and properly reward those who initiate and sustain the commonwealth multiplying ever-higher standards of performance in any and all prosocial advantage directions, options on shares in the world industry corporations will be purchasable out of the lucrative "fellowship" incomes by the computer-detected and -designated individuals who prove to be real-wealth augmentors of "important" magnitude.

All such vast considerations of "wealth" generation and regenerative distribution must start with both scientific and popular recognition of the extraordinary potential-capability value of the human beings who themselves constitute a priori automated and metabolically self-regenerating, brain-controlled growth mechanisms. The wealth-comprehending must also recognize the extraordinary potentials of the natural environment, if properly understood as a complex of complementary patterns which if properly manipulated can support total-man life. Next in importance in the consideration of the factors necessary to man's realization of nature's potential wealth comes man's experimental discovery of the leverage principle—as man accidentally steps upon the long end of a log, lying across another log, with the short end of the stepped-on log lying under a third log too great for man's lifting by the combined muscles of his back, legs, and arms. Man sees and realizes, as he steps on the log, that his relatively light weight is easily lifting the far heavier log. After much lever-exploiting experience, man next arranges a *set* of lever arms around a hub and places this wheel of paddle-tipped levers in a waterfall and is able to link up the turning water-wheel shaft by pulleys, belts, and gears—which are all lever-principle devices—to do *sustained work* greater than he can do with his own muscles; the linkage of free energies to levers belittles his own minuscule short-period efforts. With these interlinkages of the lever and channeled energy man is now in the *wealth-making business,* which is to use his brain to get nature's vast energy patterns to do the energy work of supporting and regenerating him.

All this is possible because the *true wealth of world man is mathematically inventoriable as his physically organized ability to protect and satisfy his forward, inexorable metabolic- and intellectual-regeneration needs*—which forwardly established metabolic-regeneration-capability wealth is statable in per capita forward days, safely and adequately anticipated.

The physical abilities which can anticipatorily furnish the metabolic-regeneration capabilities consist of three main components—two of which consist of energy, while the third consists of physically weightless, intellectual *knowhow*.

The first energy component is *energy as matter* out of which man fashions all his tools, each of which is a development of the fulcrum and lever or the *mechanical-advantage principle.*

The second energy component is "free" energy as *radiation* or *gravity,* which may be channeled and focused electromagnetically and otherwise to impinge on the advantage-ends of the levers to do the forward metabolic-regeneration work. Intellect shunts the free energy patterns of universe—external to man—to impinge on the big automated-leverage work complex by using man's minuscule physical (muscular and brain-reflex) capabilities, only as *self-starter* and *coordinator* mechanisms, which self-starter efforts are amplifiable by the "advantage" principle and pyramid relayingly, to finally in turn start up and coordinate the latest-biggest-system machines—by making first the small-scale tools that make the bigger tools, which in turn mass-produce the ever-bigger and more prolific—brain-reflex-emulating—automated tools.

Of this regenerative energy-wealth-intellect-knowhow operation, it may be said that the scientists assure us, by the experimentally derived Law of Conservation of Energy, that "energy may neither be lost nor created." They also assure us that the physical universe is finite—and consists exclusively of energy—therefore, the *energy content of wealth is inexhaustible;* ergo, irreducible. They also assure us that experiment shows that the *intellectual knowhow* content of wealth *is only increasable,* for every time intellect is employed experimentally, it *learns more.* It can't learn less. If it learns that what it guessed "might work" doesn't work—that is learning more; ergo, *wealth, which cannot decrease physically and can only increase intellectually* can sum-totally only multiply.

Real wealth is irreversibly self-augmenting.

Real wealth cannot be used to alter yesterday.

Real wealth can only be used to alter today and tomorrow.

The more and faster wealth is employed, the more and faster it must multiply.

Wealth has nothing to do with the *intrinsic* value "money," as metallic specie—as silver, copper, or gold coinage. Gold, silver, and copper have, however, a myriad of uniquely excellent technological-function advantages for man, for instance, in the formulation of energy-tool capabilities, that is as function #1 in the threefold *wealth constituency—energy* (M) *energy* (c), and *intellect.* Incidentally, there is a challenge to the mathematical physicists to integrate the four fundamental threefold-constituent formulations: Einstein's $E=Mc^2$; Gibbs' (phase rule) $f=n-r+2$; Euler's (topological) $V=E-F+2$; and our own wealth law $W=2E+II$ (where W is wealth, E is energy, and I is intellect). The probably ultimate identification of functions of these formulas with one another—as disclosing one generalizable law for only superficially different aspects of the same fundamentals of universe behaviorism—will bring about an enormous acceleration in the computerized establishment of man's real-wealth functioning and its regenerative investability, and thereby establishment of total man's physical success in universe.

It is an inherent characteristic of man's *intellect-organized energy wealth* that the larger the numbers served, the more swiftly the apparatus is amortized and becomes improvingly replaceable.

The larger the interactive-energy wealth system, the more efficiently does it operate. This is comprehended when we observe experimentally that when we double the linear dimensions of a system, we fourfold its surface, while eightfolding its volume; ergo, as we double size, we consistently halve the areas of surface through which the eightfolded and contained energies may escape: e.g., the larger the sun—or any star— the lower the entropic rate, and the longer does it conserve its energy. The larger the iceberg, the slower the rate of its melting, for it can only melt by inhibiting energy as heat from the rest of the universe—which it can only do through its surface. As the iceberg melts, its volume shrinks at a velocity of the third power v^3 while its surface shrinks only a v^2— therefore as it melts the rative amount of the volume as yet to be melted decreases much more rapidly than the amount of the surface area through which the energy—as heat to melt it—can be admitted. The smaller the ice mass in a given atmosphere the faster does it melt. As the iceberg grows smaller it melts faster. Conversely generalizing: as energy systems grow larger they lose energy more slowly.

The combined energy-and-intellect wealth may be distributed from the natural energy sources, which are frequently remote from where men need to use the energy, wherefore *the transmission of energy* is intimate to the omnidirectional realizations of wealth by all men everywhere.

In the transmission of energy by man from its generative source to work for other men at distances around the earth away from the energy sources, there are great differences in the efficiency, capacity, and speed of the known alternative technologies of energy transmission—i.e., by (1) continuous or batched; (2) solid, powered, liquid, gaseous, or electrical; (3) vesseled, boated, railroaded, piped, wired, or wirelessed.

All transmission systems involve original capital investments of the *energy-intellect-time wealth* to produce the transmission tools and further working capital of *energy* plus *intellectual-time wealth* to cover *operating costs.*

When we account the annual rates for amortizing the original capital—tools and structures as well as the operating costs and continuous lifelong social overhead of commonwealth responsibilities and functions—as now customarily articulated by taxes—and compare the *net delivered energy costs, volume,* and *velocity advantages* of the alternate energy-transmission systems, we find that electrical energy *delivered today by wire* (and tomorrow possibly by radio, or light, or laser beams)—is by far the most efficient, profuse, and speedy wealth-distributing system.

The history of increase of voltages, distances, and volumes of electrical-energy transmission has been tied directly to the progressive limits of practically manufacturable, installable, and maintainable equipment that could be realized from the comprehensive conversions of pure science's (subjective) discoveries into objective-use technologies—as also modified by the physical ("material") resources becoming progressively available to industrial use. (We put "material" into quotes for nuclear physics has clearly demonstrated that there are no "solid" things or "matter" in the sense in which man uses the word.)

Generally speaking, the higher the voltage, the greater both *the volumes at which* and the *distances to which* electrical energy can be transmitted. By the use of transformers, electrical energy generated at safely workable low voltages may be stepped-up to high voltage levels for transmission, and stepped-down at the receiving ends for safe domestic and industrial use.

High-voltage electrical transmission systems require many safeguarding devices, for protection of both the public and the generating and transmitting systems themselves against the otherwise disastrous voltage and wattage overloadings occasioned by the relatively frequent interactions of lightning with the conducting lines and switchyards. The systems need extraordinarily effective overload circuitbreakers, as well as insulators to support the conduction lines.

The two most limiting factors in recent years in the constant effort to increase safe, feasible, and economic electrical conduction have been (1) the limit of insulator effectiveness, and (2) the complex design and fabrication of adequately large conduction lines. The costly ceramics research occasioned by reentry problems of space vehicles, plus the large quantities of the most plentiful and economically conducting metals—aluminum and copper—now available, have provided new high-capacity electrical-transmission insulators, and higher voltage capacity in general.

High-voltage conductance—heretofore primarily at 138,000 kilovolts and at 230,000 kilovolts—has represented the maximum level of high-voltage transmission feasibility of the last two decades. The transmission distances theoretically permitted by the highest of these voltages was 1400 miles in 1936, but due to fluorescent line losses the practically profitable distance was only 340 miles. Hoover Dam to Los Angeles was a typically practical limit. Because of this 340-mile limit, industrial network systems of the major urban centers of the U.S.A. were too remote from one another to permit economically favorable integration hookups. Energy systems, as we have observed, are greatly benefited when the interlinkage is economically feasible. In addition to the "geometrical-relativity" aims of energy conservation occurring as size is increased the benefit of integration comes also from the law of averages, which allows the otherwise unused but necessarily maintained total generating capacities to flow from one system to the other, to satisfy one another's nonsimultaneous supply shortages. The costs go down, and the profits go up rapidly with transmission-network integrations.

Technological improvements are now permitting transmission voltage stepups of importantly improved magnitude—to 380,000, to 500,000, and to one million kilovolts (one million kilovolts is *one billion volts*). This new-era transmission is spoken of in the electrical industry as UHV—"ultrahigh voltage."

Contracted UHV installations are now underway throughout the U.S.A. which within a decade will, for the first time, *completely interconnect the U.S.A.'s electrical generation and transmission systems,* bringing such important cost reductions and profit increases that both the public and private ownership sectors are being vastly advantaged. The continental integrating agreements underlying the physical-network interlinkings have been accomplished without public notice of their taking place, despite that the total networks so integrated represent a capital value of $70 billion. So satisfactory to both public and private sectors has this new development become that the political voices of yesterday's vitriolic dissension between public and private sectors have been entirely stilled. They were inherently stilled because the mergers were not arrived at through the opinions of directors but by the multicomputer-cross-checked assurance of the mutual profits to be arrived at only by such merger. A preknowledge of this silently arrived-at private-public-sectors merging of the yesterday dividend sides' respective "best interests" to common bonanza accord, which took place during 1962-1963 in the electrical-transmission industry, could readily have forecast the 1964 presidential election of Johnson.

The by-product physical advantages for society of the integrated U.S.A.'s continental energy network will be many, not the least of which will be the removal of the fuel-burning prime movers of the generating systems from the major cities. Up to now, coal has been delivered by rail from Pennsylvania mines to New York City at lower energy cost than it could be transmitted by wire at 230,000 kv. The coal smoke of the electrical-generation stations has been the prime smog-maker of greater New York City. With UHV, energy will go from Pennsylvania coalfield generators to New York City at an overall 33% energy-cost reduction as compared with the previous railroading of the coal. This direct cost reduction will be minor in comparison to the indirect cost reductions, such as the dust-deposit-accelerated depreciation of all manner of goods or of lung impairments, etc. This UHV long-distance energy transmissions as from generators in Newfoundland to New York City will mean elimination of smog, not only from New York City but from the majority of all world cities.

Stepups to one million kilovolts make most economically feasible the intercontinental linkage not only of Europe, Asia, and Africa, but also of the American continents and in the not-distant future of North America linked over or under the Bering Straits with Kamchatka and thence with both the Russian and Chinese networks. This will occur in time to greatly accelerate the eastern Siberian and above all the swift Oriental energy-intellect-wealth-distribution stepups.

The *energy-intellect-wealth* advantage accruing to these last interlinkages will be the optimum because they will interlink the low nighttime loads of the progressively shadowed hemisphere of the rotating earth with the high daytime loads of the progressively illuminated hemisphere.

It is now clearly indicated that the energy-wealth advantages accruing to both private and public sectors will be so vast as to tend swiftly to cancel out the ideological differences of the respective beneficiary peoples' previous sovereign-political-system advantages. "If that's socialism—I'm a socialist" is the new-enterprise capitalists' ejaculation, and "If that's capitalism, it's ideal for the commonwealth augmentation of the masses" is the socialists' ejaculation as they integrate their respectively contributed network facilities.

These new and vastly increased energy-wealth-generating capabilities will convert to positive account the world's energy wealth now on negative account—in the inventories of atomic energy invested in destructive missiles. With the energy-intellect-wealth integrations, the *human-desire drive* for realizable physical success will swiftly outdistance man's fear-motivated weaponry buildup. There will be many energy-harvesting, -generating, and -transmitting reorganizations. For instance, led by LeTourneau's final success in developing the diesel electric all-wheel drives of large earth movers, the electric propulsion of short-haul vehicles in all urban work, combined with the swift advances in energy-storage batteries, will go on in the next decades to eliminate carbon monoxide fumes from cities.

During World War II when there was greater need for hydrocarbon products than could be supplied by the petroleum industry, experiments were conducted at the United States Bureau of Standards, using the three most popular automobile engines, which were fueled with alcohol instead of gasoline. They worked with high efficiency and only minor carburetor modifications. The alcohols came from canes and grasses. Because of exhaustion of petroleum-refining capacities during World War II, it was also necessary to allow the production of large amounts of alcohol from sugar and grains in order to produce sufficient butyl and neoprene, to in turn produce synthetic-rubber products—especially auto, truck, and plane tires. All unexpectedly, the synthetics provided far greater tire-mileage performance than had the previous tire rubbers.

By the experimental developments of World War II it was clearly demonstrated that it is technically possible for world society to live at highest conceivable standards while using only its daily energy income from the "push-pulls" of star radiation and gravity, while at the same time conserving the fossil fuels and atomic fuel "savings" of the ages. It was evidenced that all the daily hydrocarbon income of cosmically generated radiation's photosynthesis and metabolic energy harvesting in all the greenery of nature may be converted into storable alcohols from which energy as alcohol, energy as fuels, foods, or plastics, can be chemically realized—on a large scale.

In the next decade's worldizing of industrial-production systems and energy-generating and -transmission systems, we will witness the surprise solution to the establishment of world citizenship occasioned swiftly and simply by multiplication of world passenger traffic to magnitudes which will necessitate credit-card-type passports and automation of omniborder clearances; plus the amplification of the efficiencies accruing to "common market."

Compounding all the trends herewith related makes clear that the highest priority task of the International Cooperation Year will be the dissemination to all the world's peoples of the kinds of integrated trend, experiment, invention, and development information that we are considering in this review —of the Geosocial Revolution—whereby total humanity can now become physically successful, if it doesn't, through overextended and tolerated ignorance, frustrate the trends.

The important news to be disseminated continually integrates productively with other news as we realize for instance that all the energy, generation, and distribution range gaining will be coupled economically with desalination programs which can employ all the by-product heat of the electrical-generating systems to reduce the generation costs of the world networks to even more important degree—while at the same time bringing the world's deserts into ever-green operation as the most efficient sun-radiation-harvesting and -storing system of the metabolic wealth—optionally convertible thereafter into food, fuel, or plastics.

While all the metabolic gains are taking place, favorable changes in population trends will be realized. Biological population is apparently operative on a quantum basis. Nature increases the seed and fertilization starts in inverse proportion to the probability of successful growth and survival of each of the ecologically complementary species—of all of life on earth. As the chances for maple trees to survive decrease, nature starts more maple-tree seeds whirling off in their rotorships to find plantable sites.

The full range of energy events of universe impinging upon man as hurricanes, earthquakes, or mild weather changes, or even milder mosquito bites, are organized by nature on a quantum basis, whereby the more severe the energy event, the less frequent its occurrence, and conversely the milder and less disturbing, the more frequent are the energy events. Earthquakes are far less frequent than fleas, and novas less frequent than tornadoes.

In the same way, the human population's starts, gains, and

recessions are geared directly to changing survival and birth-rate probabilities. The first 17th-century European colonists in America had an average of 13 children per family. As the first waterworks and sewer systems came into use, improving the sanitary conditions and survival probability, the numbers of children per family swiftly decreased (only reversing momentarily in meager degree to rectify the abnormal death-rates of warfaring) until with full industrialization attained in America, the birthrate is now 1.9 children per family.

The more industrialized a country becomes, the more rapidly does its birthrate decrease. North America, Europe, and Russia's population birthrates are all decreasing, and tend toward swifter decline. The increase in longevity in those countries through control of diseases is alone responsible for their only temporary population-adjustment increases. World population will first stabilize, then finally decrease as industrialization swiftly amplifies to serve all of humanity. What is developing on a long-range basis is that once born, some men will probably live in excellent health and vigor to great age —possibly ad infinitum.

The rate at which each successive country, entering industrialization, accomplishes the full industrialization magnitudes per capita accomplished by the earlier industrializing economies constantly accelerates. Russia inaugurated its industrialization toolups as the U.S.A. came to the old-world pirates' 1929 financial crash (occasioned by the U.S.A.'s original industrial exploiters' too shortsighted initiatives—a fiasco which switched the prime initiative from private banking into public underwriting of the wholesale advances of technological evolution). In the early 1930s Russia purchased the prototype production plants—for all phases of industrialization—from the U.S.A.'s temporarily unemployed industrial giants, as well as from other major European industrial economies. Russia did not buy the equipment used by the U.S.A. 100 years earlier when the U.S.A. was starting to industrialize. Russia insisted upon obtaining only the most advanced equipment known to be realizable in the 1930s. As a consequence, within only 50 years Russia accomplished (approximate) parity with the U.S.A.'s industrial per capita levels. Despite Russia's high-level industrialization, its living-standard potential is as yet unrealized by its citizenry, due to the cold war's weaponry diversion of Russia's energy-intellect capital wealth.

Russia accomplished in 50 years the magnitude of industrialization which took the U.S.A. a hundred years.

China entered industrialization in 1949 at the computer-automation-atomic energy moment of history and started its tooling and instrumentation at that level. China never made or flew a reciprocating engine and propeller-driven airplane. It started in the aeronautical industry with jets. China probably will accomplish its prime industrialization in 25 years—i.e., by 1974—nine years from now. As each of the national industrializations has been accompanied by a constantly lowering birthrate, China's birthrate will henceforth decrease rapidly. China has already established effective birth control. India's, Africa's, South and Central America's industrializations will swiftly follow. The world population increase to "explosion" magnitude will never occur, but will decelerate to industrially manageable magnitude as the as yet undreamed-of higher standards of living are realized.

India, Africa, Central and South America will achieve full industrialization by 1980 when at the most disturbing prognostication rates the world population will have reached only five billion, its final peak before full industrialization's declining rate sets in. At that population peak, there will be an average of 6½ acres of dry land and 19 acres of water-covered earth for each human. The present figures are 10 acres of dry land and 30 acres of water-covered earth. The water-covered acres average a mile deep; the peak population will not come near the critical limit of metabolic supportability of man on earth.

Having climbed, figuratively speaking, to the top of the prognostication mountain range, we will now enjoy our swift ski-run back to where we started. Poised at the peak of the "run," we take our last big look around. First we see that it will be the I.C.Y.'s foremost task to clarify that the world peoples' conceptual realization that the ability to do more with less in weaponry can also be applied to livingry is a brand-new realization. It is the mid-20th century's most miraculous bonanza as realized from the cosmic treasury of the heretofore-undiscovered generalized principles which apparently govern the evolutionary operation of universe. When the world peoples' two major politicians from the maximumly opposed ideologies, Khrushchev and Eisenhower, met at Geneva in 1954, it was put in utterly surprising evidence for the first time in history that by some theretofore-unnoticed mira-

cle, it had come-to-pass that the science and commerce world
bookkeeping figures suddenly revealed that all mankind
might after all be permitted—contrary to Malthus and Darwin's "survival only of the fittest"—to be a metabolically regenerative, comprehensive, physical success on earth. Men
can't as yet believe that fact to a degree sufficient to persuade
them simultaneously to drop all their weaponry, or their
(both say "only retaliatorily maintained") defenses, or their
altogether totally obsolete bankruptcy-type economic ac-
countings. But men's imminent and total physical success is
now fact, and it makes the capability of shooting rockets to
the moon minuscule in overall significance. Not a bad thing
to have "hanging over your head"—success!

Doing more with less (ephemeralization) while only using
recirculating scrap-material resources, has never even been
thought of by politicians—let alone adopted by them—as a
realistic political strategy. They have had always to "make
do" with the most obvious and familiar "what-have-you's."
But ephemeralization is here, and the world students are the
first to develop a strategically oriented awareness of its significance, an awareness which is now accelerating and is soon to
attain world-revolution magnitude.

To man's unfavorably impressed amazement, he has now
seen, developed, and made "operational" in the weaponry arts
a package of electronic and computerized rockets weighing
less than the weight of one navy destroyer, suddenly displac-
ing all the navies and armies of the earth in a millionfold
more effective hitting power. Using his scientists-furnished
data, President Johnson likened the relative magnitude gain
of this new striking force to the graduation from one candle
light to the radiation of the sun. Man is either uncomprehending, or has become congealed in his fascination with
such a suddenly emergent destructive potential and has therefore failed almost entirely to see the significance of this
epoch-making capability to do every task related to man's
physical success on earth in fractions of 1% of the time, energy, and resources involvement per units of realized performance of each and every task as heretofore required
throughout all history.

It is the I.C.Y.'s and the world students' immediate task to
reorient man from his suicidal fixity only on the negative killing aspect of "doing infinitely more, with infinitely less" to
the realization that the design-invention revolution now em-

powers man to become a comprehensive, metabolically regenerative success in universe.

At Paris in July 1965, the world news reporters may readily catch on that design science's geosocial revolution is indeed capable of supplanting the political initiative and may indeed eliminate the seemingly irremediable world impasses. The newsmen may even see that the design revolution is civilization's last change. They may also discover that it is history's greatest news story. But, if the newsmen do not catch on in Paris, somewhere soon thereafter they will make the historic "doubletake" and report it to the world—for it is indeed history's greatest and most welcome news. Then design science's popular revolution will start rolling as more and more of the world's millions of students put themselves to work in design-science cooperatives on the world's university campuses. Thus the students will stop using their heads as punching bags, and will start to use them in the most effective functioning for which their heads were designed, i.e., to design the now, for the first time, designable physical success of all men around earth!

It is clearly the function of politics to consolidate the scientific and industrial gains. Political battling for justice, as in the present struggle for full citizens' rights, not only for all the U.S.A.'s population, but for all the world population, is highly valid. But the right to vote cannot alone feed stomachs. Only the design-science revolution can solve the problems of clothing, housing, transporting, intercommunicating, and educating all humanity, thereby to permit omni-integrating world society to have positives instead of negatives for which to vote.

The problems of private vs. public sectors is the same problem as socialism vs. private enterprise, and the same problem as man vs. men. The individual has unique capabilities, as do pluralities of men have unique capabilities. It takes two to make a baby. It takes only one to make a discovery. World society soon will comprehend and resolve these unique function differentiations and—avoiding their interferences—profit by their mutually regenerative interfunctioning. Two-headed men might make good football quarterbacks on the defensive, but they would never be able to dodge-run "slalom" in spontaneously superb coordination through a broken field. Ships of the sea and air are coordinate tool extensions of their captains. Democratic determinations of air, or sea, ship-handling, accomplished only after passenger debate, opinionated speech-making, and final majority vote would sink any ship before it reached a safe port. It is essential that world society learn to differentiate clearly which functions of man or of men are naturally most reliably and usefully operative under various tooled or nontooled, industrialized or nonindustrialized conditions. *"Don't* speak to the motorman" is as workably a sound idea as *"Do* speak to the ticket seller."

Individuals invented the radio and the airplane. Invention is an individual function. The world thereby contracted to an intimacy of all humans who had theretofore been utterly remote and unaware of one another. The airplane and radio put the politicians to work adjusting man to the intimate ecological change brought about by the inventions. It is the individuals who invent refrigeration and all the technology necessary to make the world work. It is industry's job to convert the inventions to wealth-generating functions. The politician's job is to "weed" the garden planted by the inventors and cultivated by industry—to get rid of all that is obsolete or *untrue* in order to allow the bounty to flourish. Politicians are not scientific inventors. The invention and systems-design revolution must come before the political adjustments.

Revolution by design and invention is the only revolution tolerable to all men, all societies, and all political systems anywhere. Every nation welcomed the invention of the airplane, and refrigeration. Every nation welcomed and employed the transistor. All will welcome technically economic desalinization! All the world, properly informed of the significance of the students' design and invention revolution, will applaud and support the initiative, thus seized by the world's youth.

The newspapers and periodicals of various host countries, having worked hard to get world conventions to take place within their respective countries, automatically welcome the conveners. Paris and France will of course welcome the biennial Congress of the International Union of Architects in its domestic press publications. However, none of the business transacted during any of the past Architects' World Congresses has ever been of sufficient interest to the world newsmen to be put on the international wire and wireless "services" as "news."

As before in Mexico City, London, Moscow, Madrid, etc., again in 1965 the French press will welcome the U.I.A. Congress, but there will be no world news emanating from the Congress as precipitated by its official topic, "Architectural Education." But the International Cooperation Year and the students of the world, using the U.I.A.'s Congress as a springboard, do have a story—*the greatest*—"The world can be made to work successfully for all, and we know how to do it." If the I.C.Y. doesn't say it, and the students don't say it, and the world goes on assuming itself to be an inherently self-frustrating system, then ignorant submission to the inertia of our lethally conditioned reflexes will soon push the buttons of Armageddon. We, however, are betting that the earthians will *wake up and win.*

8. How to Maintain Man as a Success in Universe

I am advantaged in many ways in our day, because I deliberately set about in 1927 to discipline myself to be a comprehensivist; thus countering the almost overwhelming trend
to specialization. I am quite certain that the most important
reason for my having known some success is that I have had
no competition.

As a comprehensivist, I have used as my guidelines the
training that once went on at the U.S. Naval Academy. I attended Annapolis early in World War I. At that time in history, the radio was still so novel and open an affair that despite coding and ciphering it was not trusted for vitally strategic messages. This meant that the naval officers who would
command the fleets of our nation's ships had to operate autonomously. They were selectively promoted for comprehensive capability. They had to be entrusted with supreme authority when at sea—for the simple reason that there was no
other authority present. Frequent decisions of vital nature had
to be made, in a manifold of categories, with no greater authority than themselves within thousands of miles. Qualifica-
tion for such supreme responsibility and initiative required
magnificently comprehensive training. The midshipmen had
to be prepared eventually to be masters under approximately
any conditions. Inasmuch as three-quarters of the earth is
water, the Navy is concerned with the whole world and the
world's relationship to America. The Navy is inherently a
world organization and is frequently in operation halfway
around the world—and one-half way around is the furthest
away from home ports.

The Naval officers, particularly the flag officers, had to be
trained to know, for instance, the aspirations and capabilities
of all countries. There was no way that a secret message
could get safely home and back, or vice versa, faster than
one of the Navy's ships could take it. There was not as yet

207

ocean distance flying. For all these reasons, naval officers had to be prepared to make comprehensive, epochal, and solo decisions on behalf of their nation. They had to be extraordinarily familiar with world commerce and the broad ranges of technology. They had to know chemistry, physics, mathematics, logistics, ballistics, economics, biology, law, psychology, and engineering. They had to be able to set up powerful, industrially tooled naval bases in foreign parts.

After World War I, radio secrecy became dependably effective through scrambling techniques. As a consequence, the U.S. Congress and the administration at last dared to trust the air waves with secret strategy messages. This meant that the top authority for all grand strategy decisions could, without loss of tactical advantage, revert to the White House.

When the President says "Hello" on the radio telephone to the admiral halfway around the world and the admiral answers back, "Hello," there is an unnoticeable lag of a seventh of a second. If the President says "Hello" to an astronaut on the moon, he will have to wait four seconds for the return "Hello" and may think the astronaut somewhat hesitant. If an astronaut gets to our nearest planet, Venus, the President will have to wait five minutes for the return "Hello" and may think the astronaut very hesitant. So also may the astronaut feel the President to be too slow in answering. Because of such lags under critical, even fatal conditions occurring remotely from earth, the astronaut may quite possibly have to exercise some autonomously supreme authority regarding surprise events occurring in his remote area of operation.

When communications are critically slow and vital decisions must be made, supreme authority and autonomy are mandatory and are spontaneously conceded by society as self-evidently necessary.

It is reported that when Thomas Jefferson was President of the United States, he said to his Secretary of State at a cabinet meeting, "Mr. Secretary, we have not heard from our Ambassador to France for two years. If he doesn't write by Christmas, we might send him a letter."

Lincoln was the first U.S. President to be wired to the battlefront with telegraph wires. Up to that moment in history, heads of sovereign states had to be present at the battlefronts to make crucial decisions. Lincoln could, if he wished, make his high policy decisions remotely and get them instantly to the front by wire. He could, in effect, be present simultaneously on many fronts.

But Lincoln couldn't communicate to the world-around-deployed ships of the Navy by wires. Therefore admirals, commodores, captains, and commanders had to be entrusted with supreme and autonomous authority.

For this reason, the training of officers for the world's top navies, up to and during World War I, was the opposite of what went on in the land universities, where the bright ones were selected and whenever possible were persuaded to go into some graduate-school field of "mastered" or "endoctored" degrees of specialization.

At the Naval Academy the authorities also deliberately picked out the bright ones, but trained them for comprehensivity.

In 1927 as an ex-"regular" naval officer, I decided to try to recall and reestablish those comprehensive disciplines learned a decade earlier. I did so because I felt that the great patterns that were developing in relation to an emergent world man would require comprehensive capabilities, but at the same time could easily be lost sight of—because men's eyes were being focused only on special parts in special and exclusive places and were failing to see whole integrated systems of socioeconomic techno-evolution and the latter's relationships to earth and universe.

Thus it happened that, for better or for worse, I am a professionally trained and persistently active, comprehensive viewer of patterns. I cannot for instance talk about manpower problems as an exclusively United States problem.

I have to start with what I think the human's function in universe may probably be. Next, I explore the way humans and all other biological species subconsciously cooperate in the successful regenerative balance of nature. Next, I think about what is "happening to" only subconsciously functioning man on earth, and next about what is happening to the chemically, biologically, invisibly, and unselfconsciously-coordinated evolution of the little spaceship *Earth,* and lastly about whither that dynamically evolute earth and its passengers are trending and wending.

And next, I review the relationship of humans to other humans on earth, and their mutual relationship to the life-supporting biosphere of earth, and next and lastly the United States, the Illinois, the Chicago, etc., relationship to that larger pattern. Finally, I study the local problems of any one man and place them in respect to the larger-scale total information and its derived theory of life.

As a consequence of this method of tackling problems—proceeding always "from the whole to the particular"—I am completely convinced, for instance, that all humanity is *swiftly* trending to discard national identities and instead to become Worldians—nothing less. I am convinced that all sovereign nations and all political theories and realized political systems, class warfaring, and charity are obsolete because they were all invented as ways for special groups of organized humans to survive a little bit better under the fundamental working assumption that there did not exist and never would exist enough metabolic sustenance to permit more than a minority of humanity to survive and live out its potential lifespan of years. For the last decade of man on earth it has become widely realized that this is not true. I am convinced that the United States is not a nation and that by the word "nations" we refer scientifically only to groups of human beings who have been isolated in remote parts of the earth for millennium-long periods, and whose respectively unique characteristics—skin color, physiognomy, etc.—are all consequences of long inbreeding of those people under the powerful influence of the respectively unique environmental conditions of all those human-life-supporting geographical areas which have been historically isolated from the rest of the world.

Russia does consist of more than one hundred of such millenniums-isolated and inbred nations. Many of the U.S.S.R.'s most vexing problems relate to the fact that the constituent nations have different languages and very differently conditioned reflexes and appearances. The United States of America is today populated by people from all over the earth, who came together on the North American continent in an already highly blended degree of crossbreeding. This is because in Western Europe—from which America's largest and most recent population migrated—during the past two millenniums there had been vastly complex and progressive westward migration and crossbreeding.

The British Isles were occupied over and over again by the westward- and northward-migrating Eurasian people who long ago displaced the Angles and Jutes. During the last millennium this great European crossbreeding began to jump westward over the Atlantic into North America, where a widely crossbreeding Mongolian-Polynesian-African-South American people already existed.

We are all on our way, I am quite confident, to what seems to me to be the completion of a second lap, or round, of westbound encirclement of the earth by universally cross-breeding humans.

Just to the south of us, in Mexico, we have the earlier world encirclement of highly crossbred people. These people probably came millenniums ago into the Central America area of Mexico, from all around the world, by drifting, paddling, and sailing across both the Atlantic and Pacific on rafts, and climbing mountains and crossing the Bering Straits.

You will find in Mexico every shape of face, eye, and lips, every shape of head, and you will find any and every one of these shapes and faces in every grade of color, from very dark to very light. The people of Mexico constitute a highly crossbred man of yesterday. He has no unique color identity. The new and second-degree stage of world-encircling cross-breeding is now taking place a little bit further to the north. As a consequence only of relative sun-radiation conditions this second-round man is a little bit pinker in average skin tone. This last encirclement probably began after the last ice age and has been in high acceleration only since the coming of the deep-seas sailing ships, steamships, and the air age.

It is possible to compare the distance covered within their total lifetimes by recent history's people. We can also ascertain the average longevity of human beings in successive years and the average distances people walk. Walking-running was measured by pedometers a great deal before the automobile era. The annually walked distances in different vocations have been methodically measured by the world's leading armies.

Up to my father's time, the all-time average of the total distances covered by human beings in their total lifetimes was 30,000 miles. That represented their total local "to-and-froing." I am much older than the average of my audience, and in my lifetime to date, I have covered three million miles. That is one hundredfold the average distance covered in their lifetimes by any of the people before us.

I am one among a class of several million who have made that much mileage. The average airline hostess, though only one-third my age, is piling up her mileage at three times my rate. When we get into the life of the extraterrestrial travelers we find, for instance, that the first two Gemini astronauts each equaled my lifetime's three million miles in their one week's orbiting.

The explosive rate of change of human life from a norm of *failure* to a norm of *success* is also manifest in the life-insurance companies' betting odds. The life-insurance buyers bet that they are going to die earlier than expected and the life-insurance companies bet the other way and have had a miraculously "good thing" in the industrial evolution. The life-insurance companies' "expectancy" tables are developed with mathematical precision from the total overall vital statistics of the national censuses. When my father was born, expectancy was fairly close to its history-long average of 27 years for a male. When I was born, expectancy for a U.S. male had improved to 42 years. I am now 70 and did not die as "expected" at 42—expectancy for a U.S. male born in 1965 has reached 72 years. Expectancy has rocketed ahead of me.

Quite clearly, man is coming into a completely new ecological relationship to his earth, and, quite clearly, we are accelerating into an utterly new relationship of man to the universe. In speaking to you I have to take that statement as my fundamental premise, not just as an interesting aside. The problems of our moment are as unprecedented as they are vast. The solutions will have to be unprecedented and vast.

I have already given several good reasons why I don't think that we can learn anything or make any worthwhile decisions about our forward undertakings by looking at problems only as they are manifest locally, within the United States, and considering them as independent of the ever-more-vast picture of man as a normally successful inhabitant of universe at large. For all the yesterdays man was normally a failure economically and physically. Now we must abruptly assume that it is abnormal for him to be a failure.

In the big picture, I see man as the first living species to *consciously* participate in the alteration of his ecological patterning, and I see that he has done this by the development of tools. Industrial tools are complex and range from simple *punch presses* to complex *skyscraper cities,* to world-embracing *weapons-delivery systems.* I am not saying that man was conscious of the overall disturbance of the ecological balance of nature wrought by his conscious participation. I just mean conscious vs. subconscious, no matter how meager the range of the conscious conceptioning.

I find that many biological species produce tools. There is the bird's nest, for instance, and the spider's web. But I see that man has employed the tool capability in importantly greater degree.

I have observed that all tools represent the externalization of originally integral, metabolic-regeneration functions of the biological species. The bird develops a nest to deposit the egg-enclosing new life so as to lighten the mother bird's weight to permit her to "fly" to reach her diet of worms and insects which regenerate her while sitting on the nested egg, to give off energy as heat, and to conserve the energy as heat to develop the new life. The nest is a heat-insulated extension of the womb's energy-conservation function.

Retrospectively, as an inventor, I am quite sure that the reason that I invent and others invent is that we have discovered ourselves repeating a mechanical or structural function time and again. We suddenly realize that we are wasting our time in repeating unnecessarily complicated steps and that a tool as a mechanism or structure, separated and detached from our integral organic complex mechanisms and structures, could take care of this special function in a much neater and energetically efficient way. This externalization, or tooled-out function, could always reward us with increased increments of our allotted lifetime to reinvest in preferred and more effective survival and enjoyment patternings.

For example, early man didn't have to invent being either thirsty or hungry: these were built-in, metabolic-regeneration "drives." But he had to discover—randomly—or invent—methodically—ways of satisfying those metabolically regenerative drives. In order to find berries enough to live on, he often wandered, inadvertently, far away from water. By the time he accidentally found water again, his thirst was often excruciating. He found that he could scoop it up with his hands more rapidly than he could scoop it up with his tongue, and that he could do better with two hands than he could with one.

Having satisfied his thirst, and knowing by experience with his built-in hunger drive that he must go away again from the water to find more berries, he thought desperately of a means for taking the momentarily plentiful water with him. And so we find *vessels*—or an imitation pair of cupped-together hands—to be among the earliest artifacts or inventions of men.

Vessels have played a very important part in our life—vessels as cups, vessels as bottles, vessels as ships of the sea, vessels of the air—carrying and moving substances from where man originally found them in nature to preferred operation points in time and space. Moving substances and later tools from here to there, man began to control the environmental conditions of his existence. All this inventing—of the environmental conditions altering controls—may be classified as "tooling." Now then, I differentiate all tools into two main categories: *craft tools and industrial tools.*

By craft tools, I mean *all of the tools that can be invented by one man, starting nakedly in the wilderness, with nobody telling him what to do.*

The child accidentally kicks a stone, then realizes that the stone can be impelled incisively in preferred directions. So the child picks it up and throws it—thereby knocking down a banana—and learns that he can alter the conditions of his environment from a distance. The child finds that, operating with a tool, he has a longer arm than he thought he had.

Accidentally a man or boy steps on the long end of a log, lying across another log with its short end wedged under a very large fallen tree, and finds out all by himself—by direct physical experimenting—that a very large tree can be lifted and moved by him—and moreover, a tree so large that he knows it to be heavier and bulkier than he could pick up by his muscles alone. Thus, the human discovers the principle of the lever and thereafter under further emergency conditions invents diverse ways of using the leverage principles—for he does not need to use the same log as in his first experience. This is to say that man intellectually harvests or generalizes principles out of special-case experiences. The brain deals always and only with specialized case experiences. The intellect detects and employs the generalized principles common to all the special cases. And thus tools became the invented means for men's increasing their physical-stature advantages over a priori environmental conditions. Humans began to work with invented craft tools multimillenniums before the beginning of written history and of necessity did so entirely on their own initiative.

By industrial tools, I mean *all of the tools that could neither be produced nor operated exclusively by one man.*

I will give you an exaggerated case, which would be the steamship *Queen Elizabeth.* It is preposterous to think of one man *producing* it, *operating* it, or even using it, as a passenger, to effect even greater pattern controls. We now have large oceangoing vessels which are almost entirely automated and may be operated by one man at a time and even by remote control. These automated ships are produced and operated, however, only as the result of the inventions of the progressively integrated experiences of multimillions of men. Automation involves a large population of producers operating in advance of, rather than subsequently to, its physical realization and operation. Tooled automation involves all the billions of men that have ever lived. Tooled automation is, in fact, our legacy of all the experience and dedication of all humanity before use. All men have always been organically and internally and subconsciously automated. Externalization of the automated metabolic regeneration of man is realized in the industrial-tool complex and its energy-distributing network, and their communications and transportation systems. Though we have not yet learned how to realize automation's energy and time advantages, we soon will, and when we do we will learn that automation can produce wealth beyond all our needs and dreams.

Within my definition of industrial tools—as advantages that cannot be produced by one man—I find that the very first of the industrial tools must have been the invention of the spoken word, which one human could not invent without another human. And with the spoken word came the ability to relate and relay need and solution experiences from one human to another in ever-regeneratively-improving degrees of common advantage gaining, and thus industrial tools multiplied all men's advantage in accelerating degree. The rate was swift and ever swifter—in contradistinction to the rate of advantage gaining by craft man, who by definition is inherently limited to his own local experience and to the availability of only those few resources which happen to occur within his leg-motion-limited exploratory area and within the amount of time that he can afford, or earn through tools, to invest in exploring.

By my definition the industrial tools represent the integrated experience of all humans, over all earth and over all history; while craft tools represent the experiences only of each very locally-restricted and isolatedly-operating human being, no matter how inspiringly ingenious he must always have been to succeed at all against such odds. It took more than a million years for craft-operating humans to make effective economic gains on earth. Those craft tools make up the mounds of billions of early artifacts found around earth.

The industrial tools are obviously more powerful tools and obviously are always gaining in advantage at an integratively accelerating rate. They start not only with two men, but they soon become extraordinarily complex and omni-interrelated.

At outset I spoke about man's consciously participating in the conversion of his local conditions by the invention of tools and in turn I spoke of tools as externalizations of our integral bodily functions. Our integral functions—our organic functions—in turn comprise the metabolic- or energetic-regeneration process known as the biological regeneration of *man,* most of which has operated subconsciously or without the knowledge of man. But the regeneration of biological man has depended upon an ecologically-supporting environment wherein—and for long unknown to consciously-cerebrating man—the air required by man has been continually reprocessed by the vegetation to render it of chemical advantage to man, and all the mammals give off all the gases essential to the vegetation.

I see then that the complex and previously subconsciously-operating total ecological support of the *metabolic regeneration of man has now been complexedly externalized into what we call the industrial system*—the industrial complex. I see that the totally-interacting effects of the single inventions by men were as unpremeditated as the a priori ecological support balances of nature were maintained without man's conscious knowledge. The industrial complex, however, now makes man progressively independent of the a priori ecological support but introduces progressively complex evolution in the development of tools to substitute for inadvertently-disturbed ecological-support functions. One of the major facts which we must now face is that the *industrial complex relates inherently to total earth*—because the resources of earth are very unevenly distributed—and relates always to the *total intercommunicated experience of all men everywhere in all time.*

What is unique about each of the 92 regenerative chemical elements is their unique *behavioral*—or *energetical*—characteristics. Through industrialization, the associable and disassociable behaviors of the elements under various conditions makes possible previously "impossible" tasks—doing increasingly *more* with increasingly *less*. For instance, we need something that is just a little harder, that can stand a little more heat, that is a little more reflective—or conductive, or nonconductive. One element is magnetic, while another is nonmagnetic, and so on. Industrialization employs these unique elemental capabilities or the myriad of their uniquely alloyed behaviors to effect uniquely new tool capabilities. But the environment alteration continually requires adjustments to inadvertently-disturbed earlier supports of humanity—frequently as a consequence of society's overspecialized, shortsighted exploitations where comprehensive training would have permitted the discovery and anticipatory avoidance of many of today's major dilemmas of world society.

In order to be able to develop the total complex of humanity's ever-improvingly efficient capabilities, we must attain increasingly swift access to all of the resources of the planet and eventually of the universe at large of earth and of the solar system and of the universe *beyond* and *within*.

Most of the resources of universe are unevenly distributed. All but one of the 92 regenerative chemical elements are very randomly distributed over a confused geographical pattern on the surface of the planet earth.

Since the last ice age melted away, three-quarters of the earth's surface has been covered by water. Ninety-nine point nine percent of humanity live on the dry-land quarter of the globe. Much of the dry-land quarter has been, and is as yet, undwellable. Man is physically minuscule and lives in scattered patches covering less than 5% of the earth's surface. As of 1965—and despite the hullabaloo about a world population explosion—all of humanity could be brought indoors in the buildings of greater New York City, each with as much floor room as at a cocktail party. All the cities of our planet cover sum-totally less than 1% of the earth's surface.

The localities in which industrialization has thus far been breeding are primarily centered around the north Atlantic basin but are now spreading to include first the western Pacific and next the south Atlantic shores, and will lastly occur around the Indian Ocean's lands. Sum-totally these geographically minuscule industrial centers now bearing the formidable name of "megalopolises" cover less than one-half of 1% of the earth's total surface.

The people who have worked industrially with the 91 chemical elements found on earth have started from a relatively few geographical points of highest initial advantage in respect to the integration of the supply of material, labor, power, distribution, capital, and other market factors.

Because of the relatively few geographical bases of high starting advantage, industrializing man has had to go—on an average—halfway around the world to find his original raw materials. He has then partially separated out the chemical-element resources from their original matrixes at the points of origin. He then forwards the wanted concentrates to pre-ferred secondary points where tools have been established and energy focused whereby he progressively and conve-niently takes the chemical elements apart. Finally "halfway around the world" again from the raw-resource origins—back at his industrial home base—he completes his ultimate de-gree of resource separation. He then starts reassociating the elements in preferred ways as alloys and compounds to do preferred tasks more effectively than in the past. Next the preferred alloys and compounds go into the production of a myriad of parts of complex machines which are progressively improved by design science to do more work more efficiently.

In order to justify his halfway-around-the-world indus-trial-traffic pattern and its enormous foot-poundage process-ing and forwarding, and the time investment in constant over-head, as well as in variable new-project costs, and in order to realize the enormous "expectancy" of increased technical advantage and the economic effectiveness of the tooling that is speculated on, industrial man has to find, educate, and en-list a very large number of customer consumers to be bene-fited by the services and retail products—as uniquely permit-ted by the anticipatory establishment, operation, mainte-nance, and constant improvement of this industrial-complex tool network.

In order to find the most people to be benefited, industrial-ly-organizing man must go halfway around the world again in all directions—for halfway around the world in any direc-tion is the furthermost point from any global point. Halfway around the world in all directions will be found all the world's customers.

Thus we find that industrialization is inherently involved in going halfway around the world twice—inward and outward bound. And the inbound-outbound industrial logistics are both characterized by vast vessel-borne tool complexes, both stationary and mobile. Thus, we discover that we can't talk industrialization unless we talk world. Industrialization is world-embracing or it is nonexistent. The regenerative forces of world industrialization are the number one forces at work today. We are on our swift and ever-swifter way toward development of a completely industrialized total world population.

The United States has developed partial resource autonomy, but only with the help of the resources of Canada, Mexico, South and Central America, Africa, Indochina, Australia, and the Near East. Russia, though abounding in chemical elements and energy, also is not only dependent on its satellite countries but also on Africa, Indochina, Canada, and South and Central America.

At no other time has either the U.S.S.R. or the U.S.A. been *completely* independent and autonomous resourcewise. In the worst hours of the "cold warring," both the U.S.A. and the U.S.S.R. have had to permit secretly-arranged trading, in order to be able to carry on. Despite the great political hazards to their respective "in" parties accruing to such trading, it nonetheless had to be accomplished. All political "bigs" have to get resources from foreign sources and often hide their economic predicaments under superficial political maneuvering.

To make it easy, instead of difficult, you must think always of the whole earth when discussing industrialization. So when I want to know what is going on in the United States of America, while recognizing that the most important factor operative in America is industrialization, it becomes clear that I must first look at the whole world to find adequate answers.

I find then that world industrialization is a self-regenerative evolutionary phenomenon which started in China at least 4000 years ago. It traveled westward completely around the earth, and has now rereached China again in vastly advanced effectiveness.

We find quaternary alloys in China, produced by scientific-industrialization principles as early as 2000 B.C.—i.e., 4000 years ago, industrialization separated out four metallic chemical elements and reassociated them in preferred and higher-performance ways as quaternary alloys. The original industrialization of the Orient produced a vast array of do-more-with-less, lightweight, segregated tension-compression products such as fans, lanterns, sailing rigs, weaving tools, mass-reproduction tools, and mathematics.

The industrialization and tooling worked westward around the world along the waterfronts of the Indian Ocean, Red Sea, and Gulf of Persia to the Mediterranean, to Europe and to America. By the time that it reached Europe, awareness of the essentiality of the chemical elements was so powerful that 81 of the potential 92 regenerative chemical elements are known to have been isolated in Europe. Of the 92, 9 may have been isolated first in Asia; only 2 were isolated by scientists in the United States. The U.S.A.'s phase of industrialization did not include the fundamental scientific harvesting of the basic resource controls. (See Figure 1, p. 46)

The U.S.A. did develop *mass production, mass distribution, mass consumption,* and *mass buying* and *mass financing* techniques as fundamental contributions to overall world industrial evolution.

In relation to the world embracement by industrialization, there are additional outstanding observations to be made. For instance, as areas of the world have graduated from isolated and simple craft, agrarian, fishing, mining, and trading activities into complex industrial-production economies, they have always commenced industrialization at the most advanced points achieved by the earlier industrial economies. They have never started back where the others started and repeated the earlier industrial development stages. You may say, "It is obvious that they would do so," but it did not seem obvious even to "experts" in the immediate past, as the following will demonstrate.

During World War II (when I was with the Board of Economic Warfare of the United States) President Roosevelt offered President Vargas of Brazil approximately anything Brazil wanted—in exchange for the United States' right to go militarily through Brazil on the way to North Africa, which was to serve as the Allied springboard to Italy. Vargas asked Roosevelt for a fundamental plan for the industrialization of Brazil.

The plans for the industrialization of Brazil, which were sent from the United States to Brazil, were predicated on U.S. leading engineers' assumption that Brazil, in order to industrialize as the U.S.A. had, would have to repeat the U.S.A.'s development—primitive step by primitive step. The U.S. plan called for Brazil's starting with railroads. This recommendation showed that the U.S. engineers were ignorant of, or were ignoring the fact that it had proven completely impractical to build and operate railroads in the major part of Brazil, which is the Amazon area—known as the Green Hell because the hard woods grew over the railway tracks faster than they could be cut away. No tools existed which could economically plow them away. The English and the Germans had both tried to introduce railway systems in Brazil and had failed years earlier. The American engineers' erroneous assumption of a replication of the U.S.A.'s industrial patterning sequence as essential for Brazil proves that the error of such an assumption was not obvious up to a 20-year-ago "yesterday" and has become so today, to the specialist mind, only through the quick adjustments of hindsight.

Paradoxically, at the time that we were giving this worse-than-useless advice to the Brazilians, the Brazilians had more licensed air pilots per capita than had the "down-its-nose-at-Brazil-looking" U.S.A. The Brazilians were already flying their goats and cows to preferred pastures. Brazil had already *started in where we had left off.*

When China began its first military flying in the days of the Korean War, they didn't start out with the Wright brothers' "Flying Jenny" of 1903, nor did they start off with the propeller-drawn American Mustang of World War II. They started out with post-World War II jets.

In the great 1929-born economic Depression, when the giant U.S. corporations were almost completely shut down, Russia found much gold in Siberia and purchased and imported the prototypes of the U.S.S.R.'s great industrial toolup, primarily from the big U.S. corporations. The biggest U.S. corporations of almost every industrial product category —glad to have any business—took contracts and put up factories for the Russians, and the Russians insisted that they be furnished the very latest machinery of which these corporations could conceive.

Thus Russia started its industrialization at the tool-design phase at which the United States had left off. As a consequence, in about 50 years the U.S.S.R. attained equivalent industrial-technique capability with the United States in respect to the production of scientifically-conceived weaponry.

China started in where Russia left off, and even though the Russians pulled out from helping them with their prototyping, China has adequate scientific capability to reestablish the

Russian line of industrial-tooling strategy. Thus China started its industrializations at the automation level. It started with computers, fission, jets, and transistors, plus a three-to-five-millenniums-old philosophic sophistication which had originated the industrialization. *It will probably accomplish its automated industrialization within 25 years. We must be realistic about that.*

By 1975 you must expect China to be the most impressively modern industrial nation, highly automated, and with one of the greatest possible benefits of industrialization—which is that they will have very large numbers of customers right at home and at their southern doorstep in India. This is a fundamental advantage, because the more customers you have, the more you can spread the cost, and the lower your prices can be and the quicker you can amortize your last tool-investment costs to enable you to acquire new and improved tools. Those who have the most customers in mass-production industrialization can undersell those who have the lesser numbers of customers, granted the same standards of technology. India and Africa, starting later even than China, will industrialize in 15 years. China is after those African and Hindu customers.

The rate of conversion from an agricultural-craft to an industrial economy is directly related to both birthrates and lifespan increase of the converted economy. The original European colonists in North America had an average family of 13 children. Many died soon after birth. Average life expectancy was 27 years. As industrial tools such as community water works, electric-lighting systems, telegraph, and telephone came into use the birthrate went down and expectancy of lifespan increased. Today the birthrate in the U.S. is less than two children per family and average life expectancy is over 70 years. Though there are larger numbers of humans now alive in the U.S.A. the total number of babies born each year is decreasing. The population increases in all the industrialized countries in the world including Russia are now holding consistently to this same birthrate decline and expectancy increase—Japan has attained approximate population equilibrium.

Because the additional, annually arrived human beings are decreasing in the industrial countries their population increase is due exclusively to people living longer. Because the highest deathrate used to occur predominantly in the first four years of life, the decline of death in these years means that momentarily the big bulge in the population increase through not dying is in the under-20-year-old people but that bulge will grow progressively older so that by 1985 the average age of people in the industrial countries will be 30 years with the birthrate so lowered as to begin to show a total population decrease. The population expansion through birth is unique to the as yet nonindustrialized India, Africa, and the Central and South American countries. China, well on its way to industrialization, has already instituted rigorous birth controls. We can say quite clearly that the craftsman's hold on life was poor and that his numbers multiplied slowly if at all. We can say that industrial man's chances of living out his "fourscore and ten" years are high. We can say that the so-called "population explosion" was a misleading name. The increase in numbers alive was due primarily to cessation of deaths at an ever-increasing age. If man is to live only to 90 then the population increase will cease when the average age of people alive is 45 years. If man learns how to keep human life going on indefinitely at a good health, vigor, and agility level then man may also stop producing new babies.

Because of the tieup of population characteristics with industrialization and the acceleration of industrialization rates of the latest countries to adopt it we can foresee a world population top in 1990 and a 21st century in which world population is beginning to decline. As the world industrialization is advanced the numbers of babies born will decrease to rates matching the accidental deaths.

Stabilization of world population will probably occur at around five billion people when there will be as yet 5 acres of dry land and 17 acres of water averaging one-half mile deep per each human being on earth. With this condition life will as yet be sparse around the surface of our little spaceship *Earth* and the natural resources for supporting human life will as yet be abundant, provided the greedy race for sea foods does not exterminate such species as the whales.

These imminent world-industrialization events are all extremely important factors in considering modifications and new undertakings in manpower policy to be developed now and henceforth in the United States. In order to survive in this kind of economic race, the United States is going, sooner or later, to have to take on full-scale automation in order to realize its regenerative industrial energy setup while also

achieving wealth, ever-lowering costs, and ever-increasing efficiency.

Foreign competition with its lower wages, permitting lower
foreign prices, will finally force U.S. labor's decision to promulgate full-scale automation as the only alternative to lowering U.S. wages and thus lowering U.S. standards of living.
Far more than just a "great benefit," automation will prove to
be our actual lifesaver. We are illiterately and shortsightedly
apprehensive about automation. We are afraid that it will
mean full-scale unemployment and therewith lack of purchasing power for the American people. I think that we will be
forced to make very logical and comprehensively-referenced
decisions in relation to automation. We are going to be surprised to find the most idealistic and hopefully daring decisions turning out to be not only feasible but also extraordinarily practical. We will find that automation will produce such
vast wealth as to permit us to grant everyone highly-paid research fellowships.

To fortify that prediction, we must introduce additional
concepts and data.

All biological life has its built-in drives by virtue of which
the various species make unwitting contributions to other species and thus to the total success of all biological life. Thus,
for instance, do the bees, intent only upon their built-in drive
for honey, inadvertently cross-fertilize vegetation by inter-
dusting the vitalizing pollens with their carelessly bumbling
tails. In somewhat the same relationship to the total success of
a totally industrializing world man's ecology, the trade-
union organizers—intent only on getting better wages and
shorter hours for their dues-paying members—have also inadvertently spread the guaranteed purchasing capability to such
large numbers of the public as to justify the banking systems'
extending loans for multiyears which have altogether made
possible mass production and mass distribution of ever larger
and costlier and more-scientifically-prototyped end products
and services. With automation able to produce more for less
for this mass-consumption capability of industrialization, automation becomes an inexorable trend which seemingly must
produce total national unemployment. As already noted, this
disemployment would seem to force American labor to oppose automation. It will, however, also be seen in broader
perspective by the labor leaders that a number of other trends
are relevant to the problem. For instance, America's big busi-

ness is now outward bound around the world in its evolutionary expansion. Four out of five dollars of all the new-plant and tooling investments by the U.S.A.'s hundred largest corporations went, in 1964, into their foreign-operation expansion.

There is also an inexorable evolutionary trend which will ultimately require an entirely new accounting of world economics which will properly explain our ever-accelerating, burgeoning production of all manner of industrial products and services and enormous expansion of the numbers benefited by industrialization. The present wealth-accounting is unrealistic. It was adopted preindustrially only for appraising the economic health of yesterday's handcraft, hand-agriculture, muscle-powered mining, hunting, and fishing trades. Our obsolete economic account is registering only swiftly-multiplying national deficits. The entirely obsolete world accounting systems fail to disclose the exclusively self-multiplying characteristic of industrialization's wealth.

The old economics accounting, which as yet prevails in both the so-called "capitalist" and "communist" countries and in their integrated world trading and industrial expansion, starts with Malthus' assumption that there is and always will be only enough of the essentials of life to support a minority of mankind. This view made failures normal. This concept is now acknowledged to be invalid. Secondly, the as-yet-employed—but now obsolete—accounting is based on the Newtonian assumption that "at rest" is normal for the universe, and that the universe will eventually "run out of juice" and "run down" or "stop." This concept has been annihilated by Einstein's *continual evolution norm* of an all-energetic physical universe with a normal speed of 186,000 m.p.s. Einstein's norm proved to be true as it explained elegantly the amounts of energy released by fission from a given mass of chemical matter. The old static norm and its "bankruptcy," "failure," and "*mort*gaged" (death-gauged) accounting assumed that the Second Law of Thermodynamics imposed ultimate failures because entropy meant that energy was always escaping from any system, including the universe, and thus fortified Newton's assumption that all systems would ultimately fail. This concept of the ultimate failure of life and universe was rendered completely erroneous and obsolete when 20th-century physics discovered that energy could escape from one system only by joining another system—that energy was therefore always 100% accountable. As a consequence, science pronounced the Law of Conservation of Energy by which it is recognized that universe's energy may neither be *increased* or *decreased*. It behaves in the Einsteinian manner of continual transformations, which transforming or *normal-change* energy-flow patterns may be shunted to impinge on man-made "levers" and thus converted to man's advantage.

The old economics assumed that metals mined and put to use would always "rust" or oxidize and eventually disintegrate and vanish from the cosmos. It has been discovered that all metals may be remelted and reused. The old economics assumed that "you can't lift yourself by your own bootstraps," ergo flying by man was impossible. It assumed that a given task would always require the same amount of material, hours, and energy. Through design science, 20th-century weapons technology has thousandfolded the performance magnitudes per ton, hour, and kilowatt invested in industrial tools and processes. The old economies knew nothing of modern chemistry's and biology's synergy which demonstrates "behaviors of wholes unpredicted by the behavior of their parts." The synergetic tensile strength of chrome-nickel steel —350,000 pounds per square inch—is entirely unpredicted by even the sum of the tensile strengths of its constituent metals as commercially produced.

	Pounds-per-Square-Inch Tensile Strength	
iron	60,000	
chrome	70,000	
nickel	80,000	
manganese plus carbon, etc.	50,000	
total	260,000	
vs.	350,000	pounds per square inch actual strength of some "stainless" chrome-nickel steel castings

The going and obsolete economic accounting says, "A chain is no stronger than its weakest link," therefore chrome-nickel steel by present economic accounting logic could not be greater than 50,000, or one-seventh of its actual strength.

The going economics fails to explain why the merger of a

dozen economic "failures" produces a "success." The American automobile industry was compounded out of many thousands of "failures" whose managements lost their credit authority but whose energy-processing real-wealth machinery assets had never failed. The accounting and the speculative funding, the promotional shortsightedness and the economic accrediting failed, but the evoluting machinery of industrialization did not. Industrialization consists of physical evolution and channeled-energy transformation which by the Law of Energy Conservation can never fail. Through traffic in interest-paying debt increases, present-day economics exploits the failure of debt crops to support the increasing numbers of humanity displaced as automatons by automation. We are in for a world of economic-accounting revision of first magnitude. We will switch from a negative to a positive world economic accounting.

In 1965 world-around industrialization produced about $2 trillion worth of "goods-and-services" wealth. This was 28 times the value of all the known gold mined and retained on earth and 50 times the value of all the world's monetary gold. Assuming a 20% annual return on capital investment this indicates the total capital value of world's industrialization plant and tooling to be $10 trillion which is 70 times the world's known total gold supply in all gold-product use or monetary forms and 125 times the world's total monetary gold. Gold is obviously inadequate, ergo obsolete, as either a monetary-exchange unit or as symbolic expression of the operative capital wealth now invested in the world's industrial systems.

In 1933 as the New Deal came into office all the world's monetary gold had been centralized in the U.S.A., not in the hands of bankers and individuals, but in the vaults of the U.S. government's Kentucky mountains, from all the nations around the earth. Gold was economically "out." All nations of the earth "went off" the gold standard. However, in 1944 the China Lobby in the U.S.A. persuaded a requisite quota of authorities that if $100 million of that gold bullion were released to them as private individuals they could corrupt China's trend to communism. They failed and that gold which escaped Pandora's Box—acting as a pump primer—began the processes of extracting that gold from the Kentucky hills and its progressive reemployment in the annual international trade balancing of the world's accounts. This gold, augmented by

Russian and African mining, now plagues and frustrates the natural expansion of the U.S.A.'s industrialization to establish a world-around means of regeneration of enough wealth to support all of humanity at an as-yet-undreamed-of advance in standard of living.

Because energy is wealth, the integrating world industrial networks promise ultimate access of all humanity everywhere to the total operative commonwealth of earth.

What do we know about wealth, stated rigorously and only in the experimental terms of science?

Answer: Wealth cannot alter yesterday. It can only alter today and tomorrow.

Multiplication of craft wealth began, as we have noted earlier, when man discovered the lever. Multiplication of industrial wealth began when man fastened a set of levers radially round the hub of a wheel, put the wheel under a waterfall and connected the wheel with a grinding mill. Thus he learned to stand aside from the work and, gaining perspective, to use only his brain to rearrange the flows of inanimate energy-transformation patterns, external to his own integral bodily energies to do more and more fundamental man-advantaging work. He did so by shunting ever-greater amounts of previously unharnessed energy to impinge upon his machine levers.

Humans found that the vast *dissociative* (radiation) *energy patternings* of universe can be harnessed, shunted, and valved to impinge at preferred times and quantity rates upon the *associative* (gravity, matter) *energy patternings;* for instance, in the form of the long ends of levers the power of whose rotating shaft can be led through trains of gears to do preferred work for man.

Man is now learning, through the repeated lessons of experimental science, that wealth is explicitly the organized tool-articulated energy capability to sustain his forward hours and days of metabolic regeneration; to physically protect him; to increase his knowledge and degrees of freedom while decreasing his interfrustrations. Wealth, he finds, is inherently regenerative, but because of comprehensive synergies of the rate of regeneration of man's solo wealth is to his commonwealth regeneration rate only as x is to x^4. As experimentally demonstrated, *wealth is: energy compounded with intellect's know-how*

Science's Law of Conservation of Energy states that "energy cannot be created or destroyed." The *first constituent* of wealth—energy—is therefore irreducible. Science states that the entire physical universe is energy. $E = Mc^2$. Some of the energy is operative in associative patterns—as matter. The associative energy as matter is organized in leverage systems to do work. The dissociative energy patterns, as radiation, are transformed into free energy to be directed to impinge on the levers.

Every time man uses the *second constituent* of wealth—his *knowhow*—this intellectual resource automatically increases. *Energy cannot decrease. Knowhow can only increase.*

It is therefore scientifically clear that wealth which combines energy and intellect can only increase. Wealth can increase only with use and wealth increases as fast as it is used. The-faster-the-more! Those are the facts of science. Those are the facts of life. The proper accounting of wealth is scientifically feasible.

We have found that: (1) the metaphysical (weightless intellect) balances the weighable physical; for the physical universe is entropic, ever-expansive, ever-diffusive and increasingly disorderly while the metaphysical intellect concentrates in ever-more-orderly fashion; (2) the metaphysical universe embraces the physical—both being finite, for the metaphysical is mathematically demonstrable as being always one tetrahedron greater than any physical system; (3) the metaphysical's generalized "capture" and identification of the physical is an *irreversible condition*—e.g., Einstein as intellect (metaphysical) apprehended and formulated the identification of the physical universe $E = Mc^2$. This formulation is irreversible—for the physical which is "disorderly" cannot "think" and make orderly statements. Energy cannot write what Einstein's intellect is. Therefore, we can say that the metaphysical is greater than, and reconcentrates and coheres, the physical.

The inherently escalating augmentation of real wealth is therefore inherently irreversible. *Wealth can only gain* and its gaining can only accelerate as in our proposition, Q.E.D.

The U.S. labor leaders will realize that automation can multiply man's wealth far more rapidly than it is multiplying at present, and that automation will leave all men free to search and research for additional income energies to shunt onto the ends of the levers and for new greater and more incisive tasks to do with those energized levers. Realizing the direct competition with foreign industry on a straight labor basis would mean swiftly decreasing wages per hour and longer hours and decreasing buying power of the public, and compounding all the industrialization trends, American labor will realize that its function is not to increase jobs, but to multiply the wealth and to expand the numbers benefited by the wealth at the swiftest possible rate. U.S. labor will then recommend to U.S. Congress and the President that as fast as anyone becomes unemployed he be given a scholarship to go back into the educational system both as a routine discipline scholar and as a search and research student. The probability figures will show that for every x thousands occupied in study and experiment one will make a discovery or invention that will care for x thousands at higher standards of living than had previously been enjoyed.

Now I want to introduce another pattern to you, in order to provide maximum cogency for anything that I have to say to you.

The following observations relate to fundamental difference between the kinds of technologies that occur on the land and the kinds of technologies that occur on the sea and in the air. First (as we noted earlier) three-quarters of the earth is covered by water, and people have lived primarily on the dry lands, and the dry lands are very widely divided from one another.

There were men who discovered, in due course, that resources of various kinds existed in many places and that you could carry much more on a raft, or in a boat, than you could carry on your back or on the backs of animals, and that resources could be integrated between various places by means of commerce with water-borne vessels on canals, rivers, lakes, and oceans. The discoverers of the world ocean used the three-fourths of the earth covered by water to provide enormously increased advantage for everyone, everywhere, through the resources they obtained from foreign countries which, when combined with local resources that had previously seemed "of no account," made them both locally successful.

The 1% of humanity that went voluntarily on the "high seas" learned that vast wealth was to be generated by virtue of this waterborne traffic, so there were great struggles of a very few men to control the high-sea trade routes. We might very accurately call them all pirates, and some were great pirates who came to master the sealanes. They were pirates because they were all "outlaws"—simply because civil laws were local to different lands, and beyond the three-mile limit there were no man-made laws—only the physical laws of nature.

Men on the land, surviving through agriculture—as good farmers or local fishermen or miners or craftsmen—were protected by strong men who preferred just to be the strong men to protect the farmsite when on frequent occasions marauders came around to try to invade and usurp their local prosperity.

So, on the land, the strong men forced the prisoners and the shiftless to build their great fortresses behind which the people could retire while the battles with the marauders went on. And the kind of buildings that we have on the land were primarily great, strong fortress-castles of great width, weight, and stability, and the heavier and thicker and higher the walls the more secure the people felt. They were structurally ignorant. Thus, buildings on land have always been extraordinarily heavy make-do contrivances.

On the sea, contrariwise, security decreased with weight. Stone boats sank. In order, then, to have a successful ship, you had to pay attention to Archimedes' law of displacement. But sailors long before Archimedes discovered that you could float only a certain amount of weight per each given volumetric unit.

The men who went to sea and mastered the important economic sea "lanes" didn't go there for defense. They couldn't afford defensive weights. They went to sea to win. They went offensively only. They built their ships for speed and seakeeping capabilities sufficient to mount a swift attack on land or sea and to carry away the booty. They needed good dry cargo space.

In the design of ships, they developed a list of essential functions to be performed. Next, they estimated how large and what shape ship would be required to mount x numbers of guns, the masts and their rigging—so much cargo, crew, and supplies to stay at sea for a given period. This finally gave them the ship's size. They then figured its displacement in terms of cubic feet of water, the weight of which told them the total weight within which they must solve their total design problem. They then made a list of the functions and assigned so much weight to each. This brought ship designing into a severe discipline of performance ratios per given weight and time and power investments—so much to make the ship strong enough to withstand and exploit hurricanes, etc.

Whoever then could get a stronger mast, or whoever could get a stronger fiber in his sail for the same or less weight, could outperform the other man, and could outrun, outmaneuver, and displace him at sea.

So in the course of world history we find the great pirates and their respective powers developing a scientific search for doing-more-with-less, going around the earth, finding more effective resources and more effective technologies that gave them ever-higher capabilities. Those who knew the most about the earth by scientific discovery and experiment were able to get the strongest fibers for their sails and rigging and the strongest timber and fittings for their hulls and so forth, and could build the best ship to ultimately rule the other men of the sea.

In no time at all, this scientific exploring, skirmishing, and development brought the great pirates to steampower and steel ships and high-power guns. With the steel they could carry much more cargo and so forth and to meet that steel-ship requirement, whereby they could "run the world" and harvest the prime wealth, they had to have blast furnaces on the land; in developing this increasingly complex logistic capability they finally had all of the steel they needed for their battleships and cargo ships. The great pirates then looked around for more and new outlets for their steel, and other science won productive capabilities. Gradually the steel was insinuated into the walls and floors of stone buildings, which made it possible to make them bigger and taller. But the land people never thought of buildings in "performance-per-pound" terms and did not alter their ignorant viewpoint about land buildings. I have asked audiences of leading architects, all around the world, "What does this building we are meeting in weigh?" They cannot answer within millions-of-tons range. They do not think that way.

Finally the ship of the sea was displaced as the number one weapon by the ship of the air. The airplane became the ship of the air because the "lighter-than-air" balloons were too vulnerable to attack.

The nonair-floating, "heavier-than-air" airplane stayed in the sky only by virtue of forward motion at approximately hurricane speed, which developed the low-pressure "lift" on top of its wingfoils. To attain such speed the airplane had also to mount and support a heavy engine and heavy fuel. In the first airplane there was just enough additional lift to carry one pilot a few hundred yards in a few seconds.

But science was put to work by the world-mastering outlaw, and in the first 50 years of the airplanes the treasuries of the major nations of the earth appropriated $2½ trillion in the direct and indirect subsidy and development of the airplane. Those sums went into hiring science and technology to *do-more-with-less* in respect to every function of the airplane as a weapon. Whoever could do the most with the least— could carry the greatest hitting power, the greatest distance, in the shortest time with the greatest accuracy and least effort —could and would rule the world!

In 1922 I went into the world of building, having been previously steeped in the Navy and its flying. When I had been in the building world for five years, and had taken part in 240 building operations, I saw that we were taking the oil burner off the battleships and into the home, so that we gave up having to stoke our home furnaces with coal. We also took the refrigerator off the battleship, and the radio and air conditioning, and brought them into our domestic buildings.

We brought item after item developed exclusively for a seaborne or airborne war technology into the home. This came about because the contractors who produced such advanced technology for the government found themselves "all dressed up" with the tools and the scientists and skilled workers, and suddenly "run out" of "defense" contracts, and the home market was an unexpected bonanza.

We have had desalinization in the Navy for half a century, and it is now about to come into our domestic economy. All the advanced technology starts under government weapons subsidy and gets into the home economy (on an average) about 25 years later.

In 1927, because of my experience with the Navy's doing-more-with-less—in the war and weaponry technology—I saw that in the building world they were not trying to do-more-with-less, and that they had never thought of it.

The principles of doing-more-with-less which dominated the science and technology of weapons development were beginning in the 1920s to affect the domestic economy where they had never thought of such a strategy per se and have continued to think of economic security only in the terms of "bigger" and "more". "Secure as the Rock of Gibraltar" is the landsman's thought.

To my excitement I saw that the drift from sea and sky to the land of the more-with-less technology might inadvertently be amplifying the economic advantage of the 99% of humanity who live on the land in sufficient degree to promise doing so much more with what we have that we might prove Thomas Malthus and the economists wrong. This is and was possible because there was for the first time in history a dawning possibility through the more-with-lessing that we might be able to take care of all humanity at higher standards than any have ever known—this in turn would, if true, eliminate the war and the war technology which was predicated on the concept that there would never be enough for more than a minority to survive and live out their potential life-span, wherefore war was intermittently recurrent.

I saw that Malthus could be fundamentally wrong because his thoughts were devoid of any sense of technology's more-with-lessing.

He saw food in the field, and he said it was going to rot because there was no way to get it to the mouths around the world. He did not and could not think in terms of the as yet uninvented quick freezing and of refrigerated transportation.

So in 1927 I made many calculations, and it seemed increasingly clear that it was feasible for us to do so much with so little that we might be able to take care of everybody. In 1927 I called this whole process "ephemeralization."

Because of ephemeralization I saw that we could have an entirely new reason for supporting science, which would be "how to maintain man as a success in universe," instead of "how to destroy the most men and the most of man's facilities in the shortest time and with least effort in order to make the little sustenance go around."

Well all that philosophy which I have recounted for you I have pursued objectively since 1927. I objectivized it by searching and planning to make man a physical success by altering the behavior of the physical environment rather than by trying to persuade man by words or political reforms to "behave" in better ways. My philosophy is to employ the inductive principles of science's exploratory disciplines. I saw that this could be done through competently comprehensive invention which would alter the physical environment to man's physical advantage in such a manner as to induce non-interference of men with one another while inducing behaviors leading to man's comprehensive physical success. For instance, we can design highways banked so that autos steer themselves safely around curves even if the drivers are drunk, or develop dams that catch rainwater to keep it until needed by man, rather than having it flash-flood him to destruction.

The foot-pounds of "work" that humans can produce per year at various age levels have been measured by the major world armies' engineering divisions. From these figures it is easy to establish scientifically a unit of physical work known as a "one manpower year."

In comparison to it, I have taken the work that is being done by all machinery and energy consumed in our various industrial economies around the world and have found, as I published in *Fortune* magazine's tenth anniversary, February 1940, issue, that in 1940 we had in the United States working for us 24 hours a day, every day of the year, the equivalent of 139 inanimate energy slaves for each U.S. animate human being—man, woman, and child.

But that figure was not arrived at by saying that all of the energy consumed by our U.S. machines was realizing 100% efficiency in its delivered work. It was predicated on the overall efficiency actually operating in our economy, which is only 4%. So I had to take the total energy, including food, being consumed by our respective economies and divide the total 100% potential energy as "consumed" by 25, which brought it down to the 4% actually realized. I divided the 4% net energy units per year by "manpower units per year" and found that we had 139 inanimate slaves per capita working for each one of us in the U.S.A.—but I also discovered that most of the energy slaves' work was going into weaponry. The energy slaves were operating throughout the local industrial network economy. Not many of them operated inside your house. The majority operated throughout the whole of the energy-production, -distribution and tools-to-make-tools system. When I subtracted the amount of energy going into weaponry production, distribution, and maintenance from the amount of energy being consumed by our total economy—the total being 695 energy slaves per each family of five humans —it was disclosed that only 100 inanimate energy slaves could do all the work necessary to maintain each family of five humans peacefully in the United States—at the highest standard of living ever experienced by any people anywhere at any time in history. This meant only 20 energy slaves per each person for peaceful existence vs. the 139 per person for living at the highest known standards while also getting ready for the next war. This meant that six out of every seven of the total inanimate energy slaves were working directly or indirectly on weapons-producing technology.

Using the foregoing criteria—20 energy slaves per each individual—or 100 slaves per each family of five—as sufficient to maintain humans at the highest known standard of living, I identified each *family of five* so maintained on earth as *an industrial have family*. Probing our technoeconomic history with this yardstick, I found that in the year 1900 less than 1% of all humanity anywhere around the world could be rated as industrial haves. However, the mechanization of World War I made such an advance in industrial technology and energy harnessing that, by the end of World War I, 6% of humanity had become industrial haves. At the beginning of World War II, despite a great increase in world population, 20% of world society were living as industrial haves; at the present moment 44% of all humanity have become and continue to be industrial haves.

It is to be particularly noted that this extraordinary increase in the percentage of all earthian humanity being supported at the highest standard of living—from less than 1% at the beginning of the century to 44% by the present moment (1965)—was all accomplished in spite of the great increase in the world population already noted, plus a constant decrease in the total amount of metals per each human being on earth. And when I say "total amount of metals," I mean all the metals which have been mined as well as all the known and newly-discovered ore bodies. Quite clearly then, the upping—within only two-thirds of a century—of the standard of living of humanity from almost total havenotness to 44% enjoying a standard of living superior to that enjoyed by any sovereign previous to the 20th century cannot be accounted for by the exploiting of more resources, because the resources per capita were constantly decreasing. This sudden transition from the persistent historical over 99% havenotness to a 44% haveness—in the face of lessening resources per capita—within two-thirds of a century *can therefore only be accounted for by the evoluting technology's accomplishing ever more with ever-less resources per each essential or desirable function.* Neither the massive corporations nor the massive sovereign states had ever set about deliberately and directly to make all of humanity successful by consciously undertaking to provide more peaceful living with ever-less resources per each accomplished task. In fact, both the corporations and the states—assuming the Malthus dictum that there were not and never would be enough resources on earth to support more than a small minority—had been intent on making themselves successful by acquiring constantly more of everything.

Obviously this utterly unexpected and unprecedented great world gain in standard of living has to be explained exclusively as an inadvertent by-product of the do-more-with-less sea- and air-warfare technology which had been secondhanded into the domestic economy from the military world. Around the three-fourths of the earth covered by water and the 100% enveloped by air, no civil law existed and warfaring has been governed only by the technological necessity to do-more-with-less because whoever could do the mostest with leastest could and did run the world.

I know that people everywhere around the world--still thinking of themselves as inherently rooted to their localities and preoccupied with their own local problems—are now noticing that technology has brought about an extraordinary and seemingly inexplicable change in their lives. I am sure, however, that they don't think of the changes specifically in terms of *industry's having inadvertently done-more-with-less, that is as an unpremeditated benefaction accruing exclusively to our massive preoccupation with the negatively-inspired production of weapons and killingry.*

What I am inferring in all the foregoing, however, is that it is unnecessary for us to depend upon the exclusively negative stimulus—of preparation for the next war—in order to accomplish the comprehensive attainment of so much to be done with so much less that within a decade we can readily and efficiently provide 100% of humanity with as-yet-undreamed-of physical and economic success.

At the present era of history, erstwhile democracy has not seen fit to give its political leaders a 100% mandate to deal centrally with all their wealth and all beings and resources— except in times of war, or in economic catastrophes, or in emergency-adopted preparation for the next war. Political leaders have been given war-emergency mandates only to get a nation out of trouble or to save it or protect it. During

peacetime, we have never given political leaders a 100%
mandate to make the entire national population physically
and economically successful. We have never thought that this
was possible. It was, therefore, a new political event when we
gave peacetime emergency powers to the New Deal as it
came into overwhelming political power in 1933, 3½ years
after the great financial crash of 1929. In 1933, we were in
such a complete financial and economic mess that for the first
time in peacetime history we gave a comprehensive eco-
nomic-initiative mandate to the political leaders, praying
that they get us all out of economic trouble. This was not
given, however, as a permanent mandate. It was a mandate to
get ourselves out of momentary and local economic trouble. It
was interpreted by the New Deal as a mandate to get the old
system going again with a few social improvements. It was
not a mandate to make everyone successful. That 1933 mandate for getting us out of what it was hoped was only momentary trouble was immediately followed by the 100%
mandate to our government to cope with World War II.
Under this mandate the enormous number of industrial undertakings and the enormous amount of energy that was harnessed to impinge on the ends of the industrial levers to produce machines and tools which produced more tools, which
in turn produced even more tools—and ultimately produced
the hitting power to destroy the enemy—brought about the
establishment of such enormous total industrial capability,
under a centralized military authority for continuous and
wholesale technical innovation, that an entirely new kind and
magnitude of commonwealth and private wealth was established as we came out of World War II.

In preindustrial history the life-sustaining wealth consisted
primarily of agriculturally-harnessed sun and chemical energy. Wars devastated the agricultural production by sending
the farmers into the army and turning farmlands into battle-
fields. Wars have in the past been characterized by catastrophic impoverishment of the nations involved. It was,
therefore, incomprehensible to society and economists that as
we came out of World Wars I and II—and especially World
War II—despite our having expended hundreds of billions of
dollars, our economy was far richer than before the war—in
fact far richer and more powerful than it had ever been.
This was because science, technology, and industry financed
by government had harnessed the flow of vast, heretofore un-
capped energy sources and had shunted them to flow onto the

ends of the industrial tools' levers. The tooled means of producing goods which sustained life through this harnessing of wealth were approximately indestructible. In all the war countries, even in saturation-bombed Germany, though buildings were destroyed, the machinery was only superficially damaged and could be removed and put to work again. Therefore, much greater wealth in the form of capability of production existed than before the wars, and for the first time the working population of the United States found themselves receiving enormously increased real incomes. This point has not been clearly established in the public mind. From a few hundreds of dollars per capita in pre-World War II U.S.A., personal income multiplied fivefold after World War II.

It is essential to note that this new wealth had not been the objective of world warring. This vast peacetime wealth-generating capability had been only inadvertently established during the development of war production. The whole of this fabulous new wealth-producing setup had been geared in by a war mandate in which the government and its military leaders were empowered to undertake the prime initiative in extending, augmenting, or evolutionarily transforming the fundamental scientific and technological energy-harnessing capabilities of society. The military were the ones who were commissioned to use the accrued capital wealth to make airplanes fly faster, missiles go further, and so forth. The new capabilities of technology permitted realization of further inventions. Accelerated technological evolution occurred as a consequence of the new environment itself. These ventures of the government, as articulated by the military defense, were of an historically unprecedented order "light-years" beyond the organizing capability of private capital venture and accomplishment.

As we emerged from World War II we were so tied up with this extraordinary new centrally-initiated and -coordinated wealthmaking capability, and we were so personally impressed with the private wealth which had come to a very large number of our population, all unexpectedly through that war, that both industry and society at large were loath to give up such a proven profitable system. As a consequence, the President of the United States, after the theoretical "peace" following World War II, was given a mandate by the Congress to continue his powerful war powers and thus to extend the technological evolution by giving billions of dollars annually worth of orders to all the great prime contractors of the national weaponry. The President was given this mandate to carry on in peacetime on the basis that it was obvious that we were going to have a Third World War, and that we would be devastated if we did not anticipate and prepare for that third war. Assuming that the U.S.A. would never again have the time to prepare, as in the past, we undertook what we called "cold warring." Thus, we continually improved the technology of war as the "other fellows"—the assumed next enemy—improved their technology. This mutual improvement at parallel rates would discourage either side from undertaking a full-scale war. This became known as the strategy of deterrence. This meant extraordinary and continuous augmentation of the fundamental scientific and industrial capability. It meant the further harnessing of vast amounts of energy which had been flowing through nature in patterns that had not previously been shunted onto the ends of the levers of the man-operative technology. As a consequence, mankind, who for millions of years had struggled around on their feet, found themselves riding around in extraordinary automobiles finer than any vehicle of any previous monarch. They found themselves traveling around the world on "wings," enjoying themselves in many extraordinary ways. Intent upon sustaining that kind of capability and recalling Malthus' warning that there would never be enough wealth to go around for all, the new successful industrial world population decided that they had better be on the defensive.

However, with 60% of humanity as yet continuing as "havenots," the newly successful have said to themselves, "Well, we can't really enjoy ourselves too much unless we act in a rather friendly and logical way in relation to the havenots, so we will try to help them to help themselves by giving them pump-priming moneys and selling them weapons and giving them economic advice; *but* they are going to have to pull themselves up."

But society has not really understood the total industrial equation. We have not understood at all how we have come into proprietorship of this fabulous new wealth. Because we don't even understand what wealth is, we revert to our fumbling understandings of the preworld-warring, preindustrial, exclusively agricultural-venture economic language. We set up a World Bank and revert to the employment of the pirates' gold-bullion wealth. We have now found ourselves in a jam because in order to expand the industrial equation to the world's comprehensive advantage—to harness more energy and produce more tools, we immediately withdraw too much gold from our U.S. gold reserves which had no technical value while stored in bank vaults. It has only a symbolic function. It does not represent the U.S.A.'s multitrillion-dollars' worth of coordinate, metabolic-regenerative capability. But because we do not have either an understanding of our wealth or a proper accounting of its regenerative employment, we shut down on the world development of industrialization by U.S. companies.

Powerful clichés have persisted for centuries which assured no important changes in the status quo, as for instance the statement, "You can't pull yourself up by your bootstraps." But we have suddenly realized a swift increase in the proportion of humanity who have become economically and physically successful. Man has pulled himself up by his own bootstraps, but the old accounting will not permit proper recognition of the fact and we keep piling up fundamentally contradictory national indebtedness.

In scientific development of their armaments, men inadvertently began to make economic sense by relying exclusively upon the laws of nature rather than upon the opinions and clichés of the ignorant, and thus inadvertently tapped the really great-capability wealth which is the development of organized-energy to deal with the metabolic regeneration of man.

Now our political leaders have gone so far as to see that we can take care of those who are in poverty within the United States. It is now also dawning upon industrial society that it could be even more successful while depending exclusively upon the potentially enormous energy income—in contradistinction to living almost exclusively by burning up our capital principal, that is our "savings-account" energy in the form of fossil fuels.

The natural energy income in, for instance, the harnessable ocean tides, wind, sunpower, and alcohol-producing vegetation, can be made to flow through the wires and pipes to bring adequate energy to bear on the levers, to step-up man's physical advantage efficiently to take care of all humanity.

Possibly the greatest limitation with which we are faced is the fact that our political leaders have mandates to look out only for their own side. All the major political states are as yet operating on the Malthusian basis that there is not enough to go around and that each nation must maintain sovereign prerogatives and egocentricity. Thus, nations merge into a few massively opposed groups. The "ins" look out only for their side. The almost "ins" get ready to switch from alliance with the havenots to alliance with the haves.

The havenots point accusing fingers at the haves as though an inherently irrevocable political class condition existed which caused their havenotness. Neither the most recently successful nor the soon-to-become-haves realize that what has changed their lot came from the scientist-inventor's discovering principles operative in nature and employing those physical laws to eventually raise the standards of all. They think their lot has improved because of their political "way of life." However, none of the great changes have occurred as a consequence of political systems. All political systems—the most highly socialized, the most aristocratic, the most capitalistic, and the most communistic—prosper equally under the operation of the dynamos and the levers. The power-driven hammers and sickles just don't belong exclusively to the socialists. The automated hammers and sickles are also being used by the capitalist to equal advantage. There is no question about the intensity of involvement in their respective ideologies of the political leaders everywhere around the world, but there is also no question about the fact that they are not inherently and irrevocably divided. Thinking of themselves, however, as irrevocably pitted against one another, they are prevented from reaching the one great solution which can be made today, which is that of making all of humanity successful. To do so would be to admit the fallacy of their claims that each of their opposed ideologies alone can solve man's survival problems.

It is now scientifically clear that we have the ability to make all of humanity physically successful. But it can be done only on the basis of making all of humanity successful. We cannot remain just half successful or with just a minority successful. Industrialization itself relates to the resources of the entire earth, the entire universe, and the entire experience gained by all men in all time. The industrial system is a comprehensive system and if reversingly fractionated will fail.

No political leader has a mandate to make the whole world work. Consequently, we cannot look for political help in turning our wealth-making adequacy toward making all of humanity successful. You might say, "I think you are wrong. Some political leaders have a mandate to make the world work." For instance, the communists say that what they are going to do is to make communism universal and then the world will work. They say, "This isn't just for Russia, it is communism for all." And the Chinese say, "This isn't China, it is communism, and communism is the best system to make the whole world work." But it is also very clear, if you listen to the communists explaining how they are going to make the world work, that they assume that there is enough to go around, so the exclusive survival means must go to the "workers" (despite the fact that automation is swiftly making the "worker" function extinct). The communists assert that they must kill off all the nonworkers in order to make their system work.

This is not a way of making the whole work. It is a way of making some people successful at the cost of others.

What is perfectly clear, as we look into the technological doing-more-with-less that I have been discussing, is that it is the scientific invention of the individual and the consequent industrial technology that produces telephones. Anyone can use the telephone. Any two can have any kind of telephone conversation they want. They can call each other communist, capitalist, or any other kind of name. The telephone works for either. But the telephone shrinks the world for both, and disasters can be averted by means of it, and when disasters occur it brings swift help from great distances. Without the telephone, the world could not be made to work for all; with the telephone, it could be made to work. It is the organized technological capability that counts and not the negative games that men are playing around the earth as to who has the best class-biased system. All political biases are now irrelevant.

In the 1950s Khrushchev and Eisenhower were both made aware by their respective militaries of the humanity-obliterating magnitude of their atomic striking capabilities, whereby the world would be left in a complete radiation mess for those few who were not killed. Eisenhower and Khrushchev determined to meet in Geneva. Both politicians knew that neither could yield politically. Neither could give up sovereignty. Neither could relax his military "preparation for the worst"; neither would discard his ideology—his socialism or his free enterprise—which concepts incidentally are confused on both sides by their respective semantic game-playing. The U.S. is by far the most socialized of all countries in the world but has socialized only indirectly by socializing only the prime "hitting-power" corporations, instead of the individuals. Indirect socialization of the individual accomplished through corporate employment or dividend distribution to stockholders hides the fact of socialism. By socializing essential institutions—through research-and-development tax subsidies and through bank-negotiable billion-dollar government "orders"—the U.S.A. has socialized "from the top down." This is too elegant for those class-warfare champions of the underprivileged who, assuming fudamental inadequacy of world resources, would first "kill off" the half of the world that is now prospering.

Communism will never admit that socializing from the top down is faster than socializing from the bottom up. Both sides attempt to put everybody on the payroll to continually match the ever-increasing productive capability of industrialization. The Western world ideologists feel intuitively (but not consciously and officially) that it is more considerate of the dignity of man to play this indirect game, which avoids the rationing and "downgrading" concepts. So in effect we are gradually making everybody in the United States the vice-president of a bank. As a consequence, we now have so many banks to store all the deposited wealth of the people that we have more banks in each city than we have ten-cent stores, butcher shops, drugstores, or supermarkets. Each one of the banks is becoming more elegant. Each is a great big "parlor" or "study," with each vice-president having a palatial residence-type library desk. But the vice-president's sole initiative and private prerogative—not covered by strict government rules—is to telephone somebody to try to take his deposit account away from some other bank. The banker, of course, is no longer dealing in his own money—the underlying safety of the bank deposits is now the *government*'s responsibility. This is a very dignified way of carrying on. Nobody realizes that he is being socialized. The idea of being socialized seems to hurt the "Western" ego and frustrates individual initiative. Those who are on the communist side say they must first level everybody. They then say everybody owns everything—theoretically—but has the use of anything or any service "according to his need" and according to availability. In the U.S.A., people pretend that they own their automobiles, but they in fact rent them as in fact they truly rent their 30-year-mortgage-"purchased" houses which they occupy—on an average—for only four years. In the U.S.A. the government is carrying the $200 billion debt load of the dwellings and always has the ultimate right to take away. The U.S. trend is in fact one also of use of wealth—each "according to his needs"—by discretion of the

U.S.A.'s Internal Revenue agents and other executive agencies of the government, as empowered by the acts of the U.S. Congress operating under duress of powerful lobbying organizations in the "nation's" capital. I say "nation" in quotes for as we noted earlier the U.S.A. is, at present, the most crossbred admixture of people from all nations of the earth. The U.S.A. is the breeding place of "world" and "universe" man.

All this confusion of identity and mutually obsolete ideologies blocks recognition of the number one big question, which is: *How are we going to make all humanity successful despite the political impasse?* Both Eisenhower and Khrushchev knew that they could not yield to one another politically —i.e., ideologically, militarily, economically, or geographically. Such an act of either would be repudiated by their respective political parties. Their parties—the "in" parties— would themselves never think of yielding because they knew if they were to yield ever so little the "out" party could effectively challenge them with treason—the most powerful accusation which the "out" party may use to displace the "in" party. Nothing could be a more important kind of yielding to the country's adversaries than to give up any part of national sovereignty. Therefore, the two greatest world adversaries' political leaders—Khrushchev and Eisenhower meeting in Geneva, knowing that neither could yield politically—sought mutually to say something to the world that had some kind of favorable promise despite the ominous existence of the great bombs. Both of them, as human beings, realized their mutual responsibility to humanity. They said, "At least we can bring our scientists together to talk to one another regarding the peaceful uses to be made of atomic power." Both opposing leaders thought they might get the world in a better frame of mind through knowing that they could be alternatives to total human suicide. So they brought their scientists together in Geneva. The scientists did do a lot of exploratory talking about the peaceful uses of atomic energy. Little atomic reactors were brought along to demonstrate how at least to generate electricity and thus to produce a vast increase in the world population of inanimate energy slaves. As is often the case, the most important event at Geneva was entirely unplanned. It was a coincidence. The Food and Agriculture Organization of the United Nations also held its annual meeting in Geneva. The world's food and agriculture scientists and administrators were assembled to take total inventory of total needs and capabilities of world man. This gave objectivity to both the U.S.S.R. and U.S. atomic scientists' considerations. One reason why Malthus had said in 1815 that there would never be enough to go around was that Malthus had to assume that much food would rot in the field and that there would not be enough ice in the iceboxes to preserve the harvested foods. Most people lived in iceless areas. Though people in hot countries used spices, these did not keep food from spoiling. While Malthus knew that a great deal of food could be raised, he thought it would never reach all the mouths of those who needed it. The scientists meeting in Geneva, a century and a half later, saw of course that atomic energies could be used for the quick field freezing of foods and their refrigerated transport and marketing. They also cited the use of energies in chemical fertilizers, as well as various ways of using energies to increase the metabolic rates of production. It became obvious that humanity could produce adequate amounts of food, could preserve that food, could distribute it under refrigerated conditions, and could keep it in perfect condition until it reached the mouths of those who needed it. Gerard Piel, publisher of the *Scientific American*, who was present, was quoted as saying that it was in scientific evidence that there could be not only enough of the living essentials to take care of everybody around the world at high standards of living, but that there also could be enough to take care of the increasing populations at ever-improving standards of living. Though this Malthus-refuting potential became obvious to the scientists, they were not impolite enough to their political hosts to say that they didn't see how this desirable potential could ever be realized in the face of fundamentally unyielding sovereignties. Though the scientists failed to make a formal statement that Malthus was wrong and that all of humanity could be both a physical and an economic success, their findings to that effect became generally known to many world scientists.

Thus, for the first time in the history of man, we have known for a little over a decade that there can be enough to go around, and that we are frustrated from realizing this epochal potential because of the one hundred or so political sovereignties which were set up for mutually-exclusive survival hopes under the Malthusian dictum.

Let us now consider what would happen if we were to take all the industrial machinery away from all the industrial countries around the earth. This means pulling down all the wires, taking up all the tracks, removing all dynamos and every motor. We take all industrial equipment away from all the countries in Europe. We take it away from Russia. We take away all the industrial machinery from China and Japan. We take it away from the United States and Canada. We dump all the world's tools of industrialization in the ocean. Within six months, two billion human beings will starve to death, having suffered greatly on the way.

Now I am going to give you another picture. I am going to leave all the industrial machinery where it is. I am going to have all the waterfalls keep on flowing and keep all the inanimate resources available, and all who are in the industrial production as workers and administrators will stay at their jobs running all the machinery. Next we are going to take away from all the countries of the earth all the politicians, all the different political ideologies and all the political party workers of every kind, and we are going to send them all off in satellites for a trip around the sun. As long as the politicians are absent, everybody on earth who has been eating is going to keep right on eating, and with all political barriers down the prospects of arranging to take care of the needs of the rest will accelerate, and humanity everywhere on earth will prosper.

This is the first time in history that we can say this on a scientific basis, because all the political systems were of course organized on the basis that there wasn't and never could be enough to go around. Because there was not going to be enough to go around for more than a small minority, political theories such as that of Marx developed to take care of a preferred group. Marx said, "Let it be the workers because they are the most deserving." But the pirates said, "Darwin says it will always be survival only of the fittest and our rugged individualism and ruthless venturing makes us the fittest." All other political systems were in between those extremes.

No one foresaw that the industrial system could make enough to take care of all. Assuming that Malthus was right, all of humanity up to a decade ago was forced to choose sides. This was and as yet is the basis for the assumption of an eternal class struggle for survival. All of the political theories have suddenly become utterly obsolete as exclusive survival systems. They are obsolete because the world-around potential abundance has not occurred by virtue of rugged individualism nor by any class warfare's cutting off anybody's head. The abundance can be accomplished without any mutually excluding interferences. We will gradually increase travel, dwelling, sustenance, and educational capacities so that whoever wants to travel can travel when he so wishes. The industrial system is gettting more effective as more and more people are able to talk to more and more people. With more and more direct dialing there are less and less busy wires. We are in for completely automated success once we get over the idea that survival and enjoyment solutions must come through politics and recognize that they can come only through unbiased, intelligently organized competence and physical redesigning of the use of the world's resources to do so much more with so much less as to be able to supply everybody with all that they need. Quite clearly it is only going to come through the development of a world consciousness of what constitutes the true problem. That world consciousness is now coming into high and swift manifestation amongst the world-around youth.

In Berkeley, California, at midwinter of 1964-1965, we have the students demonstrating a fundamental awakening to an intuitive but as yet unformulated awareness of the misconceived preoccupations of their elders in a futile shortsighted struggle leading only to utter despoiling of the earth and the end of man on earth. The young Berkeley students' specific and immediate aggravations were happenstance. The reporters, exploring the Berkeley situation, found that students in other colleges felt the same comprehensive dismay for many entirely different catalytic reasons. Inquiring of individual students, the news reporters found a new kind of student attitude. The students were not inspired by loyalty to their particular family, to their particular college, to their particular town. They were not interested in their state. They felt no loyalty to their nation. Their elders were shocked. But the students had not lost their fundamental idealism. Their idealism had lost its debilitating bias. They felt it to be immoral to be chauvinistic and patriotic. The young people were and are only interested in the whole world and in the welfare of all humanity. The average age of the Berkeley student was that of the university junior.

Since I frequently visit universities in Africa, in our own country, and in Europe, I have talked over with the Berkeley-age students the environmental factors that have been operative in their lives. One of the first things we find out about this age of students is that they were born the year of the atomic bombing of Hiroshima and Nagasaki. This is quite a birthmark. They are the first generation in the history of man to be brought up by television, which came into popular use around the earth after World War II. Even the roofs of Hong Kong, Caracas, and Accra bristle with television antennae. TV communication everywhere reaches the world's children—even the poorest.

The data of behavioral science sheds interesting new light on the significance of the TV influence. One of the important facts we have learned in the now-powerfully-exploring behavioral sciences is that the speech pattern of parents—their vocabulary, tone of voice, clarity of diction—plays one of the most important roles in the positive or negative development of their children's brains and subsequently capacity to apprehend and coordinate abstract as well as sensorial concepts. If the parents have no real confidence in their own brains or minds, they talk in clichés. They talk in the phrases of others. They accept the dictums and opinions of others. If the child finds that the parents are not using their own minds and are relying only on the brain's cunning and luck, the child relinquishes use of its thinking capabilities. Where the speech pattern of the parents indicates a desire to comprehend, to understand, and to formulate their own thoughts, to increase their vocabulary, then the child is inspired to do likewise. We have also learned that children can prosper equally with a foster parent whose speech and other behaviors favor the optimum development of the child's innate capabilities. The men and women who work on television get and hold their jobs through their diction, good vocabularies, confident tone, and pleasing personality. It is their speech pattern which is primarily apprehended by the world's listening children despite the fact that the TV actors are being hired to talk about or to sell beer, buttons, or hair tonic. The children understand games. They consider the selling as game playing. The children read through the commercials to sense the personal lives of the TV actors. The children know their television people as children of a century ago knew all the village characters. However, the children often see more of television characters than of their own parents, brothers, cousins, uncles, and aunts. I, therefore, wrap up all the television influence on children by calling the TV the "third parent."

Since World War II, the third parent has been talking to this group of young people who are now the university juniors. For 20 years the third parent has been telling all the children the news of the world every hour on the hour. And

the parents come home from the shoestore or from some
other equally unstimulating occupation and say, "Oh, I had a
terrible day. Let's have a cocktail!" So the children run back
to the TV to get the third parent's more exciting world news.
Through the years, the third parents have been telling the
children and youths about a fantastic avalanche of invention
feats of men and showing them on screen. A submarine goes
under the polar ice from Pacific to Atlantic driven by atomic
power. Next an atomic submarine goes completely around
the world submerged. Men master the virus diseases—penetrate the nucleus of the atom. Men climb to the top of Mount
Everest and they go five miles in to photograph the bottom of
the Pacific. Men orbit the earth—photograph the far side of
the moon. Men find the DNA genetic code governing the design of all biological life, and it becomes evident to the young
people that man can accomplish any physical task. So the
young people say, "We see that there could be enough of all
the essentials of life plus many luxuries to supply all of humanity on earth. Our scientists and engineers make that clear
to us. Though we can invent and do anything we want technically, we are not making the world work. The world should
be made to work, and we just haven't confidence in yesterday's negative solutions of survival as, for instance, saying
that there is not enough for more than a few so 'Let's kill off the
excess.' " They can understand yesterday's men fighting for
survival, but they think it is obsolete now that there could be
enough for all. They don't like the war concept. They want
peace. But the young people have not worked out an adequate
understanding of the comprehensive factors involved. They
don't have enough data to put together the kind of comprehensive picture that I am attempting to put together for you here
today.

The young people, thinking that the world should work,
demand of their group parent that it be made to work. The
group parent is the nearest local politician. They keep challenging the local politicians by marching in front of them in
one way or another saying, "Make the World Work"—"Let's
Have Peace"—"Stop the War." Of course the young people
are easy for the politicians and their professional subverters
to exploit. All the different and opposing political parties
around the world fog up, confuse and try to divert to their respective bias accounts the idealistic demands of the young that
the world be made to work satisfactorily for all. Most of the
young idealists are naive, so they fall for many suggestions as

to the way in which they may realize their dreams of a satisfactory world for all. Though their idealism is greatly exploited, it is increasingly manifest everywhere. Gradually it
becomes clear that there is only one way in which we are
going to be able to make the world work. We cannot have
warlessness—i.e., we cannot have peace—unless we get rid of
the whole reason for war, which has been occasioned always
throughout the ages by the fact that there is not enough to go
around.

Even now there is only enough for 44%—as the resources
are presently used. This means that 56% are going to die far
short of their potential lifespan and they are going to go
through great pains and privation. If you are going to die
without food, you have everything to win and nothing to lose
if you take up a gun and fight for it. We are going to have
wars just as long as there is not enough to go around. This is
fundamental. The young people of today are not going to get
anywhere by just saying, "Let Us Have Peace." The politician
is not able to do anything about it because he is not a scientist, engineer, inventor, designer. War is the ultimate recourse
of the politician, undertaken to fulfill or defend his political
bias. There is nothing anywhere in politics per se, political
mandates, political activity, that can in any way up the performance per pound of the world's resources and thereby
make the resources take care of 100% instead of only 44%.
This can be done only by furthering the doing-of-more-with-
less in the same way as that technological augmentation which
has occurred almost exclusively within the great weaponry programs. Ships had to float. The limit weight of floatability, as
Archimedes showed, was the weight of a volume of water
equal to that of the submerged portion of the ship's hull, i.e.,
the portion below waterline. The more you load onto and into
a ship the lower it sinks and the more water it displaces. With
enough load it will sink altogether. To make the ship go
faster and carry more hitting power meant adding to the
ship's functional inventory. To do so without sinking the ship
required that the ship designer do even more with less. Those
who became the masters of the world ocean did so by becoming masters of doing-more-with-less. The design scientists had
to do even more with less in the air. In the space technology
we have to do even more with even less again.

A fantastic degree of doing more with less occurred when
one Telstar satellite weighing only one-quarter of a ton, orbiting around earth, outperformed the transocean communica-

tions capability of 75,000 tons of ocean-bottomed copper cabling—a 300,000-fold increase of performance per pound. This is typical of the acceleration in doing-more-with-less now occurring invisibly everywhere which can be brought into play effectively enough to render the world's resources capable of taking care of all humanity.

The engineers say; "Yes, it is clear that the overall efficiency of the kind of structures and machinery we are now using is very, very low." We are operating at an overall mechanical efficiency of only 4%—as I mentioned to you a little earlier. Therefore, we find that if we increase the overall mechanical efficiency to only 12% we can take care of everybody. That threefold increase in the overall efficiency can only be accomplished by redesign. You don't do it by whipping the motor. You don't whip the inanimate slave. You make him obsolete by design-inventing a more efficient mechanical slave. You melt up the old inefficient slave and turn the same metal into two or more new and more efficient inanimate slaves. You take one of the great two-ton automobiles off the road and make two little ones that park in a much smaller space and go faster more safely on less fuel.

What we see here is that the mechanical efficiency can be comprehensively multiplied to take care of all of humanity's ever-expanding requirements. I will give you a quick meaning of "mechanical efficiency," as you may not be familiar with this engineering concept. Mechanical efficiency is stated in terms of a percentage of physical work done by a machine as ratioed to the amount of energy consumed by it in doing that work. We state the resultant relative efficiency in terms of realized work. We say that an automobile's reciprocating engine is approximately 15% efficient. That is all it is going to be able to give you because it is inherent in the reciprocating principle. After we have an explosion on top of the engine's piston, it is propelled in a cylinder. The piston is connected to a crankshaft by a connecting rod. After the connecting rod has turned the crankshaft the linkage frustrates the further motion of the piston in the direction on which it was impelled and sends it right back where it came from. This is called a 180° restraint in the mechanical linkage system. We have the same kind of piston held and restrained by a connecting rod in turbines. In the turbines, however, we have preexplosion and the expanding gases impel the blades of the turbine being introduced tangentially to the turbine rotor so that the restraint of the impelled linkage is at 90°. The rotor keeps going around in the same circumferential direction. It doesn't have to stop to come back at 180°. It is restrained at 90°. As a consequence the turbine is approximately 30% efficient—that is, it is about twice as efficient as the reciprocating engine.

In the jet engine, we have a direct thrust without any linkage restraints, so that we get about 60% efficiency. There are 12 fundamental energy directions of freedom in universe: 6 positive and 6 negative. Every time we reduce those fundamental restraints, we increase the efficiencies. All that we have to do to make the world physically successful for all humanity is to raise the overall efficiency of world mechanisms from 4% to 12%.

This obviously means a design revolution. Nothing else will do the trick—all that political revolution can do is to take from one and give to the other, with much physical energy lost in the doing. But the design revolution can't be accomplished exclusively within just one country. It has to be a total world revolution because industrialization, as we have seen, consists inherently in world-around integration of all resources—both physical and metaphysical. The resources occur randomly around the world. The only way we can operate an inherently regenerative industrial system is to hook into the universe's comprehensive evolutionary system—for the universe is the minimum and only perpetual-motion machine. Entropy frustrates perpetual autonomy of all local systems. To hook man into the universally-transforming evolutionary system involves a complete earth-around hookup. Such vast production capability involves vast investment of our already organized capabilities to deal with energy efficiencies of transformations and translations. The more people benefited by the industrial system, the more efficiently does it operate. The more rapidly you amortize the equipment, the more rapidly you can improve and buy new equipment. So industrialization, to be regenerative, must be world-around or not at all. Industrialization will only function at highest momentarily-realizable efficiency when it is world-around.

In order to be able to take care of 100% of humanity in the shortest possible time, we are going to have to stop getting our technical advantage gains only as a secondhand event realized inadvertently from the preoccupation of highest-priority science and merged resources in the production of ever-more-devastating weaponry. As the weapons contractors find their respective contracts running out because their particular product no longer is needed—a new weapons-system item having made their product obsolete—they look around in the home market for logical application of their unique research and production capabilities.

This way of gaining technical-advantage advance for societies' peaceful activities takes 22½ years, that being the average elapsed time for inventions to traverse the weapons system and fall-out into the domestic economy. We could reduce this lag to a minimum of a very few years—probably five years—by setting about directly to make all humanity both a physical and economic success. This solution is going to come ultimately through the young world's idealism and drive. That very drive is getting more and more marked because of youth's gradual realization that the solution of mankind's primary survival problems cannot occur through political means and can only occur through a design revolution.

The students—more of whom now go to the universities and stay in the universities longer and longer—going on to higher and higher levels of education—are gradually discovering that what is needed and will work is a design revolution. They are going to initiate the invention-and-design revolution in their schools. They will discover that inventors do not need licenses to invent. The Wright brothers did not have a license from society to invent an airplane. They went out to Kitty Hawk, where there were no human beings, in order to test-fly their airplane in order to avoid society's frustration of their efforts. Despite society's inertias and ignorant opposition to their salvation, inventions are gradually conveying humanity from failure to success.

*   *   *

There is already a world-around movement of students who have taken the initiative in scientific design search and research for the technical means of increasing the performance of the world's resources. They call their project the "Design Science Decade." They have inventoried the world resources—its human trends and needs. They understand that upping the performance per pound is not accomplished by reducing safety factors, but by invention of entirely new ways of doing tasks as, for instance, when we went from wire to wireless communication, thus releasing vast metallic tonnages for other tasks.

The students' design revolution relates directly to our own manpower and automation problem. It also relates to educational developments and to the behavioral sciences which I have already mentioned.

There is a professor of education at the University of Chicago—Dr. Benjamin Bloom. He is the head of the Department of Education and head of the Curricula Committee at the university. He has written a book called *Stability and Change in Human Characteristics,* published by John Wiley & Sons. It is a very good one for you to buy. He has in it the detailed year-by-year environmental case histories—from birth up to university-graduate level—of an adequate number of human beings to constitute a scientifically-controlled research.

Each and all of the case histories include identical periodic IQ tests. Whether you happen to think well of the IQ test or whether you say that it shows intelligence or not is irrelevant. These tests were designed to find out how many new apprehending and comprehending faculties had come into play in the tested brain since previous examinations and how many of the previously recorded new brain capabilities were as yet in operation.

Dr. Bloom's book is an extraordinary recording of environmental conditions characterizing specific young lives.

I am going to jump you to another scientist, Dr. Wilder Penfield, who is head of the Neurological Institute at McGill University. He is a neurophysiologist, and he is one of the most important spokesmen for the explorers of the brain with electrodes.

That electrode probing of the brain has been going forward rapidly—more than most of us tend to realize. The electroneurologists now know what part of the brain remembers names, et cetera. In the summer of 1964 Dr. Penfield wrote a very important article in the *Atlantic Monthly* on what he called the "uncommitted cortex," that part of the brain that does not get used. He shows that an enormous amount of the brain just doesn't get used or goes into disuse.

He points out that we each have approximately the same number of cells in our brain at birth. We don't get more. These cells are brought into play by a series of chromosomically-set-off alarm clocks. The chromosomic ticker-tape schedule of each human is unique. You put your finger in the hand of a newborn child and the child closes its hand on your finger. If you pull your finger away the child releases your finger with deft sensitivity. The child has been in tactile communication with its mother for many months.

Thousands of capabilities are brought successively into play in the brain at specific moments.

Eyes of children and animals have been bandaged before they came into play for various reasons and were covered at the time that the sight was supposed to commence. They were unable to see through the bandages at the critical "self-starter" moment. When the bandages were later removed the human or other animal baby could not see—the faculty, not having been used at the starting point, lost its brain-coordinated capability to function. At the time that the successive capabilities come into brain-inaugurated functioning, they must be put into immediate use. They must be put into and kept in use even though the use frequency and magnitude are low. They must also be kept in use to some minimum degree in order to remain usable.

Dr. Bloom's book shows that between the ages of zero and four years old, 50% of the capability to apprehend, comprehend, and organically coordinate come into play—that is to say "to improve the IQ." An additional 30% of the capacity to learn and improve the IQ has become operational at seven years of age—that is, at seven, 80% of the capability to learn has been brought into use. But if any of the myriad of capabilities that add up to this 80% of total capability are not properly employed, they become nonoperative. Only under extraordinary self-disciplinings can such disused capabilities be reinstated, but this reinstatement is not easy and is rarely attained.

Between seven and thirteen, 12% more capability comes in—adding up to 92%. And at seventeen the final 8% of total capability to learn has been brought into operation. Paradoxically it is primarily for students of seventeen years and more that the U.S. government now appropriates $3 billion a year in aid for education.

And we are doing approximately nothing to aid in the primary school. For zero-to-seven-year-olds we are not giving any federal educational aid in the way of money.

Dr. Bloom is able to tell us a great deal about the factors which determine whether the children will keep in use their learning capabilities after they come into play. Factor number one in the zero-to-four-year-olds is trust. Human lives are born utterly helpless and stay helpless longer than the newborn of any other living species. The biological invention of the utterly helpless depends upon the instinctive urge of the parents to take care of the child. The child has instinctive and complete trust in the parents.

The children up to four years old have to trust their parents completely. But at four they are as yet unable to go out and get their own food and are as yet dependent to a major degree on the parents. They are as yet in trust.

The trust may be easily fractured. If the child hears the parents in drunkenness speaking in ways that indicate deep irresponsibility—a mother threatening to walk out on her husband—you have a certified dropout!

There are two other main factors affecting the IQ which have been identified as operative in the first four years of human existence. One is known as "autonomy" and the other as "initiative."

Initiative relates to the fact that every child during its awake hours is a busy laboratory testing the environment resources. When the chromosomic "alarm clock" calls for it, the child has to coordinate the complex nerve and muscle capability to stand and walk. He has also to find out in advance what he may rely upon to hold onto in an emergency or to pull him up against gravity. To find out what he can trust tensilely when the chromosomic ticker tape says "go," the child has to tear things apart all over the house. This is tearing research. Often the uncomprehending parents decide to slap the children for tearing things up. This frustrates and discourages the research work in coherence.

Autonomy relates to the child's innate sense of how much space it needs for its best development. If several children are put into the same bed, their IQ suffers. If they have their own rooms, as well as their own beds, their IQ is most favored. From ages four to seven the number one environmental factor most affecting the children is the speech pattern of the parents. We noted this in relation to the effect of the TV on children.

If good books are around the home—though the child cannot as yet read them—he senses that those are the kind of books leading to greater understanding. Having confidence in his parent's determination to learn more, the child also so aspires.

All in all, we have learned that education is not inseminated by the old into the young. It is a process that takes place within the individual, which prospers or is frustrated by environment. Environment, of course, includes the people who surround the individual. Give Dr. Bloom the basic environment data regarding each of an individual's first 17 years, and he can tell you what a 17-year-old's average IQ will be to within one point. So we see that upgrading the environment is the focus of the world-around young people's design-science revolution.

Not all the TV-bristling slums are in foreign countries. East St. Louis—on the Illinois side of the Mississippi River, across from the major city of St. Louis, Missouri—has some slums worse than those of Calcutta, India. It is a place where gangsters and exploiters in general—as in Harlem, New York —keep the people poverty-captive. Their only hope is education.

They can only get out through the development of their brains by their mind. They are not going to get out through muscle. Thus there has arisen a strong representation in the Illinois State Legislature to try to get those East St. Louis people an education.

Southern Illinois University, at which I am a professor, is just a hundred miles away. It has been given the job of setting up a second campus just outside East St. Louis. We have been given 1500 acres, $32 million, and a brand-new chance at advancing educational capabilities. It became immediately evident to the S.I.U. second campus planning group that if they didn't do a very good job under these optimum conditions, with no old building or staff holding them back, future generations would not think well of them, wherefore they had and as yet have a great responsibility. They called in many advisers. They were thorough in their searching. As one of their research professors, I, too, was called upon for advice. I told them that I thought the only way they could fulfill their responsibility was to develop a powerful forecast of human needs and developments on earth to see what is coming and to set their course on such a study. The Southern Illinois University Press published my advice as a book. It is called *Education Automation*. It examines factors very comprehensively and how they impinge finally upon the new campus of Southern Illinois. This book's content is similar to my discourse to you today, but considers many points more thoroughly than we have time for on this occasion.

In it I found that we would be forced to let automation come rapidly forward in every department of our lives and most importantly in educational facilities. I would like to call your attention to the fact that we have always had automation. You are unaware of what is going on inside you in the conversion to the energy capabilities of your lunch, for the process is completely automated.

You are not consciously making chemical differentiations and sending energies to various glands. You are not consciously making each of the hairs rise out of your head at preferred rates, colors, and curves. You do not know why you have hair. In fact you do not know how or why you go from 7 to 70 pounds and then to a 170 pounds. From time to time, humans "push the right buttons" and human babies begin to grow but they do not know how to make babies. It is all automated. We have always had automation.

All tools are externalization of originally internal organisms. What is going on in modern technology is that we are externalizing that internal organic automation of the metabolic regeneration of man into what we might call a group or a continuous man where the tools are interchangeably usable. Anyone can use the hammer or pencil or airplane. This industrial, externalized, automated metabolic regeneration will work just as well for you as for me. It is an increasingly automated functioning of comprehensive man.

In *Education Automation* I noted that the automation of industrialization was evolving into existence automatically, and that there was nothing we could do to stop it. This eventuality was implicit in the automated process of the brain and the antientropy of biology. I said, therefore, that we would go through a design revolution which would progressively multiply the performances per pound of the world's metallic resources which are now totally preoccupied in machinery and structures which, operating at full capacity, can take care of only 44% of humanity. We will increase that percentage rapidly until the resources of the earth take care of all humanity at a level of living superior to that of any man's experience. In that process the crossbreeding world people on the North American continent happen to have reached a partially improved standard of living a little earlier than others within the comprehensive relay-and-regeneration process of total world industrialization.

This total evolution marks the beginning of world man demonstrating the capability to cope successfully with his environment on a conscious basis in contrast to your subconsciously experienced adjustments to environment.

We are now beginning to deal with the concept of all humanity as born to be a physical and economic success in contradistinction to the Malthusian assumption of a majority failure. There were, yesterday, three alternatives in what society could do in view of Malthus' discovery that there apparently was not enough to go around. You could either decimate all the excess people or you could divide up the inadequacies evenly, which was called socialism, and all would die slowly together. This seemed boring to those who knew about Malthus. To those ignorant of Malthus, it seemed ideal.

The third alternative was to let all the vast numbers of humans who did not know of Malthus and Darwin's "survival only of the fittest" just remain in ignorance to go on with their beliefs that their gods would take care of their salvation. This latter alternative prevailed. What we call the underprivileged countries today are those who were left out of the "informed" people's armament race.

But the potential success of all of humanity which we have now is a new challenge utterly unforeseen by Malthus or Marx, any economists, any capitalists, or any socialists.

We now have to divide up the success to be produced by the automated augmentation of wealth. We will have to abandon the negative accounting of yesterday. We will have to give up the "mortgage"—i.e., death measure—of people who were not able to demonstrate their right to live. What we will do as I prophesied in 1961 in *Education Automation* is to invest escalatingly in the successful potential of all human beings. We will start that investing by sending almost everybody back to school.

We will accomplish this by giving everybody fellowships to go back into the educational system. We have already started this by sending technically displaced persons back to school to learn new skills. But by the time each man learns a new skill, that process, too, has been automated. So he goes from one school to another. He never gets out of school.

So we might as well make up our minds to the fact that we are, all of us, about to go back to school. For the first time mankind does not have to say, "How do I earn a living? How do I prove my right to live? How may I keep my family going?"

For the first time in the history of man we are going to ask, "What would you like to do? In what direction do you have some spontaneous urge to develop or to make social contributions?" If some people say, "Well, I would just like to go fishing"—very good.

If you go fishing it is a good place to do some thinking

about what else you would like to do. You don't expect a man to come up with his best long-distance thoughts right away.

As we noted before, it is possible that, for every 100,000 we send back to school free, one in that 100,000 will make a technological breakthrough that will produce the forwardly organized capability wealth for the other 99,999.

At the present moment there is something going on that the public is not too well aware of which is of great importance and affects the general evolution toward comprehensive success. In 1900 America started to make important capital investments in countries around the world.

Before 1900, in America's early prosperity, people from around the world began to make capital investments in America. But in 1922, right after World War I, this trend changed. It changed in several ways. Up to that time more people had been coming into America than those who went out. In 1922 and thereafter more have been going out than are coming in. This was also typical of many of our import-export patterns.

In 1900 America began to go into something called "direct foreign investments." Indirect foreign investment means buying shares in foreign enterprises. Direct foreign investment means building of structures and outright production of goods.

Our direct foreign investment starting in 1900 went up to a few billions and then at the time of the 1929 Depression wavered and became depressed and remained depressed until World War II. Then in 1940 it started to increase and the rate of increase has accelerated ever since.

The U.S. economy now has $70 billion in direct foreign investments to produce goods in foreign countries for foreign consumption. That figure of $70 billion is taken after considerable amortization. That $70 billion of direct wealth-produced capability is more than all the world's gold. Gold does not produce more gold. But these foreign investments in the tools of production industry do produce goods which are not only to provide higher standards of living to millions of people but also to produce a profit to the investors and increasing wages and salaries. The additional wealth in profits produced by this foreign investment in 1964 amounted to $4½ billion.

The world's big corporations are outward bound from their sovereign identity to irrevocable world identity. Of General

Motors' $1½ billion net profit after taxes for 1964 one-third, or $500 million, accrued from its foreign operations. Despite the fact that only about 10% of General Motors' total holdings are as yet in foreign lands, one-third of its earnings were from the foreign operation.

When Conway spoke to you he talked about the grand-strategy data processing of General Motors as a big corporation intelligence system that is not available to the public sector. But G.M. are unquestionably using their computers in a very big way. Their computerized strategy is taking them out of the U.S.A. to take world-around positions.

Out of every five dollars that the hundred largest U.S. corporations spent last year (1964) in new plants and equipment, four of those dollars went to expand their foreign establishments.

American corporations are outward bound. Their evolution is, however, the evolutionary prototype for all of society. All of humanity are soon to become worldians.

Arthur Watson of IBM says that the old way of talking about "Germany trading with England" and so forth is about to come to an end. Such "nationalism" or "internationalism" is just as obsolete as talking about New York trading with Jersey City and having an annual balance of trade to be paid in gold by one city to the other after both have processed through customs and audited all the traffic between these two adjacent cities. Watson says that we are getting to the point where corporations are becoming "world" and are accounting as "world." Our annual payment in gold between "sovereign" nations is not only obsolete but is frustrating the attainment of physical and economic success for all world humanity.

In the same way all local or geographical identifications are now obsolete. People ask me, "Where do you live?" Inasmuch as I travel around the world every few months I answer that "I live on a little spaceship called *Earth*."

So I would say then in your deliberation on manpower you are in the condition where the largest of our industrial organizations are administratively outward bound. Standard Oil represents yesterday's pattern of a U.S. corporation going to foreign countries to take resources away from those countries. Mexico and other countries resented this and put a stop to it.

But in the outbound industrialization of which I now speak it is not a matter of exploiting resources, but it is of actually bringing into each country a technology—of a mass-production technique to produce more and higher performance goods and a higher standard of living for the people in those countries. For instance, foreign corporations cannot export automobiles into Mexico. However, the Mexicans want automobiles, so they invite the foreign corporations to build factories to produce the Mercedes car or the General Motors cars or the Fords. The Mexicans (and many others) want a Mercedes car and the Mercedes research work has been done all over the world. What Mexico wants is the capability and the prestige of producing that highly-evolved car in Mexico. They are not interested in starting a new "Mayan Six" on their own. This bringing of production capability to a country is very different from draining a country of its mineral or other nonselfreplenishing resources.

And as the great corporations expand supranationally without diminishing their domestic operations, their exports of end products from any one country to another of end products will decrease. The production in foreign countries at lower labor rates will affect the U.S. economy and tend to bring about either lower U.S. wages or more automation at lower costs and concomitant unemployment. U.S. labor will have to choose between lowered wages and automation which later, while disemploying men as workers, produces so much more wealth as to permit their comprehensive emancipation from physical-muscle or automation functioning and the economic support of whatever research-and-development vocation or educational undertaking most pleases each individual. U.S. labor is intelligently led and its rank and file are learning "what it is all about." Labor will support automation and will be rewarded with epochal wealth advantage.

In your deliberations here in Washington on the upheavals being wrought by accelerating industrialization you must be realistic about the U.S. people fast becoming world people. We now have three million passport-carrying Americans who are out of the country at any given time, and this number is increasing rapidly. All the other countries of the world have an increasing number of their people graduating to a spaceship *Earth*'s first-class passenger list.

We are going to have to invest that approximately inexhaustible wealth I spoke to you about on a world basis. The more we can produce the more rapidly we can increase our wealth.

So I say then that what we have to counsel for and do is to prepare American man to be world man and to begin to act and think of ourselves as world men. And with this concept comes many new kinds of understandings in relation to total world problems of mankind. Spinning through universe on his spaceship *Earth*, world man is now beginning to make sorties into greater realms of universe. In his electronic, microscopic, and telescopic probing he has already reached out billions of billion magnitudes beyond yesterday's intelligence reach. World man is already scouting the approaches to universe man.

9. Utopia or Oblivion

Astronauts, aviators, mariners, submariners, and people of all countries use and appreciate tiny transistors, because transistors do so much more, so much more reliably with so much less. So also do a myriad of invisible alloys, chemical and electromagnetic devices accomplish much more with less.

The development of these globally interacting, invisibly operating inventions was not organized as a benevolent world revolution by anyone. But their integrating and interacceleratingly regenerative more-with-lessing all together constitute a revolution which is found to be politically welcome the world around. Computers, TV's, and plastics, as superficial manifest of the invisible doings, are apparently wanted everywhere.

The centuries' long only subconscious more-with-lessing is only now entering human consciousness as constituting a unified world revolution—as inexorable and transcendental to man's will as is an earthquake. Some speak of the revolution as "the impact of technology on society," others as "automation." Everywhere people are aware of its portentousness. Few think of it correctly as "invisible more-with-lessing," the scientific description for which is "progressive ephemeralization"—99% of humanity look upon it only as more-with-more and more again.

To turn the heretofore only subconsciously regenerative more-of-every-advantage with less-of-every-resource revolution to highest human benefit in the shortest time with the most pleasure and satisfaction and with the least effort, pain, or rupture for all has become the conscious focus of a world-around university students' coordinated research. Whether this particular initiative will persist and be successful is unpredictable. But its occurrence and circumstances provide a significant case history for it brings the generalized problem into sharp, wide-angle-lensed, maximum depth-of-field focus.

As such it is probably the prototype exploration in how to make the world work satisfactorily for all.

Identified as the Design Science Decade, the world students' ten-year plan is divided into five evolutionary stages of two years each. Stage one was on exhibit in the Tuileries gardens in Paris, France, for the first ten days of July, 1965 (under the auspices of the International Union of Architects' Eighth World Congress). It confronted the world with the basic facts which led the students to the research conclusion that human survival apparently depends upon an immediate, consciously coordinated, world-around, computerized research marshalling and inception of the theoretically required additional inventions and industrial network integrations for the swiftest attainment and maintenance of physical success of all humanity.

Fortunately, say the students, such invention initiative does not derive from political debate or bureaucratic licensing. The license comes only from the blue sky of the inventor's intellect. No one licensed the inventors of the airplane, telephone, electric light, and radio to go to work. It took only five men to invent these world-transforming developments. Herein lies the potentially swift effectiveness of the world student research revolution.

While the International Union of Architects Eighth World Congress was held in Paris' Palais de Chaillot their world students exposition was deployed to the Tuileries gardens. It is worth noting in our case history that while the senior professional architects' congress was greeted cordially by the French press—the congress with its 2500 delegates from 60 of the world's nations, including the U.S.S.R., the Chinese People's Republic, and their satellites and all the major "Western" powers—neither the occurrence of the Congress nor its proceedings were reported over the international news wire services. On the other hand the World Students' Design Science Decade in the Tuileries gardens and their declared objectives did prove newsworthy and are as yet receiving wide and favorable world news coverage.

These students have no political motives. They have no formal organization—no officers or bylaws. They are not supported by any political organization. Their activities converge as spontaneously as skiers converge on the world's best snow slopes. As amateur design scientists, the students deal only in resource statistics, computation, inventions, schematics, drawings, and models which treat with the world's industrial network growth. They deal theoretically and experimentally with man's *external*, inanimate, industrial network organism in the same way that medical science deals with mankind's *internal* organism.

Their design-science findings may be employed alike by all political states, whenever, in emergencies, the students' inventions and network integrations become as obviously logical and employable as are medical science's research "breakthroughs." Anticipating critical economic, social, and technological needs, the students' design-science breakthrough solutions to the problems are placed upon the world-news-published, standby awareness "shelves" in the same way that medical breakthrough techniques and antibiotics become standby.

Because humanity has a long memory for fiascos, nonsense, and catchwords, the question has been asked several times, "Has the world students' coordinate support of the invention revolution something to do with Technocracy?" The answer is NO! Technocracy was a political organization. It was formed in the 1929-1932 economic depression. It consisted mostly of unemployed engineers. This blue-shirt-uniformed technical elite asserted that the 1932 depression would soon worsen. They announced that they would, at the right moment, set up an engineers' dictatorship. Economic recovery in the U.S.A. by Franklin Roosevelt's administration deflated Technocracy's plans. They were inherently deflatable. Engineers are too forthright. They are politically naive. As an aftermath, however, such word inventions often get into general vernacular and it frequently happens today that people who do not know the history of Technocracy refer to any engineer or scientist as a "Technocrat."

The world students' design-science initiative has no precedent. All the conditions essential to its precipitation have never before coexisted. It is the constructive outgrowth of the world-around students' ever-more-logical dissatisfaction with the inadequacy of yesterday's theories and practices to cope with today's problems and potentials. Their highly intuitive and not always clearly conceived dissatisfaction is frequently articulated only in protests over local regulations, or the right to be heard. Sometimes, in civil-rights movements, the students' spirit discloses superb courage and dedication to human justice. Sometimes—in wanton outbursts of indiscriminate disdain of the ineptness of all that is "old"—it may break windows and noses. Typical of the milder, organized protests was the recent University of California students' Berkeley rebellion.

The issues are often confused because of political tampering. It is easy for skilled operators of opposing world ideologies to surreptitiously exploit the universally persistent, intuitive discontent among their adversaries' youth by derring-do teasing in their respective directions.

Born utterly helpless, and gaining independent competence only slowly, youth's reflexes are preconditioned to expect some older authority to be responsible for its welfare. Youth assumes that the political authority is a public parent. When dissatisfied, youth protests to the authorities, assuming the authorities can, if they wish, make everything satisfactory. Often, the "authority" lacks such capability. The problems are usually beyond the scope of local authority. They demand world peace. The Mayor of Kankakee has no such capability.

The present university youth are World War II's babies, many born with their fathers away at war. Many were tended by group babysitters as their mothers worked in munitions factories. The present university students are also the first humans to be reared by the third parent—*television*—which has given them hourly news of world events. Unlike any previous generations, the students think "world." They will settle for nothing less than justice and physical advantage for all, everywhere around earth.

The third parent also taught them that no invention barriers are insurmountable to science and technology. They were born into a transoceanic, air-traveling world. The atom bomb is their birthmark. In their fourth year of life the giant transistorized computers began commercial operation. When the students were aged 9, men climbed to the peak of Mount Everest. When 10, they were immunized against polio. As they reached 12 years, the Russians' unmanned rocket Sputnik orbited the earth every hour and a half, and the first civilian nuclear reactor went into operation as an electric power-generating station. When the students were aged 13, the U.S. atomic-powered submarine *Nautilus* went from the Pacific to the Atlantic submerged below the north polar ice. In their fourteenth year, the Russians' unmanned rocket photographed the far side of the moon and returned to earth. When they were 15, the U.S. bathyscaphe took man safely to photograph the bottom of the Pacific Ocean's deepest hole. In their sixteenth year, a Russian orbited earth in a rocket. As they reached 17, the DNA genetic code for the control of the design of all life was discovered.

The students know that man can do anything he wants. However, they see world officialdom investing the world's highest capabilities only in race suicide springboards. Finding their own political demonstrations for peace or their outright revolutions leading only toward further war, a few pioneers amongst the world students have joined up objectively with the heretofore only subjectively experienced do-more-with-less design-science revolution. The students are applying general systems theory to comprehend and to utilize the accelerating invention revolution as the swiftest and only fundamental means of attaining world peace with both physical success and moral justice for all.

The students' reason:

The metals in 80% of all the scrap of yesterday's obsolete mechanics and structures have been recovered, refined as "pure metals," and put to work again.

But the rate of discovery of additional metal ores is slower than human population increase.

Throughout the 20th century, therefore, the cumulative total of world metals mined and unmined has been continually decreasing per each world man.

At the present moment the cumulative total of metals—mined and refined by man throughout all history—is wholly employed in machines or structures which, operating at limit capacity, can accommodate and serve only 44% of living humanity.

No exclusively political act of any political system can make the world's resources take care of more than 44% of humanity.

Despite the foregoing constant increase in human population and constant decrease of metals per person, between 1900 and 1965 the number of people attaining physical success as full-time participants in the highest standard of living progressively developed by world industrialization—a personal standard of living and health superior to that ever enjoyed by any pre-20th-century monarch—rose steadily from less than 1% to 40% of all living humanity.

The 40% of humanity surprisingly grown successful, despite constantly diminishing physical resources per capita, can only be explained by the doing-more-with-less invention revolution.

The success cannot be attributed to any political doctrine. It has flourished equally under opposing ideologies.

Take away the energy-distributing networks and the industrial machinery from America, Russia, and all the worlds' industrialized countries and within six months over two billion swiftly and painfully deteriorating people will starve to death.

Take away the politicians, all the ideologies and their professional protagonists from those same countries and leave them their present energy networks, industrial machinery, routine production and distribution personnel and no more humans will starve nor be afflicted in health than at present.

Why has mankind failed to perceive, understand, and respond logically to the significance of this situation? The answer is complex. But it needs answering. That will take some paragraphs. If it is to be consciously solved by man it will have to be understood well enough to be properly stated. It is the students' working assumption that "a problem adequately stated is a problem well on its way to being solved."

The problem consists of such powerfully conditioned human reflexes as laissez-faire, induced by nature's "built-in," instinctive, "game-playing" drives which are subconsciously operative in all living creatures, by which—often in lieu of intellect, they only inadvertently and unintentionally provide vital support of one another—as for instance do all the mammals respire all the vegetation's vitally required carbon dioxide, while all vegetation respires all the mammals' vitally required oxygen; or as do the honey-hunting bees inadvertently fertilize the growth of flowers with their pollen-dusting tails. It is only by the integrated coordination of myriads upon myriads of unconsciously performed inadvertencies of such "game-playing" drives that nature is able to accomplish the comprehensive ecological and metabolic regeneration of life on earth.

* * *

C. H. Waddington, University of Edinburgh geneticist, speaks of the "epigenetic landscape" in identifying the powerful effects on human behavior played by environmental factors. Waddington shows how man goes on to alter the environment and how the altered environment alters human behaviors and how the whole process becomes regenerative and continually accelerates. He does not show that the environ-

ment adds capabilities to the human's innate capabilities but
does indicate the way in which changes in the environment
permit realization of innate capabilities thereto frustrated.
Thus we see that evolution is not confined to the organic man
but consists of the combined man and his environment.* This
combined regenerative evolution has not attained a "chain-
reaction rate."

Typical of the "games" played by man which preclude his
timely recognition of the fundamentals of evolution are: vi-
sion-blinding national and local egocentricities; obsessions
with legendary "perfections" of yesterday; preoccupation with
murder and scandal news; molelike shortsightedness developed by constant attention to before-the-nose successive personal and local crises and ambitions; narrowness of focus due
to specialization; pride; inferiority complex; and spring fever.

Another important reason for world society's failure to apprehend and comprehend the significance of industrialization's suddenly obsoleting the role of all of yesterday's political ideologies is the insurmountable communications barrier between the 1% of the world population who are scientists and the 99% who are not. This is not an obstacle that
may be surmounted just by taking note of it. Many books
such as those of C. P. Snow have suggested the gap is forever
unspannable. The 1 scientist to 99 nonscientist ratio reflects
the historical fact that since the last ice age left 75% of the
world surface under water, 99% of mankind have lived exclusively on the dry land and have occupied only 4% of the
world's total surface. This 4% has been comprised of many
separate and widely dispersed areas: the most readily tillable
or minable, life-sustaining, dry lands and their fishable inland

---

Amos Hawley, "Ecology and Human Ecology," *Social Forces*, Vol. 22,
May 1944, p. 401. "It has been fairly well established, however, that the
competitive hypothesis is a gross over-simplification of what is involved
in the development of pattern, structure, or other manifestation of organization. As a matter of fact, the customary interpretation of the Dar-
winian 'struggle for existence' to mean that the primary and dominant
relationship in animate nature is opposition whether clamorous combat
or the more subtle competition, forms one of the neatest illustrations of
the 'fallacy of misplaced concreteness' that may anywhere be found. Darwin used the phrase in 'a large and metaphorical sense,' subsuming under
it all expenditures of effort to maintain and expand life. Combination
and cooperation as well as competition and conflict are embraced in the
concept. That mutual aid is just as fundamental and universal as opposition has been abundantly shown in numerous field and laboratory
studies by students of plants and animals."

or coastal waterways. Through 98% of the time, the 99% of humanity sprinkled myopically about the divided dry land were mutually unaware of one another. The local groups developed their local laws.

Those few who prospered on land fought defensively against invaders from less productive areas. The heavier and bigger their fortifications, the more secure the defenders felt. The 99% of humanity dwelling on the land built on a basis of more security always accomplished with more of everything. They shut down their work at dark, locked their doors, and everyone went to sleep.

During the same postice-age period approximately 1% of humanity went out to sea. The mariners occupied the world's omni-interconnected oceans, which together cover 75% of the spherical surface of earth.

But the sea could never be shut down. Those who went voluntarily to sea went voluntarily to fight the sea, and other men, for its supremacy and for 24 hours each day. Men on the high seas, forced by the limits of floatability, strove offensively for lightweight scientific and technical superiority— stone fortresses sank.

What we know of today as general systems theory was first practiced in the design of ships and their world operations. All the functions that the ship must perform, to be successful, and the variable limits of those functions had to be both comprehensively and specifically anticipated. Only then could the size of the ship, necessary to contain that set of essential functions, become discernible. The volume of the ship's hull next made possible the calculations of the weight of water it would displace. Then that total floatable weight had to be divided up into a tight performance-per-pound budget which assigned so much of the totally available displacement weight to each essential function. Improving the performances per units of invested resources of materials, time, and knowhow were, and are as yet, the outstanding characteristics of high-priority industrialization. Wooden structures could last long enough to make a fortune.

Because the laws of the separate lands did not extend into the sea, and those who went to sea were inherently outlaws, no nonsense such as building codes or esthetic mores limited their undertakings. They lived only by the inflexible dictates of nature's physical laws and by the law of their captain's will, wit, knowledge, foresight, and organized physical strength.

Men of the sea lived in a state of accelerated reality. Offshore navigation by the stars required the progressive discovery and swift development of mathematics. Shipbuilding required literacy and mathematics. The closer men live to reality the more daringly inventive and scientific they become and the quicker they are to adopt new ways. Thus, the sea became the breeder of science and its swift applications while the dry land life permitted and invited unscientific, massive, and inert protection of unscientific illiterate customs and habits. It can safely be said that the origins of science took place at sea and the same 1% to 99% ratio of sea people to land people as yet obtains in the 1:99 ratio of scientists to nonscientists.

Seafarers readily adopt mutually beneficial, pro tem codes of survival and prosperity. The big pirates gained power by reputations for gallantry and saved their ruthlessness only for the biggest gambles. The biggest of the pirates invented, organized, and controlled whole nations within their respective trade-route domains. After holding control of the world for years the great pirates often became so feared and respected that their fleet leaders became recognized as admirals, as they progressively differentiated and organized their merchant and fighting functions.

Both the sailors' rewards and their security lay in doing, anticipatorily, ever more within the limit of floatable weight. The more-with-less capabilities of the little pirates, with their properly equipped little ships, often overcame the big, well-manned, richly laden and less-maneuverable "venturers'" ships.

Ships had a vast number of technical and economic advantages over landborne commerce. Within a given time they could carry cargoes many thousandfold the weight transportable on the backs of men or animals, or in overland vehicles. The seas were all interconnected and the lands were not.

The pirates' more-with-less shipbuilding industry, as the prototype of all later industry, sought for the use of all the world's best materials. The pirate with the strongest, tallest masts, strongest ropes and sails, could exploit the storms and could outmaneuver the other adventurers. He found those superior resources only by voyages of discovery around the entire globe. He found better masts in the Americas, better rope in the Philippines, better cotton for his sails in Egypt. He found that the resources of the earth were unevenly distributed, and that only ships could integrate the resources to realize the industrial ever-more-with-less, competitive capabilities complex. He learned that the economic rewards for so doing were fabulous.

Because of the unprecedented wealth accruing to the ocean transport, the pirates could afford to underwrite scientific development in unique degree. Both the venturers' shipyards and the ships they built were major tool and power complexes. The opposing pirates' more-with-less sea-tool competition eventually replaced wind- and sail-driven wooden ships with steam-driven steel ships. To gain swift access to the mineral resources essential to their steam and steel shipbuilding, the pirates extended the principle of their wooden railways— developed originally only for their marine railway launchings —back inland, they mounted their ships' steam engines on metal wheeled platforms on the metal rails to go into areas of the hinterland where canals and rivers were nonexistent in order to obtain further resources to build their ever-improving steel and steam ships. Secretly dominating all the land governments, the merchant venturers, as they were politely known, obtained free franchises for their vast inland railway rights of way.

Thus began also not only the great piracy of the land, but what is known as the Industrial Revolution. The 99% of humanity preoccupied with feudally dominated farming, fishing, and crafts were unaware that they had been absorbed into the inherently comprehensive world system network of industrialization. They thought exclusively of ensuing mechanical events as products of their local ingenuity. Today's urbanism began with the pirates' inland network linkage of world transport and communication.

The scientist-artist-inventor-architect-engineers of the Leonardo da Vinci type, who had disappeared from world society when they were shanghaied to sea by the pirates at the beginning of the 16th century, reappeared upon the land again, three centuries later, in men such as Brunel and Telford—who built the railroads, bridges, tunnels, and canals by which the seaborne world industry flowed inward upon the land. As the great British geopolitician Sir Halford McKinder taught, a half century later, with the railroads the land became an extension of the ocean. Locally preoccupied landbound world man did not know what was going on.

With steel shipmaking came a whole new world of alloy

steels with unique capabilities. This brought about further scientific exploration of the earth for rare alloys. It also brought about total world interdependence. For instance, as is visible today the steel-making constituent manganese, found plentifully in Ghana, is useless to Ghanaians, who have neither coal nor iron with which to make steel. Ghanaian manganese must be transported overseas to make the steel, which will be exported back to Ghana and many other countries as tools, machinery, and structural components. Industry is inherently of world magnitude, and only works as a world system. The newly emerging nations around earth will soon have to learn that their political independence depends upon the degree to which they comprehend and voluntarily participate in the interdependence of world industrialization. Ghanaians make good airline pilots but the Ghanaian Airways equipment was not developed in Accra.

Industry takes resources from all around the world—the furthermost points of which are only halfway around the world from any one point. Industry takes the world's mined resources to a few points of maximum industrial efficiency for separation and more-with-less rearrangement in alloys, parts, and machine wholes.

In order to justify this vast expense of world pattern operation, industrialization must mass-produce and mass-distribute to obtain enough customers to divide up the total toolup and operations cost. Only world distribution provides the most customers. So halfway around the world again, in all directions, go the products and services of industrialization. Industrialization is inherently world-embracing and world-integrating.

Before the air-transport era, this vast wealth-realizing integration of the world's resources was only accomplished via the seas. Whoever ruled the oceans ruled the world.

Because a group of pirate ships could outmaneuver and surround one pirate ship, navies were invented. And the pirate navy with the best organized world-around shipbuilding yards and world bases ruled the sea.

And only the top pirates in the top navies knew what it was "all about." Thus only 1% of the 1% of humanity that went to sea came to rule the world. Secrecy was their chief weapon. The sea kept its secrets. Thus, for many centuries 99.99% of humanity knew nought of how the world was being run. But being run it was—rigorously, for the first and last time.

The rule broke down after World War I and ceased altogether in 1929.

While the great pirates ran the world only for the benefit of one-hundredth of 1% of humanity that was only because they thought—as their economist, Thomas Malthus, had pointed out—that this was the limit which could be supported by the world's resources. Their scientist Darwin confirmed this with his "survival only of the fittest." Thus the rise and fall of their world control and of the world-around economic systems which they invented is probably the least understood background of today's world problems—dry-land-preoccupied world people knew little of the vast world trade route, shipbuilding science, and economic stratagems of the pirates. Secrecy was the pirates' most powerful adjunct.

The world's peoples and their politicians think erroneously in terms of sovereign nations with colonial empires. These empires never were the product of the ambitions of the people of any nation. The British people had nothing to do with establishing the British Empire outside of being conscripted or shanghaied on board the ships by the great pirates' admirals and captains. Today's world people think naively that politicians have always run things. They never have and never will. Politicians were only the pirates' visible local stooges.

With the invention of the airplane to the point where it was able to carry a torpedo which could sink an armor-clad battleship, which it did in 1929, came the assumption that whoever ruled the sky ocean, which dominated the water ocean, must succeed to the ruling of the world. Ability to dominate the world skies was derived from the same secret and governnment-guarded science which had produced the supreme ships of the sea, so the world, though amazedly impressed, knew little or nothing of either the whyfor or the technical details of air-supremacy evolution.

What the world did not realize was that the financial crash of 1929 completely ended the great pirates' power. It died because the great pirates had let science out of Pandora's box and they could not understand science or see and control science's invisible evolution. The scientists did not revolt; but the properties of universe that they were uncovering continually broke loose from economic monopoly and the magnitude of scientific involvement developed far beyond the finance capabilities of the old pirates to cope with. Only nations and groups of nations could now cope with the magnitude of capital underwriting.

Demise of the pirates' power left the world political systems, which the pirates had invented or negatively induced, harnessed with the task of satisfying the world population's naive mandate that they—the politicians—go right on running the world realistically rather than just "acting the part of rulers," as secretly puppeted by the former pirate masters— all unbeknownst to the people.

This left the world politicians also harnessed with their newly inherited air-weaponry and electromagnetic-wave development well underway and now wholly underwritten by the "nations" because the costs of the underwriting had been bypassed to the nations' treasuries by the pirates just before the crash.

Never having known who the master pirates were and how they managed to run the world, yet thoroughly indoctrinated in all their duties, culture, and customs, people have carried on as if the old pirates' capitalism as yet existed—despite the fact that it is completely extinct. People play games of capitalism or anticapitalism or colonialism vs. noncolonialism but only because that is all they know how to play. But all the basic underwritings of new technology are now socialized, that is they are all government-financed under a complicated economic relay system which commences with national-defense hardware contracts with prime weaponry contractors.

The new air-ocean weapons race, inherited unwittingly by the world's people from the pirates along with their national identities, local laws, and mores, brought about new and increased importance of the role to be played in world socioeconomic evolution by the doing-more-with-less technology theretofore developed only by maritime evolution and now expanded by aircraft technology.

The airplane could not float in the sky. It flew only because of the negative pressure, or lift, developed over the top of its wing foils as produced only by pushing or pulling the foils at high velocity through the air. This velocity required powerful and heavy engines plus heavy fuel loads plus the weight of super-to-multi-hurricane structural strength in the airframes. The first airplanes had excess lifting capacity for only one human pilot and could fly only for short distances for a few minutes. Whoever could make the airplanes do more lifting with less material to carry the greatest striking power, the greatest distances in the shortest time, could and did run the world, but only for a few months because the technology was now geared to constant change and first one side and then the other of the weapons-race leaders could regain the design-science advantage overnight.

By exquisite probing for the means of doing more-than-before-with-less-than-before by both sides it was discovered that neither side could "run the world" so both sides continued the weapons race to guarantee that the other side should not run the world. This negatively dynamic standoff of nations staffed by an international proliferation of nuclear and rocketry scientist mercenaries or pawns finally developed into the "massive-retaliation defense posture" of the most powerful nations at the midpoint of the 20th century. And that is the condition today, at the century's two-thirds point. The vast productive capabilities of man are now locked in dynamically balanced guarantee of "nothing to be gained and everything to be lost."

In the meanwhile both "sides" burn up the fossil-fuel and atomic-fuel "savings accounts" accumulated through the ages, disdaining to invest in harnessing the vast daily income energy wealth—for instance of the ocean tides—as "uneconomical" in comparison to the "costs" of burning the savings accounts. The real cost questions which are not faced by either organized governments or businesses are what will it cost to carry on when we run out of oil, coal, fresh water, and fresh air.

In the 1920s transition from sea to air mastery of the world, the doing-more-with-less finally went irrevocably from visible technology to invisible science. Scientist-artist-inventors provided the new, do-invisibly-more-with-invisibly-less techniques. It was the cost of this new air-ocean mastering's invisible, scientific capability which rocketed beyond the purchasing means of the old pirates and ended their world sovereignty as marked by the economic panic of 1929. Only sovereign nations could now marshal the gargantuan capital venture credit required to underwrite and to command the long-term, only indirectly refunding advantages that went into the production of world air supremacy. The evolution of man's flying ran into continuous capital retooling costs eightyfold the value of all the world's gold. The economics of development of the air-ocean technology introduced a new empirical concept of wealth, which made obsolete the exclusively intrinsic wealth standards theretofore mandated and obscurely maintained by the great pirates. The new wealth was a realistically marshaled use of an ever-advancing, tool-organized, inanimate energy-capability wealth, which harvests the intellect's scientific shunting of universal energies onto the advantage end of man-invented levers, which levers also consist of associative energies appearing as chemical "materials."

Historically, the 99% of humanity based on dry land knew approximately nothing of the 1% of humanity's sea- and sky-hidden doings, and even less of its esoteric, scientific stratagems. What they were familiar with and did swallow, "hook, line, and sinker," were all the ramifications of the pirates' international accounting system—annual balances of trade and their payments in gold which had been invented by the world master pirates to keep their gold off the seas and out of jeopardy of hijacking by competitor pirates.

As a consequence of their preoccupations in irrelevancies, 99% of humanity have been historically conditioned to think of security only as more-with-more, and the bigger, heavier, and more venerable the *fortress, cathedral, mansion,* or *inventory of possessions,* the better. "Secure as the Rock of Gibraltar."

The more-with-more security finally came to its zenith in the post-World War I building by France of the Maginot Line—history's greatest fortress. The blitzkrieg, whose airpower and tank power were the technologies of the sea rolling up and flying over the land, rolled and flew over the Maginot Line as if it were not there. There were none of the anticipatorily higher-performance hardwares there to stop the blitzkrieg. It would have taken a quarter century to develop them.

As a general consequence of their preoccupation with their exclusively local affairs and of the momentum of society's confusion over technical economics and world industrialization and foreign "exchange" rate mysteries, 99% of the world population do not even now think of their economy in terms of performance per pound, energy effort and knowhow hours invested per function, let alone thinking of buildings in terms of weight. How much does St. Peter's Cathedral in the Vatican weigh? An absurd question! Nobody knows. How much does the St. Peter's-dwarfing S.S. *Queen Mary* weigh?

86,000 tons. Everybody knows that. But for the last ten years the S.S. *United States,* employing lightweight alloys and many progressively smaller more-with-less devices and weighing only 45,000 tons, has carried as many passengers and tons of cargo per year at equal transatlantic speeds as has the S.S. *Queen Mary,* all at considerably less operating costs. That is why the Cunard Line is about to do-even-more-with-an-even-smaller ship to outperform them both. We have entered into an era where visibly less than the biggest does visibly more. Now a 350-ton airliner can outperform either of these gigantic ships in total passengers carried per year. How much does the new U.S.S.R. 700-passenger airplane weigh? 500,000 pounds—250 tons, only 700 pounds per passenger vs. 1000 pounds per passenger in a Cadillac; and vs. 1400 pounds per passenger in a packed railway coach. Which of these ways of travel will get you the furthest, fastest, most safely at the least overall cost? Obviously the big airplanes are so outperforming the oldest technologies as soon to make them altogether obsolete. U.S.A.'s Lockheed Aircraft Company who are also building the 700-passenger C-5A ships at a total weight of 700,000 pounds, or 350 tons, are also working on multithousand passenger airplanes. Planes have now passed a critical point in development which permits almost unlimited sizes and shows that each time we have double the size we halve the weight per passenger. These big advanced research ships are to be literally the size of skyscrapers. The C-5A's fuselage length is that of the height of a 23-story building. This means factory production and air-delivery of skyscrapers themselves, installable anywhere around the world in a day by upending the fuselages. It also means removal of skyscrapers and their redelivery to any other points on earth in one day. This is the consequence of the chain-reaction rate now attained in the man-and-environment interregenerative evolution.

Even the architects of today are utterly ignorant of the weights of their buildings. In order to make the structural components strong enough, engineers have to calculate the building weights, but only after the owners and architects have finished the visible shape, operating scheme, superficial dimensions, and materials design.

It is fantastic that, without exaggeration, we can use the figure 99% over and over again. It is the ratio of the audience and the magician—who fools his audience into seeing him do things other than that which he is really doing. So it

had been with the old pirates who owned the scientists as
they owned laying hens. While the magician pirate is dead,
the world thus as yet carries on with the nonsense of the pirates' magic through the scientists carrying on the magician
act.

Ninety-nine percent of humanity has never thought in
terms of the do-more-with-less stratagems of the ship-,
airplane-, and rocket-designing scientists, and their military
operating personnel, who as yet constitute less than 1% of
the human population. Not one man in a million knows what
a transistor really is and why it does what it does nor how it
happened to be discovered. Not one in a million asks why a
Hindu metal worker who could qualify as a first-class tool-
maker in Detroit gets paid one-fiftieth as much for his time in
India.

Even the scientist rarely thinks realistically regarding fundamental behaviors. All the world's scientists see the sun
"going down" at "sunset"—despite 500 years of knowledge
that the earth is rotating the scientist out of view of the sun. All
scientists tell you the "wind is blowing from the west," when
a low pressure eastward of us is sucking. All the scientists say
"up" and "down" though there is no such direction in universe. The U.S. scientist on the ground speaking in the U.S.
over the television—with all the world listening—says to the
astronaut, as he is rocketing over China, "How are things 'up'
there this morning?" What he should say is "out" there. Astronauts go "out" from heavenly bodies—or "in" toward
heavenly bodies.

*　　*　　*

The public's vast ignorance of either the comprehensive or
particular nature of original undertakings in technical development has been almost certified by national-defense secrecy.
Ninety-nine percent of the original more-with-less invention
revolution has been subsidized by the weapons programs of
the major nations. Up to World War I all the drawings and
calculations of all the world's navies' ships were methodically
destroyed as soon as each ship was built, up to which moment they were the most carefully guarded of history's secrets.

During the first half century of the airplane, the major sovereign powers poured $2½ trillion directly and indirectly into
aircraft development as the new supreme weapon. Now in
one-third that time the world nations have again appropriated

almost as much capability wealth for the development of the
atomic-headed rocketry and space race, for supreme control
of the earth and its surrounding portion of the universe.

Most central to all the remote controlled more-with-lessing
of moon-landed rockets and ocean bottom exploring are the
swiftly multiplying transistorized electronic computers, one of
which can now, in one minute, print-out the solution to a
problem which a decade ago would have taken two years to
accomplish by the combined efforts of all those educated on
earth to calculate. Little wonder that 99% of humanity are
left millenniums behind, innocently and innocuously preoccupied in playing yesterday's irrelevant game of "everyday" serious "business," "politics," and "education."

Twenty-five years after the original, secretly developed doing-
only-more-killing-with-less-material-and-work-per-death as potentially realized in weapons and weapons-production technology—the, only inadvertently, *generalized do-more-with-less
capabilities*—of the tools-to-make-tools, that finally make the
special tools called "weapons"—99% of which tooling could
also make peaceful products—are secondhanded into the
domestic economics of world man to provide more life with less
effort. But this ultimate life-support upgrading occurs only after
the prime weapon contractors' respective weapons contracts ex-
pire and only as a result of the obsolescence of their respective
weaponry end-products.

While different political ideologies, as with the different
languages and customs as yet operative in yesterday's pirate-
decreed and natural-barrier-divided lands, are useful in organizing mankind's employment of the ever-swiftly improving, multiplying, and integrating industrial-tool network of
the invention revolution, by-producted from the weaponry-fo-
cused economies, it is becoming increasingly visible to ever
more people that the industrial network will soon integrate
society into a "one-town world" obliterating all national divisions of earth people, invented by the top pirates' competi-
tive-ambition strategies.

It is also increasingly clear to even more people that the
fundamental and highest priority responsibility for man's in-
terim-survival success on this little sun-orbiting spaceship,
Earth, does not fall directly within the problem-solving capabilities of political theory, nor with the results obtainable by
politics' ultimately greatest lever—war—hot, subversive,
cool, or cold. *Either war is obsolete, or men are.*

It is possible, at the present rate of performance per weight of employed resource gaining that, given 35 more years, the opposing ideologies' weapons-into-space race might go on, as in the past, to inadvertently produce enough additional by-product more-with-lessing to ultimately bring 100% of humanity into successful physical survival.

This is possible, however, only if men succeed in surviving on earth throughout that period.

During that only-by-crisis-after-crisis-stimulated 35 years development of ultra-ultra tools to make ultra-ultra weaponry the probability is close to "certainty" that one "Oswald" amongst four billion living and perplexed peoples will succeed in pushing one of the humanity-extinguishing buttons of the increasing number of sovereign possessed, omniauto-mated, interretaliation hookups to the comprehensive annihi-lation system. Assuming that humanity continues only to take the long way around by the protracted weapons-race "detour" —as the causative means of generating the new magnitude of more-with-lessing—competent scientists, integrating the proba-bility curves, now calculate that within 10-20 more years we will descend below the 50-50 chance that man will survive on earth.

But the same scientists conceded that the safe new super-highway leading directly to success for all is now ready for use. As pioneers in operating along that new highway, the world students' design-science revolution may possibly result in a general reorientation of world society's awareness, com-mon sense, and intelligence which, just in the "nick of time," will bring mankind into conscious promulgation of the do-more-with-lessing invention revolution to be applied directly to gaining man's living advantage, which can accomplish the 100% physical success of all humanity in less than one-half the time it would take to occur only as the inadvertent by-product of further weapons detouring of human initiative.

But the students are aware that in considering the reorien-tation of mankind to comprehend and directly employ gen-eral systems theory and design science that they must first clarify the history of the problem. The students recognize that the scientific development of world-holocaust weapons have thus far occurred only as the competitive, anticipatory, massive defense moves of what have been up to now power-ful but minor percentage groups of the total world popula-tion, undertaken on the economic premise of all-the-yester-days that there was not enough vital sustenance on earth to support more than a small minority of all men. This point was esoterically established, exclusively for the establishment, by Malthus and fortified by Darwin a century and a half ago. "Survival only of the fittest." As a consequence those in power in the "have" nations used their highest capabilities to back their fears for the worst. None of them was enlightened by the startling knowledge that now looms on man's horizon, that there is potentially ample for all, which can be made a reality in 20 years.

Now, for the first time in history, those in highest office in the most powerful sovereign nations have been confronted for ten years with scientific confirmation of the new economic potential, which may be realized, however, only through diversion of the high-priority science and industry from weaponry to "livingry" production. Each of the sovereign nations' "top men" cannot but wish with all his heart to move in the direction of realization of peace, through abundance for all, by risking more than perfunctory disarmament. The leaders are deterred from so doing, however, not by the intransigence or treachery of "the enemy" as the propagandized public-enemy image would suppose, but by their own political party without whose support they would have no chance of ratification of their acts. Their own party is deterred from such support by the constant threat of unseating not by the "enemy," but by their political-party adversaries within their own respective national, political systems. The opposition, counting on long-conditioned self-interest, popular skepticism, indignation, and fear, insists that any softening of military "posture" is ethically exploitable as the means of a party coup. Posture softening, it is politically asserted by the opposition, could only be occasioned by madness or by secretly treasonble acts warranting immediate and vindictive takeover by the opposition.

It comes to those who discover it, all round the world, as a dismaying shock to realize that continuation of the weapons race and of cold and hot warring is motivated only by intramural party fears of local political disasters. The world's political fate does not rest with leaders at the summit, expressing the will of world people, but with the local ambitions and fears of lower-echelon political machines, within the major weapons-possessing nations, whose vacillation is accompanied by an increasing spread of the atomic-weapons-possessing nations whose respective internal politics will forever frustrate disarmament by political initiative. All political machine professionals of all political states will always oppose loss of sovereignty for their own state. Solution of the impasse, if it comes at all, must clearly come from other than political initiative.

It is true, the world university students point out, that throughout all history up to now man has been faced with not enough to go around; not even for the survival of more than a small minority. It has always been—you or me. Swift you-or-me by the sword or gun has often been preferable to slow death by slum rot or slavery. The direct and conscious design-science revolution backed by the students can and may, by production of enough for all, accomplish elimination of the lethal you-or-me dictum and its political bias support.

Now, for the first time in history, employing its literary voices, world society can give design science its popularly mandated priority over political initiative with realistic hope as the impelling motivation. As 100% of humanity achieves, or nears, physical-survival success, past history's seemingly inexorable reason for war (not enough for both of us) will have been eliminated.

The students argue that if they can make man conscious of his design-revolution potential, and of the feasible and practical means of its accomplishment—the probability of pushing the annihilation button will be diminished from "critical" to "remote" status.

It seems apparent to students that—for whatever functional purposes man has been included in the design of the universe—nature has been, and continues to be, intent upon mankind's survival in his most physically successful and intellectually useful condition, wherefore, in view of man's historically vast ignorance and fear, nature has employed those predominant "game-motivating" negatives to impel him unconscious, even as she impelled him through the womb, toward this moment of dawning awareness of realistic hope and birth of his responsibility and intellectual initiative. The inadvertent doing-more-with-less as a by-product of the weaponry race seems, retrospectively, to have been nature's trick for developing man's highest potential, while also saving him from his own shortsighted "game-playing" ignorance.

It is inconceivable that one man, one party, one nation, or even a world congress of all mankind's representatives meeting a century ago (1865)—when a million dollars was an almost incredible sum, could have had the vision, logic, and courage to elect to invest $5 trillion in the invention and development of the then uninvented and economically unanticipated telephone; electric light; radio; airplane; jet and rocket flight; nuclear reactor; flight into space; world-around television; elimination of both bacterial and virus diseases; discovery and isolation of 60 additional chemical elements and their electrons, and nuclear components; and the genetic code; together with the ten million additional, mutually interadvantaging technical inventions and discoveries which have occurred in the last century; plus development of industrial mass production and its progressive industrial-production-capacity-geared accrediting of the paper-financed mass-consumption industry; tripling of human longevity and the support of three times as many people on earth, half of them at standards of living better than any king has ever known. Those who suggest that it might all have developed peacefully and purposefully through a shift in political doctrine are as unrealistic as are those who now think that the old public laissez-faire and political-initiative-only patterns can continue without man's annihilating himself; as are those who cannot see that the world students have found a first tiny view of a realistically hopeful blue-sky future.

When they are available to him, a healthy man each day eats 3 pounds of food, drinks 6 pounds of water, and breathes 60 pounds of air. Food has often been scarce, water sometimes scarce, but air almost always plentiful. Where there is abundance, competition is unnecessary and unthought-of. When, however, fire in a theater suffocates them, men trample one another to death in the desperate panic of the unaccustomed competition for air. There is nothing unnatural about the elimination of health competition in the presence of universal bountifulness of a vital resource. Though wars are precipitated by and identified by irrelevant and superficial yet emotionally preoccupying "causes" which are popularly sloganizable, wars have always occurred because of the underlying inadequacy of vital supplies. We will always have war until there is enough to support all humanity.

Science and engineering say the design science's peaceful accomplishment of 100% industrialization and its comprehensively bounteous support of man is eminently feasible. It is feasible because the world's economy is now operating at the appalling low overall mechanical efficiency level at which only 4% of the energy consumed is realized as effective work. Reciprocating engines are 15%, turbines 30%, jet engines 65% efficient. Efficiencies of 72% in atomic reactors

—employing their by-product heat in desalination—and up to 80% in fuel cells are now everyday design realities. Increasing the overall mechanical efficiency of the world's prime movers and machinery to only 10% from the present 4% will result in 100% of mankind being benefited by higher living standards than the present highest.

In addition to the world students' reorientation of the public from prime dependence on politics to prime dependence upon design science, there are now in evidence several other hopeful and highly realistic trends toward elimination of the political impasse to be accomplished by accelerating the more-with-lessing to the advantage of all men. Completion of the ultrahigh-voltage world network integration of electrical-energy distribution, under the Bering Straits, which is now clearly possible well within the 20-year trend, will automatically increase the world energy efficiency to an overall of 20%. This energy-distributing network linking the day and night hemispheres of earth will reduce the local standby power losses by 25%. The staggering economical advantage accruing to both public and private sectors has thus far caused both to join unreservedly in its development. The decisions of both public and private sectors to subscribe to their mutual interoperation was never taken as a consequence of interpersuasion by one another or of victory of one over the other. The persuasion came exclusively from the unbiased calculations of computers. The machine showed both sides that they would each profit beyond previous dreams by "integration." The computers will play a swiftly increasing, dominant role in the decisions of men—leading him away from "policy" or political impasse and toward total physical success.

Because energy is wealth, the integrating world network means access of all humanity everywhere to the total operative commonwealth of earth.

Wealth cannot alter yesterday. It can only alter today and tomorrow.

Multiplication of wealth began when man stepped on the long end of a log lying across another log with its short end under another big log, and he saw the big log, which was too heavy for him to lift with his muscles, lifted easily by gravity pulling his minuscule weight against the high-advantage arm of the lever. When man fastened a set of levers radially around the hub of a wheel and put the wheel under a waterfall and connected the wheel with a grinding mill, he learned to stand aside from the work and, gaining perspective, to use his brain to rearrange energy patterns to do more, and more fundamental, man-advantaging work.

Man found that the vast *associative* (gravity, matter) and *dissociative* (radiation) *energy patternings* of universe can be harnessed, shunted, and valved by man to impinge on levers and trains of gears ad infinitum.

Man is now learning through the repeated lessons of experimental science that wealth is explicitly the organized and operative tool and energy capability to sustain his forward metabolic regeneration; to protect him physically; to increase his knowledge and degrees of freedom while decreasing his interfrustrations. Wealth, he finds, is inherently regenerative. Experimentally demonstrated wealth is: energy compounded with intellect's knowhow.

Science's Law of Conservation of Energy states that "energy cannot be created or destroyed." The *first constituent* of wealth—energy—is therefore irreducible. Sciences states that the entire physical universe is ENERGY. $E = Mc^2$.

Every time man uses the second constituent of wealth—his knowhow—this intellectual resource automatically increases.

Energy cannot decrease. Knowhow can only increase.

It is therefore scientifically clear that wealth which combines energy and intellect can only increase, and that wealth can increase only with use and that wealth increases as fast as it is used. The faster-the-more! Those are the facts of science. Those are the facts of life.

The students know that they can generate more wealth through their cooperative initiative than in competition with each other. Cooperation generates commonwealth. They need not be concerned about "making a living" for themselves. By dedicating themselves to research in "how to make the world work for all in the shortest possible time" they will be realizing the only living now possible which is for all or none.

Professor John R. Platt, Chicago University physicist and biophysicist, in a thorough survey of the overall shapes of a family of trend curves which comprehensively embrace science technology and man in universe, says: "The world has become too dangerous for anything less than Utopia."

Man's reflexes are conditioned to brush aside that statement on the grounds that "Utopia" has become synonymous with the "unrealistic" or "impossible." This is because the many past attempts to establish Utopias all failed. The fact is that all past attempts were unrealistic before they started. All

the historical Utopian attempts occurred when it was assumed that Malthus was right and that there never would be
enough physical resources for more than 1% of humans to
live out their potential fourscore and ten years in comfort;
nor for more than one ten-thousandth of 1% to live it out in
precarious luxury as well as comfort; nor for any to live out
their full span in health, safety, comfort, luxury, good conscience, and happiness. The latter would, of course, be the
minimum requirements for everybody in the establishment of
Utopia. That is why their attempts were "unrealistic" in the
light of their working knowledge that those conditions could
not then be met or even dreamed of.

It was said at that time that "man cannot lift himself up by
his bootstraps." No one thought in the terms of doing-more-
with-less. No Utopians thought of airplanes as a possible reality, nor in terms of aircraft engines multiplying thousandfold
in power while simultaneously reducing their engine and air-
frame weights per horsepower by 99%. No one thought of
communications going from wire to wireless with enormous
gains in distance accomplished per unit of invested materials,
as well as a manifold reduction of weight and energy per
each frequency-tuned message circuit; none thought of a
1/10-ton Telstar satellite outperforming 75,000 tons of transatlantic cable.

The great transformation of man's physical capabilities by
scientific industrialization, which alone could provide the
physical environment and harnessed energy adequate and essential to a Utopian level of metabolic-regeneration success
for all humanity had neither occurred nor even been as yet
scientifically conceived. As so far experienced, in their day,
the would-be Utopians could reasonably think, for instance,
of bigger, more fireproof, more bow-and-arrow-proof stone
or brick walls instead of wood. They could think of common
austerity. They could think of having more cows, or more
acres, but experience, until then, gave them no thoughts of
the doing-more-with-less science and technology revolution.
Some cows gave more milk than others as some men were
taller than others. There was good or bad luck. There was
mystical blessedness or confoundment.

Not only did all the attempts to establish Utopias occur
prematurely (in respect of technological capability to establish and maintain any bacteria- and virus-immune, hungerless,
travel-anywhere Utopias), but all of the would-be Utopians
disdained all the early manifestations of industrialization as

"unnatural, stereotyped, and obnoxiously sterile." The would-be Utopians, therefore, attempted only metaphysical and ideological transformations of man's nature—unwitting any possible alternatives. It was then unthinkable that there might soon develop a full capability to satisfactorily transform the physical energy events and material structure of the environment—not by altering man, but by helping him to become literate and to use his innate cerebral capabilities, and thereby to at least achieve man's physical survival at a Utopianly successful level.

All the attempts to establish Utopias were not only premature and misconceived, but they were also exclusive. Small groups of humanity withdrew from and forsook the welfare of the balance of humanity. Utopia must be, inherently, for all or none. A minority's knowledge that the majority of humanity suffers and deteriorates while only the minority prospers would never permit a Utopian degree of contentment of the all-powerful subconscious reflexing of the human brain. In the far from Utopianly idealistic lives of history's "aristocratic" minorities, which were alone supportable by the known means and resource effectiveness of the preindustrial era, attempts were made by the successful minority to exclude thoughts of humanity's generally inexorable suffering by inventing "important" cultural preoccupations. However, dilettantism, sports, banquets, art patronage, flirtations, dueling, intrigue, and war failed to appease the subconscious reflexing of kings' and courtiers' brains. Their lopsided and twilighted conscience, therefore, imposed a code of affected blindness. This irrationality was propped up by an assumption of divine wisdom having placed a few in preposterous survival advantage over the many because of their superior wisdom, culture, and capability to fight for the less fortunate.

As a consequence, the poor illiterate masses built their churches and prayed that they and theirs be given strength to endure life, and that they be blessed—"blessed" means "wounded"—and possibly escape by death from unendurable life to a dreamed-of good life thereafter. All this is now changed, not because man has changed, but because man has found that he is endowed with a powerful brain which has found out what a few of the invisible principles operative in physical universe can do. But universe having permitted him to discover his intellectual effectiveness as well as some of universe's riches, and thus to participate consciously as well as only subconsciously in universal evolution, will now re-

quire him to use his intellect directly and effectively. Success
or failure is now all of humanity's responsibility.

The present top-priority world problem to be solved may
be summarized as how to triple, swiftly, safely, and satisfyingly, the overall performances per kilos, kilowatts, and
man-hours of the world's comprehensively invested resources
of elements, energy, time, and intelligence. To do so will render those resources—which at the present uncoordinated,
happenstance, design level can support only 44% of humanity—capable of supporting 100% of humanity's increasing
population at higher standards of living than any human minority or single individual has ever known or dreamed of and
will thus eliminate the cause of war and its weapons' frustrating diversion of productivity from the support of all mankind.

Because politicians will not dare to stop politicking, and
because income-supported individuals will not risk loss of
their incomes, and because the wage-earning world will not
dare to drop its income-producing activity to promulgate the
design-science achievement, it can only be undertaken by the
more or less freewheeling student world. If the student handling of its initiative is well done, then in the progressively
accelerating emergencies of human society, the significance of
the students' initiative will loom into increasing prominence
as their design inventions are put to work, soon in sufficient
degree to persuade the wage-earning adults to transfer their
efforts to support the student initiative. If this occurs within
the next decade, man may succeed in his continuance upon
earth. Because of the students' intuition and youth, the
chances are good!

When President Eisenhower was confronted by the data on
atomic warfare he said, "There is no alternative to peace,"
but did not define the latter or indicate how it could be se-
cured. Eisenhower's statement is akin to that of Professor
Platt's "The world has become too dangerous for anything
less than Utopia." Platt also failed to suggest how that might
be attained. Jerome Wiesner, head of the Department of Nuclear Physics at the Massachusetts Institute of Technology
and past science adviser to Presidents Eisenhower, Kennedy,
and Johnson, writing in a recent issue of *Scientific American,*
states, "The clearly predictable course of the arms race is a
steady downward spiral into oblivion." But he did say how it
could be arrested. Let us, too, at least give ourselves a chance
to vote to commit ourselves earnestly for the Design Science

Decade approach to attaining Utopia. This moment of realization that it soon must be Utopia or Oblivion coincides exactly with the discovery by man that for the first time in history Utopia is, at least, physically possible of human attainment.

10. Curricula and the Design Initiative

*Changes in Curriculum Intended to Prepare the
Individual to Take the Design Initiative in
Economic, Scientific, and Industrial
Technology Matters*

Taking the initiative means that the design scientist—like the medical scientist—will no longer operate on a basis of having to be retained by a client to carry out the client's prime design concepts.

The curriculum will prepare the design-science graduate to undertake fundamental invention, self-underwriting, development, and experimental proof of invention as demonstrated for instance by the Wright brothers wherein the design-science professional will be equipped with all of the economic, legal, and technological knowledge necessary for reducing such inventions to going industrial practice.

To realize such "breakthrough-magnitude" inventions—commercially, militarily, or even socially—involves the individual preparing himself for the competent taking of the initiative in a whole new industry and its progressive development, testing, prototyping, tooling, marketing, servicing, maintaining, operating, and phasing-in of progressive evolutionary components within the totally new industrial system together with designed phasing-out of equipment and functions made obsolete by the new industry. This, in turn, releases metals, and other materials, time, and energy resources for reinvestment in the newest phase of the evolutionarily emerging system.

*   *   *

1. The design scientist would not be concerned exclusively with the seat of a tractor but with the whole concept of production and distribution of food, which might possibly lead

293

to developing a whole new industry of hydroponic factories for automated growing, canning, and packing the food within large three-quarter-sphere geodesic greenhouses, within which are circularly operating, planting, cultivating, pruning, and harvesting mechanisms, in a treelike arrangement. He would initiate a total industry.

In short, it is assumed by the curriculum and professional initiative which I propose that the design scientist will not wait to be retained before tackling problems, and will not be concerned exclusively with carrying out the local detailing of a part of a component product within a general industrial venture system which has already been primarily designed by the *industrial client*.

2. Design-science-school students would be encouraged to organize themselves to study whole industries and the relationship of total industry to general society needs, e. g., what component disciplines such as chemistry, economics, etc., they must master will become self-evident and will be made available to them within the universities on the students' own scheduling. (See my "Designing a New Industry," 1946.)

For instance, one of the design-science schools might undertake to have all of its students spend all of their college years studying every aspect of the air-transport industry.

This study could start with the new ecology of world and space man. (See my addresses at Vision 65.) The students might undertake to redesign the whole industry of transportation service in such a way as to employ credit cards, computerized ticketing, and automated followthrough of the whole transportation process—with all its economic and technical ramifications—whereby a traveler can go to a vending machine in the nearest downtown office, or possibly to any hotel lobby or corner store. Possibly over his two-way TV facsimile, cable, or radio-beam closed-circuit system operating from any spot from which he may wish to initiate his travel. He will insert his credit card into the transmitter and press buttons showing the time that he would like to leave from one point and arrive at such and such another geographical point —anywhere around the earth, in the shortest possible time, and in the most economical way including terminal helicopter flights, automobile rentals, stopover hotel accommodation, etc.—and out will come from the vending machine a ticket printed with his routing and booked passage with the amount automatically charged to his credit card for officially automated accounting within his whole continually processed annual income and outgo along with the economic accounting of his whole social security, medicare, education, travel, and new-wealth-generating credit accounts.

Whenever necessary the traveler can cancel his ticket by putting his credit card back in any travel-vending machine and pushing the canceling button for the same routing, plus the transaction number which has been imprinted on the vending ticket when he received the machine's commitment to carry him.

Such booking-billing, clear-route-seeking, alternate-travel-plan-ascertaining computer systems will interlink the total information storage of all the airlines and their feeder systems anywhere around the world. The travel-vending machine, thus, will be able to print out commitments in split-seconds, or effect their cancellation in another split-second. The printed-out ticket will be all that is necessary for the individual to take with him as his automatic key-of-entry at the most convenient downtown embarkation point.

At his downtown airlines contact point he will enter his private traveling quarters and be transported therein to the point of major flight embarkation. His private traveling quarters will be within an angular segment of what I call a "fuselage cartridge." Each fuselage cartridge will be a circular section like a banana slice or like a Life-Saver mint candy, as one of many such circular units packed in parallel as a circular section of a cylinder cut perpendicularly to the cylinder's axis. The long tubular assemblies of these cartridge sections will fit together to form a complete cylindrical cartridge fitting neatly into the tubular-shaped fuselage of the air transport. There can be hundreds or more of these circular cartridge sections. Within any angular segment of one of these cartridge sections, the traveling quarters will provide the maximum sitting space without one human physically touching another human being. The integrity of each individual's privacy will be physically ensured by adequate space and omnidirectional design-science considerations. The planning will be omnidirectional and not just a planar expansion of the seat-row count. The sitting devices will convert to a full-length, horizontally reclining bed. The bed can move in space within the cartridge section by mechanical means.

The passenger's luggage will be stored within the same circular cartridge section in which he travels. The same circular cartridge section will hold several people and their luggage, can take a whole family, and can be curtained off for chamber privacy. All the people in any one cartridge section will be going to the same destination. A number of these circular cartridges with their passengers, and their luggage, will be joined together making an increasingly long cylinder through which runs a continuous walking passageway, or corridor, made up of the cartridge sections locked continuously together.

All of these separate destination-routed, circular, sectioned compartments, within each of which the individual may change his position of sitting to stretch out and in which whole families can be given private enclosures, each section having its separate toilet compartment, will be routed by helicopter lift from "downtown" to the dispatching airports. At the airports, the cartridge cross-sections will be loaded into the next transport bound for their particular destination, or series of destinations—the cartridges being loaded in proper sequence for detachment on jigs at their respective destinations. The combined cartridge sections, recombined at each airport, will be loaded through the open tail of the tubular fuselage as cargo loadings are made through the open tail of cargo planes.

Each of the cartridge sections will have circumferential trackage gears for smooth ball-bearing shunting into and out of the tubular fuselage or local marshaling racks on its own three annular roller bracings. The cartridges will slide into longitudinal aisle alignments and lock together, or be detached for local routing to downtown disembarkations. The cartridges, with corridors running through them, can be sandwiched together with freight and mail cartridge sections so that both passenger and cargo or freight will be automatedly dealt in or out of the various destination fuselages to be replaced by each airport's outbound cartridge group. This marshaling or separating-out and recombining of cartridge sections can be accomplished at each airport with computerized switching equipment.

The cargo sections can be swiftly let out or in at each marshaling point by gatewayed cartridge-holding tracks, which will at each point sort the cartridges anew for most economical flight aggregation, as continually processed evolutingly by the world traffic computers to most effectively integrate the unexpected new peaks and valleys of frequency and magnitude variations. Based on ever-accumulating past performance the computers will calculate probability at all times correcting as they go to the newest patterns of evolutionary changes. At destination airport, the passenger cartridge sections will be helicopter-lifted or vacuum-tube-sucked to the nearest down-town disembarkation points. The same world travel and freight traffic commuterization will not only take care of all hoteling and dwelling accommodation at "way" or destination ports but will clearly provide the guidelines for the future liv-ing-facilities industry's production and distribution require-ments. Such an overall living and travel-accommodation ser-vice industry may most probably be evolved through design science by a merging together of such present service-industry management corporations as the International Bell telephone system, hotel systems, etc.

Such general concepts can be worked on by a given de-sign-science school over a period of time as a continuing re-search in a given art. The students involved, and their fac-ulty, will be continually confronted with an awareness of all the disciplines essential to the individual in order to enable his most effective attack upon such comprehensive designing.

What will the student have to know to make it possible for him and his colleagues to reduce design-science research to effective practice, superior—in order to provoke use by hu-manity—to that already in operation?

What will those taking the design initiative need to do to eliminate frustrating contiguous industrial factors and social indifferences?

What will the students have to know, not only to make the most effective solutions, but to be able to make effectively known the results of their work to all industrial and govern-mental agencies as well as to the segments of the public con-cerned with use of their unique and comprehensive design-science innovations?

3. To undertake comprehensive, generalized system-theory research in a systematic manner by which the individual de-sign-science schools will each tackle an individual industry while correlating all their efforts one with the other on a world basis.

It will then be appropriate for the professional Design Sci-ence Society of the world and its various continental subso-cieties, as spokesmen for the profession, to coordinate the world-around design-science school curricula and to notify each and all the industries concerned of their undertakings and to make recommendations to the various industries regarding the progressive availability of the individual professional graduates most competent to carry out the finalizing phases of the new services to be provided.

This taking of the initiative and assumption of prime responsibility—vacated a third of a century ago by the "great world pirates" and left ignorantly by society to their political representations to discharge—all seems very new to the professional world of architecture, engineering, and all of the sciences other than the medical sciences. However, this is exactly the initiative and responsibility the medical sciences are already now shouldering in respect to man's internal organisms.

I propose that, in due course, design science—as the objective applied discipline accomplished by combined industrial design, engineering, architecture, and all the sciences—shall be so organized as to provide effective anticipatory strategies for formulating and managing the evolution of mankind's external, metabolic regeneration of the industrial self-organisms in the same anticipatory service manner that the medical profession has anticipatorily dealt with individual man's interior, organic processes of metabolic regeneration.

I propose that the comprehensive design initiative be officially seized by the professions. If it isn't done on the North American scene, it will be done elsewhere—possibly in Japan, China, or Russia—possibly in newly developing countries such as Africa, or Australia. It will be done! And, I am confident, in the very near future.

The professions now have the opportunity to "roll on" and "recover," and make a touchdown with the football fumbled a third of a century ago by the great pirates and ever since ineptly booted around by the world politicians in general—albeit each has "booted" the ball with his own degree of practical benevolence, according to the behavioral conditioning automatically manifest by the biases of the booters' respective environmental circumstances. Nobody has done anything wrong. We had to have almost overwhelming experience with failures to learn that we could be successful.

But from now on I think we must all assume that Malthus was wrong and thus it is normal for man to be a physical and economic success—that it is abnormal for any to be a failure —that man's preoccupation must be with his exquisite antientropic functioning in universe at-large and at-small—that by producing machines and tools that will produce more with less than was ever produced before, man must continually demonstrate the mastery of the physical by the metaphysical faculties with which he is endowed.

11. Design Strategy

Programmed to seek a weather-protected building site a worker wasp will sometimes fly in through open windows of human habitats. Failing to find the programmed requirements for a site, the wasp flies as programmed, back toward the light. Very frequently it runs into invisible window glass whose atoms are far enough apart to permit light and radio waves to pass through, but not wasps. The wasp crashes against the glass but its soft landing-gear readjusts its mechanisms whose arrested wingfoils, having lost their "lift," stall and allow the wasp to be pulled by gravity to a second crash on the window sill. From here it takes off on a spiral climb back into the room for a second and many successive flights outward toward the light. Only the "probability" statistics governing the chances of success with a half-open window and x numbers of flights, initiated from below the glazed portion of the window opening, can hold any hope for the wasp's avoiding ultimately lethal reencounters with the unprogrammed contingency—an invisible barrier.

Eddington said, "Science is the earnest and sustained intellectual attempt to set in order the facts of experience." Humans' intellects subjectively comprehend the wasp's problem but the wasp's sting is also a fact of human experience and despite a compassionate urge few humans are objective, energetic, and scientifically ingenious enough to invent safe ways of helping the wasp to escape. They think of the wasp instead of the window whose open half could be shifted from the top to the bottom—or whose glass portion could be covered opaquely with a newspaper, so that the wasp's light-seeking mechanism would steer safely only for the brightly illuminated, free, outward passage into the open air.

In short the humans spontaneously try to "shoo" the wasp, i.e., to reform the wasp's behavioral pattern instead of spontaneously thinking of how to reform the evironment so that the wasp would be spontaneously stimulated by the reformed environment to escape and thus terminate the interference episode between man and wasp.

The unprogrammed lethal frustration of wasps lends insights into many of humanity's present-day frustrated behaviors. The human's same fear-frozen, subconscious reflexes— usually mistakenly identified as apathy—plus their ineptitude in not "seeing" what to do about the wasps—is often redisplayed in their apathy and ineptitude in dealing with humanity's own sensorially inexplicable dilemmas.

Better than 99% of humanity's frustrations are occasioned by surprise encounters with the almost completely invisible evolutionary-transformation trendings of human ecology and the latter's environmental transformings. Also invisible and inaudible are the universal evolution's information-generating and -distribution systems which if adequately tuned in and integrated could warn mankind of such trendings as may be negative or even lethal to future human existence on earth.

We may bring thousands of wide-band radio sets into any room in any building anywhere around earth and tune each one in on different radio programs all of which thousands of simultaneous programs are always invisibly permeating and present everywhere within vast distances of space outward around earth. However, humanity's technical discovery and use of some of nature's invisible communication systems does not mean that he comprehends the universal evolution. Half the messages sent by humanity contradict the other half in respect to transpiring history.

During World War I—for the first time in history—industrial man's ecological-transformation processes entered into a comprehensively operating program which went predominantly beyond the sensorially apprehended ranges of human experience, experiments, communications, and realizations. In 1914-1918, humanity went from wire to wireless communication, from tracked to trackless transportation, from two-dimensional transport to four-dimensional, from visible structuring and mechanical techniques to invisible—atomic and molecular—structuring and mechanics.

As with airplane pilots operating instrumentally in night and fog, so today (1966) do humanity's myriad of specialized experts subjectively read or objectively program exquisitely differentiated, sub- or supravisible electromagnetic functions within the complex of routine or exploratory events of world embracing *industrioeconomic, ecological revolution.* The latter in turn—but altogether inadvertently—gives inex-

orable birth to a suprapolitical and suprageographical identity
—that of world man.

The essence of all the foregoing is that 99% of all important evolutionary trends are invisible. Ninety-nine percent are
either unapprehended or uncomprehended by society. The invisible, inexorable evolution will soon convert all nationally
and subnationally identified humanity into worldians, earthians,
or just plain omnispontaneously, universally coordinate, individual "people." The inexorable trending to one-world
citizenship is ignorantly and expeditiously opposed by the
sovereign nations' self-perpetuating proclivities. The sovereign nations own or control the communication systems
and preoccupy the systems with distintegrative news of the
disintegrative actions taken by the sovereign political entities.

Up to a century ago, 27 years was the average lifespan of
humanity—despite that a few exceptional humans of history
lived beyond their "fourscore years and ten," i.e., 90 years.
Up to a half century ago, it was assumed that only one
human in one hundred could be economically successful and
even then would only survive to an average age of 42 years.
Now in the 1960s, average expectancy of North American
industrialized man has reached 70 years, with two out of five
men an economic success as well. By 1970, the majority (i.e.,
more than 50% of all humans around earth) will be both
physically and economically successful—or there won't be
any humanity—save possibly a few hapless short-lived survi-
vors of the atomic holocaust.

For only the last decade of all history has total physical
and economic success for all humanity been conceded by science to be feasible. Realization of this extraordinary potential
is importantly frustrated, however, by several factors.

First it is frustrated by the as yet rigid geographical and
political partitioning of humanity under divisive and competitive ideological concepts, each purported to cope most effectively, only on a political bias basis, with locally sovereigned
groups of yesterday's on-foot to-and-froing humans and their
heretofore only but-one-in-one-hundred survival probability.
This self-entrapment by man in political straitjackets came
about through psychological and physiological events which
may be explained as follows.

Biology's two main branches—zoology and botany—disclose two main and clearly differentiated modes of survival
—static and mobile—with the giant trees and the world-
around voyaging whales at the two size extremes.

The biologically static are *subjectively advantaged*. The environment brings them what they need. The mobiles are *objectively advantaged* to "go" and get what they need or want.

After hunting fruits, nuts, herbs, as well as fish and other zoological game, fairly successfully for thousands of millenniums, man discovered that he could tame some of the game, which spontaneously performed its own regeneration. From this lesson man discovered that he could plant the vegetation's seeds and thus man started about eight millenniums ago to cease his wandering and to remain to guard the territories he found most favorable for his locally regenerative animal husbandry and agriculture.

Because man's legs are so short and the planet earth so big and because the few areas around it where he could find immediate vital support in his early days on the planet amounted totally to less than 5% of the earth's surface, man has mistakenly identified himself during the last eight millenniums with the rooted vegetation rather than with the mobile vertebrates of which type he is a member. Those few humans who found a local "good thing" dug in and the multitude of others hung hopefully and hungrily around the successful few's exclusive "property" which the economically successful successfully enacted as a concept into—strong-arm-enforced —laws of men.

Physical or "natural" law has no inherent static "property" law—only behavioral properties. Nature's laws of evolution defy all static patterns. Entropy breaks them up. "Ownership" is not immoral, amoral, or ethically unsound. Physical "ownership" is antientropic—ergo, eventually unsustainable. Metaphysical conceptualizations now are identifiable with individuals, which, in turn, are unique behavioral integrities. Democritus' concept of and sound-pattern identification of the phenomenon "atom" are forever identifiable as Democritus—i.e., as his intellect functioning. These individual metaphysical discoveries are not ownership identities. Democritus did not and does not own any atoms, but he is irrevocably identifiable with their conceptioning and naming.

Ergo: "ownership" of physical entities by man is untenable in natural law and inherently obstructive to evolution and realization of the comprehensive emancipation of man—from his ignorance-rooted failures, and from his imminently potential physical and economic success. However, unique service behaviors are identifiable with individuals and their respective creative capabilities. Only one's own "personality" and life are ownable. Only one's own inherently unique, chromosomically monitored, and experience-modified patterning integrity is ownable.

Secondly, the physical omnisuccess of all humanity is frustrated by the fact that scientific evolution—by which it could be accomplished—is almost entirely invisible and its integrated significances are too difficult for total and effective comprehension by society.

One reason for the latter frustration is that the language of science has been up to now almost exclusively mathematical —i.e., nonconceptual.

A second reason is that scientists altogether constitute less than 1% of the world population. Their thoughts are popularly unknown.

A third reason is that most scientists operate exclusively on a subjective basis—as "pure" scientists. They also operate nonconceptually. Most of the objective technologists—or "applied" scientists—are specialists and are unaware of the comprehensively integrated significance, to society, of the tasks they perform.

A fourth reason is that world society is frustrated by the communication barriers between the many languages of mankind.

For the foregoing reasons, there are only a very few humans whose experience and operative faculties permit and inspire them to inform society regarding the significance of the evolutionary trending and of mankind's now potential physical and economic success.

What could be done and up to now has been done in a big way, as a consequence of man's access to the vast energy wealth of universe, discovered by "purely" operating scientists, has not been determined by the technologists, but by their economic masters who see only the immediate highest profits—in, for instance, the exploitability of the fossil fuels, or "savings-account" energy wealth—in the most wholesale manner through national governments' commitments, most swiftly realizable in anticipation of the emergencies of total war. Science and technology operate economically and socially only as slaves of the most powerfully shortsighted cashiers of humanity's needs and weaknesses. The latter see less profit in organizing the business of humanity to survive on the energy income of the environment.

Realization of mutual success by all mankind is frustrated

also by the now entirely irrelevant and invalid "inferiority" or "failure" complex of world-around behaviors of humans, conditioned exclusively by two millions of years of experience with major failures of mankind, as well as with vital inadequacies of vital necessities; plus the ages-long, seemingly obvious, and seemingly inevitable fact that the vast majority must die at a relatively early age—either through starvation, disease, superstitiously governed human sacrifice, capital punishment, war, or dueling—as physical evolution whittled down the numbers surviving—to match the numbers supportable by the ignorantly and only opportunistically exploited—ergo, only shortsightedly and meagerly organized world resources.

The analogy to the wasp's dilemma occurs in humanity's long-conditioned, reflexively superstitious assumption that man is (with only "divine" exceptions) designed to be a failure. The "normal" human has always been a *potential* and *probable* failure. At an early age, the average human acquires a powerful inferiority complex from his exposure to his parents and his childhood community's deeply inhibited culture of *misinformation* and *misfortune*. The deep-seated proclivity of humans to gamble their moneys is founded on the working assumption of human consciousness that individuals are inherently programmed for failure and that only cultivated luck can divert the individual from his negative plight.

One reason why humanity in general loves, admires, and worships human babies is that all physically normal babies are both unblemished and are designed to be physically successful. They are swiftly blemished by man's ignorantly served love. If, despite his millenniums-conditioned failure-prone complex, man is to survive on the planet earth he must be educated to assume a new "norm" for humanity. Because of the facts world society must now assume that normal man is designed to be a success and the universe designed to support that success—for as we shall presently see, man is essential to the success of universe itself. If humanity on earth "flunks out" humanity on other planets will probably "carry-on" to perform the uniquely human, antientropic functions essential to the total regenerative evolution of universe.

To effect the successful transition of world society to the new "norm" of man as a physical and intellectual success can, and we hope will, be realized on spaceship *Earth* through the idealism of youth, as implemented by the educational-process revolution which is beginning to take place around the planet. If so, the reality of the new norm of success will be progressively fortified by the incorruptibility of the cybernated participation of man in evolutionary transformations of human ecology and on a continuous, instead of a short-term expediency basis.

And it is not a matter of being a little more farsighted and looking out for one or two more generations of man on earth. It is a matter of making man on earth a continuing success—forever.

It may be assumed that scientific and humanistic literacy must and will be popularly developed at the earliest moment in order to spontaneously obtain scientifically generalized comprehension and systematically and conceptually formulated sociotechnological answers to any and all moral economic, esthetic, and ethic questions, as well as objective answers regarding the relative harmonic desirability, feasibility, and economic practicality of any and all human preoccupations and capability commitments.

We must now ask, "What will emancipate science from its century of unnecessary 'blind flying' exclusively on instruments—as a slave profession—with lethal consequences—and without any sense of long-distance economic-success objectives for all of posterity?" We must also ask, "From whence will come the tools of conceptuality which will emancipate science and permit its assumption of the prime social, direct, conscious, sensorial responsibility?"

What can and will bring world society's leaders and world society itself to comprehend its economic potential and its essential function in universe and to its successful performance of that function—in time to permit the continuance in universe of the earthian team of humans?

It seems to me that our commitment to mutual examination of our respective functioning leads abruptly to these fundamental questions. I assume this to be so. I also assume that neither of us has innate characteristics making us uniquely fitter than others to address these questions. I assume, however, that both of us have come independently to the realization of the tasks to be done by world society and by individual men operating with integrity on their own initiative on behalf of their fellow humans. I assume that both of us has now unique experiences and organized information and accredited effort which provide us with some measurable degree

of intellectual, technical, and economic advantage in address-
ing these prime questions. On my part, I would like to contribute the following thoughts.

* * *

First, it seems to me that unless we have experimentally
demonstrable and scientifically definable meaning in our
words, we cannot communicate effectively with words. Communication is with self, as well as with others. Ergo, we may
say the degree of effectiveness of communication is propor-
tional to the degree of exactness of commonly accepted definition of meanings of the words used. This statement is a corollary of my long-held working assumption that a problem
adequately stated is a problem fundamentally ripe and potential of solution.

In seeking definitive meanings I recognize, of course, that
Heisenberg's principle of indeterminism forestalls *absolute exactness*. However, the tolerance of error is reducible. Ergo:
we may approach exactitude in progressive degree. Ergo:
what I mean by *mutual comprehension of meanings* is statable only in terms of *approximately exact meanings*.

It is also my working assumption that lacking the approximately exact meaning of the most profound generalized concepts there is little meaning and approximately no direct teleologic effectiveness in any and all special-case, local-experi-
ence communications. For instance, it is impossible to understand the previous sentence without a fundamental comprehension of the concept "teleology." It is also fundamentally
impossible for us to make conscious solution of the greatest
and prime problems and their secondary technical challenges
without use of the phenomenon teleology.

It is my working assumption that the following 40 questions must be definitively answered before we may realistically discuss our respective philosophies and grand strategies.

If we first accept mutually agreed-upon, experimentally
based definitions and answers to these questions as a priori to
our dialogue, we may then also observe the following to be
pertinent and useful to the initiation of our mutual search for
the definitive answers to the immediately foregoing set of
prime questions.

First, I refer you to my own attempts to make
experience-founded—ergo scientifically definitive—answers
to all 40 of the questions. Most of my attempts have

STRATEGIC QUESTIONS

1. What do we mean by universe?
2. Has man a function in universe?
3. What is thinking?
4. What are experiences?
5. What are experiments?
6. What is subjective?
7. What is objective?
8. What is apprehension?
9. What is comprehension?
10. What is positive? Why?
11. What is negative? Why?
12. What is physical?
13. What is metaphysical?
14. What is synergy?
15. What is energy?
16. What is brain?
17. What is intellect?
18. What is science?
19. What is a system?
20. What is consciousness?
21. What is subconsciousness?
22. What is teleology?
23. What is automation?
24. What is a tool?
25. What is industry?
26. What is animate?
27. What is inanimate?
28. What are metabolics?
29. What is wealth?
30. What is intuition?
31. What are esthetics?
32. What is harmonic?
33. What is prosaic?
34. What are the senses?
35. What are mathematics?
36. What is structure?
37. What is differentiation?
38. What is integration?
39. What is integrity?
40. What is truth?

been published in books, essays, and lectures. I do not assume that I have found the answers. I do assume that I have addressed the problems on a scientific basis for I have, as Eddington put it, "made a sincere attempt to set in order the facts of experience." I have progressively *included* and *refined* the experience basis of those meanings and have progressively refined their verbalization. I have thus discovered, for instance, that there are no nouns, for physics has found no things (static, solid phenomena)—ergo there are only verbs.

Though there are many special concepts which constantly reoccur in my day-to-day deliberations, I find that there are 14 which dominate. All of them overlap integratingly. Part of the content of one will of necessity often reappear under other concepts due to the synergetic interactions. I will group and discuss all the secondary concepts, unique to my philosophy, under the following 14 main concepts:

DOMINANT CONCEPTS

1. Universe
2. Humanity
3. Children
4. Teleology
5. Reform the Environment
6. General Systems Theory
7. Industrialization
8. Design Science
9. World Service Industries
10. Ephemeralization and Invisible Commonwealth
11. Prime Design Initiative
12. Self-Disciplines
13. Comprehensive Coordination
14. World Community and Subcommunities of World Man

CONCEPT 1—UNIVERSE

Noninstantaneity. Nonsimultaneity. Physical and metaphysical regeneration. Irreversibility of evolution. Irreversibility of metaphysical comprehension of physical.

I start with my own definition. *Universe is the aggregate of all humanity's all-time, consciously apprehended, and communicated experiences.* (The communication may be to self or others—it is the apprehending formulation of the information regarding the experiences that constitutes original consciousness.)

The physicists' Law of Conservation of Energy which states that *energy may be neither created nor destroyed— ergo is finite*—embraces only the *physical* aspects of experience. It *excludes all metaphysical* aspects of experience.

I have defined universe in such a manner that none may present experimental proof of its inadequacy for *my definition includes* both the objective and subjective: i.e., all *voluntary experiences*—i.e., *experiments*—as well as all *involuntary experiences*—i.e., all happenings.

My definition embraces both the physical and the metaphysical, the latter being all the weightless experiences of thought which include all the mathematics and the organization of the data regarding all physical experiments, science, both first and last, being metaphysical.

The metaphysical includes the mind-extracted, refiningly concentrated, and consciously formulated antientropic generalizations, in a hierarchy of progressively contracting degree, which most economically describe the working of the metaphysical subdivision of universe.

My definition of universe inherently includes all the ponderable—i.e., weighable, instrumentally detectable, associative and disassociative, material and radiational energy behaviors of the physical subdivision of universe.

CONCEPT 2—HUMANITY

Human function in universe. Entropy and antientropy.

Is the human an accidental "theatergoer" who happened in on the "play of life"—to like it or not—or does humanity perform an essential function in universe? We find the latter to be true. The discovery develops as follows.

By *entropy,* I refer to the experimentally demonstrated physical behaviors covered by the Second Law of Thermodynamics and the latter's disclosure of the omniaccelerating-acceleration of the diffusion of physical-energy patternings of universe—spoken of by the mathematical physicist as the "Law of Increase of the Random Element," which may also be called the "Law of the Expanding Universe." As the stars are all in complex motions, the radiations given off by them are ever more diffusely dispatched.

By *antientropy,* I refer to the omniaccelerating-acceleration of the clarifyingly differentiated and intercommunicated, experience-derived pattern cognitions of the human mind which progressively disclose the orderly complex of omni-interactive, pure, weightless, and apparently eternal principles governing the intellectual design and operation of the—seemingly and "suggestively" only—infinitely self-regenerative universe.

We may call this metaphysical phenomenon—which continually *simplifies* and *contracts* the generalized description of principles apparently operative in all special-case experiences —the "Law of Decreasing Confusion," or the "Law of Intellectual Conservation," or the "Law of the Contracting Universe," or the "Law of Diminishing Chaos," or the "Law of Progressive Order," or the "Law of Contractively Orderly Generalizations."

Radiation is physical, entropic, incoherent, propelling, disassociative, pushing. The logical questions arise: Is gravity metaphysical, antientropic, coherent, and tensive? Are *gravity* and *order* wrested and collected intellectually from chaos? Is intellect a priori to both physical and metaphysical universe? Is the tensional integrity of universe exclusively an intellectual-integrity phenomenon and a consequence only of intellectual exploration and measurements?

While gravity's effects are physically measurable, the *concept* of gravity is in itself unweighable. Likewise the effects of electromagnetism are physically weighable. The physicists have ruled intellectually that all that is imponderable is metaphysical. Clearly it is seen that the metaphysical is to the physical as antimatter is to matter, i.e., as the electron is to the positron.

Metaphysics and *physics* are thus seen to cofunction, to conserve progressively the self-regeneration of nonsimultaneously and overlappingly evolving universe. Man's function in universe is metaphysical and antientropic. He is essential to the conservation of universe which is in itself an intellectual conception. In 1951 I published my conclusion that man is the antientropy of universe. Norbert Wiener published the same statement at the same time. Both of us arrived at our conclusions by different routes and without knowledge of the other's discovery. I will now expand on the human's antientropic functioning.

In the above statements I am giving precise meaning to the word "metaphysics." By metaphysical I mean no more nor less than is implicit in my definition of universe. Since magic has never been experimentally demonstrated, my use of the word "metaphysics" does not contain overtones of magic or mysticism.

"Why universe?" is at present an unanswerable inquiry into the mystical. Though "mystical" sounds like a contraction of "metaphysical," they are not the same. For this reason, I consider all time spent in speculation regarding the inherently unanswerable to be inherently profitless and a squandering of the opportunity to answer those questions which are answerable by man. It is, however, experienced by us that the unanswerables provoke a sensation in us to which we allude— only intuitively—as "mysterious."

By the same reasoning, I discredit all the speculations which suggest or persuade the concept of a "beginning or ending" of universe. The most recent statements of the leading scientists hold that the concept of *original chaos* is untenable because the physical composition of universe may not be reduced to less than the orderly intertransformability of the neutron and the proton and their respective weak-effect left-ness-and-rightness adjuncts the electron, positron; neutrino, antineutrino—the positive and negative counterparts including both their negative as well as positive weights, ergo: *the average of all weight of all physical phenomena is zero.*

This is to say that the universe, both physical and meta-physical, is resolvable into a set of principles which are ever-more-accurately (but never exactly) described by the scientists' weightless intellectual generalizations. And generalized principles which are weightless cognitions of intellect have no inherent beginning or ending (nothing in human experience has ever suggested the beginning or ending of a generalized principle)—ergo the "beginning" of universe concepts together with all axioms are experimental or unproven and only superficially obvious fictions. Before the measurements of the speed of radiations, all phenomena seemed (erroneously) to be visually "instant." This gave rise to the superstitiously invented legend of a genie or god creating an instant universe. A physicist said to me a few days ago: "I have become bored with the nonsense concept of infinity—with one end closed by a 'beginning' and the other end open to infinity."

Universe, by definition, and its derivative concepts are *synergetic. Synergy,* as you know, means *unique behaviors of whole systems unpredicted by any behaviors of their component functions taken separately.*

Some of ancient Greece's natural philosophers and geometers took effective advantage of synergy when they recognized that the sum of the angles of a plane triangle is always 180°, or exactly one-half of cyclic unity—with unity taken as 360°—ergo unity equals two triangles. I assumed in 1917 that "unity is plural and at minimum two."

The stable structural behavior of a whole triangle, which consists of three edges and three individually and independently unstable angles or a total of six components, is not predicted by any one or two of its angles or edges taken by themselves. The six edges of the two triangles can and frequently do associate with one another, one as left helix and the other as a right helix, to form the six-edged tetrahedron which having four triangular faces gives synergetic demonstration of four triangles occurring as the result of associating only two triangles. Incidentally, the right and left helixes formed of the two triangles' respective sets of three edges each constitute the vectorial modeling in conceptual array of the positive and negative "half spins" or "half quanta" corresponding respectively to the proton set and the neutron set consisting of neutron, positron, and neutrino on the left hand and the proton, electron, and antineutrino on the right hand. Together these six make one quantum unit—which is identified as the tetrahedron.

Triangles as conceived by the Greeks are synergetic. The Greeks went on to demonstrate the corollary of synergy, to wit, that the known behavior of the whole and the known behavior of some of the components makes possible predictions of the behavior of each and all of the other, previously unknown components.

The Arabs' algebraic formulations and all the modern derivatives, including the calculus, are synergetic strategies.

This synergetic strategy of proceeding from the whole to discover discrete local particulars within the whole was demonstrated powerfully once again a century ago in Euler's topology which reduced all patterning of universe to lines, intersections of lines—called "vertexes"—and the areas bound by three or more intersecting lines. Euler found a constant mathematical relationship of all these three fundamental aspects of pattern i.e., $V + A = L + 2$.

The power of synergy was demonstrated once again by physicists in modern quantum mechanics—in which the assumption of a finite physical-energy universe always requires a 100% accountability of all energy transactions. Synergetic accounting of the finite system plays a major part in the success of modern nuclear physics.

Kepler's Third Law and Newton's theory of gravity provided synergetic advantage for astronomy. Willard Gibbs' Phase Rule—akin to Euler's topological equation of the relative abundance of basic mathematical pattern aspects—provided synergetic advantage in chemistry.

Synergetic behavior is omnimanifest in biochemistry and metallurgy. Synergy alone explains, for instance, why the tensile strength of chrome nickel steel is 50% stronger than the *sum* of all its constituent alloys' respective tensile strengths. Synergy is the "backbone" of general systems theory.

Despite the powerful capabilities demonstrated historically by synergetic strategy today's primary educational systems, all around the world, start the children's would-be education only with *elementary parts* of subdivisions which never explain the wholistic behaviors and thus imply that science and technology may only be successful as a myriad of separate intricate specializations which can never be subject to unified comprehension by one mind.

Specialization—therefrom today's chain reaction of the self-accelerating fractionation of all thinking into exploding categoritis—resulted from the old master pirates' pre-World War I's *synergetic strategy* by which they required that all the bright lieutenants and experts confine their labor and inquiry to differentiation, and that each must *mind his own business* and must eschew all integration which they must concede to be the old "master" pirates' exclusive prerogative.

Thus, the elementary educational system, which in contrast to synergy starts exclusively with a few parts or elements, leads at best only to differentiated *statistical probability* based entirely on the separate behaviors of those elementary parts. *Probability,* the strongest tool of statistics which deals only with parts, at its best is a weak tool. Were probability strong it would predict stock-market behavior with precision and would foretell horse race results with reliability. Contrariwise, synergy and general systems theory are *powerful* forecasting tools and have been the backbone of modern physics, astronomy, and chemistry.

My 14 concepts—taken one by one and considered only in the "separate," elementary educational manner—might seem too special and too diffuse to be effective. Taken altogether, synergetically, I hope you will find them as promising as I have already found them to be.

If I had not been consciously and deliberately pursuing all 14 concepts synergetically and teleologically for the last 38 years and if I had not obtained innumerable practical results, I would not be a position now to know you and to be asked to exchange grand-strategy information with you.

Within the last 14 years, thousands of my structures have gone to 50 countries around S.S. (spaceship) *Earth.* They were most frequently transported to their sites by air, fully assembled or in systematically coded and tightly packaged parts. I have succeeded therefore within only 38 years in demonstrating the validity of my proposal (published in 1927) to commence in 25 years—1952—the air delivery of high-performance environment controls for those of mankind's activities most advantageously performed under scientifically protected and valved conditions. In 1953 the U.S. Marine Corps made the first air delivery of my geodesic

dome, fully assembled and skinned, flying it to its site by helicopter at 60 nautical miles per hour. I prophesied this in 25
years. It took 26.

The year in which I first made this proposal—1927—was
that in which Lindbergh made his epochal nonstop New
York City-to-Paris flight in an airplane with cloth-covered
wingfoils. International airplane-passenger service was not as
yet even seriously discussed. Jet propulsion, rocketry, television, fission, transistors, cellophane tape, computers, highway
cloverleafs, staplers, stainless steel, high-strength aluminum,
uranium, the Great Crash, the Depression, Hitler, World War
II, juvenile delinquency, and atomic bombs were unanticipated, unthought-of, or held to be only fantastic possibilities
realizable, if at all, one thousand years hence. Discussions of
rocket trips to the moon were engaged in only by lunatics in
mental institutions. Only 23 years ago when I attended World
War II meetings in Washington, D.C., I was often greeted by
someone saying, "Please don't ruin this meeting by once
again introducing your preposterous, mass-produced, scientifically designed air-deliverable houses."

As a consequence of my finding both the metaphysical and
physical subdivisions of universe to be finite I have also discovered the finite, arithmetical, geometrical, energetical, rationally coordinate comprehensive mensuration system employed by nature to rationally integrate the physical and metaphysical and have thereby also provided a conceptual and
definitive bridge of understanding between the humanities and
the sciences. I am confident that the comprehensiveness of
my 14 concepts rather than being overambitious represents
the "minmaxfamfax" (minimum and maximum family of
prime variable factors) uniquely governing general system
theory.

Such (only intellectually discovered and only intellectually
employable) principles are apparently amongst the most powerful thus far to have become available to man. The a priori
(and only intellectually conceivable) complex of self-regenerative, intertransformative (macromicro), cosmic-ranging
scale of generalized principles governing nonsimultaneous
universe—thus far discovered by man only in "piecemeal"
isolations—is now disclosing a comprehensive interrelatedness
unanticipated by man at the time of the individual explorations. This total interrelatedness and its orderliness and mathematical elegance are obviously transcendental to the inven-

tive capabilities of individual man. For these reasons, taken
synergetically, there is evidenced to science an a priori, omni-
functioning intellection greater than that demonstrated or demonstrable by humans.

*   *   *

Are we not most intimate, i.e., closest with, those furthest
away from us physically, ergo closest metaphysically? No
rapport between individuals "sardine-packed" in subways and
buses. Intimacy of those writing to one another halfway
around the world. This relative intimacy may be plotted in
terms of time, history, and geography. All those who influence us daily by love, wisdom, conceptual stimulation, and
understanding are most often relatively remote both in time
and space. Most of the time the powerful influences are the
immortal influences, i.e., "most remote."

The human function in universe and its individual, fleet-
ingly sensed responsibilities—heeded or unheeded by the individual—occur as the consequence of "built-in" driving forces,
the metabolic, physical-regeneration drives of *hunger and
procreation.* The most prominent of the metaphysical-regen-
eration drives are human curiosity and the drive to demonstrate competence, i.e., to employ the abilities to subjectively
differentiate and thereafter to objectively integrate in preferred patterns or to organize events in such a manner as to
obtain answers to the questions which curiosity asks—metaphysical drives—to understand and be understood.

The dual and regenerative human functioning as successive
high-frequency subjective and objective (subconscious and
conscious) which altogether provide *angular rangefinding* and
the *teleologic irreversibility* of human articulations are implemented exclusively by two principles with which humanity
modifies his forward experiences in universe in preferred
ways. The two physical principles by which alone man may
alter his ever-evolving environment are those of *angular* and
frequency modulations. Angular modulation (cf. ruddering)
is erroneously spoken of by man as spatial modification. Fre-
quency-of-event modulation is erroneously spoken of by humanity as time modification. These capabilities of man's
senses, brain, and mind provide the basis for his strategically
selective differentiations of experience. The humans' subjective experiences are teleologically and spontaneously transformed into objective alterations of the evolutionary environ-

ment—to most effectively support man's unique brain and mind functioning in universe in the antientropic role.

It is the intent of my concept 2 to bring about most effective employment of those built-in drives of individuals in such a manner as to bring about the physical success and happiness of all humanity in the shortest time with the least effort.

It is my intent to employ the built-in capabilities to accomplish all the foregoing without ever advantaging one by deprivation of another. It is the purpose of my concept 2 to so design or control the angles and frequencies of the evolving environment events that the spontaneous reflexing of society will result in all men enjoying all of earth—and the progressive reaches of the universe about it—without mutual interference with one another's degrees of subjective and objective freedoms.

CONCEPT 3—CHILDREN

Focus of human effort on the critical first 13 years of life —wherein 98% of brain function is progressively and automatically "tuned-on," "tuned-in," "tuned-out," or shut-off in direct response to the positives or negatives of the individuals' environmental experiences and potentials.

Focus on new life. Recognizing that humanity consists of all ages, it is obvious that before any of the objectives of one have become fulfilled many human individuals and particularly the aged will have died. As a consequence, it becomes necessary to set up *time* and *beneficiary* priorities within the total scheme.

The behavioral sciences have disclosed the direct effects of the environment on new life. These are so great as to make it clear that the environment (including all the dynamic events and humans operative within the "scenery") is more than 99% responsible for lives becoming capable and happy or frustrated and confounded. And the most profound effects on human life have been completed within the first seventeen years. Ninety-two percent of the environment's positive or negative effects have been wrought upon the new life by age thirteen. Eighty percent have been wrought by age of eight, and 50% by age of four. It is obvious that effective work that can be done in advantaging life through favorable environment transformation can be realized within the first thirteen years of human life and particularly in the first four years of life.

In order for the individual to be objectively effective as a design scientist in altering the environment on behalf of his fellowman, it is necessary for him to organize his efforts so that they may become operative a sufficient number of years ahead of his original initiating to be able to transcend any frustration of his efforts by the momentum of already invested interests. This period has been discovered to be one generation, or 25 years. My work was initiated in 1927 and was designed to become effective in 1952. This proved to be a realistic forecast. In 1952, Ford Motors bought a large geodesic dome.

Combining the concept of the time lags and most effective period for advantaging life, my concept 3 came to focus on *advantaging the new life*—to protect the new life prominently from one to four; secondarily on four to seven; thirdly on seven to thirteen; and lives of the parents to be advantaged.

CONCEPT 4—TELEOLOGY

The)conscious deliberations and decisions of the human mind which reorganize the subconsciously fed-back informations. The philosophic reduction of a plurality of subjectively experienced pattern cognitions into conceptually recognized (imagined) patterns of generalized principles to forwardly control specifically anticipated events by designed modifications of environment patterns.

Generalized, comprehensive, and anticipatory design science.

The philosophy of my 14-point strategy derives from my intuition that all experiences may be progressively generalized and that man thus discovers that only a few principles govern all the multirate, nonsimultaneous, transformative interstructuring transformations of nonsimultaneous universe. It becomes obvious that the *subjectively* apprehended data and the intellectually recognized data interrelationships concerning the abstracted principles—governing evoluting universe —provide the individual with high potential for the *objective* realization of advantages for humanity. Teleology means "the intuitive conversion by brain and mind of special-case subjec-

DESIGN-SCIENCE EVENT FLOW

subjective

(search

research)

> teleology
> intuition
> conception
> apprehension
> comprehension
> experiment
> feedback

* * *

generalization

objective

development

reduction to

practice

regeneration

> prototyping #1
> prototyping #2
> prototyping #3
> production design
> production modification
> tooling
> production
> distribution
> installation
> maintenance . . . service
> reinstallation
> replacement
> removal
> scrapping
> recirculation

tive experiences into generalized principles and their subsequent objective employment in special-case undertakings."

The discovered principles governing the intertransformative structuring of universe permit the subconsciously teleological and conscious design-initiating individual to reform the environment in such a manner as to provide ultimately higher advantage for men and in such a manner as to regenerate in other individuals the drive to further transform the environment to even higher advantage for all. The design may increase the degrees of freedom of individuals by reducing environmental interferences or it may decrease freedoms as with traps and prisons.

C. H. Waddington, University of Edinburgh geneticist, speaks of the "epigenetic landscape" in identifying the powerful effects on human behavior played by environmental factors. Waddington shows how man and other factors alter the environment and how the altered environment alters the human and other biological behaviors and how the whole process becomes regenerative and continually interaccelerates. He does not show or suggest that the environment alters man's physical organism or that the environment adds capabilities to the human's innate capabilities, but does indicate the way in which arbitrarily favorable changes in the environment may permit a higher percentum of realizations and development of the innate human brain, body, and mind capabilities. theretofore inactive—only because frustrated by unfavorable regenerative alterations of the environment. Thus we see that human evolution is not confined to organic life alone, but also consists of reciprocal interactions of all the combined transformations of the environment and all it contains. This combined regenerative evolution has now attained a "chain-reaction rate" around the surface of the spherical spaceship *Earth*.

CONCEPT 5—REFORM THE ENVIRONMENT

Don't attempt to reform man. An adequately organized environment will permit humanity's original, innate capabilities to become successful. Politics and conventionalized education have sought erroneously to mold or reform humanity, i.e., the collective individual.

Reform the environment—not man. Each of my 14 concepts and their teleologically engendered strategies tend to illumine the interdependence of all the items; for instance, my item 5 is taken in consideration of all the first four but goes on to make the distinct point that my philosophy and strategy confine the design initiative to reforming only the environment in contradistinction to the almost universal attempts of

humans to reform and restrain other humans by political actions, laws, and codes. This restraining begins with the earliest parental attempts to reform their children's spontaneous
behaviors in order to conform them to "accepted" standards
and codes. The reforming of others is subsequently manifest
in attempts of grownups to reform other grownups' patterns
through politically enacted law.

My experience teaches me that all philosophic concepts
which are translated only into "bright ideas" as voiced or
written suggestions or criticisms are abortions of intellect's
higher potentials. My experience teaches me that philosophic
conclusions which are always teleologically derived may always be reduced to design-science changes of the environment which can permit other individuals' spontaneous realizations of higher destiny, i.e., behaving unconsciously in more
effective manner. For instance, a turn in the highway may be
banked angularly so that poor drivers or drunken drivers will
negotiate even sharp-radius turns subconsciously due to the
fact that the banked angles and gravity together effect the
motorcars' steering-wheel linkages in such a manner that the
cars steer themselves around the turns. In the same way,
highway overpasses allow automobilists to subconsciously
avoid crossing collisions.

In speaking of reforming the environment of man, I include a surgeon's operations on the human body for the latter
is mobile environment of the brain. I contrast the reform of
the integral or deployed physical environment in contradistinction to legal or verbal attempts to reform man's behavior
patterns. I find that there are two ways in which the environment may be altered to effect man, one positive and the other
negative—i.e., one may decrease the degrees of freedom of
humanity negatively by prisons, traps, and straitjackets and
positively by inventing better shoes for men's feet. The normal speed of universal formulations and transformative
events is 700 million miles per hour. Man's thus-far-attained
top speed of physical self-transport is 15,000 miles per hour.
Normal speed is 46,000 times man's rocket speed. Therefore,
man is—relatively speaking—almost as immobile as death.
On the other hand his environment facilities may be so ordered by design science as to give him some appreciably large
percentage communication advantage by radio which operates normally at 700 million miles per hour.

Summarizing: positive design-science reformations of the
environment must be undertaken with the intent of permit-

ting man's innate faculties and facilities to be realized with subsconscious coordinations of his organic process. Reform of the environment is undertaken with purpose of defrustrating man's innate capabilities whether the frustration be by the inadequacies of the physical environment or by the coordinated reflexes of other humans induced in those humans by the inadequacies of the environmental advantages, as for instance a mother's unreasonable punishing of a child, not for the child's direct act, but because of the mother's ever-subconsciously-present fear of the future, or of the all-history-experienced approximately complete poverty which compounded the parents' drudge weariness and failure of the physical environment to provide any hope of the parents' opportunity to protect the new life that has inadvertently been placed in their care.

CONCEPT 6—GENERAL SYSTEMS THEORY

Mind vs. brain. Generalizations as constituting the thinking of mind vs. the information storage and feedback functioning of the brain. Topology of systems. The topological hierarchy of systems. Triangulated topological-quantum coordination of generalized systems. Open and closed systems.

Comprehensivity—Theory of General Systems. As with the preceding items, we again find each and all items to induce considerations of their integrated comprehensivity. We find all the nonsimultaneous events of universe tending to effect all other events in degrees ranging from *powerful* to *insignificant.*

My own generalizations, from the total of my own special-case experiences as well as from other scientists and mathematicians—especially my experience on the sea and in the air—brought me to a clear-cut discovery of 12 fundamental degrees of freedom governing the external and internal motions and transformations of all independent systems in universe. Six of these freedoms are positive and 6 are negative; therefore, there are only 6 sets of fundamental freedoms. These cover all variable interrelationships of universe. They become the controlling facts governing general systems and thereby such supercomplex systems as the design of a nation's navy. General system's design science includes the navy's progressive fabrication and evolutionary replacement, manning, operation, establishment of naval bases, repair, maintenance, evolutionary modification, support, logistics, ballistics, and industrial tools-to-make-tools to make tools. All these functionings are *comprehensively* and *anticipatorily* undertaken—under a system of time controls and priorities which in turn are governed by fundamental resource programs and the political mandate for its existence. I have developed a completely workable, generalized systems approach —starting with the differentiation of universe, including both the metaphysical and physical—which has not only held up but permitted progressive subdivisions in cybernetical "bits" to bring any local pattern of any problem into its identification within the total scheme of generalized systems events. This means that I always start all problem solving with universe and thereafter subdivide progressively to identify a special local problem within the total of problems.

CONCEPT 7—INDUSTRIALIZATION

Definition in terms of tools. Differentiation of the tools of industrialization in contradistinction to craft tools. Industrialization only operates as a world-around system. Its inherent economic accountability as energy M (matter) × energy R (radiation) × intellect I × frequency F of evolutionary design advancements. Industrialization is the externalized complementation of man's interior metabolic-regeneration organism.

I define *industrialization* as the extracorporeal organic metabolic regeneration of humanity. Industrialization consists of tools. All the tools are externalizations of originally integral functions of humans. I divide all tools into two main classes, craft tools and industrial tools. The craft tools consist of all the tools that can be invented and produced by one man starting and operating alone nakedly in the wilderness. I define the industrial tools as all the tools which cannot be produced by one man. The steamship *Queen Mary*, the giant dynamo, the concrete highway, New York City, or even the lowly but modern forged-alloy-steel carpenter's hammer with electroinsulated plastic handles, whose alloy components and manufacturing operations involve thousands of men and the unique resources of several countries of the earth.

By my definition, the spoken word, which can only be invented by two or more men, was the first industrial tool. This is reminiscent of the biblical account, "In the beginning was the Word." In my experience appraised concepts the scriptural statement needs to be modified to read, "In the beginning of industrialization was the word." Crafts are limited to a single man and involve only very local resources and very limited fragments of earth and time. Industrialization, through the relayed experience of all men—permitted through the individualization of the spoken and written word—involves *all experiences of all men everywhere in history.*

The fundamental material resources of industry consist of 92 regenerative chemical elements—91 of which occur randomly around the earth. They are randomly disposed around the earth at an average distance of halfway around the earth from any given resource-marshaling point. The processes of industrialization take the resources from where they occur and progressively separate them from their gross-ore matrix and forward them halfway around the world for further refinement and distribution. Halfway around the earth the resources attain maximum separation. Thereafter, they are reassembled in preferred alloys and in preferred machines and structures. They are also associated and invested in progressively major tool complexes. The vast initial total cost of industrialization has to be amortized by those who need the products. Therefore, the products and services of industrialization must be mass-produced and -distributed to people all around earth to widely distribute the capital and overhead costs. The latter thus become almost negligible sums—simply the cost per pound of the product. In order to obtain enough customers to subdivide the cost it is necessary to go all around the earth, which means that the centrally produced machine, mechanics, structures, etc., must now be distributed halfway around the earth again. The logistics of industrialization therefore involves both inbound and outbound transportation halfway around the world, twice per each unit of industrial accounting. Industrialization is inherently comprehensive and omni-interrelated in respect to all humanity and all of humanity's ecological environment. This includes the sun and moon and all physical phenomena. Industrialization embraces many alternate systems, and their operators which range from private businesses to sovereign nations work inadvertently toward ultimately providing all men with higher standards of living. Although total industrialization's often negatively competitive subsystems may be motivated locally by shortsighted monetary or political profits and ambitions the total inadvertently results in evolutionarily changing the total environment to ever-higher advantage of all men and works toward the ultimate enjoyment of all earth by all men —all both economically and physically successful, without any mutual interferences or deprivations.

Though popularly unrealized—in industry there is a residual high-premium function of the crafts as basic tool and model makers which permit the original realization of individuals' inventive conceptions and their translation into mass-advantage gains for society. Crafts are ever-less-efficiently employed in the production of consumer goods, tools, and services.

Having established our first seven basic concepts it becomes clear that there is a completely separate design-science activity which is concerned with the anticipatory scheduling of all the complex interaction of the foregoing general systems events of industrialization. Design science deals in studies of the gestation rates operative in the many different constituent patterns of general world systems. For instance, it has been learned that inventions reach industrial acceptance at very different rates. Inventions in electronics are usually employed industrially within 2 years after invention. Aeronautical inventions are generally employed (after thorough testing) within 5 years. There is a lag of 15 years between railroad inventions and general use. There is a 42-year lag between invention and use in the craft-bogged building arts. There was a 50-year lag between the first blast-furnace production of steel for ships and the use of steel in a "skyscraper." There was a 42-year lag between the steel companies' by-production of Portland cement in their subsidiary companies and the time when a piece of steel fell into the setting cement to disclose accidentally the principle of steel-reinforcing of concrete.

The going economics accredits the merger of a dozen economic "failures" to produce a "success." The American automobile industry was compounded out of many thousands of "failures" whose managements lost their credit authority but whose energy-processing real-machinery assets had never failed. The accounting and speculative funding and the promotional shortsightedness and economic accrediting failed but not the evoluting machinery of industrialization. Industrialization is physical evolution and channeled energy transformations which by the Law of Energy Conservation can never fail. Through traffic in interest-paying-debt increases, present-day economics exploits the failure of debt crops to support the increasing numbers of humanity displaced as automatons by automation. We are in for a world economic-accounting revision of first magnitude. We will switch from a negative to a positive world economic accounting.

Because energy is wealth, the integrating world industrial networks mean ultimate access of all humanity everywhere to the total operative commonwealth of earth.

What do we know about wealth stated rigorously and only in the terms of experimental science?

Wealth cannot alter yesterday. It can only alter today and tomorrow.

Multiplication of craft wealth began, as we have noted earlier, when man stepped on the long end of a log lying across another log with its short end under another big log and saw the big log which was too heavy for him to lift with his muscles, lifted easily by gravity pulling his minuscule weight against the high-advantage long arm of the lever. Multiplication of industrial wealth began when man fastened a set of levers radially around the hub of a wheel and put the wheel under a waterfall and connected the wheel with a grinding mill. Thus, he learned to stand aside from the work and, gaining perspective, to use only his brain to rearrange inanimate energy patterns, external to his own integral bodily energies to do more and more fundamental, man-advantaging work. He did so by shunting energy patterns to impinge upon his machine levers.

Humans found that the vast associative (gravity, matter) and disassociative (radiation) energy patternings of universe can be harnessed, shunted, and valved by them to impinge at preferred time and quality rates upon the long ends of levers to be led through trains of gears and electric generators and conductors and motors to do preferred work for man ad infinitum.

Man is now learning through the repeated lessons of experimental science that wealth is explicitly the organized tool-articulated energy capability to sustain his forward hours and days of metabolic regeneration; to physically protect him; to increase his knowledge and degrees of freedom while decreasing his interfrustrations. Wealth, he finds, is inherently regenerative, but because of comprehensive synergies the rate of regeneration of man's solo wealth is to his commonwealth regeneration rate only as x is to x^4. As experimentally demonstrated, wealth is energy compounded with intellect's knowhow.

Science's Law of Conservation of Energy states that "energy cannot be created or destroyed." The first constituent of wealth—energy—is therefore irreducible. Science states that the entire physical universe is energy. $E = Mc^2$. Some of the energy is operative in associative patterns—as matter. The associative energy as matter is organized in leverage systems to do work. The other energy patterns disassociatively, as radiation which is transformed into free energy to be directed to impinge on the levers.

Every time man uses the second constituent of wealth—his knowhow—this intellectual resource automatically increases. He learns more. Learning is only growthful. It is impossible to "learn less."

Energy cannot decrease. Knowledge can only increase.

It is therefore scientifically clear that wealth which combines energy and intellect can only increase, and that wealth can increase only with use and that wealth increases as fast as it is used. The faster-the-more! Those are the facts of science. Those are the facts of life.

We have found (1) that the metaphysical balances the physical; (2) that the metaphysical universe embraces the physical—both being finite, but the metaphysical being always one tetrahedron greater than the physical; (3) that the metaphysical's generalized "capture" and identification of the physical is an irreversible condition—e.g., Einstein as intellect (metaphysical) writing the identification of the physical universe $E = Mc^2$ is irreversible—for the physical which is "disorderly" cannot "think" and make orderly statements. Energy cannot write what Einstein's intellect is. Therefore, we can say that the metaphysical is greater than and reconcentrates and coheres the physical.

Wealth is, therefore, inherently irreversible. Wealth can only gain as in our proposition, Q.E.D.

CONCEPT 8—DESIGN SCIENCE

Angle and frequency modulation of directions and sequence rates of least-resistant event developments. Selections of progressive, one out of 12 alternately equal least-resistant directions, i.e., the 12 fundamental degrees of freedom of intertransformative transactions in physical universe.

My concept 8 then isolates the objective and subjective design-science activities relating to the total evolutionary events of man in universe, as for instance, in 1969 the new generation of 700-passenger (or 125-ton-cargo) airplanes will be able to fly nonstop across the Pacific Ocean to establish approximate tenfold the present aeronautical transport capability within two years after their regular operations begin. Such events must be comprehensively integrated with all the other vastly accelerating environment-relationships transformations. Mining on the moon will by this time become of challenging consideration.

The rental service industry—to be discussed in concept 9 —must be compounded with time-designing doubling and possibly tripling the environment-control capabilities. World-around traveling man greatly accelerates the experience of seasonal changing between winter and summer. The regularity of days and nights will be almost obliterated by the ability to fly around the earth at the rate of its turning. He will want, however, to sleep for 8 hours every 24 hours, independent of sunlight or shadow. This may often force him to the use of a hotel bedroom one hour after it has been vacated by others. A good standard hotel bedroom and all its equipment should be indistinguishable from "brand-new." Hotel rooms may be occupied successively by two or three different humans each 24 hours, just as the airport gates are progressively occupied by airplanes which receive their rehabilitating services and move on to be immediately replaced by another plane. This new concept of man on earth is to be spoken about as frequency-modulated environment occupancies.

While this frequency-modulated use of service-industry products by humanity may seem extreme in terms of yesterday's experiences, the trends clearly indicate this mode of life will soon dominate world-around living pattern and will become the major mode of life within the next 25 years.

Lockheed Aircraft Company has a 10,000-(ten-thousand) passenger airplane on the drawing boards. These new large ships, starting with the 700-passenger, can land in unprepared fields. Length of the 10,000-passenger ships' fuselage is in the magnitude of the Empire State Building's height or the *Queen Mary*'s length. This means that within the next decade or 15 years, if man maintains evolutionary schedule, he will be able to fly a whole fleet of automated-factory-produced skyscrapers into place and upended for immediate occupancy. This is analogous to a fleet of ocean liners coming into port and taking on a city-sized passenger population on the same day. Instant city! Static urban planning will be as obsolete and inappropriate in 15 years as the attempt to build brick ships upon a stormy sea. With the computer storing and retrieving all the latest data on elevator shafting, electrical harnesses, plumbing, and manifolds, and doing the drawings, architecture and planning as now taught will be obsolete.

CONCEPT 9—WORLD SERVICE INDUSTRIES

To swiftly replace "ownership" with rentals of "new" equipment maintained at constantly renewed higher standards of performance, because more profitable and more satisfying to humanity. Service industries on world-around and year-around, automatedly accountable credit-card basis.

As world industrialization and transportation stepup increases, all humanity is gradually trending toward being worldians—all to enjoy total earth—the static-environment appurtenances of their earlier life will become progressively disused and cumbersome. Therefore, the trend to development of rental services industries will be vastly accelerated. After a half century of owning and operating 55 successive automobiles, I am now switching to rental cars. The general concept was pioneered by the telephone companies' service-maintained contact instruments which are only incidental to the service. Service industries have now grown to include automobiles, typewriters, calculating machines, and many other tools. There are a myriad of other industrial rental services. Despite the uses of the term "ownership," only a minor fraction of home and car "owners" actually own these items free of encumbrances. The quasi-owners of yesterday and today make payments on mortgages of great length in which the underwriting funds are provided by banks, labor funds, insurance companies. All are underwritten in one way or another by federal governments. The fact is the telephone in the home, though clearly rented, is as clean and new as if purchased and "owned." It is swiftly replaced by superior sets because it is owned by the telephone company whose use-frequency pays dividends and use-frequency is predicated on the relative efficiency and its induced desirability of the constant improvement of the machines.

I assume that within another two decades, the exclusively geographic identity of humanity will have given way to a general world citizenship in which it will be practical only to operate on a rental-service industry basis.

CONCEPT 10—EPHEMERALIZATION AND INVISIBLE COMMONWEALTH

The progressive doing of more with less per each and every reinvested resource unit of energy M (matter), energy R (radiation), and I (Intellect). Wealth is intellect harnessed in animate energy, tooled anticipatorily to automatically produce the forward metabolic regeneration of humanity.

A ship of the sea had first of all to float and stay on top of the water. A floating ship could and still can carry vastly larger and heavier cargoes than can be carried by men on their backs or on the backs of animals. Through shipping competition there developed swift evolution in ways of doing ever more important tasks with ever less material effort and time. This doing-more-with-less came into high magnitude of effectiveness in the development of steel steamships. Doing of ever more with ever less I identified in 1927 as "ephemeralization." It is the major control objective of design science in respect to development of airplane evolution.

As a total consequence of ephemeralization's paramount importance to the world's military efforts on the sea, in the air, and in space, men are constantly doing so much more with so much less that within the last century we have witnessed the growth from less than 1% to a benefaction of 44% of humanity with a higher standard of living than had been realized in any previous century by any monarch.

The accelerating-acceleration of doing-more-with-less will, within the next 24 years, bring an even higher standard of living to the remaining 56% of humanity, while gaining the same higher standard for the already advantaged 44%—all to be realized out of the earth's physical resources which are continually decreasing per each world man.

Ephemeralization, the comprehensive effect of more-with-lessing, is scientifically identifiable with antientropy. Ephemeralization, a product of the metaphysical conservation being more effective and coherent than physical entropy, is the number one economic surprise of world man. Up to ten years ago, all world economists counseled the world political leaders that there never had been and never would be enough vital sustenance to support more than a very few.

The development of ephemeralization has been conducted by design scientists and technologists whose numbers have amounted to a small fraction of 1% of all humanity. And their work has been focused almost exclusively upon the weaponry or defense systems. Political men dealing with the great majority of humanity were utterly surprised ten years ago to discover that their destructive weapons system had inadvertently developed a constructive by-product. This occurred when the prime and secondary weaponry contractors were displaced by other contractors with superior devices. The socially constructive inadvertencies occurred when the displaced weapons contractors turned to the domestic market for outlets for their high performances per pound and per unit of time capabilities. So much ephemeralization drifted into the domestic economy between 1900 and 1966 as to have converted 44% of humanity from "havenots" to "haves."

This ephemeralization developed by the technology which preoccupied less than 1% of humanity in weapons development had never been thought of as benefiting society. That is why its conversion of 44% of humanity from "havenots" to "haves" in two-thirds of a century has come as an utter surprise to humanity. 99.99+% of humanity don't know that this is why automobiles pack every highway and mechanical drudge-savers, iceboxes, and a higher standard of living are appearing as a flood all around the earth.

Because ephemeralization is accelerating it will complete the task of providing enough for all of humanity within another 34 years. This will occur despite the political systems which deliberately divide society and set one group against another. World man disembarrassed of political systems could accomplish universal success within 20 years. The 14-

year difference might readily be the fatal difference within which a disgruntled man might touch off the atomic-warhead retaliatory systems which would destroy humanity on earth.

CONCEPT 11—PRIME DESIGN INITIATIVE

Strategy for attaining and sustaining the comprehensive design-conception and -realization initiatives by the individual in the era of the massive world corporations and massive, sovereign, geographical states which only "seemingly" overwhelm the individual with their economic advantages in respect to investment capital, working capital, credit capital, and influence.

Economic Strategy of the Individual. Comprehensive ephemeralization involves original thought, invention, scientific calculations, technical drawings, scientific prototyping, testing, production, engineering. This brings us to the economic strategy of the individual. I have had all manner of experience in initiating the reduction of inventions to industrial use. I have experienced owning and renting shops, owning and renting tools, hiring of individuals, and dealing in the great complexes of accounting and maintenance of such high-priority technology.

I have had all manner of experience in protecting of the individual initiative and I have learned some important lessons, though frequently just short of bankruptcy. I have been able to learn those lessons without going "broke" and have managed eventually to liquidate all indebtedness. I have learned that it is fatal for an invention-developing pioneer to own his own shop and tools because it forces him to exploit his nonproduction tools with "paying" products involving repeat performances bound to vitiate experimental work. It is fatal for an inventor-explorer to build up any large staff dependent on any one economic product or focus.

The unique and superior advantage of the economic explorer maintaining his economic initiative in the face of the massive capital, staff, and equipment advantages of the large corporations and great states—who seemingly have top-heavy advantage—is demonstrated by the lone individual's complete freedom of the checks and balances of bureaucracy. Walter Chrysler found that I could produce the full-fledged operating prototype of a better, more advanced automobile than could he and his Chrysler Corporation and that I could do so with one-third the time and one-fourth the money. The U.S. Navy wrote a report which showed that I was able, time and again, to produce satisfactorily working structural-innovation prototypes in one month with an average of only $5000 and with the help of 30 university students which were superior in every way to the results obtained by the Navy Department when dealing exclusively with their prime industrial contractors which averaged them two years and $250,000 only to discover that such methods failed to produce any satisfactory results.

Quite clearly the individual initiative is at highest advantage with the least staff and property.

I have found it essential to take patents. This was proven as 50 large corporations applied to me to operate under my patents. On approximately all such occasions the attorney of the large corporation said to my attorney, "Of course, the first thing my client had me do was to try to get around your patents. The only reason we have come to you is because your patents are so well written." This was to say that the industrial corporation would have ridden over me "roughshod" if I had not protected my inventions with patents. I would never have been heard of if I had not taken patents. The monetary earnings from the patents have been negligible in proportion to the accreditation of my abilities and my theoretical activities accruing as a consequence of the economic and physical success of my geodesic domes. My accreditation as a pioneer trend navigator and environment transformer always concentrating on environment transformation was confirmed by the geodesic-dome success. I have taken a large number of patents in every country in the world in which I am allowed as an American to apply. I find that the world is so integrated that patenting within only one nation provides inadequate protection.

CONCEPT 12—SELF-DISCIPLINES

Working assumptions, cautions, encouragements, and restraints of intuitive formulations and spontaneous actions. My own rule: "Do not mind if I am not understood as long as I am not misunderstood."

Personal Self-Disciplining. In 1927 I gave up forever the general economic dictum of society, i.e., that every individual who wants to survive must *earn a living*. I substituted, there-

fore, the finding made in concept 1, i.e., the *individual's antientropic responsibility* in universe. I sought for the tasks
that needed to be done that no one else was doing or attempting to do, which if done would physically and economically
advantage society and eliminate pain.

As a consequence, it was necessary for me to discipline my
faculties to develop technical and scientific capability to invent the physical innovations and their service industry logistics.

My recommendations for a curriculum of design science:

1. Synergetics
2. General systems theory
3. Theory of games (von Neumann)
4. Chemistry and physics
5. Topology, projective geometry
6. Cybernetics
7. Communications
8. Meteorology
9. Geology
10. Biology
11. Sciences of energy
12. Political geography
13. Ergonomics
14. Production engineering

CONCEPT 13—COMPREHENSIVE COORDINATION

*Effected through discovery of nature's omnirational vec-
torial, quantum-arithmetical, geometrical, topological,
equilibriously and dynamically coordinate intertransformative system, i.e., synergetics—energetic, synergetic,
vectorial, and topological geometry.*

Self-development involved my reestablishing the self-disciplining in *comprehensivity* which I originally received at the
U.S. Naval Academy, which training countered the almost
complete trend to specialization in other universities and colleges. At the Naval Academy, the brightest were selected for
the most comprehensive training. At the other colleges and
universities the brightest were corralled and shunted into
sharp specialization. It was evident to me, specialization had
been developed by the great, master world pirates as a means
of dividing up all the bright ones, who might otherwise aspire
to displace the great ones, and thus conquering society by
keeping all powerful individuals compartmented by their specialization as the great master pirates reserved for themselves
all the integrating of the wealth-producing potentials accruing

to the specialists' multitude of special-detail accomplishments. I call them the great pirates, for they were the masters of the world commerce which took place on the oceans covering three-quarters of earth. Three miles offshore, all man-made laws were nil. Only the laws of physical universe were operative. The great masters were, therefore, inherently "outlaws."

Only the chief naval officers who maintained the master pirates' high-seas world-around fleets needed to have the comprehensive capability to be the master pirates' right-hand men.

Foremost of my personal disciplines is that I must never attempt to sell one of my ideas to others. I must confine myself entirely to the production and testing of the invention. I find that there are always capable people who learn of my activity and ask, "What is it that you are doing?" When people ask me either for an explanation or my services, I give them the best I have. I, therefore, have no promotion and allow no promotion by any associates. I have learned that when you ask people to listen to you, they become defensive. On the other hand, when they ask you to speak to them and especially when they pay a high fee, they are highly receptive.

I have learned that every consideration of my inventions and developments by others has occurred in emergencies. In effect, my work emerges through emergencies. The U.S. Marine Corps, the U.S. Navy, the Air Force, the Department of State, the Ford Motor Company have all come to me in emergencies when everything else they had tried had failed. I represented the last and most remotely possible solution to their problem.

Because I have disciplined myself and have put into operation all the strategies listed under my 14 topics, I have always had something awaiting their emergencies which I knew by experimental work would solve their problems—and do it under the circumstances which had created the dilemma. I have never had agents seeking to sell my ideas or my products. I have no agent seeking to sell my lecturing capability and have no agents trying to sell my patents.

Because I only go where I am asked to go, I am able to use the geographic and frequency of travels patterning as a trend indicator. I often gain important previews of coming events through study of my own trend patterning. Because I live in the frontiers, what happens to me usually happens to others later on. I have therefore powerful trend-prognosticating experiences.

It is part of my personal discipline to continue to try making obsolete all the inventions which I have previously developed by designing ever more effective and efficient devices for solving the complex and comprehensive world problems. I consider my patents of no consequence except for their protection of my initiative.

I do not profess anything. I am not a professional. My own description of my own work with university students is: the attempt to discipline myself to be an effective explorer in the realm of mastery of principles of comprehensive anticipatory design science.

I assumed in 1917 that nature did not have separate departments for chemistry, mathematics, physics, biology, history, etc. I decided nature had only one department and only one arithmetical angle-and-frequency modulating-and-coordinating system. I am quite confident that I have discovered an importantly large area of the arithmetical, geometrical, topological, crystallographic, and energetically vectorial coordinate system employed by nature itself. It is a triangular and tetrahedronal system. It uses 60° coordination instead of 90° coordination. It permits kindergarten modeling of the fourth and fifth arithmetical powers, i.e., fourth- and fifth-dimensional aggregations of points and spheres, etc., in an entirely rational coordinate system. I have explored the fundamental logic of the structural mathematics strategies of nature which always employ the six sets of degrees of freedoms and most economical actions.

I have been able to develop structures which are shown by engineering publications and scientific papers to be able to cover very large clearspan spaces more economically than by any known rectilinear or other shaped systems as for instance thousandfold more economically weightwise than accomplished in the dome of St. Peter's in Rome and 30 times more efficiently than this is to be accomplished by reinforced concrete or by its 10 times more complex conventional steel trusses.

Scientists operating in the area of viruses and many places elsewhere in the area of nature have found nature employing the mathematics and the structural stratagems which have come by study from the mathematics which I have discovered most probably to be part of nature's own coordinate system.

I find that there are only two possible covariables operative in all design in universe. They are modifications of angle and frequency.

Employing the coordinates employed by nature (which as yet are unemployed in any of the educational institutes of the earth and are as yet unemployed by any professional engineer or architect other than myself) and employing the contents of my 14 concepts I find I am able to effect ephemeralization in so important a degree as to make it clear that when and if world society adopts and employs my 14 strategies, mankind will always have more than adequate of everything with which to effect his physical success and intellectual satisfaction.

CONCEPT 14—WORLD COMMUNITY AND SUBCOMMUNITIES OF WORLD MAN

City today must be world-serving unit. The real urbanites of 1966 are world people like Constantinos Doxiadis. The whole of humanity is increasing not only its ecological ranging but also is accelerating its pace. The children of the Doxiadis family of Greece and the Gin Su family of Hong Kong all attend colleges and universities in America and all hands circle the world yearly as prototypes of all families of tomorrow. Yesterday only notable humans achieved travel abroad. Today anyone may expect to meet anyone else anywhere around the world (and some anywhere in space) with no more surprise than was caused by meeting one another "downtown" a half century ago. Humans are only hyperconsciously aware of themselves or their own parts—their tongues, eyes, and fingers—as constituting separate items when those separate parts get damaged. Otherwise humans are aware only of the totality of being as a coordinate part of their total environment. At such times they "feel great." When humans first acquired automobiles they were acutely aware of all the autos' separate parts because they had continually to repair, regulate, and replace them. Only muscularly powerful amateur experts could drive early cars. A half century later almost any human can drive an auto, a coordinately whole extension of their integral organism. The outcry about automation in general and its emerging comprehensivity is for the moment only provoking hyperconsciousness of society. All humans and biological phenomena have always been automated.

*There will be a gradual subsidence of humanity's con-
sciousness and specific awareness of the separate tool
parts of its complex world-around network of industrialization which is in reality only the externalized automation of its originally only-integrally-operating, ana-
tomical automation of its metabolic-regeneration functions.*

Because synergy shows experimentally the behavior of
whole systems unpredicted by behavior of the parts and because the known behavior of the whole and the known behavior of some of the parts (at least three) makes possible
discovery of the required behavior of the other parts, I assume that all planning of humanity's economic, urban, and
other undertakings must start with world trendings and possible modifications of the total or world environment.

According to my speculative reconstruction, the ecological
history of humanity around earth has two chapters. In chapter one, humanity—whose bodies are better than 90% water
—lived in huts on rafts beside the rivers, lakes, bays, and
oceans, for fish were the most plentiful food and the rafts
kept the humans safe from wild animals on the shore. Some
of these raft dwellers were blown out to sea and preponderantly eastward around earth's surface, three-quarters of
which is water.

In the second chapter of all history, men learned to sail to
windward. Following the sun, to which they intuitively attributed their metabolic regeneration, men worked westward
fighting into the headwind seas.

In Japan the originally seafaring people have an annual
"Golden Boy Day." They celebrate by flying fish-shaped kites
above the roofs of their homes—one for each of their male
children. The kites symbolize the salmon, who swims and
leaps upstream in order to regenerate. That is the Japanese
ideal.

Approximately the whole of the last 10,000 years' span of
recorded history takes place during chapter two's preponderantly westbound movement of humanity. In the Eurasian
continent, where 76% of humanity exists, this westward motion finally funnels into Western Europe. As humanity converged it crossbred. Western Europe represented an amalgam
of a myriad of previously isolated "nations." The "nations"
had developed through millenniums of inland, inbred adaptations to unique local-subsistence patterns. Along the waterfronts the sailors crossbred.

Crossbreeding Europe, intermingling with the Angles and Jutes, poured into the British Isles to crossbreed even more. Westbound Indian Ocean people inhabited Africa in ever-further-westward, tribally inbreeding, inland isolations. Then crossbreeding Western European humanity jumped westward across the Atlantic to the Americas. For ten successive generations they have settled further westward. As they moved westward they crossbred acceleratingly, not only with their own westbound, chapter-two Eurasian stocks but with the Eurasian stock of chapter one, which had drifted eastward to the American continents at least 10,000 years earlier. Into the North and South American continents and their islands there also flowed westward, both by slave trade and migration, a swiftly crossbreeding homogenization of the inbred African tribesmen.

In California, at the midpoint of the western shores of America, crossbreeding man has become so genetically integrated as to defy superficial identification with any of the earlier inbred national characteristics of Eurasia.

In California today—1966—we find an advanced phase of crossbred world man poised on an epochal springboard about to fly both skyward and into the seas' depths around the earth, thus to open chapter three of history.

In logical consequence of this historical trending the United Nations was born on the West Coast of America a score of years ago. Logically the air and space vehicles of man's acceleration into world and universe citizenship are predominantly produced on the West Coast of North America. Around the world we find nationally named airlines—the Ghana, Japan, and India airlines, etc.—but the vast majority of their vehicles are California-designed, -developed, and -produced, as are also a large proportion of the new space- and sea-penetrating vehicles.

California is in the center of the outermost jumpoff pad of humanity's springboard. From this pad, humanity is taking off from its flounder-, snail-, and crablike existence only around the two-dimensional bottom of the skyocean world—into its self-interference-free, four-dimensional occupancy of universe.

Ninety-nine point nine nine nine percent—not only of all the search, research, and development, but of all the operating controls of man's entry into the one-town world and its surrounding skyocean—are conducted exclusively in the ranges of the electromagnetic spectrum, which are infra and ultra to humanity's sensorial apprehending. Only through mind-conceived and brain-operated instruments does humanity command the operations of its birth and entry into world and universe citizenship. Education is therefore essential and central to man's successful transformation.

The fundamental concepts of humanity are transforming overnight from the working assumption of man as a physical and economic failure—as inexorably demonstrated throughout the whole of past history wherein only 1 in 1000 lived out his days and only 1 in 100,000 lived out his days in economic success.

For only the last 12 years of all history has it been scientifically acknowledged that all of humanity may now be physically and economically successful. Humanity's mastery of vast inanimate, inexhaustible energy sources and the accelerated doing-more-with-less of sea, air, and space technology have proven Malthus to be wrong. Comprehensive physical and economic success for humanity may now be accomplished in one-fourth of a century. For the first time in history it is to be assumed now and henceforth that it is normal for man to be a physical and economical success—as normal as it is for a hydrogen atom to demonstrate the success of its designed interpatterning potentials. Now and henceforth it is not only normal for man to be a physical and economic success but to be so without endangering the success of any others and without interfering with the degrees of freedom of others. A design-science revolution is underway.

In California I find a powerful latent awareness of the significance of this great moment of human transition. I find in this community a spontaneous desire to cease backing up into our future and enthusiasm for a general forward-facing of society.

Typical of the power of this West Coast springboard into the new chapter-three relationship to universe is the initiative of San Jose State College in throwing off the semantic yoke of "engineering," with all its tradition and professionally starched fabric, to reidentify the general engineering undergraduate major as the "cybernated-systems discipline," open to all undergraduates.

Such semantic reorientation is only the beginning. In my constant travel around the world I witness everywhere the swiftly accelerating birth of world man. Nowhere, in my 70 years, and in my many years of world travel, with oft-repeated visits to 174 world-around universities and colleges, have I felt the final leap into universal citizenship from the springboard of local inertia to be as imminent as I intuit it to be in California, North America.

The U.S.A. as the theater of crossbred world man best discloses the patterns coming upon all men. In the U.S.A. the population census is taken every ten years. Two censuses ago, it was found that the average U.S.A. family moves out of town every 5 years. In the last census, they are moving out of town every 4½ years. The pace is quickening. At the last (every-four-year) presidential election, it was estimated that 30 million were unable to vote because they had not been in their new homes long enough to qualify for voting. Since 65 million did vote, those disqualified by the glacial-speed reshuffling of society numbered 50% of those who did vote. Since the shift is accelerating, it is clear that within a few more national elections the majority of American citizens will be unable to vote and democracy will have to find other than a static geographical base for qualifying man to have his voice heard.

What do we know and what can we see of chapter three? Nature has devised two main and fundamental organic designs for the systematic solution of life's metabolic-regeneration requirements—the zoologicals and the botanicals. The vegetation is designed with roots to receive its sustenance at first hand by photosynthesis from the sun and sun-energized hydraulicly and pneumaticly regenerated chemical recyclings. The zoologicals are designed with high mobility to go after their sustenance and receive their sun energy indirectly by first feeding upon the vegetation. Some zoologicals feed on other zoologicals which latter first feed on vegetation. Man, though designed zoologically to go after his sustenance, found few places where the vegetation gave him fruits and palatable foods. Those who did find favorable vegetation conditions set about to guard that territory and to cultivate the most favorable types of vegetation and others hung hopefully about them. Thus, man with very short legs and a very big earth came to confuse himself with the botanicals and pretended to himself that he had roots and that he owned the favorable pieces of the earth. The swift evolutionary changes taking place invisibly are about to uproot him—all concepts of urbanization will become obsolete. Only the earth and the solar system will be his temporary home.

The swift shift of humanity from an agricultural to an industrial world economy draws men from the agricultural lands into the city. The industrialized tools and industrialized planting, cultivating, and harvesting service industries sweep over the cultivated lands.

Urbanization is only temporary as the cities become the launching pads for each human's blastoff into world-shuttling citizenship.

The centers of cities explode outwardly like volcanoes to deploy their supermarket services to ever-newer mobile traffic centers. The immobilized families and individuals begin to shuttle swiftly between high concentrations and highly diffuse deployments. They converge for the metaphysical exchange, for the brain and mind activities, for cultural and commercial exchange for museums, theaters, and university study, for broadcasting which is high-velocity publishing. They deploy for their physical activities, for the muscular and energetic activities, for mountain and water skiing, for factories and physical, archaeological, geological, and ecological research.

The whole of the urbanism is a vast oscillating system—a world-embracing entropic, volcanic physical explosion countered at increasingly high frequency with the world-embracing, metaphysically contracting, and information concentrating system which regenerates by broadcasting and publishing its progressively generalized concepts for regeneration of man's antientropic functioning that fulfills his universe functioning.

12. Epilogue

I have been asked: "What would you do if you were building commissioner of the U.S.A. or even of the world?"

I would resign!

It is popularly assumed that democracy's checks and balances—its political and economic institutions—frustrate logical housing solutions.

Many think that housing of man can be accomplished only
through a powerful political mandate. They overlook the far
vaster prerogatives of the inventor. The inventor has natural
and immediate access to all the potentials of the universe.
Edison, Bell, Marconi, and the Wrights needed no licenses
from anyone to light the night, to shrink the earth and interlink all of humanity.

Yesterday's capitalists were naturally eager to prolong the
earnings of profitable machinery investments. They disliked
inventors. Inventors made their going machines obsolete.
Businessmen were powerful enough to persuade society that
inventors were screwballs. All that is changing. Businessmen
now find change profitable. Inventors are becoming respecta-
ble.

Inventors pay no attention to manmade laws—pay attention only to the physical laws which alone govern what man
ultimately may do in universe. If humanity succeeds in becoming a total success it will have been initiated by the
Wright- and Bell-type inventions and not by the always debilitating and often lethal biases of politics.

All humans are born inventors. As children we invent
games until grownups persuade us that our inventing is futile
and that we should conform with yesterday's seemingly
proven but usually outworn inventions. But the inventiveness
remains latent in us all.

Inventors may employ man's innate capability to think
effectively in cosmic terms. As inventor I now ask the cosmic
questions. "Is man needed in the universe?" "Does he have a

343

universal function?" "If he is essential what needs to be invented to improve his functioning?" "What are the largest overall trends of human evolution that need accommodations?" If we can answer such questions we will know what to do about housing man on earth or anywhere else.

My answers to the first two questions are that man is needed to employ his mind to put things in order in the areas of universal events in which he finds himself existing. Physical universe is forever expanding and multiplying in ever more disorderly ways. This is called entropy. Biological life is forever sorting, selecting, compacting, and producing more orderly chemical substances. This is called antientropy. Human mind is the most powerful selector and order formulator thus far evidenced in universe. Mind reduces billions of special case experiences recorded by brain to a few hundred generalized principles observed to be always operative in universe. The diffuse multiplication and expansion of *physical* universe is regeneratively countered by the contractive metaphysical capabilities of human intellect. The greatest of our scientists are those who discover additional interrelationships of the comprehensive order always embracing the only at first seeming disorders of the physical. The antientropic metaphysical takes the measure of and progressively commands the entropic physical. Intellect's identification of $E = Mc^2$ is irreversible. Energy cannot identify intellect.

According to my speculative reconstruction, the ecological history of humanity around earth has two chapters. In chapter one, humanity—whose bodies are better than 90% water —lived in huts on rafts beside the rivers, lakes, bays, and oceans, for fish were the most plentiful food and the raft kept the humans safe from wild animals on shore. Some of these raft dwellers were blown out to sea and preponderantly eastward around earth's surface, three-quarters of which is water.

In the second chapter of all history, men learned to sail to windward. Seeming to follow the sun, to which they intuitively attributed their metabolic regeneration, men worked westward fighting preponderantly into the headwind seas.

Approximately the whole of the last 10,000 years' span of recorded history takes place during chapter two's preponderantly westbound movement of humanity. In the Eurasian continent, where 76% of humanity exists, this westward motion finally funnels into Western Europe. As humanity converged it crossbred. Western Europe represented an amalgam of a myriad of previously isolated "nations." The "nations" had developed through millenniums of inland inbred adaptations to unique local subsistence patterns. Forced to hibernate and cover up their skin those in the north became bleached and blond, those isolated in the hot equatorial sun darkened and blackened. Further inbreeding heightened the differentiations. Along the waterfronts the sailors crossbred and their skins became pink or swarthy.

Crossbreeding Europe, intermingling with the Angles and Jutes, poured into the British Isles to crossbreed even more. Westbound Indian Ocean people inhabited Africa in ever further westward, tribally inbreeding, ever-darkening skin, inland isolations. Then crossbreeding Western Europeans jumped westward across the Atlantic to the Americas. For 11 successive generations they have settled further westward. As they moved westward they crossbred acceleratingly, not only with their own westbound, chapter-two Eurasian stocks but with the Eurasian stock of chapter one, which had drifted eastward to the American continents between 30,000 and 10,000 years earlier. Into the North and South American continents and their islands there also flowed westward, both by slave trade and migration, a swiftly crossbreeding homogenization of the inbred African tribesmen.

In California, at the midpoint of the western shores of America, crossbreeding man has become so genetically integrated he frequently is unidentifiable with any of the earlier inbred national characteristics of Eurasia. Chapter two climaxes in the emergence of World Man.

In California we have an advanced phase of crossbred world man poised on an epochal springboard to fly both skyward and into the seas' depths around the earth, thus to open chapter three of history—that of Universe Man.

From this pad, humanity is taking off—from its flounder-, snail-, and crablike previous existence, only around the two-dimensional bottom of the skyocean world—into its self-interference-free, four-dimensional occupancy of universe. Man will free himself from local time and geographical bases and will progressively discard encumbrances, giving all heavy, static, and economically nontransportable properties to libraries, museums, and universities or scrapping them as he is able to rent superior devices and services everywhere around the earth.

For the last decade many of the world's responsible scientists have conceded for the first time in human history that Malthus was wrong and that it is physically feasible to employ the earth's energy-income resources and recirculatable metals in such a manner as to make all of humanity physically, economically, and continuously successful within 20 years. This potential is the optimum we are interested in accomplishing.

The best way to solve world housing problems is first to see how many feasible solutions there are for emerging world man and how long each would take and what its logistics are. Having chosen the optimum solutions that may be progressively attained we may see how to get from here to there— from 1966 to Utopia.

The concept of cities as they now exist developed entirely before the existence or the thought of electricity or automobiles, or before any of the millions of inventions registered in the United States Patent Office had occurred. Cities developed as warehouse trading-posts. All warehousing is gone out of the modern city. Warehousing has become dynamic. The warehousing now is mostly on wheels, wings, or in ships. The cities were later used to house vast hordes of immigrants to work in the factories which were also centered in the cities. The factories have now been deployed from the cities along with the warehouses. Cities, as we know them, are obsolete in respect to all of yesterday's functions. Trying to rebuild cities to make them accommodate the new needs of world man is like trying to reconstruct and improve a wrecked ship as the shipwreck rests upon the reef, pounded by the surf. The surf of technical obsolescence is invisible but is more inexorably powerful in its destruction than are pounding waves of the visible ocean.

Mankind is deploying all his physical activity, both the prosaic business of manufacturing and the recreational business (such as mountain and water skiing), completely out and away from cities. Mankind now converges in the old cities essentially for abstract, almost weightless, activity. Cities are great exchanges of abstract, weightless equities. Only a few cities can maintain the prestige of being the great cultural or stock exchange centers—New York, London, Paris, Tokyo, and a handful of others. These great cities will turn into great universities as automation replaces the humans functioning only as automatons.

Columbia University, New York University, Fordham

University, and City College of New York are now the prime real-estate holders of New York City. All the cities which do not have the cultural and economic exchange prestige will become totally obsolete.

It is my lifelong resolve to accomplish tasks by reforming the mechanics of the physical environment rather than by trying to reform man. I'm confident that humanity is endowed with extraordinary capabilities.

Only about one-half of the total brain is now employed.

I surmise that our higher potentials are unrealized because inauspicious environmental conditions into which life has been born have heretofore frustrated realization of most of man's potentials. We have learned much however through recent behavioral-science research, for instance that environmental conditions determine how much of the child's total brain potential will blossom successfully into coordinate effectiveness. Fifty percent of a child's total IQ capability has tried to blossom in coordinating competence by the time it is four years old, another 30% by seven, and 12% more by thirteen. At seventeen the blossoming is over. "Blossoming" frustrated by environmental conditions is usually lost.

Scientist Benjamin Bloom of the University of Chicago has demonstrated time and again that if you list the pertinent environmental conditions affecting a life throughout each of its first seventeen years, he can predict within one point of accuracy what any youth's IQ will be at seventeen. He must know —year by year—what kind of home the child lives in, whether the parents are alcoholics, etc.

Bloom validates my commitment to progressively reforming only the environment. Politics undertakes only to reform man.

When I was young, I saw that society undertook to reduce automobile accidents by attempting to reform the drivers with arrests, fines, propaganda, behavioral exhortations, and laws. I saw that instead it was physically possible to prevent accidents by split-level crossings, banked turns, and divided highways. In 1906 people said, "You can't do that, it would cost millions." After trying unsuccessfully for 60 years to reform the drivers and after a greater mortality on the U.S. highways than in World Wars I and II combined, society has at last undertaken to reform the environment with a $100 billion national highway program which has already safely multiplied the 1906 auto speeds fivefold while greatly reducing the accident rate per each accomplished passenger-mile.

Inventions alone have upped the numbers enjoying an advanced standard of living—one now superior to the best known to any sovereign before 1900—from 1% in 1900 to 40% of all humanity in 1966—despite continually decreasing metals per each human being. That same advantaged 40% are also living three times the number of years that man lived a century ago. All of that has come about through inventions which have induced appropriate social reforms but only as accessories after the facts of invention.

Take away all the inventions from humanity and within six months half of humanity will die of starvation and disease. Take away all the politicians and all political ideologies and leave all the inventions in operation and more will eat and prosper than now while racing on to take care of 100% of humanity.

My task as inventor is to employ the earth's resources and energy income in such a way as to support all humanity while also enabling all people to enjoy the whole earth, all its historical artifacts and its beautiful places without one man interfering with the other, and without any man enjoying life around earth at the cost of another. Always the cost must be prepaid by design-science competence in modifying the environment.

Man now sprawls horizontally upon the land—uncheckable by planners who enjoy only the right to "suggest." Visionless realtors, backed by government funds, operate indiscriminately in acquiring low-cost options on farmland upon which they install speculator houses. This continually reduces the productive land per capita and unbalances the ecological regeneration of life on earth. Despite the fact that the average American family now moves out of town every four years man is forced by the government-backed realtors to buy his home on 30-year mortgages which never get amortized. Man was designed with legs—not roots. He is destined to ever-increasing freedom of individually selected motions, articulated in preferred directions, as his spaceship, *Earth*, spinning its equator at 1000 miles per hour, orbits the sun at one million miles per day, as all the while the quadrillions of atomic components of which man is composed intergyrate and transform at seven million miles per hour. Both man and universe are indeed complex aggregates of motion.

Over ten million humans have now traveled more than

three million miles around their spinning orbiting spaceship *Earth*'s surface in contrast to the 30,000 miles per lifetime averaged by all humanity prior to the year 1900. So ignorantly, myopically, and staticly conceived and so obsolete is the whole housing art that its death led the Crash of 1929, since when its ghost script has been kept in rehearsal by U.S. government subsidy at a total underwriting cost to date of $200 billion.

If we take inventor heed of all the foregoing conditions and trends and if we build vertically, both outwardly and inwardly of the earth's surface, we may use less land and return good soil lands to metabolic productivity. We can also install vertical habitations upon and within the three-quarters of the earth covered by water.

The *Queen Elizabeth* is a luxuriously comfortable abode either at sea or in port. She is a mobile city. She is shaped to get passengers across oceans in a hurry. If such floating cities didn't have to speed and were designed only to be towed to an anchorage, having their occupants boated or flown to them, they might have an efficiently symmetrical shape. It is eminently feasible and economical to develop floatable organic cities of immense size.

It has been discovered also that it costs no more to go into the ground and remove earth than it does to go skyward. The great atom-war-anticipating government cave building of the last 20 years cost the same per cubic foot as building fireproof skyscrapers.

Frank Lloyd Wright designed a proposed one-mile-high tower building. His magnificent drawings excited people. But there was no engineering analysis to show whether his structure would stand under adverse conditions such as earthquakes and tornadoes. A one-mile tower is four times the height of the Empire State Building which is, as yet, in 1966, the tallest occupied building man has erected. However, in recent months calculations, only feasible by computers, have been made on a 2¼-mile-high tower habitation which will be approximately ten times the height of the Empire State. It is as high as Mount Fuji. The calculations show such a tower is physically feasible—assuming winds up to 600 m.p.h. and the tower members all encased in ice one foot thick in all directions as it is shaken by earthquakes. Though the project is feasible, the amount of steel required is formidable.

To visualize the various design-controlling conditions under

which such a high building can be constructed pinch a cam-
era tripod's legs together in parallel. Take hold of the very
bottom of the tripod in one hand and try to hold it vertically
on the top of an automobile going at 70 miles an hour over
rough terrain. But as we open the legs of the tripod, each
time we spread them, the tripod gets steadier and steadier.
This is the stabilizing effect obtained when tension stays are
rigged from top to bottom on three sides of a mast, as with
radio towers. It is equally effective to have the legs spread
outwardly as in the Eiffel Tower. When the three legs are
spread apart so that the length of the edges of their base
triangle equals the length of each of the legs the tripod attains its maximum stability. This conformation of the tripod
and its base triangle is that of the regular or equilateral tetrahedron. As the tripod's legs go further apart than the regular tetrahedron, its top can support less and less load. Thus
we learn that the most stable structure is the regular tetrahedron.

Following that design-science clue we find that a tetrahedronal city to house a million people is both technologically
and economically feasible. Such a vertical-tetrahedronal city
can be constructed with all of its 300,000 families each having balconied "outside" apartments of 2000 square feet, i.e.,
200 square meters, of floor space each. All of the organic
machinery necessary to its operation will be housed inside the
tetrahedron. It is found that such a one-million-passenger tetrahedronal city is so structurally efficient, and therefore so
relatively light, that together with its hollow box-sectioned
reinforced-concrete foundations it can float.

Such tetrahedronal floating cities would measure two miles
to an edge. That is, each of the three base legs will be two
miles long. This means that their reinforced-concrete, box-
sectioned, and frequently partitioned bottom foundations will
be 200 feet in depth and several hundreds of feet wide. Such
a tetrahedronal floating city can be floated in a triangularly
patterned canal. The structure can be assembled on the floating foundations. This will make the whole structure earth-
quake-proof. The whole city can be floated out into the ocean
to any point and anchored. The depth of its foundation will
go below the turbulence level of the seas so that the floating
tetrahedronal island will be, in effect, a floating triangular
atoll. Its two-mile-long "boat" foundation, on each of its
three bottom edges, will constitute landing strips for jet air-

planes. Its interior two-mile harbor will provide refuge for the largest and smallest ocean vessels. The total structural and mechanical materials involved in production of a number of such one-million-inhabitant tetrahedronal cities are within feasibility magnitude of the already operating steel and other metals manufacturing capabilities of any one company of the several major industrial nations around the earth.

Tetrahedra are geometrically unique in that they can be added to on any one of their four surfaces while increasing symmetrically in size. The tetrahedron city can grow symmetrically by adding to any one of its faces. Tetrahedronal cities will be symmetrically growable as are biological systems. They may start with a thousand occupants and grow to hold millions without changing overall shape though always providing each family with 2000 square feet of floor space.

Withdrawal of materials from obsolete buildings on the land will permit the production of enough of these floating cities to support frequently spaced floating cities of various sizes around the oceans of the earth at distances negotiable by relatively small boats such as operate safely between Miami, Florida, and Nassau on the Bahama Islands.

At the present time, ocean cargoes must go from one country to another, e.g., from Buenos Aires to London because ships cannot dock beside one another on the ever-heaving ocean to transfer cargo. Because the depth of their "foundations" goes below wave turbulence, permitting dropped thresholds over which the deepest draft ships may pass, such floating tetrahedron cities will permit midocean cargo transferring within their harbors and therewith extraordinary increase of efficiency of the interdistribution of the world's raw and finished products as well as of the passenger traffic. Such tetrahedronal cities floated upon the oceans will generate their own energy with atomic reactors whose by-product heat will be used to desalinate the city's water supply. All major ships of the sea already desalinate their water.

Such ocean-passage-shortening habitats of ever-transient humanity will permit his individual flying, sailing, economic steppingstone travel around the whole earth in many directions. Three-quarters of the earth is covered by water. Man is clearly intent on penetrating those world-around ocean waters in every way to work both their ocean bottoms and their marine-life and chemistry resources.

When we double the length of an airplane fuselage, we increase its surface area by four and increase its volume by eight. This means that every time we double the length of a ship we eightfold its useful cargo and passenger space while only fourfolding its surface. The amount of surface of a ship governs its friction and drag. The larger the ship, the more economically its cargo may be carried. Yesterday's limitation in relation to the bigness of airplanes was occasioned by their horizontal speeds requiring longer and longer landing strips. The new generation of large airplanes emerging, which will carry 700 to 1000 passengers and "up," are all equipped for vertical takeoff and landing, which does away altogether with the necessity for prepared landing strips. With the long landing-strip limitation removed, the size of the airplanes will multiply very rapidly.

To take advantage of the progressive economy gains of increasing size, leading airplane manufacturers already have airplanes on their engineering boards of a size adequate to carry 10,000 passengers or their equivalent in cargo. The 10,000-passenger ship has a length equivalent to that of the Empire State Building. The leading aircraft manufacturers realize that it will be possible to produce Empire State Building-size skyscrapers in horizontal position under factory-controlled conditions in mass-production jigs with mass-production tools.

Working on scaffolds, the Empire State Building was erected under approximately noncontrolled conditions of wind, rain, heat, and cold in the heart of New York City's traffic. One man was killed for every floor of the Empire State Building's 102 stories. No men should be killed in the production of the horizontal skyscraper in the airplane factory. Such skyscraper-size airplanes may then be taken from their factory and with vertical takeoffs and temporarily applied wings will be flown horizontally, with minimum effort, to any position around the world and horizontally landed. Using their vertical takeoff equipment they will be upended to serve as skyscrapers, anchored, and braced. Thus we see that whole cities can be flown to any location around the world and also removed in one day to another part of the world just as fleets of ships can come in to port and anchor in one day, or be off for other parts of the world.

In 1954, the United States Marine Corps helicopter-lifted, at 60 miles per hour, a geodesic dome large enough to house an American family. This dome had a floor area of 1000 square feet. In 1955, the Marines air-delivered geodesic domes twice that size, from aircraft carriers to the land, fully skinned and ready to occupy, also at 60 miles per hour. In 1962, the Ford Motor Company helicopter lift delivered a geodesic dome covering a five-times-larger-again floor area of 10,000 square feet. The latest helicopters being built for Vietnam can air-deliver geodesic domes, at 60 miles per hour, large enough to cover an American football field including the end zones, the quarter-mile running track and side bleachers. By 1970, it will be possible to air-deliver geodesic domes large enough to cover complete baseball stadiums. By 1975, it would be possible to air-deliver geodesic domes able to cover small cities. It is now possible with a number of separate helicopter lifts to deliver large subassemblies to complete a geodesic dome large enough to cover a large city and do so within three months' time.

Domed-over cities have extraordinary economic advantage. A two-mile diameter dome has been calculated to cover mid-Manhattan Island, spanning west to east at 42nd Street from the Hudson River to the East River, and spanning south to north from 22nd Street to 62nd Street.

When we wish to make a good air-cooled engine, we design it with many thin fins and spicules to carry away the heat by providing the greatest possible external surface area. The dome calculated for mid-Manhattan has a surface which is only 1/85 the total area of the buildings which it would cover. It would reduce the energy losses either in winter heating or summer cooling to 1/85 the present energy cost obviating snow removals. The cost saving in ten years would pay for the dome.

Domed cities are going to be essential to the occupation of the Arctic and the Antarctic. The Russians are already experimenting with them in the Arctic. The Canadians are also studying them. Mining of the great resources of the Antarctic will require domed-over cities. Domed-over cities will be used in desert areas to shield new growth from the sun while preventing wasteful evaporation of piped in, desalinized water. Gradually the success of new domed cities in remote places will bring about their use in covering old cities, particularly where antiquities are to be protected.

The domed-over cities will be so high and their structural members so delicate that their structural members will be approximately invisible. They will operate like a controlled

cloud to bring shadow when shadow is desirable and bring
sun when sun is desirable, always keeping out rain, snow, and
storms as well as exterior industrial fumes, while collecting
all the rainwater in reservoirs. The temperature inside the
dome will be so stabilized that a semitropical atmosphere will
exist. Inasmuch as there will be no rain or snow in the area,
people will live in gardens, or upon garden-terrace skyscrapers needing only local screening for privacy.

There are already 5000 geodesic domes in 50 countries
around the world, many so light and strong as to have been
air-delivered.

                    *   *   *

The great historical applications of science have been fundamentally underwritten by the munitions industries and the
weapons programs of great nations. When scientists designed
the cannon, they didn't have to do anything about the man
who fired the cannon. He could sleep beside the cannon and
there was air for him to breathe; there was water near at
hand, inclement temperature could be offset by clothing. Science produced bigger guns, floated by battleships. Men then
could sleep on the deck. However, now that scientific warfare
has gone into space, men who handle the warfaring apparatus
in space find no air to breathe and no water or food waiting
to drink and eat. For the first time in history, it has been necessary for science to upgrade environmental and metabolic
regeneration conditions of man and to package them for economic delivery by rockets. To do so requires that science understand man as a process. When the astronauts go beyond
the thermos-bottle-and-sandwich excursion limits and live for
protracted periods on the moon or elsewhere in space all the
regenerative conditions provided by the great biological interactions within the biosphere around earth's surface will have
to be reproduced in a miniaturized and capsulized human
ecology which will emulate all the chemical and physical
transactions necessary to sustain the process "Man." All the
apparatus to do so will be contained in a little black box
weighing about 500 pounds and measuring about 20 cubic
feet. Man in space with the little black box will be able to
regenerate his many organic processes, needing only small annual additions to the recirculating chemistry and physical
transforming.

The first men living comfortably in space, by virtue of the
little black box, will be watched by TV through every mo-

ment of their time by continuously rotating audiences of two billion humans on Earth. The whole of humanity will be swiftly educated on the uses and success of living with an entirely new set of environmental control mechanics.

To be successful, the new apparatus will have to operate as unconsciously, on the astronauts' part, as do all of humans' internal organic processes. Men are only aware of their internal organisms when they get a pain in the tummy, or of their eyes when they get a cinder in them.

The little 500-pound black box will have to be produced on earth. The astronauts will not be asked to produce their own black box in space. Though the first black box will probably cost the United States and Russia, combined, well over $7 billion, it will be mass-reproducible on earth at around $2 per pound. This means that a $1000 box could be rented profitably at $200 a year. Any individuals, and their families, could take their black box, costing approximately $18 a month, and go to any remote "dollar-a-year" or wilderness park lands part of earth—mountaintop or island—and enjoy essential services superior to those now available in any city complex because the sewers and energy lines will all be displaced and improved upon by the little autonomously recirculating black box.

The black box as domestic technology fallout from the space and munitions programs will constitute the first wholesale application of science directly to making man a physical and economic success anywhere in universe which of course includes "on earth." It will swiftly divert firsthand application of science from almost exclusive development of weapons and their support and the latter's heretofore almost inexorable nosedive toward self-extermination.

In 1927, a single-family dwelling machine was engineeringly proposed whose structure was similar to that of a wire wheel—laid horizontally on its side—with its axle elongated vertically to act as a supporting mast around which the circular dwelling was supported. This high carousellike dwelling machine had advanced living apparatus suitable for a family of six. It had a top sundeck above and an airplane hangar and garage below the dwelling zone. It was finally prototyped in the aircraft industry in 1944. It weighed only three tons which was approximately 3% of the weight of the equivalent facilities when provided by conventional structures and mechanics. It was popularly hailed. All that was lacking was the little black box to make this air-deliverable dwelling machine the world's most luxurious, remotely installable, and economic family habitat.

*   *   *

A one-hundred-foot-diameter geodesic sphere weighing 3 tons encloses 7 tons of air. The air to structural weight ratio is 2:1. When we double the size so that geodesic sphere is 200 feet in diameter the weight of the structure goes up to 7 tons while the weight of the air goes up to 56 tons—the air to structure ratio changes to 8:1. When we double the size again to a 400-foot geodesic sphere—the size of several geodesic domes now operating—the weight of the air inside goes to about 500 tons while the weight of the structure goes up to 15 tons. The air to structure weight ratio is now 33:1. When we get to a geodesic sphere one-half mile in diameter, the weight of the air enclosed is so great that the weight of the structure itself becomes of relatively negligible magnitude, for the ratio is 1000:1.

When the sun shines on an open-frame aluminum geodesic sphere of one-half-mile diameter the sun penetrating through the frame and reflected from the concave far side bounces back into the sphere and gradually heats the interior atmosphere to a mild degree. When the interior temperature of the sphere rises only 1° Fahrenheit, the weight of air pushed out of the sphere is greater than the weight of the spherical-frame geodesic structure. This means that the total weight of the interior air, plus the weight of the structure, is much less than the surrounding atmosphere. This means that the total assemblage of the geodesic sphere and its contained air will have to float outwardly into the sky, being displaced by the heavy atmosphere around it. When a great bank of mist lies in a valley in the morning and the sun shines upon the mist, the sun heats the air inside the bank of mist. The heated air expands and therefore pushes some of itself outside the mist bank. The total assembly of the mist bank weighs less than the atmosphere surrounding it and the mist bank floats aloft into the sky. Thus are clouds manufactured.

As geodesic spheres get larger than one-half mile in diameter they become floatable cloud structures. If their surfaces were draped with outwardly hung polyethylene curtains to retard the rate at which air would come back in at night, the sphere and its internal atmosphere would continue to be so light as to remain aloft. Such sky-floating geodesic spheres may be designed to float at preferred altitudes of thousands of feet. The weight of human beings added to such prefabricated "cloud nines" would be relatively negligible. Many thousands of passengers could be housed aboard one-mile-diameter and larger cloud structures. The passengers could come and go from cloud to cloud, or cloud to ground, as the clouds float around the earth or are anchored to mountaintops. While the building of such floating clouds is several decades hence, we may foresee that along with the floating tetrahedronal cities, air-deliverable skyscrapers, submarine islands, subdry-surface dwellings, domed-over cities, flyable dwelling machines, rentable, autonomous-living black boxes, that man may be able to converge and deploy at will around the earth, in great numbers, without further depletion of the productive surface of the earth.

It may be that after we get to the large skyscraper-size airplanes that they may be economically occupiable and economically flyable from here to there with passengers living aboard as on cruise ships.

It may be that human beings will begin to live in completely mobile ways on sky ships and sea ships as they now occupy cruise ships in large numbers, for months, while traveling around the water and sky oceans. As people live completely around the earth, changing from "summer" to "winter" in hours, the old concept of man as a cold-area or warm-area dweller or as a fixed, static dweller anywhere, and all the old concepts of seasons, or even of work as related only to daylight hours, will gradually be eradicated from man's conditioned reflexes.

Man will come to occupy mobile habitats which may at will be anchored habitats and live independently of day and night and season schedules. This will mean a much higher occupancy in use rate of environment-control facilities. Nowadays, at international airport hotels, people with one-to-eight-hour flight-transfer waitovers follow one another in rooms and beds which are made up freshly as one occupant follows the other. The rooms are occupied, not on a noon-to-noon schedule, but on a use schedule which we may call a frequency-modulation schedule. Such frequency-modulated occupancy of rented space in mobile hotels or in dwelling machines will become the fundamental patterning of man's living around the earth.

On the old farmstead there were a great many buildings to be seen—the great barn, containing hay and cows, the stables, corncribs, silos full of wet fermenting ensilage, the woodshed, pigsty, the carriage house, the cold cellar and the warm cellar. All these buildings and many others on the farms are disappearing or have disappeared because machinery in the house has displaced the functions carried on by the so-called "buildings." The small electric refrigerating device took the place of ice, the icehouse and icebox system. The electric current took the place of the wood, the woodshed and stove system, etc. In two decades the windmills, formerly on every farm, have gone.

In this way, we discover that the buildings, which controlled energy conditions of heat, cold, dry, and wet, were in effect machines because machines process and control energy. All those machines known erroneously as "buildings" have now been replaced by machines more readily recognized by us as machinery. Now however the recognizable components are decreasing as technology employs more and more of the invisible capabilities of electronics. What we are witnessing is the disappearance of the ever less economic "housing" or slow-motion phase of machinery as its functions are taken over by the high-speed machinery that brings about and maintains the preferred environment conditions at ever less cost and personal effort. This evolution is well underway, but we hide it from our awareness through semantic error, typical of which is society's noncomprehension of what Le Corbusier meant when he said, "A house is a machine for living."

When the early homesteaders went on the land with few or no tools, they had to work in the fields or build their energy-controlling structures during every minute of daylight. Spent, in 12 hours of hard labor, they slept from twilight to dawn. The design of their farmhouses told the story—little boxes with vertical walls going down into the ground. There were no porches or stoops. There were a few windows, enough for the farmer's wife to see where he was around the farm and to see if the Indians were coming. When tools, and more tools, came to shorten the time taken to do a given job, the farmer gained more time of his own. Finally, he had enough time before twilight to sit and look at the scenery, and he built porches around his house. As he began to have more and more time, he began to put screens on the porches. With ever more time, he began to put glass windows on the porches. Sitting on his porches, he watched other people go by. Then came the automobile, which in effect put wheels under his glassed-in front porch, so instead of waiting to see people go by he drove down the street to see the people. In a very real sense, the automobile was part of the house, broken off, like hydra cells going off on a life of their own. The young people who used to court in the parlor, then on the glassed-in front porch, now began to do their courting in the automobile, or the porch with wheels. Today, the young people do their courting in their parlor on wheels, driving it to the drive-in theater. Because we are conditioned to think of the house as static, we fail to realize that the automobile is as much a part of the house as is the addition of a woodshed.

In 1920, 85% of the cost of production of a single-family dwelling in the United States went into the house's shell and foundation. Only 15% of the general contract went into what we call "mechanical inclusions." In North America, that 15% covered a kitchen sink and a furnace. There was no electrical refrigeration at that time. Only a small percentage of houses had indoor toilets. A very small percentage had electric wiring. Due to the high mechanization of World War I, the postwar "fallout" of advanced technology brought one mechanical inclusion after another to be incorporated in the general contract for a single-family dwelling. Then came the electric refrigerator, the oil-burner furnace, the hot-water heater, the radio, etc.

In 1929, 28% of the general contract for a single-family dwelling went into mechanical inclusions.

In 1940, 45% of the general contract went into mechanical inclusions.

At the present time, 65% of the general contract goes into mechanical inclusions, which embraces electric wiring and plumbing, as well as the obvious machinery.

During this same time, the size of the various domestic machines has continually decreased. As an instance, the electric sewing machine decreased from a very big device to a small one. As transistors and other miniaturizations occurred, the machinery of the general contract continually produced more service with less apparatus and effort. Through the years, the cost of the electrical current to operate the mechanization continually decreased despite the increase of costs in almost all other directions.

Concurrently, the size of the houses greatly decreased as servants were replaced with machines, which eliminated servants' rooms. Sizes of families decreased as life expectancy increased. Despite the continual decrease in the size of individual homes, the cost per cubic foot of the enclosing structure has rocketed upward.

Clearly the machinery is giving man more-and-more for less-and-less, while the structural arts are giving man less-and-less for more-and-more.

The great city electric generators and the great chemical factories were once housed in vast Georgian-architecture brick factories. The chemical industries learned how to make machinery so that it would not deteriorate in the open air. The electrical industry did the same. Today we see enormous petroleum refineries and other chemical plants with their machinery completely exposed to the atmosphere—no walls. This is invisible architecture. We see the electrical switch-yards entirely outdoors, with only high fences around them. We can correlate these trends—of the single-family dwelling's swiftly transferring tasks to machinery from the relatively inefficient structural shells—with the trend of the front parlor onto wheels to go off down the street to be called the "automobile."

Because of these trends, what we now call "home trailers" are simply modern, lightweight, aluminum boxes, full of the mechanical package which constitutes the improved standard of living—minus the expensive house—compacted into usable array which mobile home packages prosper as the "regular" static home market has never prospered, despite the lack of esthetic appeal, and despite cultural inertias.

The home-trailer business has rocketed into a major industry without any federal subsidies and mortgages, while the whole home-building business has been kept going only by the 40-year government mortgage-loan guarantees, and is now in fundamental decline.

The environment always consists of energy—energy as matter, energy as radiation, energy as gravity, and energy as "events." Housing is an energetic environment-controlling mechanism. Thinking correctly of all housing as machinery we begin to realize the complete continuity of interrelationship of such technological evolution as that of the home bedroom into the railway sleeping car, into the automobile with seat-to-bed conversions, into the filling-station toilets, which are accessories of the parlor-on-wheels; the trailer, the motels, hotels, and ocean liners. All this living machinery complements the inherently transient nature of world society and its progressive emancipation from the local shackles of physical-property "machines" which were so inefficient and so enormous as to be nonportable and therefore to have imposed a static property condition upon world society which misled man into thinking of himself as geographically rooted. The new pushbutton-operating, energy-processing machinery makes operative preferred conditions on wheels, on boats, on wings, or on temporarily anchored earth beds anywhere around the earth and outwardly in space, permitting man to rest or go where he wills.

But the conditioned reflexes of society make laws that force the mobile home owner to emulate only the realtors' static horizontality. The realtors' zoned trailer parks grow up everywhere to capture the swiftly multiplying mechanical house packages. The rapidly expanding fiberglass-plastic-and-metal boat production is turning out houseboats, motor cruisers, sailing cruisers all with living machinery of the highest order of efficiently and livably compact packaging. Mooring or storing of these boats operates horizontally in harbors or marinas.

The tetrahedronal city which can be expanded from a 100,000- to a 300,000-family-supporting device consists structurally of a complex of trusses. Such tetrahedronal cities make it a practical matter for power cranes to pick up the mechanical package in the form of trailers, houseboats, or cruisers and park them on the open terraces of the tetrahedronal trusses.

One reason that we allowed 2000 square feet (200 square meters) per family on the vertically paralleled terraces of the tetrahedronal floating cities is to permit the storage of mobile trailers, houseboats, and mobile homes in general on the terraces, leaving an additional thousand square feet for a garden for each mobile tenant. These devices will be all weather-proofed and therefore require no additional "walls" or external skins to be fastened onto the tetrahedron city. Such a two-mile-high tetrahedronal city will consist of an open-truss-framework "structural mountain" whose sides are covered with parked mobile homes which at night will be ablaze with light as are the great petroleum refineries.

There will be no brick- or stone-sided tetrahedronal "mountain" cities. There will be delicate, fireproof, prestressed-concrete open-framework tetrahedronal cities consisting of hundreds or even thousands of decks one above the other on which the floatable, flyable, roadable mobile-home mechanical containers will be economically parked as their occupants dwell locally for periods during their world-around peregrinations. Each mobile home safely locked in place on its mechanical mountain terrace will provide its own all-weather skin.

As we consider these fundamental transitions in types of machinery from what seemed to be "buildings" to obvious mechanics, we realize the complete evolutionary continuity of all these trends. We realize also that the transition to the faster technologies, which will open up all oceans and skies to man's support and enjoyment, is an inevitable consequence of what is already irrevocably and inexorably underway, but has been mistakenly identified by the wrong names, wrong conceptions, and wrong categories with which man has processed his experiences.

By and large, the great world housing problem is an *educational problem*. By and large, man's inertias are only overcome by virtue of his own personal discoveries, discernment, and understanding of what it is that is happening to him. There will be no instant world housing solutions. There are fundamental rates at which the educational gestation takes place.

Publishers who try to exploit man's imagination by giving him only the end-product concepts, without showing how man will get from here to there, postpone the opportunities for helping man to educate himself on how these events may come to pass and the advantages which will be gained.

I, for one, an unwilling to allow anyone to be only amused by startling concepts of tetrahedronal cities and air-deliverable Empire State buildings while keeping from society the opportunity to understand the complex of factors that lead to such tangible results.

The comprehensive introduction of automation everywhere around the earth will free man from being an automaton and will generate so fast a mastery and multiplication of energy wealth by humanity that we will be able to support all of humanity in ever greater physical and economic success anywhere around his little spaceship *Earth*.

Quite clearly, man enabled to enjoy his total earth, enabled to research the bottom of his ocean, and to reexplore earlier patterns of man around earth, will also be swiftly outward-bound to occupy ever greater ranges of universe.

Within decades we will know whether man is going to be a physical success around earth, able to function in ever greater patterns of local universe or whether he is going to frustrate his own success with his negatively conditioned reflexes of yesterday and will bring about his own extinction around the planet earth. My intuitions foresee his success despite his negative inertias. This means things are going to move fast.

Bibliography

SOURCES OF PAPERS INCLUDED IN THIS VOLUME

1. April 1, 1967. "Man with a Chronofile," *Saturday Review*.
2. December 10, 1964. Keynote address at the National Conference on the Uses of Educational Media in the Teaching of Music, under joint auspices of the U.S. Office of Education and the Music Educators National Conference, Washington, D.C. Parts I and II published in *Music Educators Journal*, April-May, June-July, 1966.
3. October 10, 1964. "Prevailing Conditions in the Arts in Contemporary Society." Address delivered at a plenary session of the New York University Seminar on Elementary and Secondary School Education in the Visual Arts.
4. October 21, 1965. Keynote address at Vision 65, World Congress on New Challenges to Human Communications, inaugural congress of the International Center for Communications Arts and Sciences. Sponsored by the International Center for the Typographic Arts in cooperation with Southern Illinois University, Carbondale, Illinois.
5. October 23, 1965. Summary address at Vision 65 (see No. 4 above).
6. 1967. First published in this book.
7. 1965. First published in this book.
8. March 18-19, 1965. Combination of address to Brookings Institution, U.S. Department of Labor Seminar on Manpower Policy Program and to the President's Committee on Technology at the U.S. Department of Labor, Washington, D.C.
9. 1964. First published in this book.
10. February 19, 1965. "A Challenge to More Conscious Participation in Our Evolving Universe." Transcription of a day of discussion between Fuller and the American Association of University Women program staff members.
11. 1966. Statement to a leading figure in the world building industry.
12. 1969. First published in this book.